Deep Connections

For M.

# DEEP CONNECTIONS

## The Hidden Battles to Control Subsea Cables

Katja Bego

polity

First published in 2026 by Polity Press Ltd.

Polity Press Ltd.
65 Bridge Street
Cambridge CB2 1UR, UK

Polity Press Ltd.
111 River Street
Hoboken, NJ 07030, USA



ISBN-13: 978-1-5095-6587-0
ISBN-13: 978-1-5095-6588-7 (pb)

A catalogue record for this book is available from the British Library.

Library of Congress Control Number: 2026936722

Typeset in 11.5 on 14pt Adobe Garamond
by Cheshire Typesetting Ltd, Cuddington, Cheshire
Printed and bound in Great Britain by Ashford Colour Ltd



For further information on Polity, visit our website:
politybooks.com

# *Contents*

# *Acknowledgements*

An enormous amount of gratitude goes out to David Betz at King's College London, who was the first to suggest my somewhat esoteric Master's dissertation about weaponized interdependence and the history of undersea cables carried the seeds for a much more in-depth and ambitious book, and for introducing me to his publisher.

This book would also not have been possible were it not for the incredible generosity of the many dozens of people in the cable industry, government, journalism, international institutions, militaries and the wider cable research community, who agreed to be interviewed for this book and helped me understand the rather magical world of the undersea cable. I have decided not to name them here, for the simple reason that many, given their job roles, would not otherwise have been able to speak to me, because of the sensitive nature of some of the topics I discuss in the pages that follow, and the fact that I do not want to create the impression my interpretation of events necessarily represents the views of others.

I would like to thank several others in the cable orbit for the many interesting conversations about cables throughout this process: Tobias Liebetrau, Jonas Franken, Lane Burdette, Cian Fitzgerald, John Tibbles, Jonathan Reed-Winkler, April Herlevi, Camino Kavanagh, John Wrottesley, Michaela Nakayama Shapiro, Corinne Cath-Speth, Keir Giles, Pia Husch, Robert McCabe, Peter Watkins, Jonathan Reed Winkler and Benjamin Schmitt. I would like to thank Nicole Starosielski and her team at Berkeley for inviting me to present some of these ideas to their excellent class of students, and to the organizers of events that have brought me from Berlin to Oxford, from Manila to Dublin, Warsaw, Turin, Gdansk and even Valentia Island (which really does deserve its UNESCO Heritage status) to speak about the themes in *Deep Connections*. I would like to thank the generous staff at the archives and museums I consulted as part of this research: PK Porthcurno Museum of Global

Communications, the National Archives at Kew Gardens, the Kennedy Presidential Library in Boston, the BT Archives, het Nationaal Archief in The Hague, and the NATO and Margaret Thatcher Foundation's archives.

I also owe gratitude to my current colleagues at Chatham House for helping me think through some of the larger themes in this book, for their support, and, in some cases, for their patience in learning more than they ever wanted about undersea cables: Marion Messmer, Julia Cournoyer, Georgia Cole, Joyce Hakmeh, Patricia Lewis, Nayana Prakash, William Matthews, Kirsten Rousseau, Olivia O'Sullivan, Robin Potter, Orysia Lutsevych, Chris Aylett, Grégoire Roos, Elaiza Endziulaityte and Anna Morgan.

I would also like to thank my former colleagues at Nesta, the ICO and partners of the Next Generation Internet project, as well as the many great colleagues in the tech policy community, for our many hours of discussion about the meaning of digital sovereignty and helping me see the many intersections between topics that do not often get connected.

I would like to thank my anonymous peer reviewers for their time, generosity and helpful feedback. None of this would have been possible without the infinite patience of the editorial team at Polity: Olivia Jackson, Ian Tuttle, Evie Deavall, Julia Davies and, above all, Louise Knight for taking a chance on me with this project.

I would like above all to express my deepest gratitude to my family and friends who endured the many years of me working evenings and weekends, the missed Christmases, for giving up their Easters to join in cable-hunting expeditions (Andreas Bruckner and Bella Franks): my parents Peter and Jacqueline, Janneke, Gerard, Becca, Bram, Patrizia and Massimo. And above all to Marco, for always being there for me, even when I thought this book would never ever finish.

# *Introduction*

'We see you. We know what you're doing.' UK defence secretary John Healey warned the Kremlin in early 2025, in front of the Commons. He had just announced that Royal Navy submarines and warships had in the days prior chased Russian research vessel the *Yantar* out of British waters.

Russia had already been waging an increasingly disruptive and brazen campaign of sabotage operations all over Europe and beyond, especially since the start of its full-scale invasion of Ukraine in 2022 – from drone incursions forcing the shutdown of civilian airports, to mysterious fires in ammunition factories, to assassination attempts on the CEO of one of Europe's largest arms manufacturers. These were operations intended to provoke, to undermine support for Ukraine among its key supporters, and to further stoke existing political divisions in a polarized west. The *Yantar*'s activities fit this playbook, but also appeared to be about something more than just sowing chaos and disruption, however. The *Yantar* was preparing for war.

The ship, presented as a benign 'oceanographic research vessel' by Moscow, had raised eyebrows from the moment it was first launched in 2015. The *Yantar,* which carries on-board highly sophisticated monitoring equipment including two dedicated surveillance submarines, is part of the fleet of Russia's highly enigmatic Main Directorate of Deep-Sea Research (or GUGI), infamous for its deep-sea shenanigans. This was also not the first time the *Yantar* was escorted out of European waters either. Nor would it be the last. The ship had previously been spotted off the coast of the Netherlands, Belgium, Germany and France. It had spooked authorities in Ireland and Spain. The *Yantar*'s frequent covert loitering in the territorial waters of its adversaries made it quite clear it was not there just to map algae blooms or fish migratory patterns. This was a surveillance vessel, tasked with, among other things, mapping the exact locations of the undersea data cables that keep countries connected to the global internet. The kind of infrastructure one might really like to destroy in the lead up to a war.

That same war, at time of writing, appears increasingly near: in late 2025, the French government called on Europeans to get ready for a high-intensity conflict by 2030. NATO Chief Mark Rutte similarly warned a new world war may be upon us, a war which may well start along the alliance's long border with its belligerent neighbour to the East. Should the moment arrive, the destruction of submarine cables would almost certainly be near the top of Moscow's agenda, just like severing Germany's cables was among the very first things Britain sought to do in the early hours of both world wars. By mapping their routes, the *Yantar* appeared to be laying the groundwork.

## *Invisibility*

The *Yantar* was looking to make visible what had for a long time remained almost entirely invisible. Up to 99 per cent of international communications and data traffic – from our bank transfers, to our work emails, to our favourite streaming shows – travels through a global web of fibre optic cables, laid deep down on the seabed. Despite the importance of this most vital of infrastructures, it had, up until recently, received little attention.

This is not surprising. In many ways, cables are quite literally invisible, deliberately hidden away from public view. Add to this the all-too-human tendency to not pay much heed to the infrastructures that make our daily lives possible. How often do we stop to think about the water flowing from the tap, the shelves stocked full with eggs in the supermarket or the light turning on when we flip the switch? How much do we actually know about all the people – the skilled maintainers – and processes involved with making these systems function? When it comes to infrastructure, we usually only truly notice it when something breaks or goes wrong. This is even more the case for anything to do with the physical side of the internet. There is still this pervasive notion that the internet is something ethereal, which only exists in the cloud, or on our phones – not a very tangible, physical assembly of concrete boxes and polyethylene-covered wires and tubes. In the specific case of undersea cables, this 'out of sight, out of mind' dynamic is further compounded by a phenomenon maritime experts refer to as 'sea blindness', the general lack of awareness of anything to do with our seas and oceans.[1] Some 90 per cent of physical goods travels by ship; the maritime domain is vital for our way of life and security – yet most of us know hardly anything about it.[2]

All of this meant that when I first started this book in early 2023, very few people had ever heard about undersea cables. My own interest in the topic of cables was piqued in 2015, when two quite different news articles caught my attention. The first, a brief write-up in *The New York Times*, reported that NATO officials were growing increasingly concerned about suspicious Russian submarine activity near key cables.[3] The second, in a now defunct tech outlet, showed how American tech giants like Google and Microsoft were increasingly investing in and rolling out their own submarine cables, further extending the enormous reach and control these companies already wielded across the technology domain. It was an interesting contrast. One actor – Russia – was trying to flex its muscles by playing the spoiler and threatening to destroy a vital global system, while the other – Big Tech – was attempting to accumulate even more power through it. For some years, this interplay, and the wider deep-sea mystique of the submarine cable, remained a topic of casual fascination. But the more I read, the more I began to appreciate that this was about far more than just cutting cables and companies seeking to take control of yet another aspect of our digital lives. Undersea cables had been and have been incredibly multifaceted instruments of great power competition throughout their existence – from the first undersea telegraph cables laid in the mid-nineteenth century, all the way to the role they now play in the race to dominate AI. As we have once again entered an era of increasingly feverish competition between countries, cables play a surprisingly important and diverse role in it. A role which could in fact start to undermine the survival of the network. My aim with this book is not just to make visible the importance (and really also the beauty: the global cable network is a remarkable system) of the undersea cable, but also to issue a warning about the quiet but therefore no less important geopolitical forces that could start to threaten its future.

In the meantime, some of that work had already been done for me. For remain invisible, the cable did not. As I was finalizing this manuscript, it was the outside world itself that had suddenly catapulted the undersea cable network firmly into the public eye. A series of high-profile incidents in the Baltic Sea and near Taiwan, which saw cables damaged under suspicious circumstances, quickly turned this once-overlooked infrastructure into a global headline story. Politicians the world over were now giving speeches about the importance of protecting undersea cables. Tabloid newspapers splashed alarmist warnings that the internet was about to go dark, and that we would all soon return to the Dark Ages. The Kremlin liked to further fuel this kind of paranoia whenever it found an opportunity. Parliamentarians raised urgent questions. NATO launched a dedicated naval mission to maybe make this more fun. Governments began to invest in high-tech undersea drones and other gizmos, and dust off their Cold War playbooks for how to handle the ensuing panic that may follow large-scale blackouts. Think tank pundits refashioned themselves into overnight cable experts. Military officials and journalists started to flood once insider-only industry events. Media requests rather than copy edits now began to fill my inbox. When I started writing this book, still not that many people had ever heard of undersea cables; by the time I finished, there was an abundance of theories about these Baltic seabed *whodunnits*.

But though interest may have increased, that does not mean that understanding necessarily has. For the threats to the network are far more diverse and pervasive than cable sabotage alone. In this book, we will explore the increasingly entangled and corrosive ways in which countries and companies are seeking to gain control over global cable connectivity – a competition which threatens to fragment the cable network altogether.

## *The cable network*

So what exactly were these undersea cables the *Yantar* was hunting for? If you, like the spy vessel, were to go look for them, you may find it hard to know where to begin. You could start with the windowless, concrete boxes or non-descript office blocks, tucked away on the outskirts of some Kentish or Breton beach town or anonymous suburban business park. It is from there that armoured fibre optic cables begin or end their invisible journeys, disappearing first below the wind-swept car park, then onwards to the beach, where they remain underground, buried deep in trenches several metres beneath the slick or sand. From here, they move underwater and enter the sea. Once safely out of reach of any stray anchors, sand dredgers or fishing nets, these cables – no thicker than a garden hose – finally re-emerge, now lying exposed on the seafloor, the depth of our seas and oceans their main insulation as they connect together countries and continents.

There are currently some 600 undersea cables out there on the ocean floor, wiring up virtually all corners of the planet. Some of the longest systems can reach incredible lengths: Mark Zuckerberg's Meta's $2 billion Waterworth cable system, which is currently under construction, is planned to gird the globe – starting in Los Angeles, down to Australia, via India, the Seychelles, South Africa, Brazil to New York – and will come in at a remarkable 50,000 kilometres once finished – exceeding the circumference of the Earth.[4] The total length of the rapidly expanding global undersea cable network now totals 1.4 million kilometres,[5] the equivalent of 35 roundtrips around the equator.

These 600 cables and counting should be seen as the main arteries, the aortas if you will, which wire up the world. Connected together by landing stations (those bland grey boxes and office blocks), from here traffic continues onwards, through terrestrial cables – the branches and capillaries – wiring up energy-guzzling cloud and AI data centres, the internet exchange points located in cities from Amsterdam to Windhoek, the mobile cell towers that eventually get that bit of data – or maybe even the text of this very book – onto the screen in front of you.

In this book, we are primarily concerned with those key aortas, cables important enough to have names – Apollo, PEACE, Grace Hopper. These are the cables you can find on online cable maps (I recommend readers peruse the TeleGeography map available for free online, to get are a sense of the contours of the global cable network).[6] These are the expensive, strategic cables that touch on different countries, traverse their territorial waters – with all the geopolitical complexity that can entail – and are subject to the underregulated Wild West that can be the High Seas.

As the main international carriers of the internet's 'lifeblood', these cables are not only frequently very long, they can also carry unfathomably large amounts of data, and they can do so incredibly quickly. The first transatlantic telegraph cable, laid in 1858, was able to receive a single, Morse-coded – *dot dot dash dash* – message at a time.[7] When TAT-1, the first Transatlantic cable able to also carry voice calls, was completed in 1956, it could handle thirty-six synchronous telephone channels – ground-breaking at the time. The Dunant cable, a 6,600 kilometre-long

Alphabet-owned cable which connects Virginia Beach in the United States to the Atlantic coast of France, can now ferry an incredible 250 terabits of data per second,[8] or the equivalent of streaming 50 million Netflix movies simultaneously.

The speed by which data, transformed into pulses of light, travels through cables, too, only continues to increase. It initially took several hours for a telegraph message to reach the US East Coast from Europe; each individual letter of the inaugural communications exchanged by Queen Victoria and US President James Buchanan taking over two minutes to make it to the other side. The Dunant can now transmit three times the total volume of words housed in the British Library in under a second. There are whole industries dedicated to shaving off even more milliseconds of these transmission speeds – especially in the hyper-charged world of high-frequency trading, where even the most minute of increases in speed can make all the difference.

For the pivotal role they play in enabling global connectivity, and therefore much else, the cables themselves are actually remarkably slim. Most of the world's international data travels as pulses of light through bundles of infinitesimally thin glass fibres, each narrower than a human hair, whose main insulation is a relatively modest layer of steel wire and water-proof polyethylene, for a combined thickness of around 20 millimetres, or your average garden hose. It is as exposed garden hoses that undersea cables spend most of their journeys, with only these layers of protection separating them from the hazards of the deep sea. Once the cables reach shallower waters nearer to shore, they get to enjoy a bit more protection, as they now reach those segments of the sea where they are at increased risk of damage – such as from fishing gear or, say, a Russian research vessel's stray anchor.

Still, this additional layer of steel armour brings the cables up to a diameter of only around 50 millimetres – still perhaps not the robust heavy-duty cables that may have sprung to mind when we think of the key infrastructure that powers the global internet. Closer to shore still, cables tend to get buried in trenches in the seabed of one to three metres deep. Underground, the cables move onwards onto land – the transition from wet to dry. You may have laid your beach towel on top of one without ever being the wiser.

## *Cable power*

This growing web of undersea cables is far from equally distributed: some of the most popular routes, such as the transatlantic cables that connect the US East Coast to Western Europe, are served by many cables. Other places, like Antarctica and many Pacific and Caribbean island nations, do not yet have any cables landing on their shores at all. Geopolitically isolated countries such as Cuba and Venezuela live with patchy connectivity, while rising tensions between China and the United States have brought new direct cable projects between the two digital superpowers effectively to a halt.

These very different outcomes are the product of a tangled mix of geography, money, history, military considerations, legal limitations, and geopolitics. The richest countries tend to attract the most cables, a self-reinforcing dynamic, which allows them to solidify their dominance in global financial markets, technology industries, and now put themselves at the heart of the AI boom. Finding oneself at the centre of the global network brings advantages far beyond economic ones, however: they can allow countries to control global information flows and the activities they enable, project military power over vast distances and steer global commerce. They even enable the eavesdropping on our adversary's most sensitive communications (and occasionally our allies' too).

None of this is new. Ever since the first undersea telegraph cables were laid in the middle of the nineteenth century, countries and companies have attempted to control the cable network and find new ways to leverage it to their strategic advantage. In this book, we will explore many of them – from sabotage, to spying, to their use as a tool of economic coercion and influence – and meet the actors taking part in it. There are the Russian submarines lurking in the deep sea and the supposed Chinese submersibles, designed to cut cables at depths as deep as 4,000 metres. Moscow's shadow fleet tankers and Beijing's sand dredgers, dragging their anchors over undersea cables, purportedly by accident. There are the NATO planners, wargaming how to return the favour. There are the whistleblowers, who revealed the extent of American cable interception capabilities, and the Western intelligence officials who warn China may well be able to do the same. There are the tech giants – 'the hyperscalers' – who are increasingly creating their own, private cable networks, and are fuelling an AI infrastructure spending boom so large, they could send the whole cable industry reeling. We will meet the proto-tech moguls of the nineteenth century, who sparked a cable spending bubble of their own, and the disgruntled colonial administrators, disempowered by the real-time telegraph-enabled orders now arriving from the home front. We will visit the once-stuffy inter-departmental committees, whose ability to veto new cables is rewiring the network's topology; the challengers up in space, who see an opportunity to supplant the cable altogether.

This competition over cables will take us to all corners of the planet. From the Red Sea, where Houthi rebels threaten this most pernicious chokepoint in the cable network, through which 80 per cent of traffic between Asia and Europe is routed. It will bring us to the Arctic, where Europe, Russia and the United States compete to lay the first transpolar cable. To the South China Sea, where the Taiwanese coastguard faces off with suspicious cargo ships. We will visit the Gulf countries, whose dreams of a post-oil future in which they are global leaders in AI and become key cable hubs, meet the geopolitical realities of the Middle East. To the remote Pacific, where great powers battle for influence through cable diplomacy and the hijacking of new cable projects.

As we zoom in on these intricacies of the cable world, we will see that all of this is about far more than cables alone. These undersea garden hoses in many ways serve as a microcosm of the larger geopolitical battles reshaping our highly-interdependent, highly-interconnected world, where economic warfare and the weaponization of interdependencies have become as potent a weapon as cable-cutting research vessels are.

## *Weaponized interdependence*

The undersea cable came of age under Pax Britannica. From the mid-nineteenth century up until the First World War, the British Empire was able to exert an overwhelming degree of influence and control over the worldwide telegraph network, a kind of hegemony over global communications not seen before or since. Laying a telegraph cable, funding a cable, running a cable, repairing it: all involved Britain one way or another. British companies facilitated the roll-out of the vast majority of cables being laid anywhere in the world. A significant share of commercial but also military and diplomatic traffic was routed through landing stations dotting its shores. For most, the idea that London would in the future not be at the heart of effectively all facets of global communications would have long seemed unthinkable. To solidify and secure this lead, Britain set about constructing its 'All Red Line', an incredibly ambitious and expensive endeavour, which sought to create a sovereign network of undersea cables connecting together virtually all corners of Britain's vast overseas empire, while almost never touching soil not under direct British control.

This dominance and global coverage not only made it very difficult to cripple Britain's own imperial communications, it also meant that many other major powers became reliant on British cables for their own. British planners were well aware that this kind of dependency could be turned into a devastating weapon should the opportunity ever arise.

And that it did. As one of its very first acts at the outset of the First World War, Britain destroyed Germany's main undersea cables, significantly curtailing the country's ability to communicate freely for the duration of the war and forcing Berlin to rely on neutral and even British cables instead. Not only did the loss of its own cables significantly undermine Germany's war effort and the viability of its wartime economy, it also allowed Britain to gain access to Berlin's most sensitive communications. It was the fateful interception of the Zimmermann Telegram, Berlin's secret proposal to Mexico to join it in war against the United States, which finally dragged America into the conflict, and ultimately helped Britain win it.

While the British empire used its dominance over cables to great strategic effect, it also came at a cost. By making it abundantly clear – in smaller ways already before the war – just how much power Britain held over the network, it spooked even its allies into reducing their dependencies. Many also rushed to adopt new technologies like wireless, to the detriment of the cable. This is one of the downsides of weaponizing dependencies – these are powerful cards to play but showing one's hand can also undermine one's position in a network in the long run. It is what happened to the once unassailable communications hegemon Britain, which not long after had to cede this title to the United States.

It is an example today's most powerful actors in the networked economy would do well to learn from. The United States remains the most powerful player in the cable game, with especially its hyperscalers – tech giants like

Microsoft, Amazon and Google's Alphabet – now indispensable investors in the global network. By leveraging the power and global reach of these hyperscalers, Washington has made it increasingly difficult for Chinese companies to be involved in new cable projects. It has used similar, and even more powerful, levers of influence and chokepoints in global supply chains to prevent China from accessing the highest end semiconductors and microchips critical in the AI race, to name but one example.

These types of controls serve to keep the United States in the lead for now (though, as we will discuss in this book, it may perhaps already be too late for that), but have also encouraged Beijing and others to go it alone and develop their own alternatives to US tech dominance and other pillars underpinning the US-led world order. This, too, has its analogues in the cable realm. Beijing is, for example, pulling its own levers by barring others from laying cables in the South China Sea, and is actively trying to draw others into its technology orbit by exporting highly subsidized cables to the rest of the world. This rapid politicization of the roll-out of new submarine cables could eventually also begin to threaten to fragment the global network.

## *A thousand little pieces*

Such fragmentation is not new. The telegraph played a pivotal role in spurring what we now consider the first wave of globalization starting in the mid-nineteenth century, which gave rise to a period of rapid imperial expansion, of people, information and goods moving around at unprecedented speed, the birth of modern financial markets, of real-time news reporting and truly global media. But like the global order it helped birth, the cable's dominance in global communications too began to erode after the First World War, as countries turned more inward-looking, rushed to become less dependent on British cable benevolence, and newer, more glamorous technologies – such as radio, and later Space Race paragon the satellite – began to challenge the cable's centrality.

During the Cold War the cable increasingly disappeared from the public eye, sometimes literally hidden away in concrete bunkers to shield them from nuclear blasts. The companies involved with laying new cables became deeply entwined in the military-industrial complex, supporting the West in its existential competition with the Soviet Union. The network not only became more militarized, it also fragmented, with competing power blocs maintaining their own, increasingly separate spheres. This meant that while Britain had been able to intercept German communications as they arrived on its doorstep, the Americans had to undertake daring submarine capers deep into Soviet waters to tap its adversary's cables.

When we look at today's world, the Cold War echoes, too, are loud. We are now once again entering an era in which undersea cables are becoming the object of intense government and military scrutiny. Concerns about cable-tapping and hidden backdoors built into the technology see countries trying to separate their networks and weed others out of their supply chains. Technology companies – including the hyperscalers, but also China's tech giants – are once again becoming more vocal about doing their 'patriotic duty' and the important roles they can play in great power competition, especially in the AI race.

We also once again see countries and continents around the world trying to become more sovereign over their own technology, concerned that an overreliance on others may be used as a weapon against them. It was Britain targeting Germany that in part encouraged the United States to become a more strategic player in communications networks during the inter-war years. It is also what America's affronted allies are increasingly seeking to do, now that the United States itself appears to be retreating from its own good steward role over many of the institutions and systems that underpinned its hegemony.

The United States' overzealous weaponization of its hold over the global economy – whether it is the growing dominance of its tech giants over undersea cables and many other slices of the technology stack, the indispensability of its financial markets, or the role of the US dollar – sees friend and foe alike now starting to build their own alternatives. Over time, this may not just result in the chipping away at America's global power and prestige – something at the time of writing seemingly already very much underway – but could, more narrowly, also begin to undermine the global cable network's integrity. Will we be moving to a world in which the cable network, and the technologies relying on its global reach, start to fragment and splinter in different geographical spheres? A world where instantaneous global exchange is simply no longer a given?

## *Peace dividend*

After playing a more modest role for several decades, the undersea cable would make a major comeback towards the end of the Cold War – soon firmly outcompeting the satellite as the global telecommunications technology of choice. The timing of its arrival would prove providential: the undersea fibre optic cable reached technological maturity just as the Berlin Wall came down and the internet started its spectacular rise – an explosive growth these high-speed, high-capacity undersea cables in important ways enabled. Like in the telegraph era, the undersea cable thus came to play a pivotal role in fuelling this next wave of globalization too.

It would at the same time also be fundamentally shaped by it: the climate of post-Wall exuberance allowed the network to spread its reach to virtually every corner of the planet. This was the era of peace dividend thinking, in which the undersea cable became a weapon for exporting free market liberalism and economic influence, no longer just a weapon of war. As cables now quickly turned into a primarily commercial technology, rapid expansion and keeping down costs became the priority. Their security, too, would largely be left to the private sector. For many decades, this model worked well. The cable industry has on the whole been a good steward of the network: submarine cables are resilient, and the sector has been able to facilitate the astronomical increase in demand for data and connectivity, as well as further booms driven by the rapid rise of technologies like AI. The systems and processes that have kept the network running so smoothly were, however, devised for a more collaborative, secure world – where absent-minded fishermen, not Russian submarines, presented the biggest threat.

It is the kind of approach that can be seen as emblematic for what I will refer to throughout this book as 'peace dividend thinking', which prevailed in the first post-Cold War decades, during which war seemed a thing of the past and profit motives trumped most geopolitical and security considerations. It is not just in the realm of undersea cables that this kind of mentality has revealed itself to be an enormous vulnerability. Countries across the West and beyond have allowed themselves to become almost entirely dependent on others for their technology, supply chains and security, underinvested in the protection of physical infrastructures as vital as those underpinning our energy and communications systems, and let their militaries erode. Peace dividend thinking had – and continues to have – acolytes in many parts of the world but can be said to have been particularly pervasive in Europe, a continent whose three-decade holiday from geopolitics has left it especially ill-prepared for a new era of 'might makes right'. As Europe now grapples with having to relearn what it means to be a hard power actor, the need to protect undersea cables is one of those areas where it is starting to find its voice.

# 1

# *A Global Revolution*

## *The birth of the telegraph*

The invention of the electric telegraph, which for the first time allowed rapid, long-distance transmission of messages through wires, had first been commercialized at scale in the 1840s – but its roll-out had primarily been in land-based, often domestic networks.[1] The development of telegraph cables that could survive underwater, which would unlock the technology's true promise – of making it possible to communicate across continents – for a long time remained elusive. It was not until 1858, after several rather spectacular and expensive failures, that the first transatlantic telegraph cable, connecting Valentia Island, off the coast of Ireland, to Heart's Content on Newfoundland, was successfully laid.[2] Though the cable would break down again after just a couple of weeks, it nonetheless heralded in an era of unprecedented globalization and global integration, in which the roll-out of the subsea cables facilitating these transformations would become a source of great imperial prestige as well as competition.

The impact of the undersea telegraph cable was immediate and profound. Where a message sent from London via steamship would previously have taken about eight days to reach New York, this could now be reduced to a matter of hours, soon even minutes,[3] enabling the development of the modern financial system and stock markets (and bubbles). Navy ships leaving Portsmouth or Liverpool could take up to six months to reach the furthest outposts of the British empire,[4] with little communication possible in the interim. Now instructions from the Foreign Office could reach colonial administrators in near-real time. This new capability helped give rise to a period that has come to be known as 'High Imperialism', marked by rapid colonial expansion and much tighter control by European capitals over their overseas possessions.[5]

The telegraph brought not only strategic advantages, it also loomed large in the public imagination: huge crowds gathered to witness the first successful cable landings, collected postcards depicting futuristic cable-laying ships, with their enormous cable looms, which carried the thousands of kilometres of cable needed to bridge expanses as wide as the Atlantic and later the Pacific. The proto-Silicon Valley entrepreneurs, like Cyrus West Field and John Pender, who had persisted through multiple expensive failed experiments to finally make intercontinental communications possible, became global celebrities (one of the main technical challenges had been the insulation of the cables; it was the discovery of gutta-percha, a natural rubber which only dwells well in the specific parts of South-East Asia, that resolved this vital piece of the puzzle). The unofficial bard of the spirit of *Rule Britannia* Rudyard Kipling would wax lyrical about undersea cables and their deep-sea mystique ('*And a new Word runs between: whispering, "Let us be one!"*').[6]

The cable not only became an object of publication fascination, it conversely also shaped it. Cables (initially still terrestrial ones) enabled the rapid development of real-time news reporting – allowing Londoners, Parisians and Muscovites to stay up-to-date about the latest goings-on in the Crimean War over their breakfast newspapers[7] – and saw the birth of news agencies like Reuters. It even impacted the way in which people wrote: telegrams were expensive and charged by the word. Flowery prose thus soon gave way to pithy, to-the-point communications,[8] a stylistic shift which even found its way into the literature and poetry of the time.[9]

By reducing distance, the rapidly growing global telegraph network became a key enabler of the first era of globalization, but was also in some ways an object of it. The frenzied network expansion during the first decades of the electric telegraph, which lasted until the mid-1870s, was mostly driven by commercial interests and focused on the most lucrative routes, first connecting Europe and the United States, and later increasingly South America and Asia as well.[10] A flurry of new companies emerged, the most successful ones virtually all British, which capitalized on the explosive growth in global cable demand. By 1870, submarine telegraph companies accounted for nearly a third of all capital raised on the London Stock Exchange, where the vast majority of telegraph transactions took place.[11] This rapid expansion – together with the railroads, one of those other new technologies which rapidly reduced distance – helped fuel the first modern, global financial bubble as the key commercial markets started to become oversaturated. New avenues for network expansion needed to be found: it would be primarily Britain – which had taken an early lead in cable development and roll-out – that seized them first.

## *British cable hegemony*

It is difficult to overstate the dominance the British Empire was able to exert over global telegraph communications in the decades leading up to the First World War. By the turn of the century, Britain owned 60 per cent of all cables, not just those connecting Britain, but anywhere in the world.[12] Many cables, furthermore, made landfall in Britain, including those owned by other countries. The concentration of global traffic in geographically advantageous locations like Porthcurno, a small seaside town at the westernmost tip of Cornwall (Britain's West Coast remains an important node in global communications to this day) allowed Britain to wield an extraordinary degree of control over worldwide information flows, further solidifying London's position as the pre-eminent global financial centre.[13] The City of London was the place where deals were brokered and funds raised for most new cables, not just those involving British companies.

British cable giants were usually the most innovative and possessed the most technical know-how and, crucially, employed the vast majority of trained cable-laying staff, meaning British companies would even frequently be involved with their rivals' cable roll-out.[14] Control also extended to the manufacture of the physical cables themselves, and the input materials that went into them. Through its colonial possessions in the Malay peninsula and on Borneo, Britain was also able to establish a virtual trade monopoly over supplies of gutta-percha, the natural plastic vital for the insulation of underwater cables.[15] Britain, furthermore, also possessed most cable repair capacity – the dedicated ships tasked with identifying the source and location of faults out at sea, hauling up the damaged cable segments and repairing them again, a particularly effective chokepoint to weaponize in times of conflict. It above all enjoyed the protection offered by the Royal Navy, then at the height of its powers. British control over the network was near absolute – a power it would soon learn it could leverage to great advantage.

## *High Imperialism*

The strategic utility of telegraph cables as a 'tool of empire'[16] and power projection was not lost on Britain's military planners. There had been some notable early successes in the use of the telegraph in conflicts, famously in the Crimean War. At the same time, communications failures in the ultimately successful repression of the 1857 Sepoy Rebellion in India, which had resulted in delays in the deployment of military assistance, showed planners the power of rapid telegraphic communications.

It was, however, not until the 1870s that the British government and military began to play a more active role in cable roll-out and started to seriously act on the strategic advantages owning a global cable network had to offer. This involvement focused also on subsidizing the roll-out of cables to less immediately lucrative markets across Britain's imperial possessions – a new lease on life for Britain's commercial cable industry, which had saturated most of the obvious routes, and could use the government subsidies now that the commercial boom years had cooled down.[17]

This second wave of cable expansion thus began to centre around the roll-out of terrestrial and increasingly also undersea cables to connect European powers to their faraway possessions, from Alexandria to Suez, Suez to Karachi and beyond. Other colonial powers in Europe, too, endeavoured to fund their own sovereign cables and in, for example, France's case did so quite effectively, but they were not able to match the pace of British expansion, and lacked the necessary capital, industrial capacity and infrastructure to create the kind of global web Britain was now constructing for itself. [18]

Nevertheless, global cable coverage began to increase rapidly, and with it the Europeans' ability to tighten their imperial holds. Where it could previously take months for messages from London or Paris to reach local administrators on the ground – making issuing any urgent instructions fairly moot – the telegraph now made it possible to much more closely orchestrate colonial affairs directly from Europe's capitals, provided a cable was in place (it would take until the start of the twentieth century to see significant global coverage).[19] Though there is still debate among historians about whether such technology-enabled interference from the home front actually did more harm than good (Mandarins back in

Whitehall often understood little about local conditions, cultures and sensitivities when they sent over their missives), the telegraph would soon come to play an important role in, for example, more rapidly cracking down on local uprisings and stemming dissent.[20] It also allowed an intensification of trade with the wider empire, with routes to, for example, India especially lucrative. Landing stations in the colonies, which needed large staffs to receive, decode and transfer messages and maintain the specialized equipment, would become miniature Britains, Frances or Hollands overseas. Europeans who had settled in the further removed reaches of empire, such as Australia, were now far better able to stay in contact with the relatives they had left behind and remained more culturally and politically attuned with the home front, which also aided in strengthening ties.

It was not just the local populations who felt the increasingly long arm of London and its peers and the intensification of colonial presence. The technology was also perceived as emasculating by many of the colonial administrators on the ground, who now suddenly found themselves fielding far more frequent communiqués from the imperial core. Many had been used to running their own fiefdoms – far away from their employers' prying eyes – but had now been turned into mere messengers. George Orwell, who had started his career as a colonial policeman in Burma (now Myanmar), described the new dynamic several decades later as 'the one-time empire builders [having been reduced] to the status of clerks, buried deeper and deeper under mounds of paper and red tape'.[21]

Telegraph communications did not just enable London to exert much tighter control over colonial goings-on on the ground, the roll-out of telegraph cables and the establishment of landing stations in strategic locations also allowed Britain to create a global information network geared towards mapping its own and rivals' commercial and naval activities, enabling the projection of naval power over far greater stretches of ocean. The telegraph could also offer a solution to the perennial security concerns that came with maintaining a dispersed empire. The British empire spanned the globe, with many of its smaller possessions enjoying very limited colonial presence, if any at all, leaving them vulnerable to attack.[22] Contrast this with a power like Russia, one of its main rivals in this period of the Great Game – the prolonged Russo-British competition over control and influence in Central Asia – which possessed a contiguous land-based empire (and would indeed focus primarily on constructing a network of domestic, terrestrial cables).

Some of these 'neglected', vulnerable dots on the imperial map, such as the sparsely populated St. Helena in the south Atlantic (earlier in the century home to a Royal Navy base tasked with suppressing the slave trade), now turned into strategic assets as they could feature as in-between nodes connecting the far corners of the empire. In fact, Britain started to proactively acquire new possessions, such as in 1888 Fanning Island in the Pacific (now part of the nation of Kiribati), for this express purpose.[23] The telegraph not only became a vehicle for colonial expansion, its technical limitations in part also encouraged it. The logic here resided in the fact that the lengthier cables were far more expensive and technically difficult to lay and maintain than multiple shorter ones. Building in island hop points– relays – on routes could therefore reduce the cost of laying a new cable significantly.[24] Its scatterplot imperial map thus became yet another advantage Britain enjoyed in the (rather one-sided) competition for communications hegemony. France also possessed some islands and dispersed colonies it could use as a basis for cable expansion, but Germany – a latecomer to the imperial game – for example, did not, which forced it to rely on the continued benevolence of neutrals, such as the Portuguese Azores, dependencies which would prove a strategic weakness during conflicts. The telegraph may have been a tool for reducing distance and physical limits, but the cable network underpinning it was still very much tethered to the realities of geography.

The need for landing stations was not the only way in which the cable itself became the object of colonial expansion. Through its possessions in the Malay peninsula and Borneo, among the very few places where gutta-percha trees dwelled well, Britain was also able to wield significant control over supplies and trade of the natural plastic, which was crucial for the insulation of underwater cables (the Netherlands by way of the Dutch East Indies and France through its possessions in Indochina were also producers, albeit smaller). As demand for physical cable skyrocketed, Britain aggressively expanded its imperial presence there, and in the process felled so many tens of millions of the trees that it unleashed what historian John Tully has dubbed a 'Victorian ecological disaster'.[25] By the 1940s, gutta-percha was largely replaced with artificial alternatives, but not before the once abundant gutta-percha tree had been harvested to near extinction.

The telegraph was but one of the technologies that came to define, and enable, this new era of High Imperialism, which saw European powers rapidly expand and take control of most of the globe.[26] This was the era of gunboat diplomacy and in-land expansion into Africa and elsewhere, enabled by the steamship, which could navigate upriver, and advancements in medicine such as the discovery of the anti-malarial quinine; of the growth of the railways, the White Man's Burden and 'Whatever happens, we have got the Maxim gun, and they have not.'

Expansion of the cable network soon became relentless, with the technology used not just for emancipation and freedom, but also as a tool of repression and control. This breakneck expansion even moved into countries that were neither colonized nor especially keen to be wired up or integrated into Western-dominated communications networks. Qing China, which in the nineteenth century maintained a deeply ambivalent and suspicious relationship with foreign-controlled infrastructure, which it viewed as Western encroachment, had initially resisted foreign cable landings. It soon found itself facing a *fait accompli* however, after a rare collaboration between the Germans, French and British had seen the countries establish cable connections in their treaty-port concessions in Shanghai, despite fervent Qing objections. It was a move that heralded China's entry into global communications networks and served as a poignant symbol of what we have later come to refer to as the country's Century of Humiliation – an experience that still shapes China's deeply held sentiment of never allowing itself to become dependent on foreign powers for its technology to this day.

### *All roads lead to Porthcurno: constructing the All Red Line*

The critical importance of undersea cables – for the maintenance of its empire, as a weapon of war, a tool of trade and commerce – made London, despite its overwhelming dominance, increasingly concerned about the vulnerability of its cable network. Naval and imperial planners feared the rise of Germany in particular, and especially Berlin's ability to interfere with the network in times of conflict. Telegraph cables could be sabotaged, inflicting a blow 'equal to the defeat of a whole fleet of armour clads'.[27] Destroying telegraph cables was therefore perceived to be one of the few ways in which even less formidable actors could gain an advantage over the all-powerful Royal Navy – a weakness Britain increasingly feverishly sought to eradicate. 'The lines of communication that hold empires together never seem strong enough to those whose power and security depend on them.'[28]

The Admiralty as well as the private companies that owned much of the cable-laying infrastructure began to invest in hardening cables, especially nearer to shore where they were vulnerable to accidental fishing incidents, mishaps and more deliberate sabotage (for which culprits could use tools ranging from special grappling hooks to simply just their anchors). They began to fortify landing stations, which not infrequently began to resemble military outposts in their own right, or were deliberately positioned very close to British naval strongholds. Cable routes were preferably chosen to follow equivalent naval routes, which allowed some degree of implicit protection and patrolling, and made repair easier.[29]

The biggest thorn in the Admiralty's side, however, was not so much the security of the cables themselves, but the insecurity of the geographies they were routed through. Such concerns especially centred on land-based cables. Before Britain's subsea connection to India was completed in the 1870s, telegraph communications to the subcontinent had had to rely on terrestrial connections, routed from Constantinople, through the Persian Gulf, Persia and Balochistan to finish in India. Some of these places were friendly to Britain or even directly under its control – many were not, or frequently saw armed conflict, which could see cables damaged. Worse still were cables routed through or landing in territories or colonies belonging to or that were under the influence of France or Russia, or later Germany. 'Intercommunication [. . .] should as far as possible be in British hands, and should not be dependent upon the friendship or the caprice of other nations.'[30]

This sentiment is why Britain set out to construct an All Red Line, so named because British colonial possessions were generally coloured red in atlases of the time,[31] a hugely ambitious endeavour, which aimed to create a truly globe-spanning telegraph network, controlled by Britain, connecting together all its imperial possessions, and which would never land on foreign soil. The importance bestowed upon this multi-decade project, which could count on support across Whitehall (except, unsurprisingly, a wary Treasury – laying cable was not exactly cheap), not infrequently reached quite apocalyptic proportions. As one report by the Imperial Cable Protection Committee put it around the turn of the century: 'Unless we maintain our own more secure alternative routes, [we may] imperil our most serious interests, the safety of our dependencies, or even our existence as a nation.'[32]

Concerns about the costs notwithstanding, the first segment of what later came to be known as the All Red Line was completed in 1870. Constructed by a joint venture of companies led by the Eastern Telegraph Company – one of Britain's largest cable companies – and subsidized by the British government, it connected the Cornish outpost of Porthcurno to Mumbai, providing a secure connection to Britain's most prized imperial possession, via Malta, Alexandria, Suez, and the port of Gwadar in what is now Pakistan, and Karachi. The final leg of the All Red Line, which connected Bamfield in Canada with Fanning Island in Polynesia, was completed some three decades later, in October 1902, enabling Britain to reach all its major dominions and colonies, while virtually never making landfall in places not owned or controlled by London.[33] While the British government subsidized the roll-out and maintenance of its global telegraph network to the tune of nearly £3 million,[34] it still relied on partnerships with Britain's large private cable industry, which found their fortunes revived after commercial demand had dried up. Even at the height of the All Red cable rush, only some 20 per cent of British cables were actually owned by the government – the rest was all commercial.[35]

Beyond ensuring that the cables that made up the All Red line followed secure routes, efforts soon also turned to building additional, redundant cables, to allow for multiple pathways and fallback options to key locales, and to reduce the impact of bottlenecks in the network (cable routes through Egypt's Suez were already seen as a major chokepoint then, and continue to be seen as such to this day). The first trans-Pacific cables, costly endeavours of at that time still limited commercial value, were, for example, in large part constructed to bring more redundancy into the system and create alternative pathways for cable traffic, along routes less likely to form the central battlegrounds in a future European conflagration.[36] Costs kept rising, the network kept expanding, but London's planners were still not content. The Admiralty and Imperial Defence

Committee would eventually get caught in what Paul Kennedy refers to as a 'virtual fetish' for removing every possible weakness from the system and maintaining Britain's supremacy in communications.[37]

Overzealous as it may have been, the final substantive strategic assessment of the resilience of Britain's network before the outbreak of the Great War, completed in 1911, deemed that all these efforts to bring redundancy and diversity into the All Red Line had not been in vain.[38] It would require the severing of forty-nine cables to fully cut Britain out of the network – key colonies such as India were also relatively well secured.[39] Britain's rivals did not enjoy this same sense of security: despite efforts to diversify away from Britain and rapidly increase its own cable connections, by the time of the outbreak of the First World War, Germany had only two sovereign cables which served the United States, its most commercially critical route.[40] These were two cables, as it turned out, Britain would be willing and able to cut once the circumstances demanded it.

## *Britannia waives the rules*

Though the All Red Line was primarily a strategic project, the extensive involvement of the private sector also bestowed a second, highly important commercial purpose upon it. Other Western powers naturally also invested in their own cables, and sought to connect to their own overseas possessions, but could not keep up with the speed nor the eye-watering amounts of investment fuelling the All Red Line frenzy. The laying of cables outside of the North Atlantic area and some routes to key colonies like India was generally unprofitable, which meant that the All Red Line cables were the only links connecting certain parts of the globe, as there were few commercial incentives to justify the expense.[41] The upshot of this was that in some places other countries' global communications also came to rely on the All Red Line network – France, the Netherlands and Germany would all become partially dependent on various sections of Britain's web to reach even some of their most-prized colonial possessions. This left them increasingly beholden to Britain's largesse in the cable-laying domain – especially for the least lucrative routes, where it was only Britain's zeal for removing any strategic weaknesses from its network that saw cables be laid.[42]

This resulted in a situation where France and Germany, for example, had to in part rely on British cables to South Africa to communicate with their own possessions in southern Africa, such as Namibia and Madagascar, or the Netherlands, which in part relied on British cables to reach the far-away Dutch East Indies. This initially did not pose much of a problem, even as the relationships between European powers continued to fray; everyone benefitted. Britain was able to recoup some of the high capital investments required for its global cable-laying endeavours, and its customers could avoid funding their own unprofitable yet costly cables. This arrangement lasted for a while. Britain, however, showed itself increasingly willing to use the dominance this had inadvertently afforded it over global communications for its own ends. There were already growing concerns that Britain may be intercepting traffic relayed through Porthcurno, the landing site of a great many European cables, to gain an insight into its rivals' trade activities.[43] The real turning point, however, came during the Boer Wars, when Britain first censored, and later in some cases outright blocked communications going through many of its Africa-bound cables. This certainly helped undermine the Boers' war effort, but would in the process annoy, and increasingly spook, others reliant on these cables too. It would especially see Germany push to become more autonomous and less reliant on Britain for its overseas communications.

Britain also used this dominance in the network to obstruct attempts to create international rules and norms around the governance of telegraph cables. The few agreements that were brokered during the heyday of the telegraph (some of which remain in force to this day) focused on more mundane issues like disputes over fishing versus cable-laying rights, but did not meaningfully address more sensitive issues like the deliberate sabotage of cables, or interference with cable traffic. The Admiralty had not been especially keen to commit itself to pre-emptively limit its freedom to act on this front. British reluctance to put bounds on its ability to use its outsized role in the cable network to its advantage is not surprising, given the evident strategic promise of doing just this in wartime – when cutting an adversary's cables or reading along with their communications would be especially useful. It should be said that Britain was far from alone in pushing back against efforts to develop norms around, for example, the legality of cable sabotage and spying. Nor would Britain be the first to put the former into practice. That honour would fall to the Americans, who would sever most Spanish-owned cables in Cuba and the Philippines during the Spanish-American War of 1898.[44]

Britain's protectionist stance and revealed willingness to weaponize the network in its favour, however, also helped set in motion the slow decline of its telegraph hegemony. France and in particular Germany, concerned about the vulnerability this could present during a conflict that now seemed increasingly inevitable, began to rapidly expand their own strategic networks, in no small part motivated by their ambition to break free from Britain's monopoly, as they no longer considered Britain a reliable intermediary and good steward over the network.[45] These efforts, however, did not arrive in time, which meant that Britain still enjoyed an overwhelming dominance over cable communications on the eve of the First World War. Britain had control over 70 per cent of global cables in 1886; its share was down to 56 per cent by 1908 – a smaller, but still sufficiently large lead, as soon became clear.[46]

As the climate in Europe grew increasingly febrile, and the extent of Britain's dominance over the vital cable network became ever more starkly clear, Britain's rivals (and even its allies) tried to diversify from it not just by laying their own cables, but also by turning to new technologies. Wireless telegraphy, which similarly allowed communications over vast distances, was considered particularly promising.

## *A challenger on the shores*

Just as the rest of Europe, and to a lesser extent the United States, was growing wary of British cable dominance, another challenge to British network centrality emerged: the wireless, which threatened to eventually replace the need for laying cables at all. The possibility of carrying information – Morse code, perhaps even voice – via radio waves had long been anticipated in the scientific community. But it was the idiosyncratic Italo-British inventor Guglielmo Marconi who was the first to actually mature and commercialize the technology at around the turn of the century. While, just like in the early days of the telegraph, it would take some years (and many expensive failures) for wireless to live up to its promise, the scientific marvel as well as the strategic utility behind the technology were immediately apparent.

As a technology, wireless also spoke particularly well to the period's zeitgeist. The early 1900s were a time of spiritualism and belief in the occult, of seances held in the upper classes' salons, a time when even some of the most eminent scientists believed that conversing with ghosts was a perfectly rational pastime. It was also a time of deep-seated conviction that the speed and reach of technological innovation – the car, futurism! – was almost fathomless.[47] A technology that appeared to bring alive the ghost in the machine befitted these two sentiments perfectly.[48] Cables – which never fully ceased to be the workhorses of international communications – would be swiftly supplanted in the public imagination by wireless; Marconi would become a global celebrity. Though the young entrepreneur was certainly not always equally loved in British scientific circles, where many considered him a dilettante, the Admiralty had no such gripes, and in 1901 acquired wireless for Royal Navy use and helped Marconi secure a virtual monopoly over his innovations, and so obtained itself an early lead in the technology. Thus, Britain initially came to also dominate wireless roll-out and was very aware of the strategic advantages wireless telegraphy had to offer, for example in allowing one to reach ships out at sea (which cable communications of course could not). The still high degree of unreliability of the technology and its susceptibility to deliberate interference meant that Britain considered it primarily a powerful complement and fallback to the superior telegraph (having one technology serve as a back-up or complement to another communications technology is a concept I will, moving forward, refer to as 'modal redundancy').[49]

Not so Germany, which by now had started to feel that war with Britain was no longer a matter of if but when and was desperate to seize any opportunity to free itself from the yoke of British communications dominance before the inevitable came to pass. Increasingly aware that its effort to catch up with British cable-laying was permanently hampered by its limited and far-flung colonial empire, Germany began to make aggressive investments in wireless development and roll-out (though wireless also required physical stations and relay infrastructure, it was not as vulnerable to the chokepoints in between). It did this primarily through its financial and procurement support for its newly formed national champion Telefunken, a nominally private entity, which in practice primarily served to help Germany gain a commercial foothold in new markets, as well as to strengthen its security position through extensive military wireless roll-out. In the first years of the company's existence, over 70 per cent of its business came from the German military and efforts to increase German influence further afield.[50] The technology, however, remained experimental and had many limitations. It was also highly susceptible to interception. Wireless would not yet reach sufficient maturity at the eve of war for it to negate Germany's reliance on cables altogether.

There is sometimes a tendency to present the evolution of technology as a neat chronology, in which one solution passes on the baton to the next one: a new innovation arrives, making immediately obsolete all that came before. Not so in the case of the cable and wireless; undersea cables remained a bedrock of global communications throughout the twentieth century, existing in conjunction with radio and later technologies. Its footprint, and profitability, would, however, start to wane considerably from the 1910s onwards – it would not recover its lead until the dawn of the internet and the commercialization of undersea fibre optic cables starting in the late 1980s. None of this mattered yet, however, at the outbreak of the First World War.[51] Quite the opposite: the war would in many ways turn out to be the cable's finest strategic hour.

## *The Great War*

The war started with a series of telegrams, relaying the (missed) ultimatums, the declarations of war. Some historians even argue that it was the invention of the telegraph itself that was partially to blame for its outbreak.[52] Though the technology had been around for several decades, Europe's *corps diplomatique* had still not fully adapted to the speed and directness of communications it enabled, the argument goes, further fuelling the miscalculations that underpinned the July Crisis. Whatever the case, the long-anticipated war had finally arrived.

While Britain, like Europe's other major powers, soon found itself woefully unprepared for the brutality and totality of modern, mechanized warfare, one aspect of its pre-war planning it certainly did get right was its recognition of the highly strategic role that telegraph communications would play in it – and by extension the ways in which Britain's extraordinary dominance over the network afforded it the tools to weaponize that power. When the moment came, it was ready to use this to great effect.

Almost from the very outset of the war, Britain began to deploy a strategy that centred around the near immediate destruction of Germany's most strategic cables, so both throttling its adversary's ability to engage in international commerce as well as making it possible to intercept much of Germany's cable traffic, which the country was now forced to ferry through both neutral and even frequently British-owned cables. This three-pronged approach would culminate in Britain's successful interception of the Zimmermann telegram, the deft disclosure of which would draw the United States into the war on the side of the Entente, and played an important role in definitively tipping the balance in the war in its favour. The war started with a telegram; it can be said to have ended with one too.

Britain wasted no time in executing this strategy. During the early hours of 5 August 1914, hours after Britain had formally declared war on Germany and before the fighting had started in earnest, the HMS *Alert* – on board, a small, but specially trained crew – set out into the North Sea. There, in the dead of night, the vessel came to a stop not too far from the key German naval port of Emden, which was home to Germany's most important cable landing stations. There, the crew lowered their custom-made hook, lifted, and then destroyed Germany's most important undersea cables. Undetected, the *Alert* returned to port in England. Its mission, which had been undertaken at considerable risk, had been a stupendous success. Germany would not regain fully sovereign cable communications from its soil for the duration of the war.

This had a profound impact on Berlin's ability to execute its war effectively. It made it very difficult to maintain communications with its overseas empire. Even more importantly, however, was the effect this had on Germany's ability to engage in commerce, partake in international trade and diplomacy. The German economy was, for a time, an open one reliant on trade overseas – including, significantly, with the initially neutral United States. Not having access to direct, uncensored cable communications with America and others that were under Germany's own control soon emerged as a profound challenge. Any telegraphic exchange was slow, and if messages did reach the United States, they frequently needed to go through British cables, or neutral cables owned by countries like Sweden and the Netherlands, which often still made landfall on the Cornish coast anyway – providing London with a valuable opportunity to monitor and intercept a significant share of German in- and outbound communications.

Germany could not fully rely on its wireless communications as a fallback solution either. Despite Germany's early aggressive investments in wireless, virtually all international traffic still travelled through cables at the onset of the war.[53] Radio was, furthermore, still rightly seen as insecure (and in any case, the Royal Navy would also make an effort to destroy German overseas wireless stations, which were frequently co-located with its cable relay stations – soon leaving Germany with access only to its home station in Nauen in Berlin). This lack of German-controlled alternatives left Berlin in the deeply insecure position of having to rely on the impenetrability of its encryption ciphers. A serious miscalculation, as it would turn out.

British military planners had been laying the groundwork to decrypt German telegrams well before the start of the war, by building the cryptography capacity to handle the expected flow of intercepts that would begin to arrive as soon as Germany's cables were destroyed – and its sensitive traffic rerouted through cables within Britain's extended reach.[54] Communications were intercepted right at Britain's doorstep, at landing stations at Porthcurno and elsewhere, and sent onwards to London to be decrypted. During the war, much of this actual decryption work was undertaken by Room 40, a secret British naval intelligence unit, based in a backroom in London's old Admiralty building, charged with deciphering German communications. Room 40's motley crew of linguists and codebreakers, which together laid much of the basis of modern signals intelligence functions enjoyed an early boon when the Russian Navy shared with Britain a German codebook it had recovered from the sunk German cruiser the *SMS Magdeburg* in the Baltic Sea.[55] This breakthrough, and Room 40's own extensive innovations in cryptography throughout the war, allowed them to gain an insight into strategic wireless and telegraph communications that, for example, gave away planned German troop or naval movements.

This was not just about military intercepts. In parallel, a large network of censors was reading up on the enemy's commercial and logistical goings-on. Britain and its allies' dominance in cable networks thus also played a vital role in enabling them to enact a devastating policy of economic blockade, which focused on denying the Central Powers access to the vital economic goods they needed for their war efforts. Economic coercion as practised by Britain during the war was very much contingent on the increased interdependence and globalization of the world economy,[56] and far more intricate and sophisticated in its execution than just the blunt tool of naval blockade as is often believed.[57]

In broad lines, Britain's strategy focused on preventing goods from reaching Germany, and on undermining Berlin's (and its allies') war economy by throttling its ability to engage in cross-border trade. The telegraph would play an important role in both. Business traffic could be prevented from reaching its intended recipient abroad. Statements with details on shipments could be read, and shipments physically intercepted. Germany was, for example, very reliant on critical minerals and other raw resources arriving from neutral South American countries like Chile and Brazil. Eavesdropping allowed these transactions to be tracked and ships targeted or interdicted.[58] This allowed Britain to deal a serious blow to its adversary's ability to access vital goods and generate the funds to sustain its war machine.

These efforts even had a very direct impact on undersea telegraph cables themselves, by denying Berlin access to the materials it needed to manufacture new cables (not that the balance of power in the naval arena would have allowed any such cable to survive for long). Berlin had anticipated such a blockade would be likely, should it come to war,[59] and in the more specific case of telegraph cable production assumed that Britain may seek to weaponize its monopoly power over different links in the cable supply chain. Part of its motivation for funding Telefunken and wireless to the extent that it had, had indeed been to gain self-sufficiency over the full production and roll-out process.[60] With government encouragement, German scientists had by the 1910s also made progress in the development of synthetic replacements for gutta-percha, though these alternatives would not become commercially viable until the 1940s.

Britain's hegemony over global communications networks did not just allow it to target and undermine its adversaries economically, it also allowed London to put pressure on its allies and uncooperative neutrals in the conflict. A little discussed episode that illustrates this dynamic well centred on Britain's neighbour across the North Sea. The Netherlands, which was a major trade partner of both Britain and Germany (the latter two countries even co-owned several telegraph cables in Southeast

Asia) and had very little appetite to become embroiled in the fighting, had endeavoured to stay neutral during the war. This came with certain conditions, such as not engaging in the trade of what we now refer to as dual-use goods (goods which served both a civilian as well as military purpose, such as barbed wire, rubber, but also telegraph equipment), which could support either side's respective war efforts, or undermine Britain's naval blockade. Frequent Dutch violations of these neutrality agreements would become a growing source of ire in London, as its intercepts showed that Dutch investment banks were frequently secretly acting as intermediaries, allowing German banks to still access American capital markets via the heavily monitored British telegraph network.[61]

Tensions came to a head in October 1917 when it emerged that Dutch companies had enabled transactions of large quantities of sand and gravel to Germany, which had been used to fortify the latter's Siegfried Line, its 160 kilometre-long line of trenches and fortifications in Northern France. Retaliation followed swiftly. London threatened the Dutch that it would no longer allow the country to access its cable network if it did not immediately cease these activities. This was no idle threat: a complete cable traffic embargo on the Netherlands would have made it very difficult for the country to communicate with its colonies in South America and Southeast Asia. The Hague soon relented: without British cables, its communications would have crashed to a halt – another particularly illustrative case of Britain using its centrality in networks effectively.[62]

## *The telegram that changed the war*

Britain's ability to intercept and spy on German and the other Central powers' communications did not just allow it to erect an economic intelligence apparatus that enabled its campaign of blockade, it also provided it with an opportunity to use intercepted communications strategically, and use them as trump cards on the highest diplomatic stage. One famous example of this would be particularly instrumental in altering the course of the war.

The Entente powers' intensifying naval and commercial blockade certainly had its effects – but still not enough to break the stalemate. A lucky break, enabled by Britain's multipronged cable strategy, would change that. By the end of 1916 Germany's military and civilian leadership was becoming increasingly desperate.[63] The meat grinder on the Western front had devolved into a battle of attrition, which it tacitly began to recognize it would eventually lose – the balance of resources and demographics was simply not in its favour. The blockade was causing widespread famine among its civilian population. Austria-Hungary, already a far less militarily formidable ally than Berlin had initially anticipated, seemed like it may be inching closer towards getting ready to sue for peace. The events that would see Russia abandon its war effort on the other side the year after had not yet been set in motion. Though its pathways to emerging victorious were seemingly rapidly narrowing, ending the war was not an option, Berlin believed: suing for peace on such disadvantageous terms would decapitate the country, would spell a 'finis Germaniae'.[64] So if the war could not be won in the trenches, Germany did have one option left up its sleeve to tip the balance in its favour: once again unleashing the menace that was unrestricted submarine warfare.

Already Germany's U-boats were wreaking havoc in the Atlantic, sinking Entente supply ships and even neutral cargo ships that it believed were helping keep Britain and France's war machines afloat. Whatever wartime civility was left, and, far more importantly, American political and public outcry, had demanded that U-boat crews started to notify their targets ahead of time, giving passengers on these ships time to evacuate (the 1915 sinking of its passenger ship the *Lusitania*, killing 1,198, had nearly pulled the neutral giant into the war on the Entente side). Such warnings ahead of time, however, largely undid the element of surprise and by extension the effectiveness of these kinds of U-boat operations (and put a target on the submarines' backs, as cargo ships were increasingly accompanied by naval convoys). *Removing* these restrictions would allow Germany to once again unlock the full power of its U-boat dominance and provide it with an asymmetric advantage in the naval domain. Moving to unrestricted submarine warfare, Berlin knew, would, however, almost certainly result in the United States joining the war effort on the Entente side. This is where the infamous Zimmermann telegram came in. Germany needed a distraction: a distraction in the shape of Mexico.

The United States had long been concerned about the irredentist tendencies of its politically volatile neighbour to the south, which was still smarting from its loss of Texas, Arizona and New Mexico to the United States in the aftermath of the Mexican–American War (1846–48). What if, Berlin speculated, Mexico could be persuaded to join Germany's side and launch an invasion from the south, in return for German support in allowing Mexico to recover these lost lands, weapon deliveries, and much else? Washington would never see it coming and would not have the capacity to respond on two fronts at the same time, was Berlin's slightly outlandish calculus.

It was pivotal that this proposal to form an alliance, penned by German foreign secretary Arthur Zimmermann, land on the desk of Germany's Ambassador in Mexico as soon as possible – without it being intercepted by American censors. Here, German hubris would prove fatal: rather than use a human courier, a slow but generally more secure way of transferring such a sensitive document, Berlin chose to share its proposal by telegraph, relying on the strength of its encryption, which it did not know had already been substantively cracked by British cryptographers some years before. For added security, the message was sent through neutral, Swedish cables, routed through Argentina – parts of which were even leased by the United States itself; cables that also had hop points in the United Kingdom. It was in Britain that the telegram was intercepted and deciphered.

The discovery of the Zimmermann telegram would send shockwaves through Room 40 and the War Office: this was electric material; so brazen a proposal, signed by Zimmermann no less: a man whom President Woodrow Wilson considered a man of respect and civility, a potential peacemaker. It was immediately clear this was a document of immense value, the final straw that could bring a wavering United States into the war. Though it would require some deft intelligence operations to get the telegram in front of Wilson without revealing the extensive intelligence-gathering apparatus that had allowed Britain to discover it to begin with, once there, the telegram's public release generated the intended effect: following widespread public outcry, the United States formally declared war on Germany and later Austria-Hungary. The first units of the American Expeditionary Force landed in Europe in June 1917, some five months after the fateful telegram was sent. A little over a year later, the war was over.

## *Germany strikes back*

Throughout the war, Germany, too, attempted to sabotage allied cables and went about these operations in a diligent and well-planned manner.[65] The German navy, in collaboration with other Central powers, was able to, for example, inflict significant damage on Russia's ability to communicate directly with its allies to the west by severing its Baltic and Black Sea cables. It also managed to raid some of Britain's more peripheral landing stations in the Pacific, including Fanning Island, and in the Atlantic as part of some of these operations.[66] Given that Germany never had the upper hand in the naval aspects of the war, it could not, however, prevent these severed cables from being repaired again. These actions therefore served more as annoyances than as moves that could inflict lasting strategic harm. Annoyances indeed: in one particular cinematic example, British repair engineers found a message left near the landing of a damaged Anglo-Norwegian cable, which read: 'No more Reuters war-lies on this line! Kindest regards from a "Hun" and a "Sea-Pirate".'[67]

German attempts to interrupt communications between Britain and the United States after 1917, which increasingly involved the use of submarines, resulted in more permanent damage. These operations were able to destroy seven of the seventeen transatlantic cables then in service. These cuts thus did not halt traffic entirely but did result in some significant capacity issues, which made transatlantic communications more difficult. Overall, however, these efforts were of little enduring effect, proving Britain's significant pre-war investments in bringing redundancy into its networks, maintaining strategic repair capacity, as well as overall control over the oceans which allowed repair vessels to be deployed, had not been in vain.[68]

## *Interwar years*

For nearly half a century Britain had been the undisputed leader in international communications, steering the path of globalization, and wielding a degree of control over cable networks not seen since, and unlikely to ever be matched again. The sheer effectiveness with which London was able to translate this power and network centrality into strategic advantage, particularly during the First World War, would, however, also contribute to the eventual undoing of its communications hegemony. Because it had not just been Germany and Britain's other adversaries that had suffered from the overwhelming and ruthless effectiveness with which Britain could eavesdrop on, direct and scupper the flows of global communications.

Neutral countries around the world had also seen their communications censored, or severed altogether – and had been alarmed by Britain's sheer power in this regard, too.[69] The Netherlands would rapidly invest in new sovereign wireless links to the Dutch-East Indies. The United States, which up until that point had been quite content to let the market determine the contours of its own communications networks, found that its strategic interests were no longer served relying on British stewardship over the global network. Though it was not until the early Cold War that the United States definitively took over from Britain as the new communications hegemon, it was this dawning recognition – and actions that followed during the interwar years – that set the gears turning.

Washington would invest in a number of new, sovereign cables, linking directly to Europe and other markets, throughout the 1920s and 1930s. Most US investment during this time would, however, focus on investments in wireless, the cost of which was dropping rapidly – making cables a lot less competitive – while rapid gains in quality and reliability were also being made. This was an opportunity not just to immediately adopt the technology of the future, but also to wiggle out of Britain's tight hold over the market. It is actually during this period that we find the very first seeds that would eventually sprout Silicon Valley – as the US Navy began to support the newly minted wireless industries that had ventured out to the US West Coast, and had congregated around San Francisco, in a bid to compete with the British-owned wireless and cable companies, who had their American presences on the US East Coast.[70]

All of this came at a time when Britain's own role as the undisputed global hegemon was starting to wane. The war had left the country nearly bankrupt, and no longer in a position to continue the upkeep and funding of ambitious geopolitical endeavours like the All Red Line. It was certainly not able to replicate the model for the wireless age. Though the British Empire would reach its widest extent during the interwar years, the seeds of discontent were already being sown, and the first fractures that precipitated the post-war period of decolonization were already starting to be visible. Though London took a wide range of measures to keep its cable industry competitive, and prevent its high pre-war investments from becoming write-offs during this period – for example through facilitating mergers between cable and more profitable wireless companies – the decline could not be stopped.[71]

Once the Great Depression hit, investment in new undersea cables – already far less profitable on the margin than they had been in the past, and now also suffering from a precipitous drop in global demand as economic activity slumped – became exceedingly difficult to find. The upshot of this was that few cables were laid by anyone from the early 1930s onwards. As a consequence, also the cable-laying and repair fleet started to shrink.[72] This interwar retreat of the cable industry would soon also emerge as a significant strategic vulnerability once the Second World War broke out – a conflict in which the cable would have a less central, but certainly still significant, role to play.

## *The cable goes to war again*

Despite the growing role of radio, cable-cutting would still feature prominently during the Second World War. Throughout the conflict, both the allies and axis powers dedicated substantial resources to destroying strategic cables in both the European and Pacific theatres. In 1939, still during the phoney war, Britain once again cut Germany's cables in the North Sea. During the Blitzkrieg and later bombing raids, key cable landing sites were strategic targets for the Luftwaffe. Indeed, the landing station at Porthcurno was temporarily placed underground in a concrete bunker to protect it against these frequent barrages. The station survived the war largely unscathed. The Australian navy cut key Japanese undersea cables, such as those connecting Saigon to Singapore. The main objective behind these operations, beyond causing disruption, was to once again force adversaries to send their sensitive traffic through radio, which still remained a lot less secure.

Though the allies can be said to have won the battle over cables also this time around, their advantage was slimmer than it had been during the First World War. This was, in part, because of the reduced slack and waning influence over Britain's cable network and its enabling systems.

Archival materials show that when its repair ship the HMS *Faraday* was sunk off the Welsh coast, it had taken down with it not only a trained cable crew and much-needed repair capacity, but also 500 miles worth of valuable cable it had intended to lay in the Mediterranean. Though the War Office had commandeered Britain's submarine cable manufacturers to work around the clock to produce more spare cable, they proved unable to keep up with demand and the rate of destruction. Britain also turned to exploring hoisting up and diverting (now-occupied) France's cables routed to North Africa, and Italian cables it had cut earlier during the war.[73] This lack of slack and redundancy in Britain's network – a far cry from its All Red Line heyday – also showed in the country's rush to secure more repair ship capacity. After the Kriegsmarine had sunk two key British repair ships, the Admiralty had to go on a desperate mission to find repair capacity elsewhere – including by attempting to get back a cable ship it had sold off to the Soviet Union in the 1930s, a ship the Soviets were now using to ferry passengers through Lake Ladoga (the British request was refused).[74]

The early extensive cutting of German, Italian, and, after the successful wave of Nazi invasions, many other continental European cables too, would towards the end of the war also become a problem. The large-scale and ambitious allied invasion of the European mainland needed capacity and instant communications. Cables had to be restored in risky missions – the allies even laid a whole new transatlantic cable from the United States to support the war effort, as German submarine packs hunted the oceans. New cable roll-out also immediately followed the D-Day landings, as informational tethers reconnecting the allies to Europe's mainland.

## *The United States takes over*

Though the trajectory had inexorably set in during both world wars – and arguably already before that – it was during the early Cold War that the United States truly began to give shape to its conception of global superpower. This also meant it started in earnest its journey to take over as the communications hegemon. The United States, like Britain before it, saw securing and controlling global communications as key in cementing and maintaining its position as a global superpower, as well as pivotal for maintaining its lead over its emerging great rival the Soviet Union.

Already during the Second World War, the United States had started laying the groundwork for expanding the global reach of its communications power, frequently to the dismay of Britain, which had seen the United States not too gently try to wiggle itself into the monopolies Britain had held since the network's very infancy. Though this encroachment onto British positions was sold to London as a temporary wartime necessity, it was quite clear to the planners in Whitehall and the Admiralty that this was very much about dislodging Britain's commercial hold over the network once the war was over too.[75] There was, however, little that Britain could do about it, forced to come to terms with the reality that it simply was no longer able to project power in the way it once had, and now lacked the financial means to pay for the upkeep of its vast global communications network, of landing stations, telegraph relays, its cable fleet – especially as the competitive position of cables continued to wane. During the war the British government had already begun to sell off even some of its most strategic cable and radio stations to the United States, such as, for example, its cable and radio station at Horta in the Azores – once a key interchange in the All Red Line.[76]

These strategic acquisitions were just the beginning of America's cable and radio expansion. Because, while the United States liked to present itself as anti-colonial – and it genuinely was an important moral voice driving the unravelling of the European empires once the war was over – the country had also amassed its own 'pointillist empire' of overseas military bases and dependencies with impressive rapidity.[77] Existing outposts like Guam and Puerto Rico, or the scatterplot of newly acquired military bases, from Germany to Japan to Italy to Midway, formed the fabric of US global power projection.[78] To protect these assets, and magnify the power and reach that came with having such a dispersed web of bases and thus global coverage, it was important to connect them all together. Like Britain in the telegraph era, the United States too would engage in a different kind of 'island hopping', through the rapid expansion of its global network of military bases – neocolonial nodes, stitched together by radio stations and, indeed, cables.

Former British cable outposts were outfitted with radio stations. American communications expansion also occasionally necessitated the acquisition of new colonial possessions to extend the reach of signals, in a dynamic not dissimilar to the British hunt for hop points in the century before. The cable, expensive, static and, until the mid-1950s, unable to carry voice traffic over very long distances, would play an increasingly more reduced role in these activities.

## *Space race*

After the war, attention would move further away from cables. Washington had never been quite content with relying on the combination of insecure radio and static, inflexible cable and, from the 1950s onwards, also turned its focus towards the development of its own entry into the pantheon of communications technologies: the satellite. It was not alone in this, however: leveraging innovations in the rocket sphere made during the Second World War (and some of the Nazi scientists who had developed them), both the United States and the Soviet Union soon started to look at space for the next communications revolution.

The devastating technological and ideological success of the Soviet launch of Sputnik on 4 October 1957 sent these American efforts into hyperdrive, pushed forward by an almost existential fervour about maintaining its technological edge over the USSR.[79] Washington needed to show it could win the battle for technological supremacy, and winning the race over space became the symbol. For a while, Britain and especially De Gaulle's France also tried to keep up and develop their own space capabilities. France was for a while quite successful at this (and benefitted from its possession of French-Guyana near the equator, perfectly situated for space launches – in another historical parallel). Britain, too, was concerned about adopting American technology wholesale and abandoning its long-standing All Red Line-reminiscent doctrine of maintaining communications sovereignty, but eventually had to recognize financial constraints, which meant it had to let go of these ambitions.[80]

To spur adoption and innovation, the United States would also pressure its own national champions in the telecommunications realm, large companies like AT&T, to develop and adopt satellite technology as quickly as they could, even though the companies in question had often been quite content to stick with cable in particular, especially as new innovations had, for example, made voice transmission via cable possible.[81] The companies ultimately did the government's bidding and became another important source of new invention and investment.

American telecommunications companies more generally played a central role in the so-called military-industrial complex that was erected during this time. They would rely heavily on large government contracts, a lot of innovation they built on flowed out of government-funded and military-aligned research labs, and, especially during the early Cold War, private companies often also saw it as their own responsibility to play a part in ensuring the United States would come out on top in the competition with the communist bloc.

Winning the battle over satellites became a matter of great national prestige, mobilizing the power of the state, the private sector, but also the public imagination – which it soon captured. Just like Queen Victoria and President James Buchanan had exchanged messages to commemorate the first transatlantic cable, so too would early breakthroughs in satellite start to invite similar symbolic grand political milestones. Indeed, on 17 December 1958, the first human voice transmission in space took place: a message from US president Dwight D. Eisenhower wishing the American people, and the world, a Merry Christmas.[82]

This roll-out of communications infrastructure was not just a matter of ideological and scientific rivalry, but also a key tool in America's growing ambition to project its power across the globe. Washington would push the global adoption of satellite communications also as a way of growing its international influence, offering heavily subsidized solutions especially in the large contingent of countries which had recently, or were about to, gain their independence.[83] These soft power efforts cannot, of course, be seen separately from the context of Cold War competition over influence in the non-aligned world, but were also intended to dislodge Britain and France from their (former) colonies. European powers often still held monopolies over telecommunications roll-out in their overseas possessions, frequently also still after these countries had gained their independence, with telegraph cables functioning almost as physical 'tethers' of empire.[84] By exporting what it hoped would eventually become cheap, ubiquitous connectivity, the United States could root out this lingering influence. Satellites would as such come to serve as a double soft power tool: they would displace old power dynamics and bring television broadcasting to the world; that same television which would some years later allow the world to watch in awe as America landed the first man on the moon.

Though the United States, through innovation, economic dominance and territorial expansion, became the dominant communications power during this period, it never wielded the same degree of control Britain had during its heyday.[85] There were many factors driving this, but one particularly significant one was the quick succession of new, competing technologies that were coming to market. Where the telegraph remained the dominant telecommunications technology for almost a century (which allowed power to become so entrenched), radio initially still competed with the telegraph, as well as microwave systems, and later satellite, and within decades was supplanted by fibre optic again.

## *Weapon of war*

Cables may have started to lose their dominant role as the main means of international communication during the first decades of the Cold War, and especially once the high-prestige satellite came onto the scene, but the undersea cable did not lose its military utility. Because even though first radio and later especially satellite communications started to become cheaper and better able to reach the furthest reaches of the globe, both of these wireless technologies also remained insecure.

Radio traffic remained much easier to interfere with and intercept than telegraphic and later voice traffic (telephone calls) ferried through cables. Waves were susceptible to electronic warfare, which could be used to scramble signals, or prevent them from going through altogether – an art the USSR was particularly adept at. Nuclear weapons detonated in space were also seen as posing a real threat to connectivity, as the radiation from a detonation could cause a type of scattering that could severely disrupt all satellite-based communications, military planners feared.

Wireless communications were not only vulnerable, they were also a goldmine for eavesdroppers (think of the success of Bletchley Park's cracking of Enigma – which had focused on decrypting intercepted radio traffic. Intercepting cable traffic had proven far harder). While cables, as we know, could be tapped, this was still a lot more complex to do, and generally required proximity to a cable, whereas that was less the case for intercepting radio and satellite communications. This would be a problem that would go unresolved throughout the Cold War: one UK-based industry veteran I interviewed recalled receiving a panicked phone call in the late 1980s from a George H.W. Bush White House staffer, on the hunt for a secure phone line route through cables – no matter how old or obsolete – as satellite, they believed, could not be trusted.

These vulnerabilities began to become a source of major concern in NATO quarters – especially during the early decades of the Cold War, before satellites had become a more mature, stable technology, and the rapid growth in international telephony spurred renewed cable investment. Military planners became increasingly concerned about retaining the ageing cable network, which had started to erode during the interwar years and the Second World War, and could no longer meet growing capacity needs. The cable, they believed, was to be preserved as a critical redundancy to newer, more nimble, but also more vulnerable, alternative modes of communication. It was this push to maintain this type of modal redundancy in their networks that saw militaries become major initiators of and investors in new cable projects.

The most prominent such project was the laying of TAT-1 (transatlantic telephone cable), a major transatlantic cable, which connected Clarenville in Newfoundland to near the Royal Navy base in Oban in Scotland, completed in 1956. Innovations developed during the Second World War, which improved repeaters specifically, enabled TAT-1 to be the first transatlantic undersea cable able to also carry voice traffic – ensuring it also had a real commercial utility beyond just a military one. While TAT-1 was developed by a consortium of British, Canadian and American telecommunications companies, it relied heavily on government and military funding and support (all of which by extension became more wrapped up in the military-industrial orbit; while Canada and the United Kingdom maintained formal government monopolies during this period, commercial champions like AT&T in practice also became increasingly entwined – and served in support of – the US government).

## *Of sabotage and asymmetries*

As undersea cables remained so important for facilitating military, intelligence and sensitive diplomatic communications, and militaries became more prominent funders of new cables, fears about their deliberate sabotage also began to take on an even more decidedly strategic dimension. Though the Cold War did not see any major cable-cutting occur in the way that it had during both world wars – primarily because the feared all-out East–West escalation fortunately never came to pass – that did not mean it was not being planned for. While less is known about the Warsaw Pact countries' offensive or defensive cable strategies, a slow trickle of declassifications (and in some cases whistleblower leaks) have provided us with more information about how NATO, and especially Washington and London, developed their thinking about defending cable networks. These documents also offer a glimpse of their own plans for throttling Warsaw Pact communications. Indeed, cable-cutting was very much part of the strategic planning. Some now declassified materials from the period show that NATO allies were engaged in active mapping of the Soviet Union's cable network,[86] pinpointing specifically which of these cables were particularly vulnerable and strategically important, and should thus be prioritized in an attack. What is equally significant here, however, is the asymmetry at play.

The dispersal of the NATO allies' global communications networks was a strength in that it allowed global power projection, but also a vulnerability that could be exploited by the Warsaw Pact countries as it was difficult to protect such a widely dispersed network. Severing the transatlantic connections between Washington, London, Bonn and Paris, while no easy task, was not impossible and would make it extremely difficult for allies to communicate, especially if several means of communication – such as radio and satellite, in addition to cables – were to be targeted at the same time. This was a weakness the USSR and its satellite states did not have to grapple with to quite the same extent. Like Tsarist Russia, the Soviet Union and its surrounding satellite states were in effect a contiguous empire, which mostly relied on terrestrial, rather than undersea, cables for communications between each other.[87] Severing connectivity would thus be a lot more difficult as it would require penetrating deep into the USSR's heartland.

This geographical isolation also made it much harder to intercept Soviet communications. Whereas Britain had been able to read German communications as they arrived on its doorstep, a more bifurcated, disentangled network required the Americans to literally enter Russian territorial waters to gain access to strategic cable traffic. This, they literally did. The specifics behind Operation Ivy Bells, a particularly daring Cold War CIA gambit, which saw US Navy submarines physically placing wiretaps on Soviet military cables in the Sea of Okhotsk in the country's far east, will be covered in more detail in a later chapter.

The Soviet Union's cable network was not only more insular and inward-facing, it was also comparatively small, and would remain so throughout the Soviet Union's existence. This too, had a long tradition, as Tsarist Russia had already lagged behind its rivals in Europe on diffusing the key enabling technologies of logistics and connectivity that had hypercharged the late nineteenth century's wave of globalization.[88] The modest telecommunications networks Russia did have would furthermore see significant devastation during both the Russian Civil War, and then again during Operation Barbarossa. The resulting relative communications tabula rasa meant that the USSR focused on leapfrogging to new technologies as it tried to rebuild the devastated country, such as radio and later satellite, rather than try to reinvest to restore what had been before.

Significant US-led export controls implemented by the West on anything remotely dual-use that may have given the USSR a military advantage meant that accessing state-of-the-art telecommunications technology was furthermore challenging.[89] Add to this the fact that the Soviet Union was generally a far more autarkic and self-reliant economy than Imperial Germany had been, meant that, overall, cutting the country out of global communications would be a lot less impactful in a protracted, conventional conflict than it had been against previous adversaries.

The concern about this asymmetry – it would be possible to sever communications between NATO allies, but difficult to challenge the Soviet Union's own strategic depth and buffer – would become an important driving force in thinking about their protection. Despite the less eye-catching role of the cable during the Cold War decades, planning for their defence was not an afterthought, and very much securitized through a nuclear lens – the Cold War meant living under the permanent shadow of the bomb. Planning documents from the early Cold War period in particular show that planners were afraid the Soviets would target transatlantic cables in the lead-up to a nuclear escalation, and would have the know-how to do so, learned as they would have done from allied methods practised during the world wars.[90]

It was simultaneously also already clear that the Soviet Union had the capability to interfere with transatlantic radio communications (and later on also satellite communications) too. This meant that a coordinated attack, of bringing down undersea cables at the same time as other forms of communications, could make it extremely difficult for the North American and European allies to communicate.[91] This would always be calamitous, but would be especially catastrophic ahead of a feared Soviet nuclear strike.

Britain could have as few as just five minutes to prepare ahead of a Soviet nuclear strike, the US East Coast would have more time – but not much. Disabling all channels of communications in tandem – which could make mutual warnings almost impossible – would allow Moscow to gain invaluable time. This was not only a real NATO weakness in times of an actual nuclear exchange, but, planners feared, Moscow's awareness of this vulnerability in its own right increased the risk of escalation. This knowledge, was the fear, could reduce some of the deterrent effect of NATO's second strike capability – and the logic of mutually assured destruction – if the Kremlin believed it would be able to significantly undermine the alliance's ability to retaliate with a devastating strike of its own.[92]

These concerns were certainly not academic: in 1959, a Soviet fishing trawler – the MV *Novorossiysk* – was accused of having damaged, over the span of two days, several cables owned by AT&T and Western Union off the coast of Newfoundland. Though accidental damage to cables caused by fishermen was – and is – not rare, the pattern and the high number of cables affected certainly was. The US Navy boarded the ship to investigate – an extraordinarily rare occurrence, as far as cable cuts were concerned (in fact, we would not see it happen again until Christmas Day of 2024, when Finnish authorities boarded a Russia-linked ship in the Baltic Sea under eerily similar circumstances). While investigators later formally concluded that the damage was caused unintentionally, internal security briefings at the time placed some significant question marks behind that assessment.[93] This, they speculated, was the Soviet Union testing the waters and trialling new methods ahead of a more serious escalation. If Russia could hide behind accidental damage, what was to say they would not use a similar *modus operandi* ahead of an actual attack – to buy time and sow confusion? The potential for accidental escalation here had been significant: if NATO was aware Russia may potentially stage such a cable incident in the lead-up to a conflict, how would they be able to distinguish it from the real thing?

## *Protecting cables*

The increased involvement of militaries in the funding of new cables, their rising concerns about their vulnerability and the more general heady geopolitical climate of the early Cold War unsurprisingly also had a significant impact on approaches to cable protection. During the Second World War, key cable stations, such as the one at Porthcurno, had already started to be 'hardened' and hidden away in concrete bunkers to shield it from Luftwaffe raids. This push towards militarizing elements of the cable network – especially the land-based component – intensified throughout the Cold War. New cables – also those with a primarily commercial purpose – now occasionally deliberately made landfall near naval and military bases that formed the new global fabric of America's Cold War.[94]

TAT-1, as we saw, came ashore near the Scottish Royal Navy base in Oban, dug into a specialized structure, hewn into the rock base.[95] The splice of the cable that led to London ended up in the enigmatic Kingsway tunnels, a sprawling network of tunnels and fallout shelters under central London's Holborn area, which was allegedly one of the options to provide a home to the designated government in the aftermath of a nuclear attack. This hardening was more generally primarily considered through a nuclear lens – how to make sure that infrastructure would be able to best survive a first strike over the panoply of other methods and risks that may befall cables. This is a tendency we can see throughout the cable's history, with paranoia about the security threat *du jour* often becoming the paradigm of thinking about security risks more broadly: unrestricted submarine warfare kept the British Admiralty up at night and would drive cable protection narratives after the First World War; fear of terrorist attacks – though never materialized – would drive protection frenzy during the height of the War on Terror in the aftermath of 9/11.

During the Cold War, we saw a simultaneous push towards hiding the network from public view. Not only did the cable increasingly fall out of the public eye – replaced with a focus on what David Edgerton calls 'the novelty of the new', satellites and space – cables were now quite literally rendered invisible.[96] This was part of what Nicole Starosielski describes as a 'strategy of insulation', which meant that cables would quite literally go underground and become inaccessible.[97] NATO officials had also grown increasingly concerned about the amount of public knowledge that was available on the location of cables. Famous landing stations, such as the ones at Valentia Island and Porthcurno, were well known to the public, and also still saw a significant number of older cables land there, making them exploitable chokepoints in the network.[98] Fishermen had traditionally occasionally received maps to make sure they did not accidentally damage cables with their anchors and nets; military planners were becoming increasingly concerned that this information should no longer be made publicly available – even if that meant more frequent routine damage. We see this exact same dynamic recurring today: in an increasingly febrile geopolitical climate, policymakers are once again starting to favour bolstering the cable network's resilience against kinetic attacks and even all-out war, even if that can mean compromising on the day-to-day resilience of the network.

### *The Washington–Moscow hotline*

To illustrate what this type of thinking looked like in practice, let us consider the perhaps most emblematic means of communications of the entire Cold War: the Washington–Moscow hotline. The famous hotline, which allowed the leaders of the Soviet Union and the United States to contact each other directly during crises and so hopefully avert nuclear annihilation, had been initiated by Kennedy and Khrushchev in the aftermath of the Cuban Missile Crisis – the moment the proverbial doomsday clock had, up until then, come closest to midnight. Miscommunications, delays and crossed wires between Washington and Moscow had contributed to the near-escalation. To avoid such a scenario from recurring, the two leaders agreed that establishing a direct communications link, which would be as close to 100 per cent reliable as possible and be available around the clock between the two countries' highest authorities was crucial: to defuse tensions, to clear up confusion and to reveal intentions during crisis situations.

Though the direct communications link (or 'DCL') is often portrayed in movies as a red telephone ready to ring on the Oval Office's desk, the actual system consisted of a less telegenic teleprinter system; written communications were less prone to misinterpretation and mistranslations, and were at the time furthermore still a lot easier to encrypt. The system went live in 1963.

Though satellite was already becoming more mature at this time, the system would initially be made up of a set of undersea cables, connecting the Kremlin and the Communist Party's headquarters across the road on one side of the line, and the White House and the US military's main building on the other. From Moscow, the main route (though there were backups) wound up to St Petersburg, continued onwards via Helsinki, Stockholm and Copenhagen, from where it would reach London. In London, the system joined TAT-1, across the Atlantic, towards Washington. A radio circuit routed through Morocco served as the initial modal redundancy.

To ensure the system was always functioning well, the story goes that during the hotline's first years operators on both sides would exchange messages once every hour – the Soviets would send excerpts of Chekhov and other Russian literary greats during odd hours, America would get the even hours to send Shakespeare and Twain. It would not take long for the system to be first utilized for its actual purpose: the system was – allegedly – used in the wake of the assassination of President Kennedy to reassure Moscow this was no coup, mere months after the system went live. It was used again during the Six Days War in 1967, the Yom Kippur War of 1973, and the Soviet–Afghan war (1979–1989) – and several more times besides.

If the main priority was to ensure maximum survivability during a military escalation and prevent the interception of messages wired through the line, the choice to use the existing undersea cable network was an obvious one.[99] The DCL was, however, vulnerable to the kind of day-to-day resilience issues to which cables remain susceptible to this day. Within the first decade of its tenure, a copper thief stole a section of the cable in Finland, a Soviet fishing trawler severed the cable off the coast of Denmark – most likely genuinely by accident on this particular occasion – a Finnish farmer ploughed over a terrestrial section of the cable that routed through his field. Though the system never went offline entirely (it could rely on modal redundancy provided by the radio circuit), the frequent outages did become a growing source of concern. This is why in 1971 the Kremlin and White House agreed to switch over to satellite, which had become much more of a mainstay at this point in time, as the primary conduit of the DCL, while cables remained as a modal redundancy. Both the Russians and the Americans offered one satellite circuit each.[100]

The satellites used for the DCL were primarily civilian ones, but also carried a lot of key military communications – which would no doubt put them among the top targets should it come to a nuclear exchange – as would their ground stations, which were located in key military bases (the hardening of infrastructure thus became a vulnerability in its own right: proximity to high-level targets). While some of that same vulnerability existed for undersea cables, by being insulated by the deep sea and partially buried underground, cables were seen as having a higher survivability in these kinds of situations.

Since the end of the Cold War, the DCL has enjoyed several technical updates – it now relies on email, rather than teleprinters. Parallel direct video links also exist. The original coaxial cable was upgraded to a fibre optic one in 2008. But the system remains in place, and does so by necessity: at the time of writing the most recent publicly known use was in 2022, when President Biden contacted Russia's leader Vladimir Putin to deter him from making further rash nuclear threats against Ukraine and the West. The geopolitical context may have changed, the need for the hotline, unfortunately, remains.

* * *

Towards the end of the Cold War, several parallel, intertwined developments would once again change the fate of the undersea cable.

The push to securitize the network had come with a hefty price tag, and required collaboration between the private sector and governments. This was initially not much of a problem. Not only were militaries and governments key co-funders of new cable roll-out and procurers of traffic, most countries' telecommunications and cable companies were state monopolies, or, in the case of the US so intimately wrapped up into the military-industrial complex, they may as well have been. Especially in the heady early decades of the Cold War, American (and to a lesser extent European) companies were quite willing, or financially incentivized, to co-fund activities in pursuit of wider Cold War objectives.[101] This would begin to change towards the end of the Cold War, however, when deregulation (and the resulting increased market competition, which put more of an onus on minimizing cost) – and a climate of *detente* made the need for protection feel less acute. This would lay the groundwork for a more profound desecuritization during the peace dividend years, when commercial interests started to drive developments again.

Another burgeoning trend, which started to mature towards the latter half of the Cold War, was the development of a new technology that would once again put the undersea cable at the heart of global long-distance communications: fibre optics. New types of fibre optic cables would allow the development of much higher-capacity and higher-speed cable-based communications, allowing the cable to outmatch satellites to such an extent that they once again become the dominant conduit of global information flows.

The timing would prove opportune, with fibre optic cables reaching commercial maturity just as the Cold War came to an end, which would launch a new era of unbridled globalization and international economic integration that suited the cable especially well. It was especially the rise of the internet, which also started its explosive rise during this same period, that put the cable at the heart of the emerging global order.

2

# *Peace Dividend*

In 1988, TAT-8, the first transatlantic fibre optic cable, which connected New Jersey to the Cornish coast in the United Kingdom and the tip of Brittany in France, was completed. Ten months later, British computer scientist Tim Berners-Lee invented the World Wide Web at his lab at CERN in Switzerland. Five months after that, the Berlin Wall came down. These three events would shape the future of undersea cables, and the world in which they were laid, profoundly.

While subsea cables for most of the Cold War had to share the stage with other more eye-catching and dynamic telecommunications technologies such as satellites, the rapid commercialization of fibre optics technology – which relied on the transmission of light through infinitesimally small hairlines of glass – ensured that cables would soon emerge on top again.[1] Fibre optics technology, just like the World Wide Web and so much of the underpinnings of our modern telecommunications and computing systems, had their foundations in breakthroughs made by a Briton. Charles Kao, born in China but who as a young man had moved to the United Kingdom to study electrical engineering, in the early 1960s pioneered new methods for using the budding innovations in the field of fibre optics. It was Kao's inventions that made possible the telecommunications cable renaissance, earning him the moniker of the 'godfather of broadband' and a Nobel Prize for his ground-breaking research, which resolved some of the main technical hurdles that had so far prevented its use for these kinds of highly precise tasks.[2]

As with so many other originally British inventions, it took American business acumen to commercialize and scale it. It was at AT&T's Bell Labs, the iconic research lab that gave us everything from the transistor to laser, that fibre optics were turned into a usable, deployable technology. Though the undersea fibre optic cable relied on many hundreds of inventors, it was a team led by Peter Runge, a German transplant who had similarly relocated to the US to see his own pioneering fundamental research be turned into practical solutions, that was the first to make the technology actually viable for commercial use.[3] By the late 1970s, a fusion of both Japanese and Bell Labs ingenuity led to the innovations needed to roll out reliable fibre optic cables. These cables had a far higher capacity than the traditional copper-core coaxial cables, primarily used for telephony, which had made up most of the cable network throughout the twentieth century. Fibre optic cables were also able to transmit data much faster. It was these two developments which would provide a new lease on life for the cable, and once again saw it return as the main means of international telecommunications.[4]

These breakthroughs did not come about by chance. Even before the explosive growth of the internet, more rudimentary forms of data exchange by banks and other such digital precursors had begun to drive demand for more high-capacity, high-speed connectivity, which existing technologies struggled to provide. Fibre optic cables, which could now once again offer the state-of-the-art, provided a solution and began to rapidly surpass satellite in utility. Business interest, and investment, soon followed.[5]

When it came to *subsea* cables, however, a major hurdle remained. Because while fibre optic cables had already seen a rather rapid terrestrial roll-out throughout the 1970s and early 1980s, developing fibre optic cables that could withstand being laid underwater proved a lot more complex. In an interesting parallel with the nineteenth-century quest to insulate telegraph cables, finding the right materials that could protect these incredibly delicate new optical fibres once again proved the main challenge.[6]

After much experimentation, Runge's team at Bell Labs was the one which solved this puzzle. Their work not only unleashed the global expansion of the fibre optic cable, it also gave rise to one of the most persistent, and quite amusing, myths that still surrounds it. One of the group's early tests with laying fibre optics cables underwater, which it had been conducting off the coast of the Portuguese Azores Islands, had generated some rather odd outages and blips. When the engineers hoisted up the cables to investigate what was happening, marks left on the damaged lengths pointed to a rather unexpected culprit: sharks.[7] The animals, which had been attracted to the electrical current running through the cables, had left deep indentations in the cable's outer layer, throttling the connection. Further experiments showed that adding an additional layer of insulation would resolve the issue. But it did not put an end to the still-persistent media myth that it is not just the Russian shadow fleet that presents an acute threat to the global internet, hungry sharks do too.[8] Still every year the International Cable Protection Committee (ICPC) – the international industry body, which, as the name suggests, is primarily concerned with protecting cables – has to field media queries during National Geographic's famous Shark Week about this non-existent menace threatening global connectivity.

Once this final technical hurdle was overcome – and sharks effectively deterred – the fibre optic revolution could finally go truly global. More international cables soon followed. Much of the network's early growth centred around Northern Europe, but soon fanned further outwards. An especially important milestone was the completion of TAT-8, a joint endeavour between AT&T, France Telecom and British Telecom and the first transatlantic fibre optic cable. At time of launch, the cable had a capacity of 280 megabits per second, or the equivalent of around 40,000 telephone circuits. Contrast this with TAT-1, which had initially allowed for only thirty-six. Despite this massive increase in capacity when compared to previous cable technologies (some in the industry went as far as to predict there would not be any need for new transatlantic cables for at least another decade, if ever), TAT-8 would hit a ceiling only eighteen months later, with demand far outstripping supply.[9]

At the heart of this breakneck growth was a cocktail of particularly providential circumstances: undersea fibre optic cable technology matured just at the moment when the internet was also ready to undergo its first growth spurt – in fact, it was the direct link between the United States and Europe that TAT-8 provided that allowed Berners-Lee to demonstrate the World Wide Web's power. It also coincided with the end of the Cold War stalemate. In other words, the fibre optic cable would go international, just when the geopolitical and economic conditions were most ripe for the kind of hypercharged connectivity it provided. The telegraph cable had played a critical role in spurring the first wave of globalization, the fibre optic cable would in no small part help spark the second.

## *The end of history; new beginnings for the cable*

The fibre optic undersea cable came of age during a period of peace dividend thinking. The Cold War was finally over, giving way to the – in retrospect horribly naive – belief that the liberal rules-based order, at least for now, had prevailed. Erstwhile adversaries, like Russia and to an extent also China, would be on an inevitable path towards democratization and opening up. Globalization, unbridled international trade and mutual exchange would see to it. This was the unipolar moment, the period of *Wandel durch Handel.* Military budgets were slashed across the West, while the United States' extraordinarily rapid and seemingly decisive victory in the First Gulf War showed that its military and technological dominance was – at least for now – unassailable.[10] Against this backdrop, previously carefully shielded industries, aligned with the military-industrial complex and arsenal of power designed to keep the communist bloc at bay, were cut loose too and given a lot more freedom to manoeuvre in the commercial realm.

This included the cable industry, which would be significantly deregulated, loosening over a century of entrenched state involvement in the cable-laying and owning trade. The Thatcher government in the United Kingdom had already provided the starting salvo for this in the 1980s by privatizing Cable & Wireless.[11] The United States and other European countries soon followed suit and similarly deregulated their telecommunications and cable industries, with (semi-)state monopolies replaced by market-led alternatives. The parallel rise of the internet, itself a vehicle and product of increased globalization, further fuelled the commercial growth of the now unshackled cable industry.

This opening-up and commercial expansion was seen as the preferred way forwards, especially in Washington, which saw the burgeoning market for state-of-the-art fibre optic networks not just as good business, but as a means of exporting the new post-Wall political and economic order it was propagating. Cables would bring the internet, and the internet would bring democracy: a sentiment best captured by President Bill Clinton's now infamous words some years later that Beijing's attempts to constrain internet freedoms and erect the Great Firewall of China would be like 'nailing jello to the wall'.[12] The cable was still a weapon – but one to spread the gospel of globalization and free trade, not war.

This rapid about-face is well illustrated by a little-discussed episode surrounding Project Marathon, an ambitious cable project proposed by British Cable & Wireless at the very tail-end of the Cold War, which envisioned the laying of a fibre optic cable from Denmark, over land through the USSR to Vladivostok, onwards to Japan – combining undersea and terrestrial cable.[13] This longest cable yet was intended to become a global information superhighway of sorts, connecting west to east. There was one major hurdle that had to be overcome, however: fibre optic technology was then still under Coordinating Committee for Multilateral Export Controls (CoCom)[14] restrictions – the US-led Cold War body, which oversaw strict export controls on dual-use technologies to the Warsaw Pact countries and China, which the United Kingdom was also part of. This meant the project would require permission from the US government to proceed. Though Project Marathon was proposed at a time of increased detente and collaboration between the West and the USSR – this was the height of Gorbachev's perestroika – President George H.W. Bush still vetoed the project.[15] Rapprochement was all fine and good, but the United States was not going to allow the USSR access to state-of-the-art fibre optic cables, which had a significant military and strategic utility. This was in 1988.

By 1993, the Clinton Administration had not only started to lift most restrictions, but had begun to actively encourage its own companies to go and conquer the business frontiers in the east.[16] This push ensured that fibre optic cables soon came to be seen as a vehicle for commercial expansion and for bringing market liberalism to newly opened-up markets.[17] Competition soon started to centre around who would dominate this lucrative industry. Indeed, it was concerns that the United States was only harming itself by keeping the door closed, while rivals like Germany and Japan had not been wasting any time in trying to establish themselves in the Russian telecommunications market, that led the Bush White House to roll back restrictions (it was in fact a young Antony Blinken, later Biden's Secretary of State, who called the Bush Administration out on its 'Cold War hangover' in a *New York Times* penned op-ed).[18]

This push towards liberalization would only accelerate during the Clinton years. It was the Clinton Administration which in 1996 oversaw the further deregulation of the telecommunications industry, which caused the monopoly-like dynamics that had driven cable roll-out during much of the Cold War to rapidly start to erode. It was also under Clinton that the narrative of the internet as a great democratizing force truly started to take hold. As Clinton's Vice-President Al Gore described the sentiment when addressing an International Telecommunication Union (ITU) conference in Argentina in 1994: 'Information superhighways on which all people can travel [. . .] will allow us to share information, to connect, and to communicate as a global community.'[19] Cables, and the necessary deregulation, would make this happen. The world would become a global village.

Washington, as well as many European capitals, was initially not especially concerned about losing the kind of grip on the cable market they had enjoyed during the Cold War. Peace dividend thinking saw its reflection in their approach to the security of submarine cables too, which frequently began to amount to not much of an approach at all. During the early Cold War especially, it was in no small part governments who had pushed industry to harden the protection of, for example, landing stations, and, as major investors in new cables, had flexed their muscles to push for key cables to make landfall in naval and military bases (recall the landing of TAT-1 at Oban in Scotland). This would change fast.

By the mid-1990s, you would probably already have been shown the door if you had knocked on your respective navy's door and asked for your commercial cable to land on their premises, one industry expert told me. Western governments on the whole started to pay little attention to the cable industry, if they knew about its existence at all. And if there was any interest, it came primarily from the intelligence services, keen to know what was going through cables, rather than the cables themselves – a topic we will discuss in chapter 6. In policy circles, cables became largely invisible. It is only in recent years that this has started to change again, with both governments and national security communities now scrambling to understand the threats facing the global cable network, and once again recognizing their vital importance.

In the first post-Wall decades, the general goings-on of the cable industry, including their protection, were largely left in the hands of the private sector. Concerns about geopolitics and deliberate sabotage can be said to have quickly given way to a focus on the more mundane, but still very important, day-to-day challenges to the network's resilience. Less planning for nuclear Armageddon, more preventing inexperienced captains from accidentally dragging their anchors over cables. Landing stations were left unmanned to save costs. Governments and industry, already from the latter half of the Cold War onwards, also saw less of an onus to keep the global cable map restricted – which is why we get to enjoy interactive maps such as TeleGeography's today.[20] In fact, such visibility can bring resilience: the industry proactively hands detailed maps to fishermen, helping them to avoid exposed cables.

The lack of protection of landing stations especially would spark a temporary resurgence of attention and panic in the early years of the War on Terror, when the US government believed that the ill-secured concrete boxes would become a prime target for terrorist groups like Al-Qaeda and others.[21] There is no public evidence of any such attack ever having taken place. An incident with frogmen cutting two cables in the Red Sea in 2006 did briefly set alarm bells ringing – though the real culprits soon turned out to most likely have been copper thieves. This episode reflects a wider tendency to securitize the risks to a system or infrastructure through the lens of the main threat of the day. Nuclear strikes during the Cold War, terrorists in the early 2000s, and Russian and Chinese submarines today.

It is important to note that this steady path towards the 'desecuritization' of subsea cables, and prevailing peace dividend thinking, did not mean that protection became an afterthought: in some areas protections were instead actively bolstered. From the 1980s onwards, the practice of burying cables became more commonplace for example, with segments of cables nearest to shore now placed in trenches several metres deep. This was an expensive process, necessitating specialized machinery effectively ploughing the seabed, but helped prevent fishermen, dredgers and other users of the maritime domain from accidentally snagging a cable. As there was now a lot more demand for cables again, and a reduced ability to fall back on other forms of connectivity such as satellites, it also became a lot more financially viable to bring more redundancy into the network, especially on the most commercially lucrative routes. This also improved resilience. The lens through which these protections were put in place were primarily market-driven, however, and no longer necessarily fuelled by the sort of Cold War concerns we discussed in the previous chapter.

## *Boom, bubble, bust*

All of these changes to the cable industry happened against the backdrop of the explosive growth of the internet throughout the 1990s. What had started as an academic (and military) experiment had grown over the decades, and a more mature ecosystem had started to take shape. It was Berners-Lee's World Wide Web that really catapulted the internet from a close-knit community of researchers to something with global commercial appeal. More people wanted their own home computers that could connect to the internet. Offices started to embrace email. A wave of new companies arrived on the scene looking to place themselves at the heart of this revolution. This all required a lot more connectivity. When TAT-8 was laid, it was expected to deliver sufficient capacity, and satisfy transatlantic demand, for at least a decade. In practice, it hit a ceiling within just eighteen months. More capacity was needed, and soon. There was both a need for new terrestrial cables to better connect emerging digital hubs, but importantly also for more intercontinental submarine cables, which would make collaboration and expansion across the world possible.

These were the early, heady days of Silicon Valley's dot-com boom, where incredible fortunes were made and the future was being engineered;and everyone could strike it rich.[22] The explosive growth of the internet soon turned into a gold rush, with a flurry of new internet companies (or 'dot-coms') entering the market. Investors soon wanted in on the action too. In 1999, the NASDAQ went up 85 per cent in a single year, largely fuelled by the growing interest in internet stocks. Companies which appended a .com to their name saw their stock values skyrocket. Many of the companies that mushroomed seemingly out of nowhere did not need more than half an idea to attract investment, easy money which some went on to spend on Superbowl ads and Gatsbyesque launch parties before they even completed a single sale. The imperative was to build market share and name recognition quickly: the internet would continue to grow astronomically, and you had better get in there early, or you risked missing the boat.

Every gold rush needs its shovel salesmen. In this case, it was companies new and old which saw an opportunity to lay the infrastructural foundations, to build the 'super highways', that enabled the rapid growth of these e-commerce and other internet businesses. This explosion in demand, combined with the deregulation of the telecommunications sector (which allowed the entry of new challengers, including cable companies) gave rise to a Silicon Valley-centred subsea cable bubble of proportions not seen since the 1870s.[23] Over a period of three years, global telecommunications capacity would increase *a hundredfold*. Billions were pumped into the undersea cable and wider telecommunications industry. Dozens of new international cables were laid all over the world, many largely on spec, based on the assumption that demand would invariably follow.[24] Massive investments also flowed into new cable-laying and repair vessels which would be needed to actually roll out and maintain all of this new fibre. These investments in capacity rested on the assumption that the predicted growth in internet usage would continue to be an exponential one. There were 4 million internet users in 1991. By 2000, there were already 400 million. One only had to imagine how many there would be by 2010 – and how much cable their demand would require.[25]

It could not last, and indeed it did not. At the turn of the millennium, the bubble deflated, and the dot-coms – and their exuberant investors – would lose their shirts. The Dow Jones would go on to lose 40 per cent of its value.[26] Many of the new upstarts would disappear just as quickly as they had appeared on the scene, their stocks now effectively worthless. In February 2001 – slightly lagging behind the wider dot-com bust – the market for fibre optic cables collapsed quite spectacularly as well. Far too many fibre optic cables had been laid, the demand wasn't (yet) there, and prices for those who wanted to buy capacity were falling precipitously. Telecommunications companies lost a staggering $2 trillion in market capitalization due to this correction.[27] Half a million workers employed in related industries lost their jobs.[28] Many of the new infrastructure companies that had sprung up, enabled by deregulation and encouraged by the *hausse*, just as quickly collapsed again.[29]

## *Dark days, dark fibre*

The spectacular bursting of the dot-com bubble had a profound and lasting impact on the cable industry, one that in many ways reverberates to this day. After the market for new cables largely disappeared overnight in 2001, it took almost a decade for demand to slowly begin to recover.[30]

In the interim, most of the plucky new challengers that had entered the cable trade during the heady nineties went out of business.[31] Illustrative of the more hands-off approach that Washington in particular would take when it came to the telecommunications sector, was its decision not to intervene and 'let free market forces prevail', which contributed to the United States' steady retreat from telecommunications hardware, an industry which it had come to see as low-margin and low-prestige. This was to be a fateful decision which has become a significant source of geostrategic angst in recent years, as we will soon see.[32]

While the (precursors to the) current giants French ASN, American SubCom and Japanese NEC did manage to weather the storm, they emerged far from unscathed. There was now so much excess cable supply lying on the seabed that cable owners saw little need for much additional roll-out.[33] The financial disaster the market's collapse had left in its wake would, furthermore, for a long time leave banks and other investors very wary of putting up any financing for new projects, which further hampered the industry's recovery. After the completion of the Apollo cable in 2003 – which connects New York and New Jersey to Brittany and Bude in Cornwall – no new transatlantic cable would be laid for another decade.

As new cable roll-out ground to a halt, the wider web of companies in the cable orbit all felt the pain. So many engineers, trained cable crews and other specialists left the industry during the early and mid-2000s that the battle scars are almost literally visible to this day. During industry events, attendees joke about how everyone there either has grey hair or is 'a spring chicken': a whole generational cohort – those now roughly in their late thirties to mid-fifties – is simply missing. As the most experienced industry hands now start to retire, this leaves a concerning void in an industry that is very dependent on institutional knowledge.[34] This skills gap is not the only legacy of the dot-com infrastructure bubble that has impacted the cable network's resilience.

The dot-com trauma has also imbued the industry with a deep sense of conservatism, which has left it very cautious about expanding capacity and making large capital investments across any rung of the cable supply chain. This is perhaps most visible in the cable ship fleet, the highly specialized ships used to lay and repair cables. Very few investments in new cable repair ships have been made since the early 2000s. Though the cable network is on the whole rather robust, cables do occasionally break or get damaged – some 150 to 200 times a year, in fact.[35] Though the handful of incidents where there is the suggestion sabotage may have been involved receive a lot of media attention, the vast majority of these faults are accidental: some 86 per cent of cases of damage to cables can be attributed to human error. Think here, for example, of commercial ships dragging their anchors over cables or dropping their fishing gear in the wrong place. The remaining 14 per cent is largely accounted for by natural causes or technical faults.[36] The cable industry's biggest nemeses are fishermen, not Russia – or so it likes to joke.

In order to keep the network functioning properly and minimize the impact of these kinds of faults, cables need to be repaired as quickly as possible. We will discuss the intricacies behind this process in a later chapter, but in the meantime it suffices to say that it is important to have specialized repair ships on call that can quickly reach the site of an incident. There are currently only around seventy ships out there that can be used for this purpose; and only twenty-two of those are in the cable repair business full time.[37] These ships are distributed across the world in strategic locations and permanently on call. Twenty-two may not sound like a lot especially when we consider the vital importance of the global cable network. Indeed, according to many experts, it is too few for comfort – especially now that many ships in the repair fleet are reaching the end of their lifespan, sparking concerns about the future resilience of the repair ecosystem.[38] Remedying this gap is, however, not straightforward, especially as new ships are expensive: a new repair vessel can cost up to $100 million.

These are investments the industry has been hesitant about making. Though there is certainly demand for more cable ship capacity – as we shall discuss soon, the market has recovered and is once again going through a boom cycle – only a handful of new repair ships have been delivered since the dot-com era.[39] Under ideal circumstances, cable ships have an effective lifespan of around thirty-five years. Some of the ships now still operating are approaching forty years of service. This is not a bottleneck quickly fixed: any initiatives to build new repair capacity will take at least five years to deliver, and trained crews, too, remain in increasingly short supply. It can take about a decade for a crew to fully learn the ropes of the trade. In the meantime, repair ships continue to age out of the fleet, leaving a dangerous vulnerability in the interim, which market forces alone are unlikely to resolve.

## *Filling the void*

The slowdown in the market was to a large extent driven by the glut of speculative supply the popping of the dot-com bubble had left in its wake. Seabeds were now riddled with a lot of finished or near-finished undersea cables, for which there was suddenly no longer the promised rapid growth in demand. As the dust settled, there was now so much spare capacity, or 'dark fibre', in the global network, especially on the most saturated routes, that it would be able to satisfy the actual growth in internet use and connectivity well into the late 2000s. Cables have a long lifespan – they last on average twenty-five years – and can be upgraded while already laid on the seabed by 'lighting' more dormant fibres retroactively or upgrading systems, so that even when some of the initial capacity ceilings were hit, existing cables would suffice. All this unlit dark fibre and ability to upgrade would prove ruinous for the cable industry, but a boon for others, as we shall soon see. In the meantime the traditional cable market, then still dominated by Western companies, largely stalled.

Not everyone was sitting still, however. Entering the cable market as a new cable-laying company is notoriously difficult. The upfront capital costs involved with establishing the infrastructure to lay cables are high, and building trust in your wares in this conservative, close-knit industry is a real challenge. Beyond the big three of ASN, NEC and SubCom, few have managed to eke out a significant market share. One country, however, was keen to upend this balance, well aware of the strategic utility that becoming a big player in the telecommunications sphere offered.[40] This country was China.

Beijing, from the earliest days of its opening up in the Deng era, saw the importance of telecommunications both as a point of entry into high-end production, but also as a lever for global influence. Aspiring hegemons, it had learned from Britain, Germany and the United States, needed communications power. Cables were one of those 'forgotten' links in the telecommunications stack that could help China get there.

It also spotted an opportunity. Western cable giants had traditionally shown less interest in launching cable projects in lower-margin markets in much of the Global South, leaving especially parts of Asia and Africa very underserved in the network, due to the low commercial viability of these projects.[41] In parallel to this, the United States in particular had apparently also not been too concerned about ceding control of the telecommunications plumbing more generally, considering it less prestigious than some of the far more profitable software-based companies built on top of it. This combination offered China an in. The technology companies the Chinese government had helped cultivate, chief among them hardware giant Huawei – famous for everything from its smartphones, to 5G infrastructure to, indeed, the design and laying of submarine cables (through its subsidiary Huawei Marine Networks, which had started in 2008 as a joint venture between Huawei and British Global Marine Networks, but had become increasingly Chinese) – and some of the country's biggest telecoms providers such as China Telecom, worked in close symbiosis to fill this gap by bringing their own, often state-backed cables to places previously left behind in the digital divide.[42]

There were many advantages to this strategy: it allowed an ambitious Beijing to spread its global influence, especially in the Global South, in a way not too dissimilar to the manner in which the United States had brought low-cost telecommunications to the non-aligned world during the early Cold War. It was also an effective way for Chinese companies to build experience in the cable industry in what they perceived to be a lower-stakes environment, and, in due course, showcase to the rest of the world that Chinese cable companies, contrary to the then-still prevailing stereotype, could deliver high-quality engineering and trustworthy technology. Their success meant that most cable industry experts I interviewed for this book now – often somewhat begrudgingly – admit that China's cable sector is now as technically reliable as that of the Western incumbents, if occasionally not even more so.

Beijing's strategy was focused not only on bringing low-cost cables elsewhere, but also on improving its own connectivity and centring itself in the global cable web. China was a relative latecomer to the undersea cable game. It received its first fibre optic cable only in 1993, which connected the country to Japan. It had only very limited participation in international cable networks before then.[43] Chinese companies had some catching up to do, and did this by focusing initially on rolling-out terrestrial cables, connecting the country to its fourteen direct neighbours, with the Eurasian continent an especially major area of focus of early expansion. As it began to saturate those nearby markets, Chinese companies increasingly pivoted towards more lucrative markets overseas – not just in the Global South, but also Europe, and increasingly the United States too, in part relying on the then still relatively politically neutral cable landing hub of Hong Kong to serve as an intermediary.

So its footprint grew: in 2005, Chinese cable companies were still only involved in a handful of cable projects. By 2019, its cable champion Huawei – and successor HMN Tech (Huawei Marine Network's new name, after Huawei had found itself forced to sell its stake, amid ongoing US pressure) – had accrued itself a market share of around 20 per cent in planned projects.[44] 2019 proved to be a temporary peak in China's cable rise, however. By this time, the strategic value of cables, and telecommunications infrastructure more generally, had once again started to come on the radar of national security officials in the West, especially those in Washington. China's rapidly growing cable footprint began to spark alarm and would face increasing backlash – a still-growing rift we will explore in detail in later chapters.

## *The hyperscalers era*

It was not just China which would upend the existing balance in the cable trade. A second new cable actor would similarly disrupt the close-knit cable community during the late 2000s and 2010s. These were the so-called hyperscalers.

Most of the casualties of the dot-com bubble left little in their wake, beyond cautionary tales (who remembers Pets.com?) and a thriving second-hand market for ironic merchandise given away during extravagant launch parties. The remnants of the enabling fibre bubble would instead have a far more tangible legacy; one which would turn out to be highly consequential. When, after several years of slowdown and increased whispers that this whole internet thing had turned out a dud, a new crop of technology companies slowly began to rise out of the ashes of the dot-com debacle,[45] and they would be able to do so on the cheap. The abundance of available dark fibre and oversupply of other digital infrastructure had driven down cost, survivors had bought up distressed assets for pennies on the dollar, which had made it easy and cheap for new businesses to access effectively unlimited high-speed connectivity and data centre capacity.

Web 2.0 startups, like Facebook, YouTube and Twitter, all thrived on being able to facilitate their initial growth on a low budget. As a lot of the excess capacity was concentrated in the places which had enjoyed a lot of investment during the dot-com era, especially Silicon Valley and the wider Bay Area, new startups had even more reasons to flock there, further cementing the West Coast's leading role in the digital economy. So while the bursting of the bubble caused a lot of suffering in the cable industry itself, the dark fibre glut has also been credited with helping create the conditions that allowed the next, more profitable, wave of Web 2.0 companies to emerge. This is one of the interesting aspects of infrastructure bubbles: they can wreak a lot of destruction in their wake, but – when the conditions are right – can also serve as catalysts for future innovation.[46]

The arrival of the next generation of internet companies meant that demand for subsea cables would start to pick up again from around 2007 onwards. The growth of several of these new tech companies would soon turn stratospheric, along nearly every dimension. The Big Tech companies would start to accumulate user bases in the billions. They collected trillions of data points every day. The internet had long been something that existed only for an hour a day after school on the family computer, but would now become an ever-pervasive presence, never more than an arm's-length away. This next step in the internet's growth was all about binge-watching streaming shows and uploading pictures onto social media, not old-school plain text forums and emails. It was thus not just the amount of usage, but also the nature of it that required more and more connectivity, data, traffic, computing power, things. Some survivors of the dot-com era, like Amazon, Google and Netflix, as well as newcomers like Facebook, began to buy up more and more capacity on the existing undersea cable networks, as they began to consolidate their rapid ascent and hold over the global digital economy.

As they grew, the business activities they partook in would also expand. For companies initially known for being agile and largely intangible, the Big Tech giants began to build edifices of very tangible infrastructures to facilitate their growth. As they started to invest in hardware and infrastructure of their own, such as their own data centres, this then necessitated more capacity on existing cables to ferry data between them.

It was this move into operating massive, global cloud and computing infrastructure – especially large data centres – that would earn some of these companies the moniker of 'hyperscaler'. Firms such as Microsoft and Amazon soon also began to monetize this foray further down the physical side of the so-called technology stack, by becoming purveyors of cloud-based services. This allowed other companies and private consumers to essentially 'rent' some of the growing capacity the hyperscalers now had at their disposal – tapping into their data storage facilities or computing power, so that they could, for example, run their own apps or store the files of large user bases, without necessarily needing to maintain their own large physical servers. It was also in this hyperscaler business that some of these companies started to make a lot of their revenue. A company like e-commerce giant Amazon has long generated more profit through its cloud service AWS than the retail business it is perhaps best known for.[47] For others, this provision of cloud services has become a key lever for selling other services – notably software (the Microsoft and Google suites both come with the convenience of more or less seamless cloud integration – which has helped further cement their market positions over their competitors) and now increasingly also AI solutions.

Initially, the slack in the existing cable network could meet this increased hyperscaler demand. But towards the beginning of the 2010s, as the hyperscalers and other tech companies began to purchase more and more capacity on existing cable systems, and their data flows continued to increase exponentially, the network on some routes began to reach a bottleneck. Many of the existing undersea cables, such as many of the transatlantic ones, could initially be upgraded to increase their capacity. Eventually, however, they too would hit the so-called 'Shannon Limit', the point at which (slightly simplified) lower-capacity cables can no longer be further retrofitted and re-engineered to facilitate more traffic in a cost-effective way. Eventually, Big Tech's needs started to outstrip the available lit and unlit fibre. The hyperscalers needed new cables. They also needed new routes (to connect their data centres, which were not necessarily located in the same places traditional demand was concentrated). So they changed tack – with profound consequences for the cable industry as a whole.

Because the hyperscalers had now become active players and owners in the undersea cable market themselves. Google would be the first of the hyperscalers to invest in a new cable directly, when in 2010 it joined a consortium that was funding the laying of a new cable between Los Angeles and Japan.[48] The endeavour proved a success. Other tech giants soon followed suit. The four biggest hyperscalers, Amazon (through AWS), Google's Cloud, Microsoft's Azure and Meta, which together account for over two-thirds of global cloud capacity, had by 2017 cumulatively invested in twenty subsea cables.[49] By 2024, this number was reportedly already up to sixty. Google's mother company Alphabet that same year was the part or sole owner of thirty-three submarine systems – including, at time of completion, the highest capacity cables in the global network: the Dunant and Grace Hopper cables – both of which are wholly Google owned.[50] In 2025 Meta announced its new $1 billion Project Waterworth cable, which is planned to be the world's longest cable, coming in at an incredible 50,000 kilometres once completed. This cable too will be entirely owned by the company. As per 2025, at least one American hyperscaler was involved in or would have outright ownership over approximately 40 per cent of upcoming global cable projects,[51] with their footprint especially large in the most ambitious, expensive and highest capacity new cables. In 2012, the share of undersea fibre optic capacity accounted for by hyperscaler consumption was still less than 10 per cent, but by 2022 their share had shot up to nearly two-thirds – fuelled primarily by incredibly high-intensity data centre to data centre exchange.

This rapid ascent of the hyperscalers, and the advent of the internet before it, has fundamentally altered the economics behind the undersea cable industry. Where owning and running cables were previously the main sources of revenue for companies in the cable trade, now the profit made from the data running *through* cables has become largely decoupled from the business models behind the running and owning of the cables themselves. Where telecommunications companies and other cable owners could in the past make a healthy profit from owning and managing the world's informational plumbing, for hyperscalers this is not generally a priority. We should instead see these forays into cable infrastructure ownership as capital investments: the critical plumbing that makes possible the data flows, cloud services and the applications that run on top. Because it is these more 'virtual' activities that are now making the real money.

Using the internet itself is becoming cheaper (compare the cost of 10 gigabytes of mobile data today, to what we would have paid just a decade ago), and other uses of cable capacity, such as landline phone calls, are declining steeply. This means that owning a cable is becoming an increasingly marginal business, which has created some challenging new dynamics in the cable sphere. The entrance of the hyperscalers has in many ways revived, some may argue even saved, the industry: it injected a lot of money, created new jobs, financed cables to previously neglected geographies, and brought a lot more vibrancy into a market that was still licking its dot-com wounds and had by all accounts become rather stagnant.[52] But there are reasons to be wary of the hyperscalers' growing hold over the cable market.

The reinvention of Big Tech companies as key funders, and increasingly also as cable owners, has allowed these companies to even further consolidate the already outsized power they have accumulated over the internet and all that it enables. These companies already increasingly determine what we see, what we read, what we buy, and who we can vote for – and now also control the digital underpinnings enabling that.[53] The consequences of this are rather profound.

At minimum, one could argue that these companies have not always acted as good stewards over an industry that has increasingly been stretched to its limits. Hyperscalers have become such prolific investors in new cables – including their own proprietary projects – that they are hogging up more and more cable-laying capacity too. This hoarding comes at the expense of smaller cable projects, which could serve to fill important gaps in the network, and makes it hard for individual countries to retain sovereign control over their connectivity.[54] New Jersey's SubCom, which traditionally managed cable projects for all kinds of customers – especially those involving the United States – is now reportedly so oversubscribed with Alphabet's demand alone, that according to many industry experts, it has little time for anything else. Meta appears entwined in a similar dynamic with French ASN, which instead finds its most important customer in Mark Zuckerberg's growing conglomerate. Where many hyperscaler projects previously were joint consortium efforts or left spare capacity on new cables for others to buy and benefit from, allowing a certain degree of piggybacking on their investments, the hyperscalers are now also reserving new cables for their own use alone.[55]

There is also the question about the role the hyperscalers ought to play in ensuring the wider vibrancy and resilience of the cable value chain. While it should be said that a lot of the cable engineers that work at these companies are active and enthusiastic participants in the close-knit cable community and contribute to, for example, improving cable repair processes, there are questions about whether these companies – given their deep coffers – should take on a greater financial burden. Take, for example, the looming shortage of repair ships. The hyperscalers are arguably among the only commercial stakeholders in the space for whom a capital investment in new ships would be a relatively low cost to bear. It appears that none, so far, have stepped in to fill that void, however, leaving the (far less profitable) cable-laying and maintenance companies or, more likely, taxpayers, to cover the cost of renewing the cable fleet. Some in the industry also quietly express dismay about the fact that the hyperscalers, which increasingly run their own large engineering divisions, are able to offer the highest salaries and so are hoovering up a lot of scarce talent from the industry. This is of particular concern in the Global South, where the trained pool of experts is the smallest.

Most worrying, however, is the degree of power over the cable network the hyperscalers have been able to accrue by becoming so indispensable as investors. Large projects in practice now usually need a hyperscaler as an anchor tenant to secure financing. With the exception of the Chinese companies, no other major actors in the global network can afford to get in the hyperscalers' bad books, which, as we shall see in the next chapter, gives both these companies and by extension Washington a lot of power to determine the future contours of the network, and the ability to decide who can be involved in expanding it. The decisions behind routing and ownership are already opaque and now concentrated in very few hands.

The dominance of the hyperscalers is only set to increase in the coming years. While the overall share of the hyperscalers in the network is already high, when we look at new builds and upcoming cables on some of the key routes, this dominance is even more disproportionate. Many of the current transatlantic cable systems that *are* still owned by the traditional consortia – many of them dot-com era projects – are ageing, and will one by one be phased out of the network, leaving the old players even further marginalized.

This is a particularly concerning time bomb on the transatlantic routes, where by the end of the 2020s most, possibly even all, cables may be (partially) hyperscaler-owned – raising serious questions about the sovereignty of those countries and actors that rely on these vital arteries of global connectivity. It certainly affords the handful of players in control of those sections of the market with an incredible amount of power, as it does the US government, with which they are in an increasingly symbiotic relationship. The current economics of the cable market, however, make it very difficult for other commercial actors to fund ambitious projects of the scale the hyperscalers can, absent substantial government subsidies – or at least, not profitably. For many countries, the only alternative to US-backed hyperscalers is therefore now Chinese infrastructure – an increasingly uncomfortable binary in a world tilting towards ever more fractious great power competition and coercive practices targeting smaller powers.

## *AI Ai ai . . .*

The current boom in investment in artificial intelligence (AI) infrastructure and solutions is set to again quite radically upend the status quo, and further entrench the role of the hyperscalers. Companies like Microsoft and Alphabet have effectively staked their future success on becoming market leaders in the technology – and are now once again pumping eye-wateringly large amounts of investment into new underpinning physical infrastructure to create the capacity for all of this assumed future growth.[56] Much of this AI infrastructure spending has focused on building specialized data centres that house the sophisticated highest-end microchips used to train and run AI models in a bid to secure so-called 'compute'. This rapid expansion does not come cheap: in 2025 alone, estimates suggest the hyperscalers invested between $550 billion all the way to $1 trillion on AI infrastructure. According to management consultancy firm McKinsey, AI-related spending may reach a cumulative $5.2 trillion by 2030 – or roughly the equivalent of Germany's annual GDP.[57] While the hyperscalers, as we have seen, are among the few with the kind of cash reserves to be able to splurge in this way (again making it difficult for others to catch up), their battle chests are not infinite – and spending is by some measures already exceeding the height of the dot-com bubble, with the AI boom, at time of writing, not yet showing any signs of cooling off.

All this spending has an impact on cables too. The vigour with which these companies are pursuing this AI build-out is hogging up even more cable-laying capacity – and putting even more strain on the system. An even larger share of new cable projects is now made up of proprietary cable expansion, as the hyperscalers seek to wire up their AI and cloud data centres, which are increasingly located in remote, cheaper locations, rather than in hubs of traditional cable demand, such as large financial and population centres.

There is reason to believe that all this hyperscaler investment is fuelling another, far larger, infrastructure bubble. Ever since the current boom in generative AI spending started – largely in response to the remarkable success of ChatGPT 3.0's release in late 2022 – a growing cadre of market analysts have placed question marks about the actual return on investment the technology is able to generate: training frontier AI models is incredibly expensive, and consumers' and businesses' willingness to actually spend on the technology remains feeble. A lot is therefore riding on companies like OpenAI, Anthropic and Google making the promised breakthroughs in AI, which they predict will so profoundly alter our societies and economies, that putting themselves at the heart of this is worth the upfront investment. The Magnificent Seven (the group of seven stocks made up by hyperscalers Alphabet, Amazon, Meta and Microsoft, as well as Apple, chipmaker Nvidia and Tesla), which together drive most of the AI-related stock market rally, cumulatively, accounted for more than a third of the S&P 500's market capitalization between 2023 and 2025.[58] According to some estimates, without AI infrastructure spending, the US economy would have entered a recession in 2025.

Unlike in other links of the AI value chain, the cable industry has so far been more hesitant about growing its capacity and jumping on the AI bandwagon. They know a bubble is brewing when they see one. The upshot of this is that waiting times are becoming even longer and capacity constraints more pernicious – even if the cable industry wanted to rapidly ramp up undersea cable roll-out, the crews, vessels and equipment simply are not there.[59] Regardless of the caution with which the cable industry is treating this current AI bonanza, if the bubble were to eventually pop, the pain will inevitably be felt by the industry as a whole. A Magnificent Seven licking its wounds would not be good for new cable investment – a serious weak spot of an industry whose fortunes are increasingly dependent on the spending power of a handful of companies.

Whether a potential bursting of the AI bubble would spark the kind of innovative wave we saw in the aftermath of the dot-com collapse remains to be seen. For now, it seems the conditions are not as ideal as those that followed the previous bubble. AI infrastructure and compute, especially the highly bespoke chips made by manufacturers like AI chip giant Nvidia, have a far shorter shelf-life than, for example, undersea cables, and may – when used intensively – last only as little as two to three years. They are potentially also less easily repurposable for other ends than some of the dot-com infrastructure was, constraining the options for what would come next. No doubt, some of the existing giants will jump in to buy distressed assets, and other new entrants may seek to reuse some of this excess capacity for new ways of turning AI into profitable products. Whether it will spark a new tech renaissance is anyone's guess.

## *The people who keep the network running*

Before we move on to the next chapter, in which we will discuss how geopolitical and economic forces came to give the cable network its current shape, it is important to understand that these cables are made up of far more than just garden hoses and concrete boxes. They are reliant on a web of complex and truly global supply chains and industries making this rather magical technology actually work.

The cable network is in many ways a remarkably resilient one. Though cables do occasionally break or get damaged – human error, such as fishing vessels accidentally snagging a cable with their nets or anchors, or natural causes, such as earthquakes and mudslides, are the most frequent culprits – it is relatively rare for internet users to actually notice them. A cable break or outage on average takes place every three days, for around 150–200 cable faults a year. This is a number that has remained relatively stable over the years, despite the rapid expansion of the network in the digital era.[60] This resilience is in part a function of the amount of redundancy in the network – the principle that when one cable sees an outage, traffic can be fairly seamlessly diverted through other cables that follow the same routes (or reach the same endpoints). It is also a credit to the wide set of actors – a diverse and truly global industry – involved with maintaining and repairing the network.

First, there are the companies involved with planning and laying the cables. Doing this is no easy process, and involves extensive mapping of the seabed and finding secure new routes for cables to be laid along. Specialized marine survey and route-engineering firms conduct detailed environmental analyses and seabed mapping to determine where cables can be laid safely and efficiently.

The cables themselves also need to be manufactured, an art of highly precise engineering. It involves constant innovation in fibre optics and other technologies to improve the performance of individual cables and meet the breakneck increase in demand, which looks at reducing as much as possible latency, the inevitable delay that comes with having to route traffic over vast distances, and increasing the capacity, or bandwidth, of cable systems – the amount of traffic a cable can carry at a time.

Then the cables actually need to find their way down to the seafloor. This requires the use of specialized cable-laying ships, which roll out the sometimes thousands of kilometres of cable along the intended routes. It also requires special machinery and vessels involved with digging the trenches nearer to shore in which cables are buried.

There is a panoply of smaller and larger firms involved with aspects of this process. Four main 'cable giants', however, dominate this more physical aspect of the cable industry: the traditional big three, French ASN, Japanese NEC and American SubCom, and more recent challenger, Chinese HMN Tech. Then there are also the actors taking care of the intangible aspects of the cable-laying and owning process. There are, for example, those involved with navigating the actual legal paperwork and licensing – making sure that cables do not do undue damage to the natural environment and meet local requirements, as well as handling the unfortunately growing number of governments who are weaponizing international law to make it difficult or expensive to route new cables through their waters. This is a process that can take many years and one that is, as we shall see, getting more political.

Then there is the – incredibly important, but often unsung – matter of cable repair, which sees highly specialized companies send out vessels to as quickly as possible identify the source of cable faults, hoist up the cables, and repair them again. In the case of high-profile incidents involving damage to cables in the Baltic Sea in 2023 and 2024, it took only days or at most a few weeks before the cables were up and running again, ensuring the actual impact on local connectivity was fairly limited.[61]

Cables owners – the companies that actually invest, own and operate undersea cables – are another diverse category of actors involved. Traditionally new cables were often funded by cable consortia, frequently made up of telecoms companies based in countries where the cable was going to make landfall, which would team up to make these often expensive projects happen. As we have seen, this ownership structure has begun to change in recent years, as large American Big Tech companies have increasingly begun to join consortia or self-finance their own cables.

Though global and diverse, the cable industry is also a small and close-knit one. The domain of submarine cables may have long been a largely invisible one to the outside world, within it, the main players all know each other, gather at annual conferences in hotel lobbies from Singapore to Honolulu to Lisbon to share the latest gossip. Processes like maintenance and repair were largely self-managed within this community, with the 'g' word (geopolitics) best avoided.

The recent increased scrutiny and heightened political tensions around submarine cables have changed this. Government officials and military planners are now regulars in the room. Countries around the world are releasing undersea cable security strategies and prodding industry to become involved in actually executing them. Submarine cables are no longer seen as the relatively apolitical, hidden plumbing which make highly geostrategic technologies like AI possible. They are now at the heart of geopolitical struggles in their own right.

3

# *Contours of the Network*

That leaves us with today's highly complex network of now nearly 600 international cable systems, whose funding, laying, running and maintenance involve an ever-growing and increasingly more global constellation of actors. In its complexity, variety and purpose, the cable network and the data it funnels around the world can arguably be seen as one of the most globalized infrastructures to ever exist, perhaps only vying for position with the global financial system, the murky world of international shipping, and hydrocarbon and similar commodity markets – all of which, it should be noted, the cable network helps enable.

Virtually every corner of the globe now has an undersea cable landing on its shores, with only the most remote, sparsely populated outposts, such as parts of the Pacific and Antarctica, still not wired up. And even that may not be the case for much longer: the United States' National Science Foundation is at the time of writing still considering the feasibility of laying a cable to connect its McMurdo Research Station (winter population: 150) to either New Zealand or Australia.[1] Such a cable would improve research capacity and relieve the scientists working there from having to rely on patchy satellite connections to phone home (a Starlink satellite connection has already brought some recent respite).[2] Strategic considerations – which in both Antarctica and the Arctic frequently take the form of staking a claim by growing a country's research presence – are no doubt part of the equation as well.

Though undersea fibre optic cables now span the globe, that does not mean their reach is evenly distributed. It takes only a cursory glance at the TeleGeography cable map to notice how some routes on the map enjoy a far higher density of undersea cables than others do. This is no accident. Indeed, a combination of economic, geographical, geopolitical, regulatory and military forces old and new have each contributed to shaping the network's contours and topology.

Ultimately, cables follow demand. Traditionally, major financial and economic centres such as New York, Singapore and London have been the key hubs at the core of the global cable network. These metropoles are not just home to many nearby cable landings, they are also often especially well connected to each other, reflecting the enormous amounts of data that flow between these most central nodes. More recently, the explosive growth of the hyperscalers has seen this topology change somewhat, as their mission to connect together their data centres – which also follow cheap energy, land and water, not just population density – has started to impact cable routing.

Other places, already left behind in the digital divide, instead rely on sparser and frequently ageing cable connections, or do not have any cables landing on their shores at all. Countries on the periphery of the digital network also often depend on intermediaries for most of their traffic, which can leave them beholden to the whims of the countries located in between – as will be discussed later in this book. Up until recently, most flows between South America and Africa were routed either via the United States or through Europe, for example. There are still no cables directly linking otherwise well-connected Australia to anywhere on the continent of Africa. The completion of Umoja (the Swahili word for Unity), a planned cable announced by Alphabet in 2024, is set to change that, however.[3]

The reason why some countries have more cables than others is far more multifaceted than a simple function of economics and demand. Geography and habit mean that established pathways and landing sites have a tendency to become entrenched, which can help cement the centrality of places, such as the United Kingdom and Singapore, which were traditionally already better linked-up in the network. Geopolitics and legal tugs-of-war, too, play no small role in determining the topology of the network. We see some routes, nodes and geographies quite deliberately bypassed for political reasons, for example. Israel has few connections with its direct neighbours, Cuba virtually none at all. Other countries are instead quite deliberately woven into the network, not just for commercial but also for diplomatic or strategic reasons. These different factors often work in tandem, and thus can reinforce each other. To understand how this can work in practice, we will now explore each in turn.

## *Geography's revenge*

Undersea cables are intimately tied to the natural environments they are laid in. Fibre optic cables are in the end only the thinnest of hairlines of glass, fortified by a relatively modest coating of steel, copper and polyethylene but otherwise laid bare to face the elements down in the deep: shifting sediments, sharp rocks, coves, mountains and trenches, undersea earthquakes and currents, volcanic eruptions. It is an inevitability that, subject to such constant wear-and-tear, cables will occasionally break. Much avoidable damage can be prevented through careful route planning and the bypassing of the highest-risk obstacles. Indeed, within the pantheon of actors that make the cable network work so well, it should come as no surprise that there is a sophisticated surveying industry concerned with analysing the seabed to help select the best possible routes for new cables. This task is far from straightforward: it is often said that the surfaces of Mars and the Moon have been mapped at a finer-grained level of detail than Earth's seabed.[4] The selection of a route is therefore a delicate art, which can be expensive and time-consuming.[5]

At risk of grossly oversimplifying, decisions about routes effectively boil down to a balancing act between minimizing the length of a cable needed to connect our desired location A to B, and avoiding geologically disadvantageous features and conditions along the way. Every kilometre added to a cable system costs an estimated $30,000–$50,000, so diversions are preferably avoided. Repairing a fault on a cable, however, also comes at a cost – around $500,000 to $1 million for the average fault, depending on the location and severity of the damage.[6] Frequent outages can also make customers start to question the reliability of a specific system and take their business elsewhere.

While high-level cable maps present cables as straight lines, we should keep in mind that, because of this balancing act, they are in practice all but. Cables will be serpentined, zigzagged, wound around obstacles to avoid danger zones. The somewhat enigmatic Mariana Trench in the Pacific Ocean – nearly eleven kilometres deep at its nadir – is preferably bypassed in route planning, though some cables do cross it. In other cases, cables are left suspended over short distances to avoid sharp chasms and canyons. Though planners prefer to avoid seismically active areas too, that is not always possible, especially not in the Pacific

Ocean, surrounded as it is by the 'Ring of Fire': the tectonic belt of volcanic hot spots and activity that stretches along the Pacific coasts, starting in southern Chile, up along South and North America, via the Bering strait down to Japan, coastal China, South-East Asia to end in Oceania.

Route surveyors also prefer cables to be laid in deeper waters, where they are less vulnerable to fishing mishaps and other human interference – the cable repair industry's main source of headache. The selection of landing sites is a similarly delicate art. Continental shelves, the submerged final stretches of continental landmasses, made up of solid rock are not among the first choice for landings, as it is difficult or frequently even impossible to bury cables there. Sandy, gently sloping beaches are preferred over rocky or soft, shifting shores.

Risky geologies cannot always be bypassed, however. Taiwan, one of the world's high-tech hotspots and global foundry of the semiconductors that underpin much of our modern economies, finds itself at the confluence of a number of particularly unfavourable environmental and geological conditions. Though the island is connected through relatively many international cables – around fifteen in total to the namesake main island of Taiwan – it has been a particularly frequent victim of widespread cable outages.

First, there is the fact that Taiwan lies along the Ring of Fire. Submarine mudslides triggered by the 2006 Hengchun earthquake damaged virtually all of the island's cables and caused significant internet disruption across East and South-East Asia, which even affected financial markets.[7] When it is not earthquakes, there is also the elevated risk of strong typhoons. Typhoon Morakot, a particularly violent 2009 storm, once again took out several of the same cables the Hengchung earthquake had also damaged, prompting further investments by Taipei to better protect its network.[8] The Luzon Strait separating Taiwan from the Philippines to its south is bisected by several mudslide-prone canyons, which cables cannot avoid having to pass over. This has proven another source of faults. To the north-west, in the narrow band between the Chinese mainland and Taiwan itself, lies the Strait of Taiwan, one of the world's busiest shipping lanes – which poses its own risks, due to intense maritime activity. It is clear that, even absent the increasingly tense geopolitical situation in the Strait, Taiwan's connectivity is vulnerable.

Another place subject to a perfect storm of unfavourable conditions is the remote Pacific island nation of Tonga, some 7,000 kilometres to the east of Queensland, Australia. The 170-island archipelago, famous for its whale breeding grounds and for being among the first countries to herald in the New Year, has only one single international cable connecting it to the rest of the world – the Tonga Cable, which links to Fiji. When the underwater Hunga Tonga-Hunga Ha'apai volcano erupted on 14 January 2022, the debris and resulting tsunami not only caused a humanitarian disaster, it also severed said Tonga Cable (as well as a second short domestic cable), leaving the country almost entirely cut off from the global internet.[9] It would take days before the Tongan government was even able to broadcast a message to the world to call for help.

The cable break would ultimately take five weeks to repair – leaving the Tongans relying on old transistor radios and other makeshift solutions in the interim. On some of Tonga's many outlying islands, restoring connectivity had to wait even longer: it would take eighteen months before the domestic cable became operational again. This delay was both a function of the complexity of the fault – the broken segments were buried under sediment dislodged by the eruption – as well as the sheer distances involved. The nearest available repair ship, the *Reliance*, stationed in Papua New Guinea, had to travel for more than ten days just to reach the site of the break.[10]

This lack of resilience is a problem for Pacific island nations more generally: cable faults here take far longer to repair than they do in other geographies because of the remoteness of the islands, lack of repair capacity, and higher frequency of breaks due to seismic activity and prolific illegal fishing. Nor is Tonga the only country in the region that relies on precariously few cables: the Solomon Islands, Cook Islands and others are similarly only wired up by a single cable. Places that rely on so-called 'thin lines', very few connections, are generally more vulnerable to outages and faults, because they do not enjoy sufficient redundancy to fall back on.[11]

It is not only remote, thinly connected places that face elevated risks: a lack of geographical diversity in routes can also create systemic vulnerabilities. In early 2024, several major undersea cables serving West Africa were disrupted simultaneously, resulting in serious outages throughout the populous region. While many media outlets were quick to speculate that sabotage may have been involved, the actual cause was later attributed to a natural event, most likely an undersea mudslide along the continental shelf near Côte d'Ivoire.[12] The reason the outage was able to have such an outsized impact on connectivity was because many of the key West African internet cables follow more or less the exact same path, leaving the still modest redundancy the network enjoys in the region far from robust. Recent initiatives by the hyperscalers, national governments and international consortia to deploy new cable systems are, however, beginning to improve both local diversity and resilience.

## Geographical chokepoints

This lack of redundancy and route diversity tends to be a product of simple economics: it is expensive to lay new cables, especially in places where demand does not justify the upfront investment. The sparsely populated Pacific countries have a combined population of only around 2.3 million, distributed over some 25,000 islands (of which about 1,000 are inhabited) and dispersed over a distance east to west of nearly 10,000 kilometres: the tricky business case is obvious.

In some cases, geographical chokepoints are caused by too much cable, not too little. Perhaps the most infamous geographical chokepoint where that is the case is in Egypt. Ever since the Suez Canal was completed in 1869, allowing vessels to avoid the volatile and long route around the Cape of Good Hope and so cutting the length of the journey from Europe to Asia by half, the canal has been a strategic boon to whoever was in charge of it at any given time. Retaining sovereign access over the Suez Canal was important enough for Britain to join forces with France and Israel and go to war over it with Nasser's Egypt in 1956, and in the process shred the last morsels of its credibility as a global hegemon. Egypt closed the canal down for eight years in response to the Six-Day War with Israel in 1967. The slightly unedifying image of the South Korean container ship *Ever Given* stuck in the narrow waterway in 2021, thus throttling traffic for days and severely disrupting global supply chains, costing the global economy tens of billions in the process, revealed the vulnerability that comes with relying on a single, vulnerable maritime chokepoint.

The Suez bottleneck also has a cable analogue, which in its own right arguably forms the most pernicious weak spot in the global cable network. The Isthmus of Suez – in the Egyptian desert – is a stretch of land around 100 kilometres long, which cables connecting the Mediterranean Sea to the Red Sea need to bridge on their way from Asia to Europe. Seventeen per cent of global internet traffic – and the vast bulk of Europe-to-Asia communications and data exchange – has to route through this isthmus, forming such a critical bottleneck that it finds itself frequently referred to as the internet's Achilles heel.[13]

Alternative routes are currently limited. Though there is a growing number of cables winding around Africa, going south around the Cape of Good Hope is expensive due to its length, and introduces significant latency (though this is becoming less of a problem as technology advances and the nature of data demand changes). Many terrestrial routes from west to east – through Russia, through the volatile Middle East – have proven geopolitically wrought, especially after Russia's full-scale invasion of Ukraine. Other options are in the works, but nascent. This situation leaves Egypt with a lot of power over global connectivity.[14]

This is not new. There were only two real weak spots on Britain's All Red Line. The first was a cable landing in Portugal, which was deemed relatively secure, as the country was a close ally (Portugal in fact remains Britain's longest-standing ally – a diplomatic alliance that dates back to 1373). The second was a small section of terrestrial cable, routed through Egypt's Suez zone – initially not yet a British protectorate. Targeting this small section, the Admiralty was well aware, could technically sever the British Empire in two – at least when it came to communications. While there are now both far more cables and more terrestrial land routes through Egypt than there were in the nineteenth century, these cables, and the astonishing amounts of traffic funnelled through them, remain at the mercy of a government which has certainly not always shied away from taking advantage of its key role in the network, this to the deep frustration of many in the cable industry. Licences for cable landings and routing traffic are exorbitantly more expensive in Egypt than they are mostly anywhere else.[15] More significantly, having so many key cables concentrated in one place is also a source of great fragility, and creates an especially valuable target for those with ill intent. The chokepoint this has created is increasingly being weaponized in the Red

Sea, the direct extension of the Suez strip, as we will see later on in this chapter.

Geographical chokepoints are usually here to stay. We humans may have been able to reshape much of the planet in our favour, but we have not yet been able to move mountains and oceans. But geography gives and takes. One upshot of the melting of the polar ice caps is that it may make it increasingly possible to lay cables connecting Europe to Asia through the Arctic, either via Canada and the United States or over Russia. These would be far shorter routes that could help bypass the volatile Suez Canal and Red Sea altogether. Laying Arctic cables would be extremely expensive and technically challenging to be sure, and increasingly brings its own geopolitical challenges (a topic we will discuss in the next chapter). However, this appears to be a price governments and investors are willing to pay in a bid for resilience in an increasingly uncertain world.

## *Historical inertia*

Cable routing also frequently exhibits a great degree of historical inertia, in no small part driven by the force of habit. If we were to take an old telegraph cable map visualizing the full network on, say, the eve of the First World War and compare it to TeleGeography's most up-to-date releases, they would not look too dissimilar.

The transatlantic routes were among the most important routes then, and remain among the most important ones today. Europe and North America are still especially densely connected, though new key hubs have emerged since, especially in Asia. Some places have seen a degree of retreat. In a more cooperative and intertwined Europe, Germany, which does not have the most favourable geography for cable landings – and tends to be more focused on terrestrial connectivity – no longer has the same incentives for maintaining its own sovereign cable network as Wilhelmine Germany used to do. On a more granular level, historical hubs such as Porthcurno (though cables are now more dispersed along the Cornish and Devon coast) and Guam remain well served to this day. Though the network is by no means static, it can be said that its overall sketch lines and contours exhibit a great degree of permanence.[16] This stickiness is dictated by logic, convenience, market demand, but also by habit.

Establishing new cable routes is, as we have seen, risky and expensive; following the same pathways that have been proven to be reliable over many decades, sometimes centuries, has obvious advantages. Places with many existing cable landings will already have a more mature land-based backbone of digital and telecommunications infrastructure to connect to, and frequently benefit from a well-established cable industry, skills base and existing know-how, which helps attract future landings. Some industry experts warn that this self-perpetuating cycle can have an impact on the resilience of the network, as it discourages the diversification of routes. This dynamic can also entrench and reproduce existing power structures – even if those actual power dynamics themselves are no longer necessarily there.

The legacy of colonialism, for example, remains starkly visible in the network to this day.[17] One of the reasons so many of the West African cables follow the same coastal routes is because a lot of African traffic – even those data flows that remain on the continent – is routed through Europe. A message sent from Accra to Kampala may still go through Marseille, as Africa's network of terrestrial cables has historically been underdeveloped (though it is now rapidly expanding). The main cables from Latin America to Europe still land in Portugal and Spain. Precursors to French ASN traditionally got a lot of their business in Francophone Africa and elsewhere in France's expansive former empire. Cable & Wireless used to enjoy the same position in the United Kingdom's former overseas possessions and long continued to serve the countries of the Commonwealth. Military bases like Guam, which were important bulwarks already at the turn of the twentieth century, remain so today, and even see some of their *raison-d'être* revived, as the United States and others seek to find safe harbours for their cables amid growing concerns about Chinese interference. Cable routes can replicate even older patterns and lines of communications, as the original telegraph routes frequently followed important trade and naval routes.

Historical inertia can also help cement the power that central actors in the network wield in other domains. When the European Central Bank studied the post-Brexit prospects of the City of London's continental competitors such as Paris, Amsterdam and Frankfurt, it too pointed to the surprising staying power of fibre optic cables.[18] London, despite a variety of homegrown own goals and external pressures, would in part be able to retain its pre-eminence as a global financial centre, the study found, because the United Kingdom enjoyed such a long, historical legacy of network centrality in undersea cable networks. This would continue to provide the City with an advantage, especially when it came to facilitating the kind of high-capacity, instantaneous trading that has become so pervasive in modern finance. This built-in infrastructural advantage, according to a related research paper, boosted global turnover in foreign exchange transactions in London by as much as one-third.[19]

Another reason why the City has remained one of the few true challengers to New York, despite the waning role of both Britain and sterling in international markets, was London's early ability to act as a conduit to Asia, especially China, in part through its continued relationship with Hong Kong (first formally, and then by tradition and inertia after the handover in 1997). As the bridge between the West and the burgeoning economies of East Asia, Britain could remain a key spill in this reconfiguring global economy, as Hong Kong served as an important entry point into China's, and the wider region's, rapidly expanding markets. Undersea cables arguably played a role in facilitating the continued exchange between the two cities, as Cable & Wireless, long after the company had lost its influence in many other places in the world, remained a key telecommunications player in Hong Kong into the early 2000s.[20]

## *Power begets power: economic heft*

One of the clearest relationships we have traditionally been able to discern in the geography of the network is in the link between economic heft and cable-routing. Large, populous financial centres are home to a lot of nearby cables and tend to have more spare capacity to allow for future growth. Places on the economic periphery have few, and find themselves left with ageing systems, and difficulty attracting new investment. Traditionally less digitally-developed places that do function as important cable landing hubs due to their specific geography – countries such as Djibouti, which serves as one of the key secure hubs on the horn of Africa – do not always necessarily see these connectivity aortas translated into digital capillaries stretching further back into their hinterland, where they could benefit their own domestic populations. Some critics argue that this leaves them relays in the global web, rather than nodes with agency in their own right.

Having a lot of connectivity has traditionally also tended to beget more connectivity, and thus further opportunities for economic growth. On some of the most popular routes that already have the most capacity, such as those between the US East Coast and North-West Europe, investors were traditionally more willing to support cable projects laid 'on spec', where not all the potential capacity of a new system had already been accounted for ahead of time. Demand for such 'unlit' capacity would invariably follow once the cable was completed, was the calculus. This spare capacity ready for the taking, in turn, can attract new businesses with high bandwidth needs, such as those in the highly lucrative financial and technology sectors. All the dark fibre left behind in the ravages of the dot-com bubble arguably created the conditions for the companies that drove the Web 2.0 revolution, such as Facebook and Twitter, to scale at a relatively low cost, setting in motion a self-perpetuating cycle.[21]

Since the entrance of the hyperscalers into the cable market, this relationship has started to weaken somewhat – with the economics of cable-laying now increasingly requiring upfront hyperscaler participation in a project, as traditional cable owners no longer have the financial resources to take the kind of investment risks they used to. Though hyperscalers therefore play a decisive role in shaping especially the most ambitious projects (at time of writing, all upcoming transatlantic cables projects involve a hyperscaler) – which has, for example, put more emphasis on data centre locations over direct customer demand – this Global North versus Global South dynamic persists.

This interplay has created some digital infrastructure, and by extension cable demand, hotspots. One acronym you hear bandied around in the industry a lot is 'FLAPs', to signify Europe's most important financial centres: Frankfurt, London, Amsterdam and Paris. Occasionally, you might find a D appended at the end, for Dublin, reflecting the large number of large technology companies that have decided to domicile themselves in the Irish capital.

On the US East Coast, the corridor between New York and Washington, DC plays a similar role. Singapore is one of the main hubs in Asia. These places are home to industries where having access to abundant, reliable and importantly also ultra-low-latency connectivity (in the case of financial markets) is vital. In the world of modern finance and high-frequency trading, shaving even a microsecond off the processing speed of a transaction can make the difference. Optimizing for speed means having access to a state-of-the-art digital infrastructure backbone: data centres, high-performance broadband, internet exchange points and – as nearby as practical – cable landings.

From the 2010s onwards, connectivity planning has become less driven by demand for real-time end-to-end communications and data exchange, but instead about connecting together data centres, many of which are owned by the hyperscalers. This has an impact on the topology of the network.

Within the FLAP-D, the Netherlands, which in the heady growth days of the 1990s emerged as one of the key digital hubs of the early internet, was one of the first countries to capitalize on rapidly growing data centre demand. Its early advantage as a digital hub (it remains home to one of the world's largest internet exchange points),[22] the country was later able to translate into attracting significant data centre investment, with concrete boxes now dotting its lush green polders.[23] In the United States, it was in the hinterland of Wall Street, where land was cheap and ample – New Jersey – and near Washington, DC – with its enormous flows of national security data – that the data centres started to mushroom (the initial growth of the data centre economy near the US capital was in part driven by demand from the NSA, CIA and other US intelligence agencies – another case of government–private sector symbiosis).[24] The nearby Virginian counties of Fairfax and Loudoun – which many readers may be most familiar with as bellwether nail-biters during US elections – are home to the highest concentration of corporate data centres in the world.[25] Data Centre Alley Loudoun alone is home to some 200 data facilities, taking up more than 45 million square metres of land – or equivalent to 3 per cent of the county's total land area.[26]

While these places have seen almost unbridled growth in recent decades, with the requisite added undersea cable capacity growing in tandem, it now seems like this expansion may be hitting a wall. On a local level, data centre demand has already started to skirt the edges of planetary bounds. Local electricity grids and water supplies in the most densely data centred geographies, like the Netherlands, Singapore, Ireland and the hyperconnected counties of northern Virginia, are stretched to their limits and risk reaching saturation. Both Amsterdam and Singapore have at different times put in place temporary moratoria on the construction of new data centres, as their energy grids and water supplies were buckling under the strain of unrestrained demand.[27] Singapore even temporarily banned the landing of new subsea cables on its shores. In the United States, the concrete data boxes are forced further and further south into Virginia and into new states, as land and power is running out, and public opposition mounts. Bloomberg found that communities near data centres saw their electricity costs shoot up by some 267 per cent over the period 2020–25,[28] driving increasingly vocal local resistance. As infrastructure investors, such as the hyperscalers, are forced to also look elsewhere to satiate their connectivity needs (and for AI data centres they certainly are), cables will eventually follow suit.

Indeed, the relationship between economic activity on the one hand, and density of cable routes and landings on the other, had long been a near-absolute one, but appears to be breaking down. This is in no small part driven by the rapid growth in investment in artificial intelligence, which requires access to unfathomably large amounts of data, as well as so-called 'compute', the processing power needed to train the models underpinning the heralded AI revolution, and access to energy to power it all. To accommodate this explosive growth, the data centre and cable industry is at the time of writing going through one of its periodical spending frenzies. Especially AI data centres, which house the GPUs and CPUs – specific types of microchips used for training AI models – are in high demand. By some estimates, in 2025 around 70–80 per cent of new data centre capacity coming online was driven by AI and cloud investment by the hyperscalers, many of which have bet the house on the success of the technology.[29]

As AI gobbles up enormous amounts of power, energy constraints have started to become an even more important determining factor when it comes to picking new data centre locations, and by extension the routing of the new cables leading to them. Where data centres were traditionally built relatively near the source of demand, this is furthermore a lot less necessary when it comes to AI training facilities, as latency is not as big of a concern when data do not need to be moved around in real time.[30]

This has allowed previously digital 'backwaters', which offer access to cheap land and abundant energy and water, to suddenly find themselves home to state-of-the-art AI facilities. Several of AI giant OpenAI's ChatGPT models were trained on a supercomputer cluster in Iowa, not in California. Rural counties in Montana, Wyoming and North Dakota, not Fairfax county, are now topping the US data centre growth tables. In Europe, countries like Spain and Poland are starting to catch up to the traditional FLAP-Ds.[31] In the hunt for land, water and power, the cost of fibre roll-out has become an afterthought. One can question the logic dictating some of this new infrastructure build-out – data centres, cables, local energy infrastructure – for the sole purpose of servicing AI needs. Should demand for this specific use case ever wane, it may leave investors with a lot of stranded assets, which may not be so easily repurposed as the infrastructure left behind by the bursting of the dot-com bubble.

While this has started to raise alarm bells among growing segments of the cable industry, and far beyond, many governments are nonetheless keen to hop on the AI bandwagon and are now trying to tout their wares – cheap energy, cheap land – to lure in new investment and establish themselves as key cable and data hubs. Often, the hope is that the physical presence of cutting-edge AI facilities may also lead to innovation further up the technology value chain and attract or ideally even result in new tech champions within their borders. The Gulf States have been especially forceful in positioning themselves in this way, with Saudi Arabia and the United Arab Emirates not just funnelling astonishing amounts of money into AI through their sovereign wealth funds but also providing a home for new AI and cloud infrastructure roll-out. Cheap energy and land aplenty.

Investment in digital, especially AI, infrastructure forms a key pillar of Saudi Arabia's Vision 2030, which aims to prepare the kingdom for a post-hydrocarbon future, in which it is no longer able to count on its vast oil revenues.[32] The aspects of Vision 2030 – the brainchild of the country's idiosyncratic Crown Prince Mohammed bin Salman (or MBS) – which have attracted most public attention are the ambitious, some would say grandiose, mega-projects it proposes. MBS's plans include the construction of the Line, a 170-kilometre-long horizontal city entirely covered in glass, which has raised eyebrows among investors, architects, urban planners, environmentalists (a 500-metre-high, 200-metre-wide mirrored wall is quite the obstacle for migrating birds) and human rights activists alike. As the blueprints have started to meet physical reality, ambitions have quietly started to be scaled back. Also in the works are Aquellum, an upside-down skyscraper touted as 'the subterranean digitalized community of the future', and an outdoor ski resort out in the Saudi desert, set to host the 2029 Asian Winter games. NEOM, the Kingdom's new innovation zone, or 'living laboratory' – the name a portmanteau of Neo (new) and the Mohamed Bin Salman's first initial – will provide a home to many of these projects. Some aspects of NEOM are, however, a lot more mundane, and dare we say practical, and focus on improving the country's digital connectivity. This is especially because Saudi Arabia, like several of its other oil-rich peers in the Gulf, is keen to become a prime global digital and AI hub, and has begun to court – and bankroll – the US hyperscalers such as AWS and Oracle and AI giants like OpenAI to encourage them to set up shop in the country. The case the Saudis present is a credible one: the country is relatively well positioned to form an alternative to the chokepoints in the Suez zone, and as a geopolitical swing state, it is increasingly considered a lower-risk option in the region (or was, at least, before the outbreak of the war in Iran, which has seen Tehran deliberately target hyperscaler data centres across the Gulf). In the cable domain, its strategy has started to pay dividends: because beyond several dozen new data centres, the Kingdom has also been able to attract cable landings such as the Blue-Raman system, a major Alphabet project connecting France to India. Saudi Arabia now forms a landing spot for twenty undersea cables and plans to add another seven by 2028 – and is thus becoming an important new node in the network.[33]

## *Geopolitics, influence and diplomacy*

Cables and cable routing are about more than just business. They are also shaped by, and can be tools of, geopolitics, influence and diplomacy. The All Red Line was a fundamentally geopolitical project, which has left its traces in the network to this day. Ireland, when it was still under British control, was a major cable connecting point – it was from Ireland's west coast, after all, that the very first successful transatlantic cable departed. The island would, however, rapidly lose this favoured position from the 1920s onwards, even though its geographical position remained advantageous.[34] At the root of this decline were the Irish Civil War and the country's staunch policy of neutrality – it was accused of maintaining an at minimum rather questionable relationship with Germany during both world wars and never joined NATO – which left especially Britain wary of routing sensitive traffic through the country, already during the war.[35] Ireland was briefly considered as a landing site for TAT-I, but amid the heightened tensions of the early Cold War, a landing in a rock face near a Scottish NATO naval base soon emerged as the more prudent choice.

France, too, became a source of headache after Charles de Gaulle took the explosive decision to take the country out of NATO's integrated military command in 1966.[36] Archival documents show a scramble at NATO headquarters, hastily relocated from Paris to Brussels, to find and fund new sovereign cable routes and landing sites for sensitive traffic that now no longer just had to bypass Franco's Spain, but also a suddenly unreliable France as well.

Saudi Arabia's ambitious plans to become the Middle East's pre-eminent digital hub are in part also predicated on delicate diplomatic wrangling – in this case with Israel. The aforementioned Blue-Raman cable system is split into two nominally separate sections (part 'Blue', and part 'Raman'), a separation widely speculated to in part be chosen to avoid creating the impression that Israel and Saudi Arabia would have agreed to connect directly to each other.[37] Such a two-pronged arrangement was reportedly necessary, because of the high degree of sensitivity that exists particularly on the Saudi side when it comes to engaging with Israel, a country whose sovereignty Saudi Arabia at the time of writing has never formally recognized. But it seems that even such artificial separations may now no longer be necessary. Several, rather opaque, cable projects are now reported to be underway, which will link Israel and Saudi Arabia directly. These cables will move largely over land, from Israel's Mediterranean coast, and continue through the narrow Gulf of Aqaba in the Red Sea, to connect to the small Saudi city of Haql (quite literally at the intended end of The Line).[38] These projects are believed to have come about under the banner of the Abraham Accords, the first Trump Administration's efforts to normalize relations between the Gulf States and Israel.[39] It is not clear how the wars in Gaza and Iran have impacted these plans.

Beyond the diplomatic considerations and regional interests that underpin these cable projects, their development also makes a lot of practical sense. Saudi Arabia is keen to attract more cables to its shores, but does not have direct land access to the Mediterranean. Routing through Israel offers a relatively stable and quick path, and could bring a much-needed alternative to the Egyptian desert bottlenecks. In September 2023, Israeli Prime Minister Benjamin Netanyahu called these kinds of projects 'an example of the most obvious [advantages of normalization]. That's the shortest route. It's the safest route. It's the most economic route'.[40] Because of its extraordinarily complex relationship with its neighbours and mutual concerns about cable traffic tapping, Israel had up until then been largely disconnected from other countries in the region, with almost all of its outward cables routing directly to Europe. This has generally meant that Israel has fewer local cable connections than one would expect given the country's heft in the global digital economy (it has the highest number of tech startups per capita in the world, sometimes earning it the moniker 'startup nation').[41] It has also meant that the alternative routes it could offer to bypass Egypt have not been exploited.

Israel is not the only country where geopolitical and security considerations have played a key role in determining their position in the global network. Unsurprisingly, North Korea does not have any undersea cables landing on its shores at all. Venezuela is another example of an under-connected country. While the country was originally not far behind its South American peers when it came to its outward-facing cable connections, the complex domestic context has seen the country fall increasingly behind. Since the early 2000s, it has only added one new cable system, connecting it to Cuba.[42]

Cuba itself has not fared much better. Because of the United States' ongoing embargo against the island and Havana's ambivalent view when it comes to opening up internet access to its people, Cuba has long been largely isolated from the rest of the global internet (if we disregard two US government-owned cables connecting Guantanamo Bay). The island only received its first cable landing in 2013 – Alba-1, that same one connecting to Venezuela and Jamaica – and had prior to that been entirely reliant on less powerful satellite connections.[43] Though the record of success of the internet bringing liberalization and democracy has so far proven to have been a rather patchy one, the Obama Administration's official Cuba policy encouraged the laying of further subsea cables to the island as a way of dislodging the sitting regime. However, when an initiative to do just that was up for approval in 2022, it was Washington that blocked the endeavour – citing national security concerns.[44] Connecting the United States to Cuba directly would mean the country would start to serve as a conduit for some American internet traffic. This would allow the Cuban authorities to potentially access sensitive information, which it could share with Beijing and Moscow, was the verdict. An initiative supported by France has since filled the vacuum, and a new cable connecting Cuba to Martinique has been laid.[45]

Geopolitical considerations do not only keep certain countries out of the network, they can also bring them in. Amid mounting global competition, cable roll-out has emerged as an increasingly active strategic arena, with China, the United States, Europe, Japan, Australia and others all competing to invest in the roll-out of new undersea cables to places which do not currently enjoy much connectivity or lack the means to fund their own.

As of 2026, China has been involved in, maintained and supported perhaps as many as 100 subsea and terrestrial cable projects, as part of its Belt & Road Initiative and other investment mechanisms through which it brings state-backed undersea and terrestrial cables to especially South-East Asia, Africa, the Pacific and Central Asia. These cables are seen as tools not just to grow China's own cable industry and generate business for its national champions, but also as a means through which to export a Chinese model for the internet to be solidified on top of this physical infrastructure, and to grow China's influence, markets and military power in new regions.[46] Europe's Global Gateway programme, launched in 2021 in part in response to the Belt & Road Initiative, had by 2023 committed €420 million in spend on new subsea cables, which the European Union sees as a means to bolster its own autonomy, foster closer ties with so-called swing states, and to counter China's influence in its perceived neighbourhood.

Geopolitics are becoming an increasingly important driving factor in the determination of new routes, and in attracting commercial investment in new cables. In the early stages of my research on this book, the 'G word' was still carefully skirted around during industry events – something we all best pretend is not there. Towards the end, more and more companies in the cable industry started to actively tout the resilience and robustness against geopolitical risk as a major selling point of their new projects.

## *Governance and lawfare*

In the Netherlands, humanist Hugo de Groot – also known by the latinized Hugo Grotius – is best known for his daring caper of fleeing Spanish captivity in Slot Loevenstein, a fortress castle at the confluence of the Maas and Waal rivers, by being smuggled out in a book chest. The rest of the world primarily knows the Dutch theologian and legal scholar as the popularizer of the concept of 'Mare Liberum', the idea that the High Seas – those zones of our oceans and seas that fall outside of any nation's direct jurisdiction – should be freely navigable and open to all. The concept of Mare Liberum was originally seized on as a challenge against the somewhat grandiose Treaty of Tordesillas, the Portuguese-Spanish 1494 *pas de deux*, which divided the newly discovered non-Christian world into a half to be controlled by Lisbon – the Indian Ocean and South Atlantic – and a half – the West Atlantic and the Pacific – that was to be dominated by the king of Spain. It was initially emerging naval powers like the Dutch Republic and later also Britain, wanting in on the increasingly lucrative trade with the New World and Asia, who promoted the concept of freedom of navigation on the High Seas.

Just as the challenger powers would soon win out over their Iberian competitors, so would their conception of the maritime sphere as a commons, in principle free to use by all – a notion that continues to underpin maritime governance to this day. The High Seas – initially defined as any unenclosed stretch of saltwater beyond the length of distance within which a country could meaningfully defend itself from land ('the reach of a cannon shot'), would be treated as a global commons, open to trade, discovery, fishing and also the 'privateering' that would bring the Dutch Republic and the British Empire such unimaginable riches. Still today, the concept of Mare Liberum and freedom of navigation remain key pillars of the global maritime order, and the globalized trade regime it empowers – making it possible for container ships, oil tankers and their naval protectors to cross the globe relatively unimpeded.

The concept of the High Seas and freedom of navigation also figure prominently in the maritime and other international law rulebooks that govern the roll-out of new undersea cables. Under international maritime law, anyone is in principle free to lay any new undersea cable wherever they want to in the High Seas, without needing anyone's permission.

This right is critical: if every bit of the 1.4 million odd kilometres of subsea cables out there were subject to a complex web of intersecting jurisdictions, it is hard to imagine the network would have ever grown as expansive as it has.

Countries, however, do have more latitude to refuse or set the conditions for the roll-out of new subsea cables within their own territorial waters (now defined as up to twelve nautical miles, or approximately 22 kilometres) – and, to a more limited extent, their exclusive economic zones (EEZs) – the area defined as extending out 200 nautical miles (or approximately 370 kilometres) from shore. Some governments have made grateful use of these powers. This can be quite benign: the US state of California is notorious for its strict environmental rules for new cable landings,[47] which has seen Oregon and others nearby try to seize the opportunity to present themselves as the less regulatorily cumbersome cable gateway to the West Coast. Other, especially more unpredictable, regimes – especially several in Africa – have instead made it incredibly difficult or expensive to land cables on their shores or traverse their waters, for example by blocking or placing exorbitant costs on permits, or making it difficult or lengthy for repair activities to be undertaken in their jurisdictions.[48]

This is no longer just a tool used by the small spoilers of this world, however. In a more geopolitically charged climate, in which international law holds progressively less sway or is even turned into a weapon, the frameworks governing the roll-out and protection of submarine cables are creaking at the seams. And this legal toolbox was already rather limited and difficult to enforce to begin with. Many of the rulebooks we rely on have not been updated in decades, sometimes in more than a century (in arguably yet another case of sea blindness).

The oldest in-use cable treaty dates back to 1884,[49] and is still firmly rooted in the context of the telegraph era. The United Nations Convention for the Law of the Seas (or UNCLOS, for short), in force since 1994, remains the most important piece of international law governing subsea cables, signed by over 160 countries, but was never ratified by key actors like the United States[50] or signed by Turkey. UNCLOS is now also increasingly being weaponized and contested by actual signatories like China, whose expansive interpretation of its maritime sphere of influence has seen it try to curtail the roll-out of new cables in the South China

Sea.[51] This relative lawlessness of the High Seas and the lack of robust and enforceable legal frameworks has also left concerning gaps when it comes to damage to cables and especially their deliberate sabotage, a topic we will discuss in detail in chapters 6 and 7.

Regulation and jurisdictional muscle-flexing are not just affecting the physical places in which cables are laid, but also the data that flow through them. Attempts to steer data flows – while seemingly more deterritorialized – also impact the cable network's geographical contours. Many countries and regions around the world now expound their own interpretations of 'data sovereignty', the idea that data – an increasingly valuable commodity in modern, tech-mediated economies – should preferably stay close to home and under domestic control.

In the case of techno-authoritarian countries like Russia and China, such sovereignty efforts focus primarily on restricting the access of domestic populations to supposed harmful external influences.[52] In the case of, for example, the European Union, this can take the shape of policies like data localization, which stipulates that sensitive data on European citizens should ideally be held on European soil, and can only be stored in, for example, data centres located in the United States under the strictest conditions.[53] Countries around the world are increasingly starting to put an emphasis on achieving cloud sovereignty – the idea of not having their data sit in hyperscaler-owned data centres which they cannot fully control. In Europe, for example, some 70 per cent of all data – from the continent's healthcare systems to its most sensitive military data – is housed by US cloud providers like AWS and Microsoft – which gives these companies, and by extension the US government, a lot of leverage and ability to weaponize this dominance.[54]

The growing push to build and bolster domestic cloud providers, and accompanying data centre infrastructure, will in the long run too have an impact on the physical layout of the cable network. Brexit, for example, may not have spelt the end of the City's financial pre-eminence in Europe, but it has started to have an impact on the United Kingdom's continued role as the continent's chief cable hub, with cable owners moving landings into the European Union out of concern about how regulatory divergence and different standards for data protection could complicate free flows of information in the future. Countries like Ireland and France have been beneficiaries of this uncertainty.[55]

In still other cases, it is concerns about the security of the cables themselves that can impact the geography of the network: America's Team Telecom, a powerful grouping of regulatory bodies and government departments tasked with assessing the national security risks of any new cable project planning to land on US soil, has used its powers to, for example, prevent the landing of cables in Hong Kong, mainland China and – as previously mentioned – Cuba, citing concerns that Beijing may interfere with sensitive data.

## *Rue the* Rubymar

To illustrate how all of these different vectors of power and influence on the network can come together and frequently also reinforce each other, let us consider one especially notorious incident involving damage to cables: the sinking of fertilizer freighter the *Rubymar* in the Red Sea in March 2024, which resulted in a significant loss of connectivity on both sides of the vital chokepoint – with especially South-East Asia and East Asia badly affected. When the news broke that three key telecommunications cables had been damaged off the coast of Yemen, some of the more sensationalist media was swift to draw its conclusions: this had to be Houthi sabotage.[56] The Houthis are an Iran-backed Yemeni rebel faction which has been able to seize control of vast swathes of Yemen (including its capital Sana'a) since the start of the country's devastating civil war in 2014. The conflict was long one of those unjustly 'forgotten conflicts', which simmered in the background, despite the humanitarian catastrophe it has unleashed on Yemen's civilian population (nearly 400,000 people have died since fighting commenced). The aftermath of Hamas's October 7 attacks against Israel changed that, as it has so fundamentally changed much else in the Middle East, firmly pushing the Houthis – who would become a significant actor in events – back into the global headlines.

The Houthi's official mission statement – 'God is the Greatest, Death to America, Death to Israel, Curse be upon the Jews, Victory to Islam' – leaves little ambiguity about where the group's loyalties lay in the Gaza war. The group, which has acted as an effective, though frequently hard-to-control, proxy for Iran, announced in November 2023 it would start to target any ship with ties to Israel traversing the Red Sea, in solidarity with the plight of the Palestinians. The Houthis soon made good on this threat and began to target commercial and other ships for which it could establish even a tenuous link to Israel (its expansive definition meant effectively all Western ships now had a target on their backs), using both Tehran-supplied and increasingly also self-manufactured missiles and drones.

The impact was immediate and profound: shipping through the Red Sea, the key gateway towards Suez and as such a conduit of approximately 12 per cent of global maritime traffic, slowed down to a trickle, as many ships sought safer routes around the southern tip of Africa. In the first year since the start of what effectively amounted to a naval blockade, transit volumes through the Red Sea dropped by some 70 per cent, shipping costs jumped by 250 per cent, and resulted in a noteworthy rise in global inflation.[57] The US-led multinational Operation Prosperity Guardian, which sought to counter the Houthi threat (often using multi-million dollar missiles to shoot down $3,000 drones) had proven unable to fully reopen the vital Red Sea lanes by the time the *Rubymar* commenced its journey.

So when a massive connectivity outage – seemingly originating in Yemeni waters – sent alarm bells ringing across the operation rooms of several global data providers, it was no surprise many quickly pointed to the Houthis. There had been rumours for some time that undermining global trade was no longer enough for the group: it also had plans to cripple the critical data infrastructure powering the global internet conveniently located on its doorstep. The fact that a Telegram channel linked to the group had posted detailed cable maps of the Red Sea, accompanied by an ominous message that said that: 'There are maps of international cables connecting all regions of the world through the sea. It seems that Yemen is in a strategic location, as internet lines that connect entire continents – not only countries – pass near it', added further lustre to these warnings.[58] The group did not just have motive, it also had opportunity: beyond its terrestrial occupied lands in Yemen, it also controlled most of the territorial waters through which the Red Sea's undersea cables are routed, and would thus have been in a prime position to interfere with this key artery of the global network.

Houthi leadership was quick to deny any involvement in the incident, however, and issued an official statement making clear that it was 'keenly interested' in protecting the submarine cables that routed through its waters, and would 'provide all services and grant necessary permits' to help facilitate speedy repair.[59]

The truth lay somewhere in the middle. The cables had indeed not been deliberately destroyed by Houthi rebels, but nor was it true that the group had nothing to do with the incident. The link was simply less direct. This now finally brings us to the *Rubymar*, a heavy freighter which, in a typical case of maritime convolution, was Belize-flagged but owned through an opaque structure involving the United Kingdom – the national link which had seen it singled out for attack – the Marshall Islands and Lebanon. The ship had been on its way from the United Arab Emirates to deliver fertilizer to Bulgaria, when it had been hit by a Houthi anti-ship missile.

Sent adrift, the hole in its hull leaving an oil slick some 70 kilometres long, the ship's loose anchor had inadvertently snagged and broken three key undersea communications cables (the AAE-1, Seacom/TGN-EA and Europe India Gateway) – taking out some 25 per cent of Euro-Asia cable capacity in its wake. All this before the *Rubymar* would eventually sink, its crew fortunately successfully evacuated. The *Rubymar* so became one of the first and to date most high-profile casualties of the Houthi blockade.

The reason why the sinking of the *Rubymar* had such an outsized impact on global connectivity was because it took place in the Bab-el-Mandeb, or Gate of Tears, the narrow strait – only some 26 kilometres wide at its narrowest point – which divides Yemen from Eritrea, and forms the gateway from the Arab Gulf into the Red Sea and by extension the Suez Canal chokepoint. At the time of writing, eighteen cables route through the strait, most of them laid in Yemeni waters.

A discerning reader might wonder why so much cable connectivity would be routed through the waters of a country with a political situation as volatile as Yemen's. The answer is that there is little alternative. Part of the story is geography – the Yemeni side's seabed is more favourable than the Eritrean – but it is above all because the warring parties in Yemen have ironically proven more reliable business partners than the Eritreans. Eritrea, which remains one of very few countries effectively cut off from the global internet, is not a signatory of UNCLOS, and its idiosyncratic regime effectively operates as a complete black box. It is not that the cable industry has not reached out about permits and potentially laying cables in the African country's territorial waters; it is simply the case that Eritrea does not respond. Email requests go unanswered, phone calls ignored. The sanctioned-to-the-hilt Houthis may be far from ideal interlocutors, but at least it is possible to have a conversation.

And that was a conversation that indeed urgently needed to be had. Not only had the *Rubymar*'s dragging anchor taken out several important undersea cables, including several of the highest-capacity systems – the ongoing exchange of fire, extreme volatility and legal complications meant that repairing the cables would become an odyssey in its own right; one which would take nearly five months to complete.[60] This hold-up was caused by a number of factors, above all of course the fact that the damaged cables were located in a highly-active war zone. Even if there had been repair ships and crews willing to brave the prospect of being fired at with missiles and chased by drones while they were undertaking the precise and lengthy task of hauling up the cables and addressing the multiple faults, they would have been hard-pressed to find an insurer willing to take on the risk of underwriting such an operation without serious security guarantees.

Then there was also the matter of sanctions levied by many governments against the Houthis, with countries affected, such as the United States and Saudi Arabia, having designated the group a terrorist organization. Where the Houthis had previously run a rather professional and efficient ship – the group derives significant profits from acting as the gatekeeper to the Red Sea and Suez – the type of backchannel negotiations involved with this now had to happen against the backdrop of literal missile fire being exchanged between several of the countries involved. It would in the end require no small amount of backdoor diplomacy, mutually agreed security guarantees, and the Houthi government itself having a significant interest in seeing the problem resolved (Yemen's own internet connectivity suffered significantly from the outages), before the repair process could finally get started.

While the cables were soon up and running again, the problems with shipping in the Red Sea remained.[61] Egypt has emerged as one of the blockade's biggest losers, as revenues from the Suez crossing have dropped precipitously (ceasefires have brought some respite). Most international shipping rerouted around the Cape of Good Hope, at significant cost to the shipping industry. The environment suffered; doubling the length of the trip by waylaying traffic means increased emissions, not to mention the risks of environmental catastrophe emerging from active exchanges of fire in the Red Sea itself. And we must also not forget about the crews on these ships, who now face even longer and more arduous journeys.

The visceral way in which the Houthi's weaponization of the Red Sea has revealed the fragility of this chokepoint has also put new impetus behind investments in alternative cable routes. Countries like Turkey, Saudi Arabia, Israel and Iraq may all be beneficiaries from an increased willingness to put up with the risk, diplomatic ramifications and added expense of laying more terrestrial cables over the Arabian peninsula.[62] Though these projects were initially conceived as ways of bypassing Egypt, it is events in the Red Sea that put serious momentum behind them. Some of the most ambitious hyperscaler cable projects which, like much of the shipping sector, seek to wind under the Cape of Good Hope, are similarly in part intended to bring more resilience through diversity – extra costs and length absorbed as an unfortunate but unavoidable consequence of a more insecure, complex world.

Economic, geographical and geopolitical factors mean that some countries are able to position themselves as key nodes or chokepoints in the cable network, whereas others struggle to wiggle themselves out of the periphery of global connectivity. Being at the centre of cable networks brings more advantages than just speedy, high-capacity internet and communications. As history has shown us, there is much to be gained from playing a leading role in communications networks and supply chains, to be the place where many cables land. We have only to look at Britain's experience during the nineteenth and early twentieth centuries to see how much power can be derived from being the central node in the global web of cables. The United States enjoys a similar position today – though its current adversarial approach to foreign policy and relationships with allies and foes alike may begin to chip away at this advantage.

The United States could find itself losing out in a number of ways. Placing oneself at the core of the network does not only help cement economic and financial power in an interconnected, globalized economy. It can also serve as a tool for controlling and intercepting information flows, for wielding military power, and bringing others into our orbits of influence. Well-connected countries and companies are also at an advantage in the increasingly feverish global race for technological supremacy, especially AI. We will explore the ways in which big cable players can derive power from the network in the next chapter.

4

# *Cable Power*

## *A weapon of war*

The contours of the cable network are not only shaped by those actors with most power – who are and who own the best-connected nodes at the heart of the network – cables are also important tools of power in their own right. Ever since the first undersea telegraph cables were laid, cables have been used as weapons of war, enabling communications and power projection over vast distances. This allowed the more effective cracking down on uprisings in the colonies back then, and the funnelling of the vast swathes of raw data collected by drones, satellites, sensors and the other hyperconnected tools of modern warfare today.

Undersea cables are also instruments of control. Countries and companies at the centre of the network can play an important role in determining who gets access to connectivity and all that it enables and who does not. Owning the underpinning infrastructure can thus provide countries and companies with an incredible amount of say over the data and information that flows through these cables and the structures built on top of them.

Cables can also be used as expressions of soft power. In a world where being connected to the global digital economy is an increasingly indispensable precondition for growth and economic success, laying cables to those places which still lack physical connections – or are trying to attract data centres and other infrastructure they believe are needed to compete in the AI race – can be an effective lever to gain influence and sympathy. This cable diplomacy can then be used as the basis to export one's vision for the wider technological sphere in the process – and lock others into one's strategic orbit.

This chapter charts some of the ways in which these different forms of cable power interact but can also contradict, and how major powers have increasingly started to weaponize their advantage. The stakes involved are high: the cable network has become an important flashpoint in a wider, globe-spanning geopolitical and geostrategic competition, which stretches from the Pacific Islands to the Arctic.

## *It's logistics, stupid!*

For as long as humans have been waging wars, we have been looking to leverage technology and innovation to gain an advantage over our adversaries. We have looked for *Wunderwaffen* – from the longbow to hypersonic missiles – to tip the balance of power in our favour. We have established new doctrines, hypothesized about revolutions in military affairs and the ways in which new technologies may be able to upend existing orthodoxies. As a species, we also continuously redefine what we consider war at all – with conflict creeping into the nebulous grey zone, into the economic sphere, to the heavens or the deepest depths of our oceans. The character and ways in which we wage war is a continuously evolving, ever-ongoing dance, in which technology and scientific breakthroughs are but one input.

Underpinning this dance, however, we can identify some universal dynamics that have driven forward the general evolution of warfare and the role innovation plays in it. When we look over the centuries and millennia, technology has allowed us to project power over ever larger distances and allowed us to bring more distance between ourselves and our adversaries in a bid to minimize casualties on our own side, and increase lethality on the other.[1]

Hand-to-hand combat, legs and fists gave way to clubs and swords, to bows and arrows, catapults, machine guns and V-2 rockets. The longest-range intercontinental ballistic missiles available today can now bridge distances of over 16,000 kilometres. While we have moved further and further away from our opponents, we have also tried to hit them with ever more precision. During the Second World War, American and British bombers still had to physically fly over German factories to target them, guided by navigators with paper maps and charts in hand. Success rates were low and rates of attrition abysmal. Today, drone operators sitting in Nevada can watch their targets in Yemen or Somalia enjoy their lunch, before they push the fateful button. The Israel Defense Forces (IDF) now claim their AI-enabled tools can hit targets with over 90 per cent precision.[2]

All this distance and precision are predicated on having access to more and more information and data, in order to lift the proverbial 'fog of war'. Intelligence satellites and drones have enabled battlefield visibility, and a degree of insight army planners and field commanders of the past could never have dared imagine. The radio in part challenged the cable because it was able to reach ships out at sea, and later also troops on the move. Both sides in the war in Ukraine have found themselves empowered by the hyperconnectivity and mobility enabled by satellite systems such as Starlink.[3]

What all these dynamics and trends have in common is an increased reliance on technology and the underlying connectivity that enables it: satellites, sensors, data centres, AI-fuelled command and control hive-minds, and the unsung hero enabling much of this, indeed, cables. The data needs of the US military, still the pre-eminent and one of the most high-tech militaries, are quite astonishing – and continue to increase. At the height of the war in Iraq, already 75 per cent of the intelligence, surveillance and reconnaissance (ISR) data collected, and ferried through a set of dedicated fibre optic cables laid to help facilitate the invasion, comprised drone footage.[4] Many militaries' new love affair with AI systems, which can speed up target identification and battlefield decision-making far beyond normal human abilities, will require even more data and thus even more bandwidth. While the 'final mile' collection of lots of this data will be wireless, the bulk of the information collected on the battlefield still ultimately needs to travel through undersea cables to make its way to the home front or overseas bases.

## *A perfect symbiosis?*

While militaries and governments will occasionally possess their own cables, they are heavily reliant on the commercial network for moving around all this information. By most publicly available estimates, around 95 per cent of US government traffic runs through regular commercial cables, the very same cables our bank transfers and WhatsApp messages are routed through.[5] Though no longer as important a customer as they had been in the semi-state monopoly days of the Cold War, governments remain important sources of funding for new cables. They are especially indispensable when it comes to wiring up under-connected geographies or routes that are not especially lucrative but deemed politically important.

A lot of this kind of funding is rather mundane: governments or institutions like the World Bank or European Commission will provide development support for cables, which would otherwise struggle to get the green light, for example because of their relatively low expected usage – think here of cables connecting small, sparsely populated islands.[6]

Some of these publicly funded cable projects have a decidedly more geostrategic flair, however. A 2023 Reuters investigation found that the US government had quietly funded SubCom, the New Jersey-based cable giant, to lay a secret cable splice off of a more conventional commercial project connecting Australia to India and the Middle East the company was involved with. The branch in question would serve to connect the US military base on Diego Garcia to the global cable network.[7]

Diego Garcia, the southernmost of the Chagos Islands, has been home to a secretive joint US–UK military base since the 1970s (a relatively late addition to Washington's pointillist empire). Diego Garcia's geographical position, as well as deep-water port, airfield and surveillance infrastructure, are strategically vital for US power projection in the Middle East and the Indo-Pacific – in fact, many of the air operations targeting the Houthis were launched from there. Diego Garcia is, however, also extraordinarily remote. It lies roughly mid-way between East Africa and Indonesia, deep into the Indian Ocean. The wider Chagos island group is furthermore very sparsely populated, meaning that it had so far not been wired up to the global network, and has had to rely on patchy satellite connectivity.

Given the nature of the acknowledged and unacknowledged activities taking place on Diego Garcia, the base would benefit greatly from fast connectivity and gaining the ability to quickly relay high volumes of data back to the United States, the United Kingdom and the other Five Eyes partners Australia, Canada and New Zealand.[8] But despite the Pentagon's deep coffers, it would have been expensive for the US government to lay a completely dedicated cable system just to connect a single, remote, base. More importantly, it also would have been difficult to keep details of such a project away from prying eyes. Piggybacking off an existing cable system made connecting Diego Garcia a lot more achievable.

The US government is believed to have a permanent retainer in place with SubCom – worth several million each year, though the total may be higher – which allows it to disperse funds for projects such as the Chagos splice, without such endeavours necessarily attracting the kind of attention and scrutiny they would do if they had to be put up for more traditional Congressional budget approval.[9] Given the sensitivity of some of the projects it presumably uses these funds for, for Washington working with a US company like SubCom is an especially good fit. This relationship with SubCom can be said to be a symbiotic one, and dates back nearly a century: the company is a spin-off of AT&T, which sat at the very heart of the Cold War military-industrial complex. The company and wider cable industry benefit from government funding – it reportedly coughed up about one third of the cost of the main commercial cable as well, not just the splice. The Pentagon, meanwhile, benefits from getting to work with a trusted partner which can be relied upon to keep any talk about the project to a minimum.

### *A different kind of dark fibre*

While US military and government communications rely on commercial cables (and the same will be the case for most other countries), it is generally agreed within the industry and the cable research community that the US military and intelligence services also own proprietary cables. Some of these cables are a matter of public record. Scouring through the Pentagon's procurement database, we find scores of contracts for fibre optic cables laid on US domestic or overseas bases. In the 2010s, for example, the United States acquired two new cables connecting its base in Guantanamo Bay.[10] The US military also owns other types of undersea cables, not used for communications. It has power cables. It also had its Sound Surveillance System (SOSUS) and its successors, the elaborate underwater listening and sensing cable and hydrophone system first launched during the Cold War, which was used to monitor Soviet submarines in the North Atlantic.[11] Fallen into disuse in the post-Cold War era, the Pentagon is now reportedly reviving and modernizing these systems, at a time when Russian subsea adventurism has once again become a source of great concern.[12]

Whether the US has its own international communications cables solely for its own use – the splice connecting to Diego Garcia could be one such example – is a matter of more debate. Speculation about the existence of such cables has a long history. During the Cold War, TAT-1 and its successors funnelled an important share of the sensitive communications being ferried between the US and its European allies. Some historians suggest that there may have been further, secret, government-owned cables in place as well, which allegedly made landfall in the heavily fortified UK naval bases like RAF Bude in Devon and at RAF Skewjack in Cornwall, and would have carried sensitive military and intelligence communications and secure calls between the US and UK. Such cables may very well still exist today. Many in industry and the research community certainly believe so.

Unsurprisingly, given the highly sensitive nature of the communications that would presumably be carried by these cables, their location, even their very existence, is kept opaque. Dark fibre of a very different kind, if you will. These cables do not appear on TeleGeography's cable map, nor on the far more precise maps shared with fishermen and other prolific commercial cable snaggers. It is these kinds of highly strategic cables that ships like the *Yantar*, the research vessel spotted in many European countries' waters, are especially intent on finding. Militaries and intelligence agencies prefer for these secret cables to occasionally get damaged as part of a routine accident, rather than have their exact location become known to adversaries with bad intentions. This appears to be the risk calculus. Similar to the philosophy that prevailed during the Cold War, minimizing the much rarer but highly impactful risk of state interference with an undersea cable outweighs concerns about the cable's day-to-day resilience and protection.

That, however, does not mean that no precautions are being taken. These kinds of cables still need to share the seabed with more traditional commercial cables – if any crossed wires or accidental entanglements can be avoided, that is naturally in everyone's interest. It is therefore apparently not uncommon to find representatives of the US military listening in at the back of the room during industry gatherings and events, keeping a keen ear out to find out more about the kinds of routes new commercial projects have in the works. Nor would it necessarily be unprecedented for some of these companies to receive the occasional phone call, urging them to 'move their cable just a little bit further south, if you can. Well maybe not quite that far south'.

These kinds of government cables of course do not materialize out of nowhere. While the US Navy does own its own – ageing – cable-laying repair ship, the USNS *Zeus* (which helped lay the cables to Guantanamo Bay),[13] it does not have its own shadowy cable-laying crew which goes and spools out mysterious new cables in the dead of night. Here too, a symbiosis with industry exists, which supports the routing, laying and maintenance of new cables – not much different from the public-private partnerships that maintain and build the other structures that underpin the US military's global reach. There is a trusted circle of individuals in the cable industry who know where these cables are. It is a small one.

## *Infrastructural power*

This symbiotic relationship between telecommunications companies and the US government dates all the way back to at least the First World War.[14] Before that, Britain's communications hegemony was similarly predicated on the fusion of commercial and strategic interests. This is not the case for all segments of the current US tech industry, however. Up until recently, the relationship between Washington on the one hand, and America's hyperscalers and other tech giants – shorthand Silicon Valley – on the other, had proven more complex. It is in some ways intimate by inevitability – one could not exist in its current form without the other – but Silicon Valley had for some time also taken great care, at least publicly, to maintain an air of distance and of projecting a global, neutral and supra-jurisdictional image. Its products existed in the cloud and were decoupled from physical geography and materiality (their large data centre footprints notwithstanding). Its companies were simply so big, so powerful – they existed above the state, were increasingly states in their own right. Silicon Valley did not shy away from doing business with China (or at least the companies Beijing allowed in. Most American social media platforms have long been banned in the country). When it was forced to comply with American court orders, the Silicon Valley giants liked to create the impression that they refused to play ball or only complied begrudgingly.[15]

From the late 2010s onwards, this dynamic started to shift. To understand why, we need to take a step back in history, and zoom in on the evolution of the relationship between the US tech industry and

Washington. Though Silicon Valley likes to tout its hippy, counter-cultural antecedents, its roots lie firmly in the military-industrial complex and the generous military contracts that funded its early post-war growth.[16] The semiconductor industry, to which Silicon Valley owes its name, came of age in the 1950s and 1960s with the birth of companies like Intel, whose initial growth and innovations were in no small part driven by Pentagon demand. Defence giants such as Northrop Grumman and Lockheed Martin all maintained large presences in California. The RAND Corporation, the illustrious defence think tank, was founded in Santa Monica, not in Washington, DC.

The internet itself, too, has its roots in the military: the original Advanced Research Projects Agency Network (or ARPANet) was funded by the Pentagon. This precursor to the internet was in part conceived around the idea of distributing and decentralizing information flows by design, so that no single node or chokepoint could be targeted to bring down the whole network, again recalling All Red Line logic. Some of these early decentralized nodes of the network were housed in universities such as Berkeley and Stanford, which would both emerge as important intellectual feeder institutions during the early commercial internet's 1990s boom years.[17] These were to be the new core nodes around which the expansion that put the region at the centre of the global economy would increasingly revolve.

This intimate relationship – and particularly Silicon Valley's reliance on military contracts – started to cool after the end of the Cold War. Especially here, the spirit of peace dividend thinking became a key driving force, as military spending soon saw significant reductions – and with it, a drop in lucrative Pentagon contracts.[18] While military spending was on the wane, the simultaneous rapid growth of the digital economy meant that there was now a lot more money to be made with commercial applications, as the trillions generated in California since attest to. This was about more than just making money, however.

Pursuing Pentagon contracts during this period came to be seen increasingly as anathema to the Silicon Valley ethos of 'moving fast and breaking things', the kind of work that would get bogged down by bureaucracy and tedious, slow procurement processes. Frontier technology development and investment at the same time also moved, at least optically, away from hardware – semiconductors, telecommunications equipment, cables! – towards higher-margin and sexier software, giving a certain sense of de-territoriality to the tech trade. Tech was now borderless. Less glamorous manufacturing, the actual making of things, that could all be outsourced abroad.

Perhaps most importantly of all, Silicon Valley's hyperscalers came of age at a time when working with the military came to be seen by many as uncouth – a trend that is now slowly starting to reverse. Perhaps most emblematic of this changing relationship was the 2018 outcry over Project Maven, a Pentagon programme which enlisted the help of companies like Google to allow the US military to actually analyse all these massive reams of strategic data flowing through the cable network. When Google staff got wind of the multi-million dollar deal, they staged a walk-out and in an open letter demanded the cancellation of the project, or at least their employer's involvement in it.[19] Amid the more liberal climate that still prevailed in California's tech industry at the time, Alphabet's leadership soon heeded these calls and temporarily abandoned the project (the company, however, never fully severed ties with the Pentagon, but kept the collaboration discreet – staff may have been opposed, the board room was not necessarily). It was not just staff opposition, however, that prevented these kinds of collaborations.

The whole culture in Silicon Valley can be said to have been shaped by this idea that it was above government. So above government, in fact, that it was just a matter of time before it would make wasteful, sluggish governments obsolete altogether.[20] In recent years, as the world has turned more insecure, insular and geopolitically tense – and the borderless trade Silicon Valley relies on is no longer a given – the tech industry has come to recognize again that it may need government after all. It has also once again grown more interested in exploring the dual-use and defence applications of their tech solutions – driven by a combination of patriotic sentiment, as well as the promise of high levels of investment, amid a rapid rise in global defence spending, especially since the start of the war in Ukraine. This rapprochement and return to the kind of entanglement, of a kind not seen since the Cold War, has taken on an especially intimate dimension during the second Trump Administration.

It was to be a picture for the ages: the grouping of tech tycoons from Mark Zuckerberg to Jeff Bezos – then worth a combined $1.35 trillion – lined up alongside each other to witness Donald Trump's second inauguration. None had deigned to make an appearance during the first one. Where the Bay Area had long been known for its liberal inclinations – it still votes overwhelmingly democrat – now several of its leaders openly admitted to donating to the Trump campaign, and were later revealed to have contributed generously to the president's inaugural ball and the construction of a $300 million White House ballroom.[21] Some of the tech luminaries – most notoriously Elon Musk – even joined the Administration to bring the 'move fast and break things' ethos to the administrative state. Silicon Valley had entered politics and wanted its *quid pro quo*: get into the White House's good graces, and buy its global muscle to push an antiregulation, pro-tech agenda, and promote its AI wares both domestically and abroad.

It relied on more than just the White House's coercive strength. The world had changed dramatically since 2016 – as had the economics behind the tech industry. Rising geopolitical tensions, global regulatory pushback, especially in key markets like the European Union, a slowdown in traditional venture capital investment (outside of AI) and pace of innovation, and later also growing concerns about returns on investment on the industry's massive AI infrastructure expenditures, had made chasing government contracts more appealing for tech companies big and small.[22]

The numbers showed it: the Pentagon signed contracts with hyperscalers worth an estimated $53 billion between 2018 and 2022 alone.[23] Most hyperscalers and frontier AI labs like OpenAI and Anthropic started to provide services to the Pentagon. Technology was also becoming more physical again – with all the investment in data centres, chip hardware and, indeed, cables (significantly, Silicon Valley's two largest companies by market cap – Nvidia and Apple – are in large part focused on selling hardware). The Valley itself could no longer pretend it was not firmly rooted in geography, and fundamentally tethered to its own home country – the United States – and, by extension, its geopolitical destiny.

This was also about ideology. Major tech leaders called on US tech firms and new startups to do their 'patriotic duty', in the mounting competition with China.[24] Companies like Palantir and Anduril, both major US champions in the booming defence tech sphere, present themselves as explicitly working in support of US power and Western values worldwide.[25] Leading frontier AI labs have started to compare America's AI mission to the Manhattan Project and begun to suggest that Washington foot more of the ballooning bill for the infrastructure underpinning AI development, lest it loses the existential race for supremacy over the technology. A more cynical onlooker may interpret these calls also as attempts to have the government save the day as the bet on AI threatens not to bring the promised commercial returns on investment. It certainly brings to mind the way in which the telegraph cable industry staved off collapse because of the British Admiralty's growing belief in the existential need for the All Red Line, just as the commercial market started to be saturated.

But these overtures do go both ways. The Pentagon, in turn, increasingly believed it could only retain its global supremacy if it became better able at leveraging Silicon Valley's innovative heft. While during the Cold War new technologies frequently emerged out of the military-industrial orbit and government-supported research labs (recall Bell Labs' fibre optic breakthroughs), this direction of travel had now largely reversed, with Silicon Valley's leading-edge companies driving frontier innovation, and the Pentagon increasingly struggling to fully harness it. The push to remedy this was driven by an increasingly frenzied bipartisan fear in Washington that, though the US military remains the world's largest, its capabilities were atrophying, while more nimble rivals (above all China) were rapidly catching up.[26]

The Pentagon launched its dedicated Defense Innovation Unit in 2015, which would make it easier for Washington's colossal procurement apparatus to work with more experimental and faster-paced tech companies. Key pillars of Biden's technology and economic policy agenda – from the CHIPS Act to export restrictions on strategic technologies – were framed through a national security lens and intended to enable US tech to retain its edge over Chinese tech challengers. The Trump Administration walked back many of the regulatory guardrails put in place by previous administrations in order to unleash AI's full potential and teamed up with its AI champions to export their solutions, and so influence, abroad.[27]

Silicon Valley is once again firmly weaving itself into the military-industrial complex, becoming more geopolitically involved across all layers of the technology stack. There are reasons to be wary about this increased symbiosis. In his final address, President Biden cautioned about the emergence of a new type of tech-industrial complex, in a clear echo of his predecessor Eisenhower's similar warning during his farewell address to the nation.[28] What this kind of entanglement will certainly do is provide Washington with even more powerful levers to shape global technology networks – including undersea cables.

### *The state meets the quasi-state*

Washington has made effective use of the outsized role of the hyperscalers in global cable networks, but has not always done so with the full support of said companies. As we shall discuss in depth in chapter 7, America's Team Telecom, the government body made up of the US Departments of Defense, Justice and Homeland Security as well as the Federal Communications Committee (FCC), which is in charge of approving new cable projects which land in the United States, has used this power to make it increasingly difficult for new cable projects which land in China or those that involve Chinese suppliers to join the global network. This has primarily affected several marquee hyperscaler projects – which were partially blocked on national security grounds.

But this dynamic does not always have to be coercive. Just like the relationship between Big Tech and Washington appears to be growing more intimate, also in the cable space do we see increasingly how both government and hyperscalers can benefit from collaboration. Operating as they now do as quasi-states, the hyperscalers are becoming increasingly sophisticated geopolitical actors in their own right. According to several people in the industry, Google's mother company Alphabet has ambitions to effectively create its own globe-spanning cable system, which will connect together its overseas data centres and key traffic hubs;[29] a modern All Red Line if you will, but one run by a private company, not a state. In this new conception, data centres are the military bases, and access to cheap energy and information flows the new resource extraction. We live in an era of networked power after all.

Presumably as part of these efforts, Alphabet has announced the construction of a number of new cables which follow less than traditional routes. In 2024, it announced its new Umoja system, which will connect Australia to east Africa.[30] The route has been considered somewhat unorthodox by many in the industry – the amount of direct traffic flowing between the two is arguably not (yet) sufficient to justify the laying of an expensive, high-calibre cable such as this. If you are looking for geopolitically resilient alternative routes that steer clear from China, however, these kinds of interconnections start to make a lot of sense. Meta's Waterworth cable is a similarly inherently geopolitical endeavour. Announced in early 2025, the fully Meta-owned and funded cable project, which at 50,000 kilometres will be the world's longest, will touch on five continents – connecting Australia, via India, South Africa and Brazil, to both the US west and east coasts – entirely bypassing the traditional routes through the Red Sea, Europe and the South China Sea.[31] Again, this is a project as much about resilience as it is about commercial utility.

These growing hyperscaler ambitions benefit Washington, which is thus even better able to leverage the strength of its tech industry in shaping the contours of the global cable network – now not just blocking or piggybacking on new cables, but shaping entirely new routes and connections. As hyperscalers are now among the very few actors who can undertake these kinds of large-scale projects, this kind of symbiosis has the potential to reconfigure the network's overall contours. As we know, Washington has its annual retainer with SubCom.[32] Some industry observers suspect that Washington may be indirectly supporting certain hyperscaler cable routes too – in a dynamic not unlike the Diego Garcia project described previously.

All sides benefit from these arrangements. Alphabet finds itself one step closer to achieving full coverage and improves redundancy in its network – and could in future benefit from the increased usage on Africa's east coast, as the continent's internet adoption continues to grow exponentially. Washington, in turn, finds itself with an entirely new, secure route from east to west that bypasses the geopolitically charged South China Sea, and indirectly bolsters its influence on the continent. The cable industry also benefits – monetarily and security-wise – from these closer ties between governments and the tech sector.[33]

As we shall see in later chapters, the increased politicization of cable routing and permitting in the Indo-Pacific has made some traditional cable routes and landing sites no longer as viable as they used to be.[34] Hong Kong, for example, used to be one of the primary cable landing hubs in the region, but amid growing concerns in Washington about the city's increasingly authoritarian turn under pressure from Beijing, and

China's moves to complicate the roll-out of new cables in what it believes to be its maritime sphere of influence, it has effectively been taken off the map. The Pacific Island of Guam, acquired by the United States in the late nineteenth century in part because of its strategic position as a cable landing hub, has been emerging as an alternative. This is not an unwelcome development for the cable companies, given the implicit security and protection that comes with landing one's cables on an island with significant US military presence.

## *One Belt, One Road*

Cables are, however, not just instruments of hard power – whether military, or of economic coercion. They are also tools of influence, tools for setting technical standards or for making diplomatic overtures. They are sometimes all of these things at once. One country that has been particularly adept at combining these different levers of cable power is China, which has long recognized that placing itself at the centre of global communications and trade networks was a vital ingredient in achieving its goals for global influence.[35] One of the main vehicles through which China has sought to expand this reach is through its Belt and Road Initiative (BRI), its grand infrastructure funding vehicle launched in 2013.

The BRI was in many ways China's way of showing it was no longer content to 'wait and bide its time', but was now ready to meet the world.[36] By 2024, the Belt and Road Initiative had around 140 members (though some countries, such as Italy, have since left again) and is estimated by its tenth anniversary to have channelled more than $1 trillion into infrastructure projects around the world. Cables were always at the heart of its approach: during the inaugural BRI Forum, Xi Jinping stressed the critical importance of China becoming a leader in developing and exporting technologies that underpin the 'digital economy, artificial intelligence, nanotechnology, and quantum computers, and promote the construction of big data, cloud computing, and smart cities'. The laying of telecommunications infrastructures was the *sine qua non* enabling all of this. China, too, recognized the power of connections and being at the heart of global information flows – a datafied All Red Line, if you will.

So it was only logical that, as part of the Belt and Road, China in 2015 announced the Digital Silk Road (DSR), a separate arm of the initiative specifically focused on the roll-out of digital infrastructure, notably also submarine cables.[37] Since the DSR's inception in 2015, China has backed dozens of cable projects, often co-financed through BRI mechanisms, linking partner countries across Asia, Africa, Europe and beyond. These cables are usually laid by national champion HMN Tech (previously Huawei Marine), and are supported by Chinese telecommunications companies. The crown jewel of the Digital Silk Road's cable effort is the PEACE cable ('Pakistan and East Africa Connecting Europe'), a $425 million project spanning from China to France via Pakistan, Djibouti and Egypt, which since its completion in 2022 forms one of the key arteries through the Suez chokepoint.[38]

It has not all been smooth sailing for the Belt and Road Initiative. In recent years, China has been met with increased pushback and counter-initiatives from Western countries, who warn about the national security implications of China's growing global infrastructure footprint, as well as the economic coercion, anticompetitive dumping and alleged debt trap diplomacy recipient countries risk exposing themselves to by welcoming in Beijing's generosity.[39] Many BRI recipient countries, too, have become wary of the excessive corruption and slowdowns behind many of the projects (as have Chinese planners), the cost overruns which have landed several of them close to IMF defaults or in need of (Western) bail-outs, and a growing awareness that many of these new bridges, trainlines and cables arguably appear to above all serve Chinese resource extractivism rather than their own citizens.

Beijing itself too is reining in some of the largesse – with spending having tapered quite significantly over the past few years, amid fiscal headwinds in Beijing, due to a persistent property crisis, weak domestic consumption and other pressures.[40] That has not meant a move away from new cables and digital infrastructure, however: the new, pared down Belt and Road now focuses above all on the roll-out of new digital and green infrastructure, two ingredients of the approach through which China hopes to become dominant in the new economies of the future.[41] The Digital Silk Road, for now, continues apace.

## *Ulterior motives?*

Beijing's largesse has proven a powerful vehicle for creating a global market for Chinese exports, such as steel, cement and solar panels – especially as its own domestic market struggles to absorb all of its production and manufacturing capacity. The BRI is also a highly visible tool to show China has arrived on the world stage, and can now wield its influence as a global power and back that up with cash and tangible investments.[42] We should see the Belt and Road, and the Digital Silk Road, ultimately as mechanisms to put China at the heart of a new, alternative set of global networks, centred around Eurasia – in a true revival of the Ancient Silk Road – in a rather Mackinderian vision for global supremacy.[43]

The Belt and Road should thus certainly not be mistaken for a soft power instrument alone. Just like Britain and the United States employed investments and subsidies as tools to solidify their respective communications hegemonies and fuel their (neo-)imperial expansion, the Silk Road's cables, too, serve a dual purpose for bolstering Beijing's hard power and coercive interdependencies.[44]

Unlike some of China's other forays into the global economy, the launch of the Belt and Road Initiative did immediately spark alarm in Washington, which worried that the initiative intended to supplant America and its allies in the Global South, trap beneficiaries in asymmetrical dependencies, and – importantly – allow China to also expand its global military footprint and technological influence and standard-setting power. Indeed, Washington has repeatedly warned that many of the cables China has been rolling out as part of the BRI were about much more than just bringing connectivity, but served a clear dual-use – both military and civilian – purpose.

There is a strong, bipartisan, view in the Beltway, that the Chinese Communist Party (CCP) has mobilized all of China's growing industry and economic power in the service of its 'civil-military fusion' doctrine, a long-standing ambition which has only increased in intensity under Xi's leadership of the party, which posits that China's commercial sector should be more involved in building up the People's Liberation Army (PLA), and support any future war effort when the time comes.[45] It should be noted that some China scholars express some scepticism about the degree to which this notion of civil-military fusion is in fact an actual, integrated whole-of-society strategy, rather than mostly just an aspiration, something for senior-level CCP officials to bandy around in speeches and for captains of industry to pay lip service to, to please Beijing.[46]

Nevertheless, there is certainly good reason to believe a secondary military objective may be behind the roll-out of some of these DSR cables. Rick Umback has aptly pointed out the similarities between Huawei's initial growth and Imperial Germany's Telefunken's in the early twentieth century.[47] Both companies initially relied on strategic military investments and government subsidies which aimed to create a global market for their wares. Both also sought to challenge entrenched incumbents (British cable giants then, and today the large Western telecommunications companies and hyperscalers).

This dynamic goes beyond leveraging military spending to achieve growth. The PEACE cable, which touches primarily on major communications hubs along its route, also notably makes landfall in both Gwadar in Pakistan, and Djibouti. Djibouti, highly strategically located in the Horn of Africa, also happens to be the location of China's very first overseas naval base.[48] The port town of Gwadar in Pakistan has long been rumoured to soon become one too.

Gwadar was long a relatively sleepy and underdeveloped backwater on Pakistan's south coast, whose population of 90,000 largely relied on fisheries. The port city's strategic location, however, also means it serves as an endpoint of the $46 billion Pakistan–China Economic Corridor – a new alternative, land-based route for energy and goods transportation, which connects China's Xinjiang province directly to the Arabian Sea, and so avoids the contentious Strait of Malacca (the critical shipping lane between Indonesia, Singapore, Thailand and Malaysia – another key maritime chokepoint).[49] Gwadar has been among the most-feted recipients of BRI funding. The city is now home to a Chinese-funded deep-water port, Chinese-funded airport, and new railway lines, highways and energy projects: infrastructures which, according to local critics, appear to primarily serve Chinese strategic interests. There is perhaps some historical irony in the choice of Gwadar: this is also the place where the original telegraph cable connecting Britain to India, the crown jewel of the All Red Line, made landfall. Empires come and go, but geography is permanent.

The roll-out of Beijing's subsidized cables is also believed to serve as a Trojan horse of sorts for the wider export of Chinese technologies and standards. First, you send the means to connect, then you control what runs on top of it, then you set the standards to ensure this entanglement persists into the future, runs the logic. This is about power and lock-in but also has a clear ideological component: China has a well-developed vision for its own domestic internet – it heavily limits outside information coming in, and restricts its own information space to conform to party lines. Beijing sees an opportunity to export that vision to the rest of the world.[50] Like the ways in which Big Tech companies wield their infrastructural power, China too wants to expand its influence across all layers of the stack, locking others into its model.[51]

To do this, Chinese companies and government bodies have in the past decade become increasingly active in the alphabet soup of international standard-setting bodies that shape the protocols, norms and standards that make the internet function – from setting standards for how new technologies, such as facial recognition systems, work, to the most foundational of underpinnings determining how traffic is routed through the global system.[52] China has also focused on bringing others into its technological orbit through technology exports. Despite the setbacks Huawei has faced in the West in the past decade amid mounting US pressure, the company remains a market leader in much of the Global South.[53]

And it is not just Huawei. Smartphones, telecommunications equipment, the tiny but vital screw needed to make a widget work, high-end satellites, energy infrastructure, top range electric vehicles, almost everything else: they increasingly come from China. Though long written off for only being good at hardware and cheap gadgets, Chinese software is also making in-roads: super-app WeChat is the application of choice for everything from chatting with friends to online payments in much of Asia; Indonesian taxi drivers use Chinese Didi, not Uber; TikTok has young eyeballs glued to the screen all over the world. The country's AI models are increasingly able to compete with the American market leaders. Chinese electric cars whizz through Europe's capitals, and have the best software. The China stack is expanding its reach.

Beijing has accomplished this not just by creating an increasingly more competitive offering, but also by quite literally bringing connectivity to new places, creating a new customer base in the under-connected Global South, and then using that as an in to sell a wider philosophy, tech paradigm and set of tools, to new markets. Especially those governments with less robust democratic credentials are all too often glad to adopt Beijing's model. The delivery of BRI hardware connectivity has indeed frequently been followed by the export of surveillance technologies like Chinese facial recognition tech, internet censorship tools, as well as recipients' support in multilateral bodies for China's technology standards.[54] Once countries embrace a technology stack, it can create a dynamic of lock-in that is hard to break out of again (something many European countries are now waking up to in the context of their reliance on US solutions) – creating a realm of interdependency in which a Chinese model for the digitization can start to reign, and its own infrastructural power can expand.

Washington, in particular, has been concerned not just about what it perceives to be an insidious lock-in of recipient countries, but also about how Chinese infrastructural expansion could open the door to interference with the network more generally. The more wired into the cable network China becomes, the more global traffic flows through its own mainland or places like Hong Kong; the more information is routed through the cables it has manufactured, the more power over others it can wield. Becoming more central in the network could hand China a lot of control over others' communications and information, all the while keeping its own citizens' data close to home. As we will see below and in later chapters, these concerns have led to a concerted push back by the United States and its allies to limit this rapid roll-out of new Chinese-linked cables.

## *Pacific power games*

One relatively early example of how countries can find themselves in the middle of this competition between China and the West over subsea cables is the case of the Solomon Islands. Australia, by some margin the wealthiest and most powerful country in Oceania (it is home to a full one third of the continent's population, and accounts for around 85 per cent of its GDP) – has, unsurprisingly, traditionally been the most influential actor, as well as biggest funder of development projects, in the vast archipelagic region.[55] Australia's position in the Pacific was only truly challenged once – by Imperial Japan during the Second

World War – and Canberra is certainly not keen to let that happen again. The United States, too, considers Australia, and by extension its own, continued pre-eminence in the Pacific a priority. For Washington, especially the region's western flank has historically been particularly strategically important, as its close geographical proximity to Asia makes it a useful staging grounds during a potential conflagration in the Indo-Pacific, as the bloody Pacific battles of the Second World War viscerally remind us of. Australia and the US in the post-Cold War decades had, however, started to take their influence in the Pacific for granted and did little to continue to cultivate their relationships with the small island states.

Enter China. Beijing has a significant interest in growing its influence in the region. The scattered island nations offer a fertile ground for – legal or illegal – fishing. They attract much tourism, and have long been home to substantial Chinese diasporas. Because of the islands' wide dispersal, their exclusive economic zones are especially large, and their seabeds believed to be home to sizeable mineral deposits – for example cobalt and manganese. These are resources which are important for electric vehicles and batteries, and the manufacturing of other goods on which China is keen to lead.[56] Many of the islands – especially those closer to the Asian heartland – are highly strategically located, and a target for Chinese expansion. As we have seen, every aspiring hegemon needs its own set of overseas bases. China as a rule does not maintain any formal treaty alliances (North Korea being the exception), which limits its global military reach. Pursuing the development of new bases and security partnerships of its own has therefore become an important objective in Beijing. The Solomon Islands have emerged as a prime contender for such expansion, and cables one of the early tools of influence of choice.

Beijing's early moves in courting the Solomon Islands involved the laying of a subsidized subsea cable. We have previously discussed how the often extremely sparsely populated, relatively poor, and extraordinarily remote islands that make up Oceania are currently not well served by the global cable network. Australia, like most of its Western peers in the peace dividend era, had, however, not paid much attention to the important role strategic investments in communications infrastructure, and cables in particular, could play in binding countries to its sphere of influence.

China did.[57] In July 2017, Beijing and Honiara signed a Memorandum of Understanding setting out that Huawei Marine would lay a cable connecting the Solomon Islands to Sydney, as well as build an additional domestic network within the archipelago itself.[58] The undersea cable, which would be the Solomon Island's first, would primarily be funded by China, informally under the banner of the Digital Silk Road.

This announcement came at a time when the United States and Australia, both members of the Five Eyes intelligence alliance, were in the middle of feverish debates about whether to remove Huawei's 5G solutions from their own domestic telecommunications infrastructure. Both countries unsurprisingly responded with alarm to the news about the agreement, seeing the cable not just as an effort to win hearts and minds, but also as an important dual-use project which would help the PLA achieve its Pacific ambitions (and perhaps tap sensitive cable traffic in the process). Canberra soon flexed its regulatory muscle to put a stop to the project, by denying the licence needed for the cable to make landfall on Australian soil.[59] Washington and Canberra also recognized, however, that weaponizing its permitting powers here was not enough; if the object was to claw back influence over the wavering Solomon Islands, denying it an important and much-needed infrastructural investment would not be the way to regain sympathy.

The next act in the competition with China for influence over the Solomon Islands and the wider region was thus for Australia to step in and fund the cable project instead. Its overtures were successful: the Coral Sea Cable, which became operational in 2020, now connects the Solomon Islands with Australia via Papua New Guinea, and was largely funded by the Australian government. Australia has since significantly increased the funding it has made available for this type of cable diplomacy and works closely with its partners in the Quad – a widescoping security partnership between India, Japan, Australia and the United States – to ensure China's expanding cable reach in the wider Indo-Pacific, and beyond, can be countered. While this power move may have for now put a halt to China gaining a cable foothold in the Solomon Islands, it certainly did not end Beijing's wider Pacific ambitions: in 2022 it was announced that China had signed a sweeping security pact with the Solomon Islands' ruling party, which in due course may even involve a naval base and significantly increases China's reach.

## *The Empire strikes back*

China's growing footprint in global infrastructure roll-out, especially in the Global South, has been a growing thorn in the side of the traditional leading donor countries in the West – who both fear the growing web of influence Beijing is spinning in this way, but also feel they themselves are not getting sufficient credit for their own activities. Western countries, particularly in Europe, the United States (at least until the arrival of the second Trump Administration, which put a wrecking ball to USAID, its influential development spending vehicle) and Japan, remain by some margin the largest funders of global development projects – whether directly, or through mechanisms such as the World Bank. This funding frequently does not receive much recognition, whereas the Belt and Road Initiative has rapidly become a household name.

There are a number of reasons for this discrepancy. First, there is the marketing issue. Western aid can be fragmented and less visible. To put it in slightly cruder terms: putting a discreet plaque with a European Union flag on a new school building may be the more elegant, but not necessarily the most eye-catching, promotional strategy. Western aid traditionally also suffers from a preconceived notion that it comes with too many strings attached, including 'moralistic' preaching about human rights and sustainable development goals: 'When China comes to town, we get a bridge. When the West comes by, we get a lecture', as the cliché goes. This is perhaps further amplified by a – difficult to overcome – sense that Western aid perpetuates existing colonial relationships, whereas Chinese aid instead provides a more aspirational example showcasing that non-Western countries can also make it big.

This PR challenge is also a product of the kinds of projects and activities that get funded. From the end of the Cold War onwards, countries in the West started to move away from funding large infrastructure projects, such as media-genic bridges and hospitals, in favour of 'softer' support, such as educational and capacity-building projects and anti-corruption initiatives. It is, however, a lot more appealing for a local decision-maker to get to cut a ribbon in front of a new dam, high-speed rail line or other infrastructural edifice of modernity than it is to announce a new round of vaccines – no matter the actual human impact one or the other may have.

Spurred on by China's charm offensive and growing influence in places like Africa and Central Asia, Western countries have recently recovered some of their zeal for funding infrastructural projects of their own (even if overall development funding is under strain). Clever recipient countries have not hesitated to begin to take advantage of the *potlatch*-like dynamics between West and East this has set in motion – also in the cable space.

The United States under the Biden Administration had tried to make its own fist against China's BRI by becoming a more generous funder of infrastructural projects around the world. Through partnerships with the G7 nations and others, it sought to mobilize $600 billion to counter China's development frenzy (at this stage, the Belt and Road itself had, however, already begun to rein in some of its ambitions) – and as part of this specifically pinpointed undersea cables as a strategic priority.[60] So far, the specifics behind these endeavours have remained rather vague, and it is as of yet unclear what of them remains under the Trump Administration. Beyond this, the American approach can be said to also be a more ad hoc one, where opportunities are found to dislodge China around the world, or leveraging the investment clout of its hyperscalers to shape the contours of the network – as discussed earlier in this chapter. These deals may have real strategic utility – and bring real connectivity to previously underserved places – they do not always help bolster Washington's visibility as a generous supporter of cable roll-out.

The United States and China are, of course, not the only significant players. Australia, as we have discussed, has significantly increased its cable funding. Japan is traditionally one of the major infrastructure providers in Asia (and beyond), and has leveraged its own national cable champion NEC to lay new cables in the region.[61] But the actor that is arguably making the biggest fist against China's Digital Silk Road is the European Union.

### *A gateway to the world: Europe finds its voice*

The Global Gateway programme was launched with much fanfare by European Commission President Ursula von der Leyen in December 2021, and touted as Brussels' answer to the Belt and Road Initiative: 'We want to show that a democratic, value-driven approach can deliver on the most pressing challenges.'[62] To do so, the ambition was for

Global Gateway to mobilize €300 billion worth of both private sector and member state investments ('Team Europe') by 2027 to help support the building of new transportation links, digital and green energy infrastructure and other tangible strategic projects around the world. The programme operates globally but its main emphasis is on its eastern neighbourhood, the Indo-Pacific, Latin America and especially Africa – which, many European leaders fear, has increasingly traded its historical ties with Europe for closer relationships with both China and Russia. Global Gateway is the kind of geostrategically ambitious initiative that befitted Von der Leyen's first term, which she herself dubbed the first 'Geopolitical Commission'.[63]

Writing in early 2026, the initiative has so far not been without criticism. First, there is the fact that several years since its launch, Global Gateway's name recognition remains far more limited than the Belt and Road Initiative's. Though it is true that the BRI has enjoyed a head start of nearly a decade, it is difficult to deny that the European Union does not excel at marketing itself. While China enthusiastically drums up the BRI links of even mostly commercial projects, Europe can be said to rely too much on 'actions speaking for themselves'. Other criticisms of the initiative point to the Global Gateway's scattershot approach and lack of a clear strategic focus – and importantly – an appealing and convincing story it wants to tell the world. China had used the BRI and the Digital Silk Road as ways to present a new version of itself, and its new priorities. The European Union does not yet have a fully formed vision for the kind of geopolitical power it (again) wishes to be – or the strategic levers it is willing to pull to get there. Europe, however, finds itself with an opportunity to finally remedy that: at a time when its two main rivals for global influence – China and the United States – both face growing concerns about their reliability and benevolence as actors on the world stage, being the trusted third pole, which adheres to the rule of law and is unlikely to chaotically retreat from its commitments, may become a rather attractive alternative.

It is too soon to offer much judgement about the success of the Global Gateway programme itself – inchoate as it is. What is clear is that the initiative so far amounts to more than just rhetoric, and has translated some of its big ambitions into substantial investments. By 2025, the initiative already counted more than 250 flagships projects, and upped its funding goal from €300 to €400 billion by 2027, after the previous target had been reached earlier than expected.[64] Its activities in the cable-laying domain can be seen as especially successful. It is no surprise that the Commission has focused some of its efforts here: because unlike many other slices of the technology stack – where it is currently not as well represented as one might expect of a continent of its economic and historical technological heft – Europe remains a formidable actor in the cable-laying sphere. French ASN is among the biggest cable-laying companies. In 2024, when the French government effectively nationalized the company, it did so in recognition of its 'important geostrategic importance' in furthering Europe's strategic autonomy.[65] Europe has a competitive ecosystem across other links in the cable value chain as well – from cable manufacturers to maritime engineering and maintenance firms to telecommunications companies – which, too, have been mobilized in support of Europe's cable diplomacy efforts.

By 2025, four years after the European Commission started this investment drive, it has invested in approximately fifty strategic cable projects – and has committed to allocate more than €500 million to cable resilience and roll-out by 2027.[66] Through a smorgasbord of acronymic funding instruments, the European Union supports new cables to bring more resilience, diversity and connectivity to all parts of the union itself – think here, for example, of cables connecting less well-served Greek islands, or some of the far-flung places that either still belong to the Union, or its member states maintain strong post-colonial ties with – such as Martinique and the Netherlands Antilles in the Caribbean or the Faroe Islands in Europe's northernmost reaches.[67]

And then – most relevant for the current discussion, there is also a renewed push to lay new strategic undersea cables connecting the EU to non-members, especially those in its so-called near neighbourhood in Eastern Europe and North Africa. These projects serve to position the EU as a global connectivity hub and to literally and figuratively strengthen ties with recipients at the other end of the line. Two particularly significant examples of efforts of this kind are the Medusa Cable and an as-of-yet unnamed Black Sea cable project.

The Medusa Cable will connect and importantly create landing sites in eleven countries bordering the Mediterranean Sea. The cable will link Portugal, Spain, France, Italy, Greece, Cyprus, Egypt (landing, where else, in Suez), Libya, Tunisia, Algeria and Morocco – only missing the Levant and Malta. The cable, whose western branch was ready for use in 2025, and the eastern part the year after, is in some ways quite a revolutionary project in the cable world.[68] Because though there are certainly plenty of undersea cables that traverse the Mediterranean, these mainly treat it as a thoroughfare to the Red Sea, connecting the major European hubs, such as Marseille, to the Indian Ocean and the Pacific, but offer little to many of the North African countries that border it.

The European Commission and European Investment Bank are providing subsidies and loans worth €140 million for the cable, which amounts to approximately half of its total cost.[69] The cable is not only commercially interesting – demand for additional connectivity between the Maghreb and Europe is expected to surge in the coming years as North Africa's digital economy continues to grow – but also has significant strategic utility. Europe has long been accused of paying insufficient attention to its neighbours directly to its south, but geopolitics have caught up with this dynamic. Pressures around the migration waves that arrive over the Mediterranean have seen the EU sign controversial deals with Tunisia and Libya to keep flows at bay – with increased investment being part of the *quid pro quo*. Especially Algeria's strategic importance to Europe has increased, with the country rapidly emerging as an important source of European natural gas imports since the start of the full-scale invasion of Ukraine, which forced the continent to finally wean itself off its Russian gas addiction.[70] As the global order becomes more chaotic and multipolar, and the continent is less able to rely on the United States, Europe is seeking to strengthen its ties and develop its own bilateral relationships with strategic partners, of which North Africa has several.

Another project spurred by the war in Ukraine is a proposed cable connecting mainland Europe to Georgia, by way of the Black Sea.[71] Georgia is a major recipient of Belt and Road funding – historically appropriate perhaps, given that its strategic position connecting East to West was already well-recognized during the times of the original Silk Road, which routed through it. Keeping the Caucasus country close has also emerged as a particular strategic priority for the European Union. Georgia – which became a candidate for EU membership as part of the same enlargement wave that saw the applications of Moldova and Ukraine rapidly expedited the year before – is increasingly dependent on energy and data flows routed through Russia.[72] This is a liability and chokepoint that can be weaponized by Moscow at any opportune moment. These cables and pipelines currently serve as an uncomfortable tether to a regime, which unfortunately can again count on the support of the Georgian government (even though its population remains overwhelmingly in favour of pursuing a European future).[73] The realization of the ambitious Black Sea submarine cable project, which combines the laying of a power cable alongside a data cable, could be an important lever to keep the country close.

## *Coming in from the cold: wiring the Arctic*

The small mining town of Kiruna, population 17,000, in Sweden's highest north, may at first sight appear an unlikely place for the European Union's top brass to gather. Especially in January, when average temperatures can fall as low as −20°C (−4°F). But there was a good reason why Sweden invited Commission President Ursula von der Leyen and the rest of her cabinet to travel north and stay over in the local ice hotel rather than in Stockholm, for the inaugural meeting of the Scandinavian's country rotating EU presidency back in 2023. Places like Kiruna, and Europe's Arctic belt more generally, are home to vast resource deposits: mines near the town currently account for 80 per cent of Europe's iron ore production and are an important source of other minerals as well. The opportunity offered by the Commission's high-profile visit was seized to announce the recent discovery of an additional one million tonnes of rare earth oxides and iron ore in Kiruna's Per Geijer deposit – currently Europe's largest known such supply.[74] This, according to Swedish energy minister Ebba Busch, could be a find as significant as Norway's discovery of off-shore oil in the 1960s – a find which made its neighbour one of the richest petrostates in the world.[75]

Indeed, Kiruna's minerals could be critical for achieving the Commission's green, digital and defence ambitions, which rely on sovereign, secure access to rare earths and other critical minerals such as lithium. Mining in the Arctic could also leave the continent a lot less dependent on especially Chinese dominance over the key resources that are likely to underpin the new energy order (for some critical minerals, China controls up to 95 per cent of global supplies – a dominance it is increasingly willing to weaponize, as we shall see in chapter 8). 'The EU's self-sufficiency and independence from Russia and China will begin in the mine', in Busch's words.

Between Finland, Sweden and Denmark, the European Union has three member states which are also Arctic nations (completing the list are the United States, Canada, Iceland, Norway and Russia). The EU is keen to translate this significant territorial footprint into economic and military gain. Indeed, amid growing geopolitical tensions in the Arctic, the US President's increasingly explicit territorial designs on Greenland, Chinese economic expansionism, and increased Russian hybrid activity and military muscle-flexing, European countries have been bolstering their own presence in the Arctic – both through NATO, and through deeper coordination at a European level.

As such, the High North is emerging as a prime theatre through which Brussels wants to give substance to its geopolitical and geoeconomic objectives – not just vis-à-vis usual suspects Russia and China, which both have their own ambitions in the Arctic, but also in countering an increasingly belligerent United States. In a world where hard power has once again become the most important currency, European leaders have started to recognize that they need to increase their physical presence and sovereign claims in the High North. One way it could do that is by laying the first trans-Arctic, intercontinental, undersea cable.

## *An Arctic cable*

The possibility of laying a subsea cable across the Arctic has been speculated about in the industry for decades, but apart from the construction of some short cables connecting, for example, Svalbard to the Norwegian mainland (several of these Arctic cables have fallen victim to mysterious outages in recent years – more on those later),[76] financial and practical hurdles have prevented such a project from becoming a reality. Climate change and the thawing of the Arctic ice – which now retreats at an average of 13 per cent each decade, as temperatures here rise nearly three times faster than they do elsewhere – could make such a project more feasible.

There is much to be said for laying a cable through the Arctic. While no one would dare call the Arctic a geopolitical backwater, especially not under the second Trump Administration, it is still less wrought than the currently dominant Europe-to-Asia cable routes, many of which traverse multiple active war zones. There are traditionally three dominant pathways that connect the Eurasian landmass from east to west: through the Red Sea, directly through Russia via primarily terrestrial cables, or cables girding the globe the other way around, via the United States. The previous chapter already explored the chokepoints, bottlenecks and tinderbox that characterize the Red Sea lines, which account for over 80 per cent of traffic between Europe and Asia. Relying on terrestrial cables through Russia is unsurprisingly no longer considered a secure option either, especially not since Russia's full-scale invasion of Ukraine. Terrestrial routes through the Middle East are in the works but bring their own volatility. The third route going west – for example through the United States – is very long and suffers from high latency (a problem still for real-time financial traffic, for example).

Within this constellation, an Arctic cable could present the holy grail. It would not just bring more redundancy into the global network, but also more resilience and diversity by introducing a new route altogether. Such a cable would also be much shorter than those that follow paths laid nearer to the equator. Among the currently most mature transarctic cable project proposals is the Polar Connect, which looks to connect Finland, moving north-west over Canada, to Japan. While the distorting effect of traditional world maps would not suggest it, such a cable would, at 10,000 kilometres, be substantially much shorter than, for example, a cable connecting Scandinavia to Singapore via the Red Sea routes – which generally are around 16,000 kilometres long, depending on their exact routes. An Arctic cable would allow a stock market transaction from a bank in Tokyo[77] to one in London to arrive an estimated 40 per cent faster than it does through the current pathways.

This is not just a boon for flash traders. Arctic cables would serve a dual-use purpose too, as NATO members are intensifying both their research and military activities in the High North.[78] The Arctic's short routes are not only commercially interesting, they also offer the shortest distance a missile from, let us say, Russia, would have to travel to Europe or the United States – the Arctic is therefore home to many missile defence and monitoring assets. It has also traditionally been important for many space activities, particularly for communications with satellites in polar orbit, all of which would benefit from additional, high-speed connectivity delivered by new cables.

The harsh conditions of the Arctic could also offer security. Cables would be laid under the thick pack-ice of the Arctic, which would be 'as tight as cement', especially in winter.[79] Thick enough that not even the heaviest anchors could pierce through it, the pitch goes. This natural protective layer could make the cable hypothetically more interference proof too. If it is challenging to lay the cable under the ice, it is equally difficult for anyone with nefarious intentions to get near it.[80]

But for all these advantages, an Arctic cable would not come cheap. Where a cable route serving Northern Europe to Japan through the traditional pathways cost about €200 million to lay, the cost of the transpolar Finland–Japan cable (the Polar Connect) has been estimated at €1.2 billion.[81] The additional expense would be hard to justify from a purely commercial point of view, and would require significant government subsidies to be realized.

The endeavour is expensive for a reason. First, this is an entirely new route that needs to be planned out in a part of the world that has only very recently become semi-navigable. The cable-laying process itself can only take place in a brief window during the summer months, when the ice is at its thinnest and there is sufficient daylight. The cable-laying ship will also need to be supported by special custom-made icebreakers, to keep its path free – ice-breakers which at present have not yet been built, and would need to be specially made (Sweden is currently doing so). Given that ice floes move, some industry experts suggest faults in certain segments of the cable are actually likely to become a lot more frequent – making the 'tight as cement' a double-edged sword, as far as repair is concerned.[82] Indeed, there is no small degree of scepticism among some segments of the cable industry about the viability and commercial justification for the endeavour.

All of this notwithstanding, it presently seems that the European Commission is likely to give the plan the green light.[83] It has already funded several feasibility studies exploring the viability of the endeavour. If it does fund the cable, it is an example of how considerations around security, sovereignty and geopolitical manoeuvrability have now started to be weighted quite differently in the balance against purely financial considerations, with the scales now increasingly starting to tip towards the former. Projects like the Polar Connect are, however, about more than resilience alone. According to several people I have spoken to about Europe's Arctic ambitions, the success of the transpolar cable mission has become a point of personal pride for the decision-makers in the European Commission. The laying of an Arctic cable is an opportunity to show that Europe, a continent too frequently written off as being stuck in the past, can still accomplish great feats of ingenuity and engineering, and breach new frontiers.

## *Mounting competition*

Europe is certainly not alone in its ambitions in the Arctic. Climate change, the hunt for shorter trade routes, the North Pole's strategic utility and its incredible resource riches have made several countries – and not just those who hold territory above the Arctic Circle – increasingly interested in staking their claim. In the emerging Great Game over the Arctic, cables like Polar Connect are also not the only challengers.

### Russia

Russia, which has most territory in the Arctic, is one of the most active actors in the region, and keen to show it.[84] When in 2007 Russian submarine *Mir-1* planted a titanium flag on the seabed at the geographic North Pole, Russian commentators described the feat as akin to the moon landing. But unlike Neil Armstrong, who heralded his first lunar step as a triumph for 'all mankind', *Mir-1* expedition leader Artur Chilingarov said the main objective behind his mission had been to prove that the 'Arctic was Russian'.[85] By solidifying its sovereignty and claims in the High North, Russia is not just keen to secure access to the pole's mineral wealth and oil and gas reserves, it also sees an opportunity to recentre itself as a key conduit of global trade.

In 2017 Russia achieved another Arctic milestone by completing the first non-ice-breaker-supported journey through the Northeast passage, a route coveted for centuries. The Northern Sea Route, passing over Russia, can effectively halve the time it takes a ship to reach the port of Hamburg or Rotterdam from Shanghai. The journey through the Suez Canal – even absent any Houthi interference – currently takes 35 days;

going north has proven to shave that down to around 18 days. Though the route is far from a fully reliable one yet, climate change-induced thawing could see the first ice-free summers in the Arctic arrive as soon as 2040. Already this northern passage – which Russia envisions as a future nerve centre for global trade – is seeing increased use, though volumes by tonnage remain low and, post-2022, dominated by energy exports to China, as Moscow finds itself more economically isolated.

Russia's commercial ambitions in the Arctic significantly interact with its expanded military objectives here. Presence in the sparsely populated Poles equals sovereignty – and Russia has been making rapid strides to make its military muscle be felt here, by expanding its infrastructural footprint, rebuilding and expanding old Cold War bases and bolstering its naval presence.

To support these efforts, Russia, too, has been laying its own, more enigmatic, Arctic cable, which, when finished, will bridge the vast country's northern coast from east to west. The Polar Express, which is being laid by Russian state vehicle Morsvyazsputnik and about which details remain rather sparse, is believed to be planned to start in the hamlet of Teriberka, near the town of Severomorsk, home to Russia's important northern fleet, and a less than two-hours' drive from the Finnish border. By the time of its projected completion in 2028, the cable will make a final landing in Vladivostok, near the base of its similarly important Pacific fleet. Though there were earlier plans for this cable to be extended to Norway, Finland and China, a change in the geopolitical tide interfered. Chinese cable champion HMN Tech is believed to be playing an important role in laying some segments of the Polar Express – which, by being laid further south in the Arctic, is technically less challenging than projects like Polar Connect, which will move closer to the Arctic's magnetic pole. Given the currently limited commercial value of this project – which is presumably why the extension into China has not been completed – suggestions that the cable is very much a dual-use endeavour do not appear wide of the mark.

## China

Despite being thousands of kilometres from the North Pole – its northernmost provincial capital, Harbin, lies at the same latitude as

Venice – China has put serious effort into positioning itself as a 'near-Arctic power'.[86] It has secured observer status in the Arctic Council, the intergovernmental forum of Arctic countries, has been working closely together with Russia to cultivate shipping routes there – of which it would be one of the chief beneficiaries – and is also eyeing the region's vast untapped energy and resource riches. In the same way that Beijing has grand plans for a Digital Silk Road, China also has a strategy to create a Polar Silk Road.[87] As the country lacks any credible territorial claims on either pole, it has, for example, focused on leveraging scientific diplomacy as a tool for getting a foot in the door, including through establishing research partnerships and bases in Finland, Sweden, Iceland and elsewhere. Concerns that China's Arctic research initiatives and space activities are once again exponents of its civil-military doctrine and serve a clear dual-use purpose in the Arctic too have begun to spark alarm.[88]

The Arctic is also one of the places where Sino–Russian partnership is intensifying, and it is in the Russian Arctic where most of China's investment in the polar region is concentrated.[89] China's push to expand its access to the Arctic's resources and roll-out of new infrastructure – such as through HMN Tech's role in helping Moscow realize its Arctic cable ambitions – has not been uniformly welcomed in Russia, and is seen by some policy elites as dangerous encroachment. In an increasingly uneven partnership, where Russia has had to accept the status of junior partner, the Arctic is one of the few spaces in which it still has the upper hand. Though there are few signs to suggest the Russia–China relationship may be fraying, the Arctic may yet prove to be the place where the cracks in Xi and Putin's 'limitless partnership' first start to show.[90]

## The United States

The United States – which owes its Arctic state credentials to Alaska – too, sees the growing strategic utility of the Arctic in an era of energy transition and increased resource competition. Trump's increasingly aggressive moves to dislodge Greenland from Denmark and ambitions to secure access to its mineral wealth attest to that. The United States has frequently framed its Arctic ambitions as led by national security concerns and in direct opposition to China and Russia's growing footprint on the pole. Its planned trans-Arctic cable, Far North Digital, a project the country is pursuing in collaboration with Finland and Japan, and which would run through the Northwest Passage and around Greenland, should be seen through this lens.

This growing strategic competition over the Arctic is getting increasingly hot. Not for the first time: already during the Cold War, it was a key battleground in US–Soviet competition.[91] As the shortest missile flight path between the two nuclear superpowers, both maintained extensive reconnaissance and other military assets there. The GIUK gap — the area between Greenland, Iceland, and the UK — was a vital NATO naval chokepoint, which could be disrupted to sever direct lines of communications and resupply between North America and Europe (and conversely made it difficult for Russian vessels and submarines to reach the United States unnoticed). This necessitated a permanent military presence and extensive infrastructure to monitor Soviet activity.[92] When the Cold War ended and the era of peace dividend thinking dawned, this tension would soon start to defuse. The United States closed its naval air base in Keflavik on Iceland in 2006, Denmark dismantled its entire submarine fleet, and Russia's once-feared Arctic fleet was left to rust in the desolate ports near Murmansk. The Arctic became 'the Great Exception' – a place where cooperation – on scientific projects, on climate change monitoring – was possible, even when geopolitical tension was mounting elsewhere.

This consensus collapsed after Russia's full-scale invasion of Ukraine – and with it any illusions of Arctic exceptionalism. Russia's membership of the Arctic Council, the cooperation forum it had helped found in 1996, was frozen. Sweden and Finland, which had previously acted as relatively neutral stabilizers in the region, joined NATO. Virtually all actors in the region are rapidly remilitarizing and as part of that are fortifying their presences above the pole. The Arctic is emerging as one of the main geopolitical battlegrounds of the coming decades: if it were to come to blows between major powers, it may well happen here.[93]

The Arctic is presently already a hotbed of greyzone activity. Russia has been accused of weaponizing migration flows along Norway's border. Its submarines, but also civilian fishing vessels, map infrastructure and gather intelligence, while its drones fly over Nordic airports and energy hubs. Provocative Russian troop movements and exercises on the Kola Peninsula, the nucleus of its Arctic military presence, near the Norwegian and Finnish borders, are intensifying. These activities also involve cables: on several occasions, communications cables near Svalbard and those serving some of Norway's northernmost military bases, have sustained mysterious damage. To quote the words of Admiral Rob Bauer, then chair of NATO's military committee, in a 2022 speech in Reykjavik: 'in the Arctic, NATO has no other choice than to prepare for the unexpected'.[94]

# 5

# *Anatomy of a Fault*

## *The* Newnew Polar Bear

It was the gas companies that first raised the alarm on 8 October 2023. Pressure in the BalticConnector — a key gas pipeline linking Finland and Estonia through the Finnish Gulf — had begun to drop precipitously. Not long after, Swedish authorities reported disruptions in two undersea communications cables in the near vicinity of the connector. Was this just another accident or was there something more nefarious going on? It had barely been a year since the dramatic sabotage of the Nord Stream pipelines, and authorities were still on high alert. No definitive blame had ever been apportioned as to who was behind the destruction of the highly controversial gas pipelines, with theories ranging from the Russians to capers involving Ukrainian frogmen on sailboats, to a joint venture between the American and Norwegian special forces. Whoever may have been behind the Nord Stream pipelines' demise, the incident had made it abundantly clear how vulnerable the Baltic seabed was to this kind of wilful interference.[1]

And it soon seemed that deliberate sabotage was back on the menu once again. A few hours after the news broke, the Finnish coast guard released a statement suggesting that the damage to the BalticConnector and the two undersea cables (the EE-S1 connecting Sweden and Estonia, and the FEC-1 linking Estonia to Finland) – had been caused by an hitherto unidentified 'external force', and may well have been the product of an intentional act[2] – echoing Nord Stream. It did not take long for the incident to invite commentary on the highest levels. Estonia's President Alar Karis took to social media: 'We know the cause is not nature, but probably human activity. Who, why and how? Negligence or intent? These questions have yet to be answered.'[3] Then-NATO Chief Jens Stoltenberg, mobbed by the gathered media, called for a 'united and determined response' from the alliance to help better protect critical infrastructure out at sea.[4]

For the Baltic and Nordic countries, threats to maritime infrastructures, from cables to wind farms, were no light matter. Their shared sea was becoming increasingly important, not just for fishing and trade, but also as a hub for mutual interconnectivity, and for providing its energy needs and independence amid mounting Russian aggression. The BalticConnector, completed in 2019, had been conceived of as a project to bring more diversification, independence and resilience to the Baltic region's energy grids.[5] A growing number of power cables and interconnectors, which ferry electricity between countries, as well as offshore wind farms out in the Baltic, help serve a similar purpose – especially post-2022. But now, these purported sabotage incidents appeared to show that these infrastructures, out there in under-governed and under-secured international waters, were becoming vulnerabilities in their own right. There was some irony then, perhaps, that in a bid to reduce their exposure to the Kremlin's energy blackmail, these countries had created new vulnerabilities which could be exploited by that very same actor.

Given these optics, and the wider geopolitical context, many of the countries affected almost immediately pointed to Russia as the likely culprit behind this most recent incident. Surely these events could only be understood as Moscow's retribution for Finland joining NATO earlier that year, and as an attempt to undermine the country's ability to satisfy its energy needs, just as the bitterly cold Nordic winters were around the corner? President Putin, in turn, was quick to write off these early accusations as 'rubbish' and attempts to distract from the act of 'Western terrorism' that had been behind the destruction of the Nord Stream pipelines.[6]

As this speculation and back-and-forth were playing out in the global media and on social media, the details behind the damage to the cables and pipeline itself for some time remained nebulous. Norwegian authorities initially believed explosives had been used to destroy the BalticConnector, with the impact on the two nearby communications cables likely collateral damage. Once Finnish investigators had made their way over to the site of the incident to collect evidence, the emerging facts started to point to a rather different cause instead. Not explosives, but an old-fashioned anchor drag had damaged the pipeline and cable segments.[7]

Large commercial vessels carry anchors weighing up to several tons – roughly equivalent to the weight of a delivery truck. Heavy enough to puncture through the soft Baltic seabed and snag cables, even those buried for their protection. Evidently also heavy enough to inflict serious damage to the concrete protection that enclosed the BalticConnector. It is important to note that it is not per se unusual or suspicious for commercial vessels to occasionally sweep their anchors over seabed infrastructure such as cables – especially in crowded, shallow seas like the Baltic. Such drags can go on for some time, and over extended distances: rather like a plough tending the seabed. In fact, accidental anchor drags are among the more frequent sources of cable damage – especially so under adverse weather conditions, during which captains can find themselves struggling to keep their ships under control.

But the fact that such anchor drags are part of the pantheon of routine accidents that can befall undersea cables means that they would hypothetically also make for a clever *modus operandi* for those with more shadowy intentions. It could allow one to credibly dress up such an act as an accident, for example. Anyone with access to a sufficiently large ship and a willing crew would technically be able to execute such an operation, and hide behind the cloak of plausible deniability.

After the investigators had found the tell-tale signs of an anchor drag on the Baltic seabed – which, as it later turned out had reportedly lasted for a rather staggering 100 plus nautical miles (or 185 kilometres), *not* the norm – they next turned to identifying the vessel which had left these marks. The investigators soon zeroed in on a somewhat surprising offender: the *Newnew Polar Bear*, a Hong Kong-flagged but Chinese-owned commercial freighter, which, according to its transponder data, had been present at the scene at the time the cables and pipeline had been damaged. The ship had not long after been photographed, now safely docked in the Russian Arctic port of Arkhangelsk, conspicuously missing one of its two anchors. That same missing anchor was recovered from the seabed very near the site of impact two weeks later, speckled with deep red chips of paint that were a seeming match with the colour of the hull of the 169 metre-long freighter.[8]

Though the incident had taken place in Finland's exclusive economic zone, by the time the offending ship had been identified, the *Newnew Polar Bear* had already made its way north, first to St. Petersburg, then reportedly even further up to take the Northern Sea Route over the Arctic, from Murmansk to the Bering Strait, with plans to eventually dock in the Chinese port of Tianjin. This, some reporting suggested, however, not before changing its ownership structure from a Chinese-owned company to a Russia-registered one, adding even more complexity to the murky circumstances surrounding the vessel.[9]

The ship's rushed escape and flagging situation – it is the country whose flag a ship sails under which is responsible for investigating any potential wrongdoing or negligence it may have engaged in – made it especially difficult to investigate the circumstances and intent behind the incidents, which many experts assumed was yet another dangerous escalation in Russia's (and potentially now also China's – this was a Chinese-linked ship after all) greyzone war against Europe. It also meant the respective owners of the cables and the BalticConnector would be unlikely to get their day in court and would be left to foot the bill for the repairs – unfortunately not uncommon in the maritime sphere.

In the end, the harm caused by the damage to the undersea communications cables had been quite limited. There is generally sufficient redundancy in the Baltic Sea's cable network, so traffic could be rerouted relatively smoothly. Internet users in the region had not felt a blip. Both cables were repaired speedily and up and running again within days. But the same could not be said for the BalticConnector, the damage to which was a lot more significant and longer-lasting. Not only are pipelines and power cables a lot harder to repair than data cables – it would take nearly six months for the BalticConnector to be fully operational again, racking up a bill into the hundreds of millions in the interim – they also tend to enjoy far less redundancy, making the impact of incidents such as this all the much higher.[10]

Despite these complex jurisdictional circumstances, both the Finnish and Estonian authorities would undertake their own investigations[11] – still ongoing at the time of writing – in hopes of providing a more definitive answer to whether the damage to the cables and pipeline had in fact been caused by the *Newnew Polar Bear* and, if it had, whether its crew had done so intentionally. Beijing agreed to cooperate with these investigations and also conducted its own – but in the end allowed little involvement from the countries impacted by the incident. In May of 2024, the Chinese authorities released a report concluding that the *Newnew Polar Bear* had indeed been the one to sever the cables and to damage the gas pipeline – but had not done so deliberately. Not nefarious intentions, but a storm, it found, had caused the freighter to let its anchor run rampage through the Baltic seabed.[12] This conclusion has so far not been corroborated by the European investigators.

It seemed China would leave the matter at that. The case would, however, have a further interesting coda. In May 2025, Hong Kong authorities, presumably at Beijing's instigation, unexpectedly arrested the *Newnew Polar Bear*'s captain, citing reckless criminal negligence as the charge.[13] What to make of this decision – an admission of guilt, a gesture of goodwill at a time when China appeared keen to mend its ties with Europe (and capitalize on mounting transatlantic tensions); an attempt to create a sense of distance from Russia's escalating campaign of hybrid mayhem, or simply due process – remains a question open to interpretation.

## *The* Yi Peng 3

A year and a month would pass until a second, remarkably similar incident would again shake up the Baltic Sea. On 17 and 18 November 2024, two further undersea cables were damaged in quick succession: first, there was the BCS East–West Interlink Cable, which connects Lithuania to Sweden's island of Gotland (since Sweden's accession to NATO, an increasingly important strategic stronghold in the alliance's plans to protect its eastern flank), followed the next morning by the C-Lion 1 cable, which connects Finland to Germany.

Analysis of the maritime traffic data in the area quickly zeroed in on the *Yi Peng 3*, a Chinese-flagged, Chinese-crewed freighter ship, which had left the Russian port of Ust-Luga (an important oil transporting port several hours south of St Petersburg, and notorious hub for Russia's sanction evasion activities), on its way to bring fertilizer to Port Said in Egypt.[14] Just like the *Newnew Polar Bear*, it was the ship's anchor that had snagged the cables, and though the *Yi Peng 3* had not lost its as part of its 330 kilometre-long dragging ordeal, the anchor had sustained significant and very visible damage, as had the ship's own hull, as later picture evidence would reveal. While it is not especially uncommon for a ship to sail onwards with its anchor still down, it is also not something that is likely to go unnoticed by a ship's captain or their crew – and would usually see them take quick action.

The news about this new round of cable breaks reached the global media soon after. Given the stark similarities with the October 2023 incident, many politicians in the region were quick to draw their conclusions. German defence minister Boris Pistorius commented in front of gathered cameras that 'no one believes' the cables 'were accidentally cut', before the repair ships sent out to investigate the incident had even arrived at the site of the cuts.[15] Gabrielius Landsbergis, then still foreign minister of Lithuania, took to X to similarly express his scepticism about the potential accidental nature of the incidents: 'If I had a nickel for every time a Chinese ship was dragging its anchor on the bottom of the Baltic Sea in the vicinity of important cables I would have two nickels, which isn't much, but it's weird that it happened twice.'[16] Finland and Germany issued a joint statement, citing that 'European security is not only under threat from Russia's war of aggression against Ukraine, but also from hybrid warfare by malicious actors.' Though no leader in the moment directly accused either Russia or China, their implied meaning was clear. It certainly was to Russia, which, unsurprisingly, once again dismissed any suggestions of its involvement.[17] Authorities in Beijing, too, denied all knowledge of events.[18]

Where the *Yi Peng 3* incident instead differed quite significantly from events in October 2023 was the response from the countries on the receiving end. Where the *Newnew Polar Bear* had already sailed off into the night before its crew could be brought in for questioning, the *Yi Peng 3* was still making its way through the Baltic Sea when investigators zeroed in on it. This allowed the Danish Navy to stop the ship and force it to drop anchor in the Kattegat, the narrow strip of sea which separates Denmark from Sweden, in a section of Denmark's EEZ. Repeated attempts by the authorities to encourage the ship to allow itself to be escorted into Swedish territorial waters were, however, not heeded.

The rumour mill soon began to churn. First, the story started to spread that, even though the *Yi Peng 3*'s crew was Chinese, its captain was actually a Russian national – someone who may well have been persuaded to do Moscow's bidding, therefore. That turned out to be untrue. Then the story changed to the Chinese crew of the ship having been paid – or perhaps pressured – by Russian intelligence to conduct this low-tech sabotage operation and keep shtum after the fact. But when Swedish authorities wanted to board the ship and interrogate the captain and his crew to explore these theories, Chinese authorities in Beijing initially refused access.[19]

Here the fact that the damage had been sustained in international waters became especially important: UNCLOS, the main international legal framework that governs these kinds of incidents, stipulates that the country under whose flag the ship involved is flying is in charge of the investigation when it happens outside anyone's direct jurisdiction – ergo, in international waters.[20] In this case, therefore, that meant it was China that was in charge, the very country – or at least its nationals – suspected of having participated in this potential greyzone operation.

There followed more than a month of diplomatic stalemate, during which Danish and German naval vessels carefully monitored the ship from a distance as it laid anchored beyond their legal reach. Some Swedish observers (but not the criminal prosecutor in charge) were eventually allowed to board the ship – a full month after the incident took place – but had to do so under close supervision of Chinese authorities now present on the vessel. This was to be an investigation in name only: the observers were refused the opportunity to record interviews with the ship's crew, and by this time a lot of data collected by the ship – critical information usually used to piece together a vessel's movements and actions in the lead-up to an incident – had already been meticulously wiped.

Eventually, the Danes were forced to let the vessel leave to 'ensure the physical and mental wellbeing of the crew' (to use the Chinese authorities' words) – the matter still unresolved and evidence in either direction significantly lacking.[21] The investigation into the potential liability of the *Yi Peng 3* remains ongoing at the time of writing.

## *The* Eagle S

It did not end there. Not a month later, with the dust barely settled on the *Yi Peng 3* incident, a *third* case of cable damage in the Baltic

Sea took place. It was Christmas Eve of 2024 when the Finnish coast guard received the call: it was Finnish energy company Finngrid warning authorities about an acute outage of the Estlink-1 power cable – one of two key power cables connecting the Nordic country to the Baltics. The Estonian and Finnish coast guard deployed immediately, in hopes of still catching the perpetrator *in flagrante*. The Estonian coast guard never made it – the stormy weather conditions too unpredictable for them to brave the Finnish Gulf. But the Finnish coast guard did – and just in time: the offending ship – which had already damaged two communications cables in addition to the Estlink-1, had been about to sever the Estlink-2 as well, the only other power interconnector connecting the Baltic countries to the Nordics. Had both these power cables been taken out of action, it would have left a risky gap in the region's power supply.[22]

The suspicious vessel in question was the *Eagle S*, a 230-metre long, 74,000 ton oil tanker, which was flying under the flag of the Cook Islands, but owned by an Emirati company, apparently managed by an Indian company; its captain a Georgian national, as was part of its crew, most of the others were from India.[23] Such a panoply of nationalities is far from atypical in the maritime sphere, but it also showed a degree of obfuscation and complexity that pointed to one specific category of ship in particular: Russia's shadow fleet. Russia's shadow fleet comprises an estimated 500–1,500 vessels, which Moscow employs to evade the oil sanctions that have been imposed on it by Ukraine's supporters in the wake of Russia's brutal invasion.[24] These ships are characterized by their advanced age – the average lifespan of regular commercial vessels such as oil tankers is around fifteen years; many shadow fleet vessels are pushing twenty or beyond (the *Eagle S* entered service in 2006 – by 2024 firmly in shadow fleet territory therefore). These ships usually lack proper insurance and other necessary paperwork, have extremely poor maintenance records – and are as such ticking time bombs for environmental disasters – and are frequently noted for their convoluted ownership structures, making it difficult to trace them back to Russia.

The *Eagle S*, which, like the *Yi Peng 3*, had just left the Russian port of Ust-Luga (a notorious hotbed for shadow fleet activity), had been Egypt-bound, its hull full of Siberian crude. There was already a growing clamour of voices suggesting that Russia was no longer just using these shadow fleet ships to sell its oil on the cheap to less scrupulous recipients –

these ships were also increasingly serving as arm's-length hybrid weapons of the Kremlin. The *Eagle S*, for example, had in the past already been singled out by leading shipping information provider Lloyd's Register as potentially carrying Russian spy and monitoring equipment on board – used to map the shipping lanes it frequented.[25] This, then, was perhaps a more immediately likely candidate for a ship that could orchestrate a greyzone attack at the Kremlin's behest than its Chinese predecessors. The possible use of such a shadow fleet ship simultaneously also seemed to signal that the Kremlin was becoming more comfortable with revealing its involvement in these alleged attacks (Moscow formally, of course, once again denied everything).

The *Eagle S* had not made it particularly far either before the incident took place. It had barely made it out of the Finnish Gulf – just a couple of hours from its point of departure, when it had slowed down, dropped its anchor and dragged it through the slick for over ninety nautical miles (or 166 kilometres), destroying the trio of cables in its wake.[26] The sheer force with which it had dragged along its anchor had eventually led it to lose it on the seabed altogether, where it was not much later recovered by Finnish investigators. Pictures taken of the hull of the ageing tanker revealed significant damage sustained by the weight and pressure of the anchor's heavy chain as it has been forced along.[27]

This time, however, the culpable vessel would not be able to get away with it. When the Finnish coast guard had intercepted the *Eagle S* and had forced it to a stop, it had also – successfully this time – urged the ship to follow along from the international waters where the cable snags had taken place, into Finland's territorial waters. This was a major coup. Once under Finnish jurisdiction, Finnish special forces were able to board the ship – dramatic footage of which was soon broadcast all over the world: black and green night vision scenes of uniformed men jumping on *Eagle S*'s deck from a helicopter, apprehending the crew.[28] This far more forceful approach by the Finns marked a clear departure, as well as evolution, in the approach the European countries had taken when it came to these incidents. The *Newnew Polar Bear* had been allowed to leave without much consequence. The *Yi Peng 3* had been temporarily apprehended, but authorities in the countries concerned had been wary about undermining international maritime law by taking more forceful action. The Finns had seized the ship and amped up the dial of escalation in a bid to get accountability for this incident, and deter similar dangerous adventurism in future.

As all the countries who had seen their undersea infrastructure damaged during these successive incidents were (by now) NATO members, the military alliance had a role to play as well. Its responses, too, began to take on an increasingly more forceful tone. NATO members immediately collectively condemned the *Eagle S* incident – though never calling out Russia by name – and in early January launched operation Baltic Sentry, a special mission which would see intensified naval patrols and surveillance of the Baltic Sea. In the words of newly minted NATO Chief Mark Rutte, who had just taken the helm of the alliance: 'Ship captains must understand that potential threats to our infrastructure will have consequences, including possible boarding, impounding, and arrest.'[29]

Like with the previous two incidents, the undersea communications cables involved proved a lot quicker to repair and more resilient against this kind of damage. Internet traffic had been rapidly rerouted through other undersea and terrestrial cables, ensuring the impact on connectivity in the region had been limited. The quick response by cable repair ships already stationed nearby had meant the cables were working again by the first week of January. Not so for the Estlink-1, which was not repaired until June 2025.[30]

In the meantime, the *Eagle S* remained impounded in Finnish waters – its captain and part of its crew eventually charged by the Finnish authorities. Finland's extraordinary move to escort the ship into its territorial waters – the first time Finnish forces had seized a foreign ship in this manner since the Second World War – may have pushed the boundaries on Europe's response, but serious legal snags remained. The Finnish courts in October 2025 ruled that, even though the ship was presently in Finland, the incident had still occurred outside of it. The prosecutors' attempts to interpret UNCLOS and the other relevant rulebooks in such a way that they could be used to hold the crew and its owners to account, were rejected and Finland ordered to pay for the legal costs incurred. At time of writing, the case is being appealed.

## *Aftermath*

The fallout from these incidents was immediate and immense. While the protection and vulnerability of the undersea cable network, and Russia's apparent interest in monitoring and mapping it, had long been a simmering topic in national security communities – with the post-Cold War revival of these concerns dating back to at least 2015 – these incidents had suddenly propelled the topic into a highly charged global news story. Some of the more sensationalist media outlets speculated breathlessly about how these incidents were just a prelude to Russia throttling the global internet, which would soon leave us all in the dark. National security omni-pundits rapidly seized the hype cycle to share their views about the fragility of a system few had more than a cursory understanding of. Governments and militaries had to be seen to be acting decisively to counter these now seemingly increasingly frequent incidents.

After the third highly publicized incident, NATO, as said, launched its new mission, Baltic Sentry, which would see navy frigates and drones deployed to better monitor the Baltic Sea and prevent further attempts to deliberately – or accidentally – damage critical undersea infrastructure in the region. There were also questions about what other legal options were on the table which could help deter malicious actors from repeating this playbook. Not wanting to appear weak, governments found themselves facing the difficult dilemma of wanting to act more forcefully to stop such purported Russian (or Chinese) aggression, but in the process undermining some of the key pillars of maritime security and openness of navigation, and – worse – risking escalation with its nuclear-armed, increasingly belligerent neighbour.

The once so invisible cable industry, not used to finding itself at the centre of a global geopolitical firestorm, valiantly tried to cut through the noise to correct some of the more alarmist assessments in the media.[31] But their calls for restraint, and to wait for the outcome of at least the preliminary investigations before turning to overly feverish conclusions mostly went ignored. Where some governments were at risk of over-reacting, elements of the industry were arguably at risk of doing the exact opposite. By continuously stressing cable outages were par for the course, and that even the suggestion that deliberate sabotage may have been involved amounted to uninformed fearmongering, they were also prematurely trying to shut down any kind of discussion about the possible intent behind these incidents – and the role governments and the private sector play in addressing them.

As all of this was playing out on the global stage, it became increasingly clear that there was all but universal agreement that these incidents had in fact been cases of sabotage. The sceptics argued the incidents in the Baltic Sea looked exactly like conventional accidents – which, as we have explored, are not especially rare. What real proof was there that these were not just further examples of the kind of routine damage the industry deals with on an almost daily basis? All that was really different was that these faults happened to have occurred in a geopolitical powder keg, the argument went: no camera crews had showed up when similar incidents had happened elsewhere in the world during the same time period. Those never even made the news. Others, however, argued that there was no denying an obvious pattern.

It is exactly this kind of ambiguity and the difficulty of delivering definitive proof – and the disagreement that can emerge from it – that makes these kinds of alleged greyzone incidents so effective. In all three of the cases, the culprit had been quickly identified. Despite the opacity that tends to characterize the maritime environment, hiding an oil tanker or large freighter in a place like the Baltic Sea is difficult, their routes traceable even by amateur ship-tracking enthusiasts. The challenge, then, had been proving intent. Here, anchor drag incidents such as the ones explored in this chapter differ quite fundamentally from other greyzone activities, such as cyber attacks or the sabotage of the Nord Stream pipelines. In those cases, it is often quite clear that a crime has been committed – explosives placed on gas pipelines leave little room for debate. It is the attribution to a specific actor that is usually the difficult part. The cable cutters, instead, may have relied on strategies of plausible deniability. In the absence of a clear smoking gun – a money trail, a captain's confession – proving in court that whoever was behind the damage intended to cause it was always going to be especially challenging. The investigations into these incidents may indeed never prove conclusive. This continued ambiguity leaves space for doubt and division, and undermines governments' ability to take concerted action.

Indeed, it is not just elements of the cable industry (which, a cynic may argue, would have good reasons for wanting to minimize the fallout and the increased government scrutiny it has since evidently invited) that professed scepticism about the deliberateness of these incidents. In the months following the Baltic cable trilogy, it became clear that there was also a growing split between governments *within* NATO about what this had all meant. In many ways, these diverging views reflected their respective stances when it came to countering Russian greyzone activity more generally. Many countries in the region – especially those most exposed to Russian aggression and with long histories of finding themselves at the receiving end of Russian 'active measures', had little doubt about who the mastermind was here, and were pushing for the alliance to step up its responses. Others, instead, had counselled restraint and had perhaps hoped for the whole episode to soon be forgotten. When Russia was concerned, it was best to steer clear of doing anything that may lead to escalation.

The fallout from a January 2025 *Washington Post* article perhaps showcases this tension best.[32] The article, which reported that anonymous sources within Western intelligence services now claimed that there was 'an emerging consensus' that the Baltic cable incidents had been accidental, was soon written off by many commentators as an attempt by a cautious White House to change the narrative. What the *Post* claimed was 'an emerging consensus' was really just the United States, perhaps joined by some of the other European NATO countries further south and west (to whom the Russian threat felt less visceral), pushing their agenda, the argument went. Several regional experts and government authorities involved with the investigation went on record to dispute that any such consensus had been found.[33] Beyond revealing some of the emerging fractures beneath the 'one NATO' veneer, the *Washington Post* episode arguably pointed to something else significant: it suggested that the Northern and Central European countries were now increasingly setting the tone on shaping NATO's response. Where in the past it may usually have been Washington that would have taken the lead in determining the response to incidents like this, this was now an apparent case of the Europeans taking matters largely into their own hands and setting out their own red lines. Baltic Sentry, the NATO surveillance operation, counted on the participation of ten initial European countries – but notably not the United States (though Washington did provide critical operational support, such as providing certain space-based intelligence capabilities Europe still lacks).

This does not mean that there was a full consensus within the Baltic littoral about the cable incidents either. As time passed, officials in the countries involved, such as Sweden, also began to go public with their own early findings, showing that no proof of foul play had been found yet – but also not yet any exculpatory evidence to the contrary.[34] Many officials still insist – some in off-the-record conversations, others in more public fora – that at least some of the incidents clearly bore all the hallmarks of intent (with the *Yi Peng 3* the one mentioned most often).

So where does that leave us? With the outcomes of the final investigations still forthcoming, this book goes to print at a time when many of the details still remain murky and consensus far off. In some ways, if these disruptions were indeed acts of sabotage, this confusion and discord they have sown could be considered their greatest success: losing an anchor is a small price to pay for the amount of heated debate, scrambling of resources and noise these incidents have unleashed. So who was right? Rather than commit my own theories to print, I will present you with some of the arguments both competing camps have put on the table. I will leave it to you to draw your own conclusions.

## The case for the prosecution

Let us start with the arguments in favour of at least some of these Baltic cable incidents having been cases of deliberate sabotage. In this camp we primarily find the Russia analysts (most familiar with Moscow's ways), those in the national security community and think tank trade, maritime security specialists, those in shipping ('no captain would be that inept'), no small number of cable industry experts, and many European governments – especially those in the Baltic and Nordic region itself.

First, they point to the nature and mechanics of the damage itself. It is true that the vast majority of cable faults are caused by human error. It is also true that such errors not infrequently involve the dropping of anchors on cables – and may even see a vessel lose one in the process. But not all accidents are made equal, and dragging an anchor weighing multiple tonnes for 100 nautical miles – in the case of the *Yi Peng 3* even over 300 miles (555 kilometres) – is very much out of the ordinary and at minimum presents gross incompetence, many maritime professionals I have spoken to argue. An anchor drag of this kind would have reverberated with such force through the ship, that it would have spurred any experienced, responsible crew to slow down the ship and to hoist the anchor back up again. They certainly would not have continued onwards with their journey for, in the case of the *Yi Peng 3*, nearly a day (fifteen hours separated the first and second cable snag). The pictures taken of the damage to the hull of the *Eagle S* reveal the sheer force with which the ship must have hauled its anchor along, as it ploughed through the seafloor. For a crew to make that kind of mistake in a specific geography once? Perhaps. But for such ineptitude to be showcased three times in a row in relatively quick succession, and in such similar ways? That is highly unlikely, the argument goes.

The pattern does appear hard to dismiss outright: in each case, a commercial vessel, supposedly caught unawares, drags its anchor over vast distances and damages multiple cables and other structures in the process. The C-Lion 1, a cable owned by the Finnish national telecoms champion Ciena, even got caught twice. Each of the three ships had either frequented or were on their way to Russian ports. Two left from Ust-Luga. Coincidences happen, but for them to happen in such a geopolitically tense geography riddled with greyzone activity? Open source investigators calculated the odds based on publicly available data on cable faults, and gave it a 1 in 10,000 to 100,000 year chance.[35] Based on the pattern alone, there was at minimum enough there to warrant further investigation.

But there was more. There were also the suspicious circumstances surrounding the ships themselves. Each of the three vessels had been shown on marine traffic trackers to have been sailing in odd zigzag patterns in the period leading up to, and during, the respective incidents. These furthermore were not clean sweeps, but the nature of the breaks suggested some cables had been avoided in one-two-hops, some insiders I spoke to confided. The Swedish coast guard had furthermore found that the *Newnew Polar Bear* had not been alone at the 'scene of the crime', but had likely been accompanied by the Russian nuclear-class icebreaker the *Sevmorput* around the time the BalticConnector had been damaged – the two vessels had reportedly even headed to Kaliningrad together after the incident. That very same *Sevmorput* had been spotted surveilling the future blast site of the Nord Stream sabotage in the months leading up to the pipelines' destruction. The *Yi Peng 3* had, according to some reporting, earlier in 2024 already come worryingly close to damaging cables in the Baltic Sea, and had turned off its transponder at the time of the successful October incident. Prior to the cable damage, the *Eagle S* had already been reported on as potentially wearing a dual hat, not just as a proud member of Russia's sanctions-evading shadow fleet, but also as a potential spy vessel.

And then there was the matter of timing. Mere weeks before the *Yi Peng 3* incident, then still secretary of Russia's Security Council and Putin confidant Nikolai Patrushev had told Russian newspaper *Kommersant* that not only were the US and UK behind the Nord Stream sabotage – a plot hatched in London (few believe as steadfastly in the continued reach of the long arm of London as Moscow does) – they were now also scheming to imminently 'throttle the global internet' by destroying undersea cables.[36] As an informal law of Kremlinology would posit: whenever Moscow accuses someone else of planning something, it is usually a prelude to something they themselves have in the works. While Patrushev's claim was broadly dismissed as baseless, it followed a familiar pattern of anticipatory disinformation used by Moscow to muddy the waters ahead of its own actions.

The timing of the *Eagle S* incident on Christmas Day was similarly suspect: it followed just weeks before the widely telegraphed date by which the Baltic countries would fully decouple their energy grids from Russia's, an important historical, psychological and logistical milestone towards energy independence from their hostile neighbour.[37] Was it really a coincidence, therefore, that two power cables critical for achieving this decoupling had both been targeted during the incident: the Est-Link 1 had been seriously damaged – necessitating an expensive and lengthy repair, and the *Eagle S* had only been minutes away from similarly snagging the Est-Link 2.

These incidents, furthermore, did not just appear to fit a pattern when it came to critical infrastructure damage in the Baltic Sea, they also seemed to bear all the hallmarks of Russia's wider hybrid warfare playbook. Russia has long operated in the grey zone, disrupting and sabotaging its way through Europe and beyond. Since the country's full-scale invasion of Ukraine, such tactics have only intensified and become more brazen – from mysterious fires in factories to drone incursions shutting down European airports. Russia also had form when it came to targeting cables. There had been warnings issued by NATO and others going back at least a decade about Russia behaving suspiciously near key undersea infrastructure. The Baltic incidents were not the first ones around which an aura of suspicion clung: there had been similar incidents near Svalbard and Norway's military bases in the High North – incidents we will discuss in the next chapter.[38] Mounting such operations in the Baltic Sea – a strategic waterway Russia considers to be firmly in its sphere of influence, but fears is slipping from its grip – only seemed like a logical next step up the hybrid escalation ladder.

Taken together, camp sabotage likely will have felt they had a strong case. But then those arguing that the damage had been accidental also had their own arguments, which we will assess next.

## The case for the defence

The second camp is made up of those who believe the uproar about the Baltic subsea cable incidents was a 'storm in a teacup'. While the initial circumstances may have seemed suspicious, especially to those new to the cable industry, skimming beyond the surface would show these events were a lot less extraordinary than they may at first have appeared. More than yet another gambit in an escalating shadow war, these were simply just routine examples of the everyday chaos that characterizes the maritime sphere, especially in such congested and fault-prone waters as the Baltic Sea.[39]

In this camp, we find many – but certainly not all – members of the cable industry. Here we also find several Western governments and intelligence services, especially those in countries not immediately adjacent to the Baltic Sea. Less credible expert witnesses that also dispute the intent behind these incidents can, unsurprisingly, be found in the Kremlin and Beijing. We will not feature the latter two's arguments here.

Critics of the saboteur theory pointed to the fact that, if it had been the case that some of the vessels involved belonged to Russia's shadow fleet, their poor seamanship should hardly come as a surprise. The most experienced, responsible crews and captains do not tend to opt to join shadowy, uninsured and leaky ships if they have the choice. This argument holds well for the *Eagle S*, which has long been believed to be part of Russia's oil sanctions-evading armada. The same, however, cannot necessarily be said of the Chinese and Hong Kong-flagged *Newnew Polar Bear* and *Yi Peng 3*, which were by all accounts rather regular cargo vessels – though in the occasionally murky world of global shipping, that is no guarantee of crew competence.

Weather conditions had also played a role: the *Newnew Polar Bear* and *Eagle S* had both met stormy conditions when they had lost their anchors. Adding to the impression that this had all just been accidental was the fact that the *Eagle S* had heeded warnings and stopped its rampage course when it was requested to do so, and even voluntarily allowed itself to be escorted into Finnish waters. As the vessel had been so close to also severing the second power cable connecting the Baltics to Finland, would it really not have kept going on just a little bit longer, if more significant, durable energy disruption had been its objective?

There was also the lack of a smoking gun. Because, while many analysts and politicians had been quick to point the finger at Russia, no one had been able to provide more than circumstantial proof of any link between the Kremlin and these vessels. Many ships that sail through the Baltic Sea frequent Russian ports. It appeared that none of the three vessels had any Russian nationals on board, or Russian ownership links (the *Newnew Polar Bear* eventually apparently would, but only after it had already fled the scene). As far as such information is available in the public domain, no incriminating evidence has been found on board any of the ships either. Nothing more has been released about the *Eagle S* potentially holding sophisticated spy equipment. None of its crew members – not even after weeks of confinement on their ships – had been persuaded to cut a deal with the local prosecutors or confessed. If we assume that the investigators had also attempted to follow the money trails, what they found had not provided them with irrefutable proof. No uncles or second cousins who had suddenly come into money, no wads of cash under sleeping berths. Sometimes, one might argue, the lack of evidence can be considered evidence in its own right. And as the supposed motive – monetary reward – for the offending crew was missing, so was, the naysayers argued, a convincing rationale.

Because why would Russia engage in these kinds of operations: their tangible impact on the region's connectivity had been negligible. Internet users in the countries affected would never have noticed anything amiss, if it had not been for the global media reporting on the incidents. If this was indeed a case of deliberate sabotage, it had accomplished little, but had instead revealed much about the Kremlin's strategic playbook. Because had it not now pushed European countries, and even the rest of the world, to significantly up their efforts and investments to improve the resilience and security of their cable systems (a topic we will discuss in the next chapter)? By playing the sabotage card now, Russia lost the element of surprise, which may have given it an advantage during a potential more serious escalation, such as an attempted invasion of the Baltic countries. Through its actions, Moscow had also invited further scrutiny of its shadow fleet, which had become such an important economic lifeline for a country that remains incredibly dependent on revenues from hydrocarbon exports.

What's more, Russia allegedly even inflicted damage on itself: weeks after the *Eagle S* incident, it was revealed – to far less fanfare – that another cable had been damaged: the short data cable which connected the exclave of Kaliningrad to the Russian mainland, its landing near St Petersburg.[40] Russia's own investigation eventually apparently settled on the theory that the cable must also have been collateral damage caused by the *Eagle S*. This then begged the question: would Russia deliberately undermine its own connectivity in support of a greyzone attack?

The main argument the camp of sceptics appeal to is, however, a statistical one. Cable faults are, as we have discussed, not especially rare, and in the vast majority of cases – 80 per cent, give or take – caused by human activity: anchors, trawlers, dredgers. The heavily trafficked Baltic Sea, with its shallow waters and soft seabed, was certainly no exception. Accidents rather similar to those in the Baltic Sea were almost daily occurrences – they just never invited that degree of scrutiny and public attention.

A case in point is a *fourth* incident involving damage to cables that took place in the Baltic Sea during that same time period: in February 2025, news broke of yet another cable fault in the Baltic Sea, off the coast of Gotland this time, during which a cable connecting the island to Ventspils in Latvia had been damaged, once again by an anchor drag. The cause of the damage was determined to have been the *Vezhen*, by all accounts a rather conventional freighter, flagged under a Maltese flag and owned by a more by-the-books Bulgarian company – both EU and NATO members. A vessel which did not fit the usual picture, therefore. It was indeed quickly concluded by the investigators in charge that in this case, the damage had genuinely been accidental – adverse weather, poor seamanship – even though the circumstances of the incident looked similar to the others. After an initial flurry of feverish reporting, the *Vezhen* incident was just as quickly forgotten about again – an unfortunate blip confusing the wider sabotage narrative.

The cherry-picking of data, and omission of counterexamples, allows one to make a pattern out of a biased set of data points, and so create a misleading narrative (*lies, damned lies and statistics*). The analysis that had been conducted using the database of publicly reported faults had relied on incomplete data, as many cable owners prefer to keep outages to themselves (having a cable seen to be down too often is not good for business). If you instead looked at the full, proprietary dataset of faults, only available to some in industry, it showed that the rate of incidents in the Baltic was far from out of the norm, a statistical outlier neatly flattened. And if there was a bit of a peak, this could be explained by the rapid uptick of shadow fleet activity in the region. While it is certainly true that more complete fault databases do exist, the cable industry has at the time of writing unfortunately not yet shared its Baltic analysis with the general public.

## The China question: a no-limits partnership?

As the dust has begun to settle on the Baltic cable incidents, one aspect that remains particularly puzzling and has not yet been interrogated to a satisfactory degree – or at least, not in the public domain – is the wider implications of the collaboration between the two alleged actors involved. Because the story remains an incomplete one. Though politicians and military leaders were careful not to point the finger directly at Russia in the absence of any concrete proof, reading between the lines, the implication was clear. If these were deliberate acts of sabotage, they must have been orchestrated by – or at the very least have involved – the Kremlin.

But what, then, to make of the fact that, while the three respective vessels' links to Russia remained somewhat tenuous, two of them *did* have very clear ties to China? While Moscow's potential involvement received a lot of airtime, the idea that Beijing may have played a central role never entered the narrative in any major way. Perhaps the political and economic implications were simply too profound: Europe may have severed most of its ties with Russia, it certainly has not with China. There were tensions to be sure, for example over Beijing's trade and industrial practices and (increasingly less) tacit support for Russia's war against Ukraine. China has also on numerous occasions been accused by the intelligence services of the UK, Netherlands, the United States and others of waging widespread cyber campaigns against Western countries. Beijing willingly involving itself in such a visible and brazen series of kinetic attacks against European countries would, however, present a concerning next step on the escalation ladder. Had the CCP turned its greyzone playbook up a notch, or was there a different explanation? We are left with several possible scenarios.

*Scenario one*: Russia *was* the architect behind these operations, and China was only an unwitting participant. In such a scenario, operatives in one of Russia's more entrepreneurial intelligence agencies could have, for example, bribed the crews of the *Newnew Polar Bear* and *Yi Peng 3* to take part in the rogue operation. Russia's intelligence services are known to have developed a taste for recruiting foreign nationals to execute their greyzone activities. This to create a degree of distance and deniability. But this will frequently concern nationals from nearby European countries like Poland, Moldova, Belarus and Ukraine itself – not usually its more powerful partner China. Russia's decision to recruit specifically *Chinese* ships for the cause would be a peculiar one if Beijing had no active part in it or did not at least give its tacit approval. The incidents had necessitated no small amount of Chinese diplomatic damage control and had once again put a spotlight on its respective relationships with Moscow and the West. Would Beijing look kindly on its – for all intents and purposes – junior partner putting it in this position, not just once but twice?

*Scenario two*: Russia orchestrated these incidents, but was in fact in cahoots with Beijing – or, even worse, was following its lead. The implications of this scenario would be rather consequential. Because even though China has itself also not shied away from conducting greyzone operations in Europe, its proactive part in the highly visible incidents in the Baltic would signal a new level of brazenness, openness as well as depth of its no-limits friendship with Russia.

What would China have to gain from providing Russia with plausible cover in this particular instance? There are certainly signs that the partnership between the two countries has been intensifying since 2022, and any attempts to effect a so-called (reverse) Kissinger, of driving a wedge between the two (as the Trump Administration, for example, has attempted), has proven a folly. China of course also has its own gripes with NATO and incentives to try and exploit the growing divide between Europe and a United States it accuses of trying to prevent its rise. Sowing discontent within the alliance and disagreement about how to respond to these kinds of provocations may help accelerate such a separation. It may also be a useful way of testing the waters: how *will* European countries respond to these kinds of activities, in their own waters, or elsewhere?

As we shall discuss later in this chapter, China has also been accused by others closer to home – especially Taiwan – of having orchestrated cable damage incidents of its own. Was this then a case of two partners learning or perhaps even mutually supporting each other? Russian surveillance and shadow fleet vessels had been spotted near Taiwan in the past, and accused of suspicious behaviour. Were China and Russia perhaps executing an elaborate subsea 'Strangers on a Train' scenario, in which both were helping each other out – to strengthen their mutual cases of deniability?

Another possibility raised by some China experts I've presented this conundrum to is that this could have been a case not so much of masterminding by the upper echelons of the CCP, but instead one of ambitious government apparatchiks further down the totem pole wanting to make a name for themselves. How well such hypothetical entrepreneurialism would have been received is guesswork. Because even though Chinese authorities may have made it extremely difficult for the Europeans to investigate the *Newnew Polar Bear* and *Yi Peng 3* incidents, they did eventually publicly apologize for the first ship's involvement – something the CCP notoriously does not like to do. This apology is significant, and perhaps suggests that the operations had not been greenlit on the very highest levels, the same China experts suggest.

*Scenario three*: the damage was, in fact, accidental and just a particularly unfortunately timed sequence of events. A storm in a teacup.

At the time of writing, we do not yet have any final resolution to this deep-sea *whodunnit*. Future updated editions of this book may be able to provide readers with a final answer.

## *Into the grey*

Whether recent undersea cable incidents were acts of sabotage or not, one thing cannot be disputed: Russia has been waging an increasingly aggressive and disruptive greyzone warfare campaign across Europe and beyond. This playbook, which has a long legacy harkening back to the Soviet Union's active measures, as well as subversion campaigns during the reign of the tsars,[41] has been revived and reinvented under Putin, and, especially since the start of the country's full-scale invasion of Ukraine, has taken on an increasingly irresponsible turn. Director General of British intelligence agency MI5 Ken McCallum described Russia's escalating campaigns of disruption and chaos as a case of the Kremlin's agents having 'gone feral', causing 'sustained mayhem' all over the continent.[42]

Almost nowhere is this felt more acutely than in the Baltic countries: Lithuania, Latvia and Estonia. These small countries, whose combined populations of six million are dwarfed by Russia's 140 million plus, are in the direct line of fire of any expanded Russian ambitions that could see Moscow set its sights on NATO next. Though the Russian military has taken a significant hit as a result of its ill-fated invasion of Ukraine, Western officials assess that Moscow could reconstitute its forces to a sufficient extent to mount a serious campaign against the Baltics by the end of the 2020s.[43] During a 2025 speech at London think tank Chatham House, NATO Secretary-General Mark Rutte warned that Russia could be ready to use military force against NATO within five years.[44] The French government has warned about the high risk of a major high-intensity war in Europe, involving European allies, by 2030.[45] Some analysts suggest Moscow may take the plunge even sooner – with the Kremlin well aware that Europe's rapid military build-up will likely start to bear fruit by the end of the decade and tip the balance increasingly in the latter's favour. No countries are more bellicose than those who fear they are running out of time.

An incursion into NATO territory – such as into the Baltic countries – would make good on a long-standing obsession of Vladimir Putin, who considers them as forming an integral part of the so-called *Russkiy Mir*, or 'Russian world', the country's natural, historical sphere of influence. It is an eerily similar justification to the one Putin used to defend the annexation of Crimea in 2014 and his horrific war of conquest targeting the rest of Ukraine launched in 2022.[46] In the eyes of the Kremlin, the independence of the small Baltic states, which were repeatedly forcefully colonized by the Soviet Union and before that by Imperial Russia, is a historical aberration. Reclaiming them would help solidify Russia's re-emergence as a great power and make right what Putin once called 'the greatest geopolitical catastrophe of the 20th century', the dissolution of the Soviet Union and with it the fall of Russia's stature on the global stage.[47]

Moscow has not shied away from making this displeasure about the Baltics' European turn, away from Russia, be felt. Few places have borne the brunt of Russian hybrid warfare, aggressive rhetoric and other provocations as frequently and intensively as the Baltic countries, signalling both the degree to which Moscow still perceives these countries to be in its sphere of influence, as well as its longer-term objective of sowing disruption to aid in what it believes may lay the groundwork for more formally bringing the Baltics back into its strategic orbit.

In 2007, Estonia was hit by one of the first nationwide cyber attacks in history, likely in retaliation for its decision to move a controversial statue of a Red Army soldier from its prominent perch in the centre of its capital Tallinn to the city's outskirts. The statue's relocation sparked an outcry from elements of the country's sizeable Russian-speaking population, as well as the Kremlin, with Foreign Minister Lavrov calling the removal a 'vengeful policy toward Russians living in Estonia and toward Russia'.[48] Soon afterwards Moscow showed off its own vengeance: the attacks, which are widely believed to have been orchestrated by Russia, crippled many key systems in the country – from Estonia's banking system to its traffic lights, prompting weeks of disruption. The events should have presented a stark warning for the rest of Europe about the dangerous turn Russia had taken under Putin, who many Western European leaders at that stage still believed they could do business with. It was a warning unfortunately not heeded.

Today, Russia's hybrid playbook has become only thicker. Russia's intelligence services and their proxies run large-scale disinformation campaigns to undermine cohesion and sow distrust – which, in the case of the Baltic countries, have in particular targeted the countries' substantial Russian-speaking populations.[49] There is the widespread GPS jamming and spoofing all over Eastern Europe in particular, which, by scrambling signals, endangers both military and civil aviation.[50] The Russian state runs ever more disruptive cyber operations, and has handed an apparent carte blanche to its domestic cybercriminal networks to run wild and sow disruption.[51] A 2024 cargo plane crash in Lithuania sparked questions about possible Russian involvement.[52] Twin fires – setting ablaze both one of Warsaw's largest shopping malls and an IKEA in Vilnius – led to prosecutions in 2025.[53] Agitators who defiled a Jewish graveyard and Holocaust memorial in France with swastikas and other antisemitic symbolism turned out to likely have been on Moscow's payroll.[54] Then there were mysterious fires in factories and weapon depots in Germany, the United Kingdom and elsewhere.[55] There was the assassination attempt on the CEO of Rheinmetall, Germany's largest arms manufacturer.[56] Mysterious power outages and train disruptions in the lead-up to the opening of the 2024 Olympic Games in Paris and the 2025 NATO Summit in The Hague, raised eyebrows.[57] Russian fighter jets have been violating Baltic and Nordic airspace for years. Moscow has learned that the weaponization of immigration flows along the Nordic, Baltic and Polish borders, originating from Russia and Belarus, makes for a particularly potent political weapon.[58] In the autumn of 2025, an epidemic of mysterious drone incursions ground to a halt air traffic from Copenhagen to Brussels, Munich to Oslo.

And then we have not yet mentioned Russia's alleged hybrid activities in the maritime domain. Zooming in on the Baltic Sea alone, there is more Moscow is doing beyond targeting undersea cables. There's the Russian border guards moving buoys along its frontier with Estonia.[59] Its submarines are frequently spotted acting suspiciously all over European waters. There's the activity of its shadow fleet – which not only helps sustain Russia's war machine, but also presents a clear danger to maritime security in the region (these often ageing and badly maintained ships, manned by inexperienced crews, are an environmental disaster in the making). There are growing suspicions that Moscow also uses these ships more entrepreneurially – for surveillance and monitoring (recall the *Eagle S*, which allegedly at one point had spy equipment and intelligence agents on board), but also a launching platform for hybrid attacks. The mysterious drones, which shuttered Copenhagen Airport in September 2025, for example, were allegedly launched from shadow fleet vessels.[60] These greyzone operations often happen in conjunction – Russia's disinformation mongers will throw conspiracy theories into the ether, to rapidly create multiple false narratives and stories ('these were Ukrainian drones! This was a British false flag!') – in the hopes of sparking panic, but also ensuring many possible truths can take hold at the same time, further fracturing polities in the countries targeted.

Another way in which Russia clouds the picture is by making it difficult to determine not just who is behind an incident, but whether it was a case of hybrid warfare at all. Vanishingly few of the above-mentioned incidents have ever been decisively proven to have been orchestrated by Russia. They can be made to look accidental – as may have been the case with the Baltic cable incidents. In other cases, irrefutably tying an event back to Russia is the main challenge. Many of Russia's sabotage operations now rely on local criminal networks in the countries targeted, disenfranchised immigrants and increasingly even gig workers recruited on apps who are promised a quick buck.[61] This remote cultivation of agents is a means to an end (many of Russia's local intelligence networks were dismantled when their embassy-based handlers were sent back to Moscow by their host countries after 2022) but also help make the case for plausible deniability.

The strategic calculus behind these greyzone activities is multi-layered. On the most basic level, these types of low-cost operations help Russia inflict significant economic and political costs on European countries and others at the receiving end. Every cable that needs to be repaired or airspace closed comes at a cost. Countries find themselves forced to dedicate scarce military and other resources to better guard critical infrastructure systems and upgrade protections from a peace dividend world to a new era of global disorder. NATO's Baltic Sentry sees finite European naval assets deployed to monitor infrastructure in the Baltic Sea. In response to repeated drone incursions in the autumn of 2025, the European Commission is at the time of writing mulling over the specifics of its multi-billion investment into the development of a so-called drone wall, an elaborate curtain of sensors and counter-drone systems meant to stop or limit incursions from the east.[62] By the time such protections are in place, Russia's game of whack-a-mole may already have moved on to the next infrastructural weak spot.

These kinds of greyzone operations, Russia hopes, will also weaken societal resolve and democratic resilience in the countries targeted – through the spread of divisive messages and support of pro-Russian, anti-EU political forces, but also at bringing home the cost of supporting Ukraine in a rather visceral way.

Moscow also uses these actions to send a message and voice its displeasure, by timing highly visible operations around significant political events. It is likely no coincidence that the *Eagle S* would have arrived on the scene mere weeks before the Baltic countries were finalizing their transition away from Russia's power grid. Drone incursions targeting Copenhagen were timed to take place mere days before a high-profile EU leaders summit in the Danish capital – and days after Denmark announced it would support Ukraine develop long-range strike capabilities that could allow it to more easily reach Russia. Maritime greyzone activities in the Baltic specifically helped Russia signal that the sea, despite some of the boisterous talk that Sweden and Finland's joining of the alliance had turned it into a 'NATO lake',[63] was all but invulnerable.

This is not just about psychological and economic warfare, however. The more recent pattern behind these activities, according to many in the intelligence community, points to something much more disturbing. These are no longer just provocations: they are rehearsals. Especially Russia's shadowy activities in the Baltic Sea appear to suggest the country is gearing up for a more serious escalation. It is pre-positioning capabilities (perhaps even placing explosives on seabed systems such as cables and pipelines), running sophisticated reconnaissance missions and mapping critical infrastructure (including subsea cables) ahead of time. It is seemingly also assessing alliance responses: how exactly will NATO allies react to provocations? This is important. It is highly likely that Russia would target the Baltic countries' undersea cable network in a bid to isolate the countries ahead of a possible invasion – recent incidents may just be the first pinpricks to test the waters.

Unfortunately, isolating the Baltic countries is very much within the realm of possibility. Geography, the fate of nations, is especially unkind to the Baltic states. The small and exposed countries share extensive land borders with Russia's most developed and heavily militarized parts. The

Estonian border town of Narva lies only some 50 kilometres from Ust-Luga – and only 500 from St Petersburg. Trains in the Baltic countries still run on the same pre-tsarist train gauges; many of their highways lead straight across the border. Its long, densely forested borders – though hard to penetrate (and currently being dressed up in barbed wire, turned into peat bogs and swamps, and lined with landmines to slow down any Russian advance)[64] – are also difficult to defend. Unlike Ukraine, which at twice the size of Germany benefits from significant strategic depth, the Baltics are small, meaning any initial deep Russian troop penetration from the east risks rapidly becoming a *fait accompli*, something the Baltics' own sizeable (and often underestimated) reserves as well as the promised NATO reinforcements may struggle to reverse.

Compounding this problem is the Baltics' reliance on the so-called Suwałki Gap, the narrow corridor linking Poland to Lithuania, flanked on the west by the Russian exclave of Kaliningrad and on the east by Russian satellite Belarus, which is the only land route connecting the Baltic countries to the rest of NATO. If the narrow corridor, which is only 65 kilometres wide at its narrowest point, were to be seized early on – many analysts warn – the Baltics would effectively be cut off from NATO's main land-based reinforcement routes. This exploitable vulnerability has earned the gap the moniker of NATO's Achilles heel. The accession of Finland and Sweden to NATO has alleviated some of this problem (St Petersburg is well within striking distance from Finland, and Sweden's Gotland, 'NATO's unsinkable aircraft carrier' similarly allows power projection across the region); nevertheless, the danger is a real one.

If the objective is to quickly isolate the Baltic countries and limit their lines of communications, cutting off the Suwałki Gap and sea routes – and indeed, the undersea cables that route through both – would mean near-total isolation, both digitally and operationally.

## *China enters the fray*

China's possible role in the Baltic Sea incident in late 2023, involving the *Newnew Polar Bear*, and then the *Yi Peng 3* in 2024, remains a disputed one. But its involvement – intentional or otherwise – in a series of disruptive episodes much closer to home, targeting Taiwan, is a lot more direct. In the period between 2019 and 2023, Taiwan has been on the receiving end of thirty-six incidents involving damage, or attempted damage, to its undersea internet cables – with several of these occurrences apparently linked to China.[65]

The most famous of these episodes took place in February 2023, when the two undersea cables connecting Taiwan's main island to its outlying Matsu Islands were severed. Taiwan's control over the sparsely populated Matsu archipelago, located just a few miles off the Chinese coast, has long been a geopolitical flashpoint and source of ire in Beijing, with the popular tourist islands almost visible from the mainland – but not under its control (something Beijing certainly would like to remedy). A prime target for greyzone escalations, therefore. The incident followed a pattern we are now all too familiar with: a Chinese-registered sand dredger and fishing vessel in rapid succession damaged – purportedly by accident – the then only two cables connecting the Matsus to the main island of Taiwan, fully cutting them off from the global internet.

Here, the risk of bottlenecks in repair capacity became abundantly clear – with no repair ships immediately available (Taiwan has no sovereign repair capacity of its own and relies on ships from Japan, Singapore and South Korea), it would take several weeks for the cables to become operational again, leaving Matsu's population in the dark in the meantime. While some residents joked that the internet blackout helped them 'find themselves', the implications of the incidents were abundantly clear. As a geographically small island, with an economy heavily dependent on high tech, Taiwan's dependence on the cable network is a profound one – a vulnerability China is seemingly keen to show it can use against it.[66]

Any suggestions that China may have deliberately caused these incidents were rapidly brushed aside by Beijing, with an official spokesperson declaring that: 'While the basic facts and the people responsible for the accident have not yet been clarified, the Democratic Progressive Party authorities [then Taiwan's ruling party] have deliberately exaggerated the situation in an attempt at political manipulation, which will not enjoy popular support.' It later even accused Taiwan of having orchestrated the incidents, to spark anti-Chinese sentiments and elicit foreign sympathy.

While China – like Russia – may have relied on plausible deniability, here too the circumstances of the case were noteworthy to say the least. The incident involving the Matsu Island cuts, and similar ones before and since, all relied on *modus operandi* eerily similar to those we have witnessed in the Baltic Sea. They also followed repeated warnings by Taiwanese authorities that China had been mapping maritime infrastructure in its near-environs and had been using fishing vessels and dredgers (China needs incredibly large amounts of sand to fuel its construction boom) to intimidate and cause economic and environmental damage by disrupting the seabed. Adding to the heated debate was China's publication in 2025 of a patent that showed it had developed a special type of submersible, which could be used to cut cables at depths as great as 4,000 metres. While this type of device has a clear commercial utility, we should also certainly expect it to be used as part of a wider effort to cut cables in a conflict scenario.

Just like Russia's activities in the Baltic Sea and beyond, China too has long been waging its own greyzone campaign against what it considers its 'wayward province', its approach similarly combining disinformation (an art, it has to be said, it has mastered less well than its partner in Moscow), cyberwarfare, economic coercion, and other greyzone activities. The aim is not only to take hits at Taiwanese morale and perhaps over time coerce a bloodless surrender, these kinds of actions similarly also appear to be testing the waters and to be in preparation for a larger escalation. Especially in Washington, many China hawks now believe that Xi Jinping's move to take the island – an ambition China's leader has pledged to achieve by 2049 – may arrive a whole lot sooner, perhaps as soon as 2027.[67] Taiwan's twenty-four submarine internet cables (fifteen linking it to the world, nine domestic ones connecting its own islands) would no doubt be among the first targets.

Since the Matsu Island incident in 2023, several further incidents involving damage to Taiwanese cables have followed. But just like it appears that Russia and China have been borrowing and iterating on each other's cable cutting practices, so too have those at the receiving end of these alleged greyzone operations honed their own responses. In early 2025, Taiwan's coast guard – emboldened by the Finnish response, it seemed – intercepted the *Hong Tai 58*, which had just damaged submarine cables on Taiwan's southern coast, after being spotted zigzagging suspiciously. The Togo-flagged but Chinese crewed ship has since been found in court to have deliberately caused the damage, its captain – a Chinese national – jailed for three years. This is something European countries have not yet managed to do.

To Taipei, these are not matters to be taken lightly: 'Some scholars have said that World War III could begin with the cutting of undersea cables. I think that's quite realistic', Herming Chiueh, Taiwan's deputy minister of digital affairs said to the BBC about the affair.[68]

## *How big is the risk?*

While the recent spate of possible greyzone incidents may not have caused any serious or long-lasting damage to connectivity, are there scenarios imaginable where they would? Is there a possibility one could use kinetic – or other forms of force – to cripple large sections of the global network and leave many, if not all of us, disconnected?

Despite apocalyptic warnings from Nikolai Patrushev and assorted tabloid media that hybrid attacks on undersea cables could bring about the demise of the internet, the actual risks such incidents pose – especially in well-connected geographies like the Baltic Sea – are largely manageable. Internet users barely registered the Baltic disruptions, thanks largely to the high levels of redundancy built into the region's cable network. Despite the now frequent talk about the fragility of undersea cables, the network is, in many ways, actually a quiet triumph of fault-proof engineering and solid industry practice. In each of the three Baltic Sea incidents, cable repair ships were on the scene within days, sometimes hours, investigating the incident sites, assessing the damage, and had the cables working again within a week. There are even seemingly counter-intuitive arguments that can be made that this leaves the network almost *too* resilient and may so actually invite disruption – aware that these kinds of provocations have relatively little impact, bad actors may be quite willing to take the risk, conscious that the potential for overreaction on the receiving side is quite limited.[69]

Of course, as we have discussed, these incidents are not without cost. There are the cable and telecommunications companies, who face increased risk premiums, uncertainty, difficult questions from investors and, given the limitations of international law in this domain, little hope of ever seeing accountability, let alone recoup the costs of legal support, repair and loss-of-service. These incidents also sow disruption and panic among the general public, test the target's resolve, and tie down finite resources – both NATO countries and the Taiwanese coast guard are now actively monitoring their respective waters, for example. They inflict costs, but are also designed to remain more limited in scope, and deniable, so as not to invite a more forceful, or even a kinetic response.

Those who are concerned that the 'cable panic' of the moment is perhaps overblown are not necessarily incorrect as far as greyzone incidents are concerned – no rogue anchor is going to cripple the global internet. Where the potential impact *could* be a lot more significant is in the lead-up to an all-out conflict or war.

Defence planners around the world recognize that the severing of cables would in all likelihood be among the first things their opponent would seek to do. Let us not forget how the Royal Navy cut Germany's cables as one of its very first acts during both world wars. Though (to my knowledge) never executed, archival documents from the Cold War similarly show that effecting such an immediate and thorough communications black-out was a core part of the planning[70] – both defensively, but certainly also offensively. Western militaries may be looking at ways to stop Russia and China from inflicting such an early blow, but they are also getting ready to return the favour or launch the starting salvo.

While those in the security community are naturally tight-lipped when it comes to revealing their own offensive hand, several have gone on record to say that Russia has long been developing the capabilities to effect more widespread damage against critical undersea infrastructure in NATO countries and elsewhere. This is not just evidenced by GUGI's prolific seabed mapping activities, but also through its development of the kinds of equipment that would allow the crippling of infrastructure at a large scale – an ability Moscow has continued to invest in since at least Soviet times.

Any attempts – whether by Russia, China or anyone else – to rapidly and decisively throttle connectivity in the early days of a war would have to rely on damaging or severing many cables at the same time, and would almost certainly not involve the use of regular commercial ships dragging their anchors. Action would need to be swift, and decisive. This could, for example, involve the prepositioning of explosives on cables in several hard to reach or defend locations. Submarines or naval vessels with grappling hooks could also be used; China's dual-use submersible – capable of reaching great depths, where repairs bring their own challenges – could be used for such purposes. Beyond acquiring the technical abilities, executing an operation of this kind also requires careful planning and intelligence gathering ahead of time. You need the technical means, but also know how, and where, best to deploy them. This is the kind of reconnaissance spy vessels like the *Yantar* are accused of engaging in. An effective cable-cutting surprise would also need to be executed without the adversary tipping its hand. If such preparations fail to remain under the radar, there is the risk they may prematurely alert the target that a wider escalation could be imminent.

Such planning is well worth dedicating resources to. Throttling the network ahead of an invasion has a very clear strategic utility – which is why we have seen it happen so often in the past.[71] Cutting a sufficient number of cables would mean a given geography's international exchange would slow down significantly or even grind to a halt. Financial systems could be crippled (which in turn would inflict serious economic damage and make it hard for countries to sustain their war efforts). It would cause panic and, importantly, would make it far more difficult for the country at the receiving end to practise effective military command and control, if no backup systems remain in place (space-based systems and other back-ups would presumably be similarly targeted).

Taiwan and the Baltic countries are not only considered likely subjects of future invasions, but both geographies are unfortunately also isolatable, and cutting many – if not all – of their undersea cable connections could sever their communications in the above ways at a critical moment. While places like Estonia and Taiwan are particularly vulnerable, that does not mean that it is only countries at the immediate frontline of a conflict that could be targeted. We should also expect such an operation to be mounted against countries much further in the rear. Places like Ireland – home to an especially large number of cable landings, which the militarily neutral country is ill-equipped to protect, as we will discuss in the next chapter – while far from any frontline, would be vulnerable.

Even a far better-connected island nation like the United Kingdom with its sixty cables would not be able to withstand a significant assault on its cable network, especially as not all cables connecting a place need to be severed to significantly degrade international traffic. Some assessments suggest that neutralizing even just a third of the United Kingdom's network could already significantly hamper real-time flows of, for example, financial traffic. In a country – and global financial system – that is very reliant on the goings-on of the City of London, this would be a significant source of disruption.[72]

It is not very likely that the United Kingdom or Ireland would find itself facing an invasion on their own soil, but targeting their undersea connectivity could sow chaos and so complicate a European response further east. Disrupt the rear, essentially. Cutting key European and transatlantic cables could help sever key lines of communication and significantly complicate military coordination between NATO allies. A loss of high-speed communications could delay the allied response, and make it much harder to quickly send the promised troops and equipment to the eastern flank.

It is this kind of wartime sabotage of key sections of the cable network that should be the primary source of concern among planners. But that certainly should not mean we should forget about the grey zone. Greyzone activities owe their names to their ambiguity: not quite war, not quite peace – provocations skirting the very limits of what we may consider an act of war. That also makes them especially high-risk endeavours. And this is perhaps the point where some actors' alleged actions in the cable domain do carry the potential of catastrophic escalation, even in the absence of a wider conflict. If countries continue to allow these kinds of incidents to go unpunished, it encourages the perpetrators to keep pushing the envelope further and further, take it just that bit further each time. This will not only see the frequency and magnitude of hybrid provocations increase – with all the costs that involves – each such occurrence also increases the chances of miscalculation. A provocateur seeking to find red lines may find itself inadvertently crossing them.

As the severing of a large number of key communications cables would likely be part of the preamble to a wider, conventional war, a large-scale, manmade outage of cables – even if intended as a smaller provocation, or even one caused entirely by accident – may well be misinterpreted by those at the receiving end as a prelude to something far more serious. Such a misinterpretation could set in motion a series of escalations that may be hard to pull back from. Through its increasingly more brazen hybrid activities in the maritime domain and elsewhere, Russia is playing with fire. The disruption of how many cables at at time can a spoiler in the system like the Kremlin get away with, before the target considers it a declaration of war? NATO members triggered Article 4 of the alliance's collective defence agreement (a rare event, only invoked nine times in its more than eighty-year history – two of which in 2025), in response to Russian hybrid mayhem involving drones and fighter jet incursions. Is there a threshold by which an alliance member may even invoke Article 5 – the cornerstone of NATO's collective defence commitment, which posits that an attack on one is considered an attack on all? The lack of a rulebook and clarity on red lines to counter some of these actions leave incidents like we have seen in the Baltic Sea at risk of unintentionally tipping over into something far more serious.

We will be discussing these kinds of risks, and what countries can do about them, in the next chapter.

# 6

# *Cutting the Cord*

It was the incidents in the Baltic Sea that catapulted the security of cables into the global headlines, but the issue had already quietly resurfaced as a topic of conversation in national security circles quite some time before that.

The enigmatic Russian research vessel *cum* infrastructure mapper the *Yantar* (which we visited all the way back in the introduction) had been an object of curiosity, if not outright apprehension, from the moment the ship became operational in 2015. It was that same year that US officials first started to publicly air concerns about suspicious Russian behaviour near important submarine cables, which they warned suggested 'Russians might be planning to attack those lines in times of tension or conflict.'[1] Concerns voiced in proverbial smoky backrooms will likely have gone back quite a few years further than that.

Also think tanks and journalists had already slowly started to bring this topic to the public's attention. In 2017, a new backbencher in the UK parliament, who would not much later go on to become Prime Minister, Rishi Sunak, wrote a report for Westminster think tank Policy Exchange, raising the alarm about the susceptibility of undersea cables to deliberate weaponization: 'We have allowed this vital infrastructure to grow increasingly vulnerable and this should worry us all.'[2] According to an insider who had been in government at the time, the responsible civil servants in Whitehall had been unsure how to respond to some of the storm whipped up by the release of Sunak's report: a difficult choice between publicly acknowledging the validity of its conclusions, which in the halls of Whitehall were agreed to be mostly very valid and risk drawing attention to the issue, or was it better to let it disappear to gather dust in a digital drawer? The UK government ultimately opted to err towards the latter strategy, but that did not mean it forgot about the issue.

In a speech in 2017, then Chief of the UK's defence staff, Sir Stuart Peach warned that strategically severing undersea cables could 'immediately and potentially catastrophically' hit the economy.[3] Other countries were concerned too. France released a dedicated seabed strategy in 2022.[4] The US Congress launched an inquiry into the vulnerability of submarine cables in 2020 – and also expressed particular concern about the ability of adversaries to potentially listen in on cable traffic. For some time, the cable sabotage question remained a largely academic one: it certainly appeared that Russia – through GUGI, its enigmatic Directorate of Deep-Sea Research (or deep sea spy agency) – and perhaps also China, were laying the groundwork to potentially interfere with global cable connectivity at some undetermined time in the future and were rapidly developing the capabilities to do so. While interference with traffic may already have been actively happening, at least according to US security assessments, neither country had, however, put these new sabotage playbooks to the test yet.

This would all change in early 2022, in the weeks leading up to the full-scale invasion of Ukraine, when the undersea cable linking Norway's mainland to the highly strategic and increasingly contested Arctic island of Svalbard was cut, the result of what the Norwegian authorities officially attributed to human activity.[5] As with other similar incidents, while no definite proof has yet emerged in either direction, the smoking guns were several: a trawl by investigative journalists through the data revealed that a Russian fishing vessel, later identified as having likely been behind the damage, had traversed the cable in question some 130 times in the period leading up to the incident (the very same trawler was likely involved with a similar incident in Norway's High North the year before).[6] Pictures released by the Norwegian police of the damaged cable itself suggested significant force had been involved.[7] Several deep indentations into the seabed spotted near the cables – likely caused by anchors or dragnets – similarly raised eyebrows: perhaps someone had had a stab at damaging the cables before. The timing of the incident also suggested potentially nefarious intentions: this had all the hallmarks of a shaping operation ahead of the invasion of Ukraine only weeks later – cables in the High North such as the one connecting Svalbard are important for space-based intelligence capabilities, with the ground-based elements of many systems of military importance situated there – the sort of capabilities Ukraine's Western allies would need access to more than ever in the near future.

Though the incident received far less attention than the later Baltic cable episodes, it provided a harbinger of what was to come. The Svalbard cuts also remain among the few cable incidents almost everyone I have spoken to on this topic quietly acknowledge was likely the product of deliberate damage. Despite all of this, it was not until the sabotage of the Nord Stream pipelines some months later that the topic of infrastructure out at sea was catapulted into the public consciousness. Since then, we have seen a rush – from the media, from policymakers, from defence companies, from think tank pundits – to talk about the need to better protect cables and ready them for a new era of geopolitical competition.

Some in the cable community are minded to treat the current securitization of cables as a moral panic of sorts, where militaries and navies use the increased, and in their view frequently overblown, attention being paid to cables and the wider 'resilience' buzzword as a convenient excuse to plead for more resources or to drive investment into new undersea gizmos. For some, we see the exact opposite: the growing threat to submarine cables and seabed infrastructure is increasingly being framed as an existential one, symbolic of a far broader reassessment of their security role.

## *Ireland*

Take, for example, Ireland, a country which has long prided itself on its neutrality. It is one of only four EU member states not part of NATO, and maintains only a relatively small and modestly resourced military.[8] The country owns no submarines, no battle tanks, its army ranks 125th in the world by number of active personnel. Ireland's position of neutrality was borne from a matter of principle and values – the country, for example, does play a proactive role in global peacekeeping missions – and its extraordinarily complex history and relationship with its larger neighbour. This philosophy has now become so entrenched in its political culture and identity that few politicians dare even broach the topic. Up until recently, that was also not especially necessary. Ireland has long been able to maintain this posture because of its relatively sheltered position on the continent – with NATO members, such as the United Kingdom and France, serving as buffers (despite this history, Dublin continues to rely on the Royal Navy for aspects of its security),[9] and far removed from the continent's increasingly hot eastern flank. No longer so.

In an increasingly geopolitically volatile world, where greyzone escalations are becoming more commonplace and aggressive, Ireland's lack of formal Article 5 protections, limited ability to defend itself against these kinds of threats, and heavy reliance on digital infrastructure for its economy – the Irish permissive tax regime has lured large swathes of the tech industry to Dublin, including many hyperscalers – leave the country the weak zebra in the herd. This has become a growing source of concern, and not just in Dublin.

Ireland is home to a sizeable percentage of Europe's data centres and is now the key landing site for many transatlantic cables. Other countries too, therefore, depend on the country as a conduit for their international exchange and connectivity. A well-targeted attack, bringing down several of Ireland's cables, or, perhaps even easier, the interconnectors that help power its significant data centre economy (which now accounts for approximately 20 per cent of the country's electricity use), could thus have serious spillover effects into other countries as well. This vulnerability and relative importance of its connectivity mean that Ireland may therefore be a prime target in the lead-up to an incursion on NATO's eastern flank, disrupt as it would connectivity in the alliance's hinterland, and the ability to rapidly move troops and supplies east. Another NATO Achilles heel, perhaps.

Europe's adversaries appear to be cognisant of this vulnerability. Russian spy vessels the *Viktor Leonov*, the *Yantar* and others have been spotted in the Irish Sea on a number of occasions, with navy and coast guard ships escorting the prying vessels away again.[10] These incidents can be seen as small game provocations, singling out a weak link in Europe, but are again also potential probes and exercises to test the waters.

These incidents certainly appear to have stirred decision-makers in Dublin into action. In a speech in October 2024, then foreign minister (and at the time of writing Taoiseach) of Ireland Micheál Martin, who had made, like us in the audience, the seven-hour trek from Dublin to the highly symbolic Valentia Island, from which the first transatlantic submarine cable departed, raised the centrality of the issue to Ireland – and transatlantic – security: 'Our maritime footprint – our Exclusive

Economic Zone is seven times our land area – is currently home to the majority of transatlantic data communications.'[11] It arguably thus behoves, is increasingly the view in Dublin, that the country equip itself better to protect it. This is not just critical national infrastructure, it is arguably critical *European* infrastructure – and Ireland cannot continue to just rely on others to secure it. Countries like France and the United Kingdom, which have lost a lot of digital business – and resulting tax revenues – to Dublin, may start to wonder whether it is right that they should continue to foot much of the bill for protecting it. Major investors, such as the hyperscalers, may start to wonder whether relying on a country not presently sufficiently well-equipped to defend these assets is not becoming a source of geopolitical risk – in a historical echo to the way that Ireland lost its position in the cable network in the early twentieth century, when it was similarly political concerns that drove this decline.

Ireland is starting to take action: the country in 2026 launched its very first maritime security strategy, is slowly but steadily beginning to build up its capabilities to defend maritime infrastructure and is seeking closer ties with its neighbours, primarily through EU mechanisms (joining NATO would be a bridge too far), to address the threat.[12] According to some in the Irish security community, this is about far more than just undersea cables: Irish policymakers are using the issue as a less-sensitive entry point (few would disagree that keeping cables secure is a bad thing) to slowly crack open the highly sensitive door to get the Irish public ready for a wider reconsideration of the country's position of neutrality.

## *Europeanization of NATO*

Just like cables are becoming the starting point for conversations in Dublin around its evolving security role, they can similarly be seen as an emancipating issue for many other European countries, especially those in the north and east of the continent. They can even in some small ways appear to serve as a means for the long-anticipated closer integration of European defence. As Europe grapples with the generational challenge of a seeming US retreat from the continent and falling away of the certainties offered by America's post-war security umbrella, the protection of infrastructure in the Baltic and North Sea is emerging as a domain where European countries are increasingly formulating their own responses and are setting their own red lines – notably without explicit leadership or visible involvement by the United States.

The Joint Expeditionary Force (JEF) – a grouping of ten naval-minded countries in the North and Baltic littorals, led by Britain – is one such example. The JEF, which notably does not include the United States, had first been formed in 2014, but has since found an important part of its *raison d'être* in the protection of maritime infrastructure. NATO's Operation Baltic Sentry similarly also only involves European ships. As European countries give shape to what this kind of mini-lateral or even pan-European collaboration and integration can look like and consider what kind of military powers they may again want to be, preventing Russian seabed shenanigans is emerging as a testbed of how this may be put into practice.

## *Vulnerabilities and weak spots*

Contrary to the popular belief that has taken hold, the cable network is not actually all that fragile. As the network continues to expand, the absolute number of annual faults has remained remarkably stable. In many ways, submarine cables are some of the most reliable technologies on the planet, with failure rates on cables trending towards zero per billion hours of operation.[13] Individual cables usually last several decades. A well-oiled repair and maintenance machine, sufficient redundancy and industry collaboration mean that when faults and outages do occur, they can usually be repaired quickly, and traffic diverted elsewhere in the interim (in the better-connected geographies that is; this is certainly not the case everywhere around the world, as we have seen).

But these systems, processes and procedures were, however, largely built and devised for a climate of peace dividend thinking, an era of higher trust and collaboration, in which planning for deliberate sabotage or concerns about interference did not feature high on the list of priorities – if they featured at all. This has left weak spots in the network. I certainly do not intend for this book to be a how-to guide to cable sabotage. Nevertheless, to analyse the current actions many governments have started to take to improve the network's resilience, it is important to understand which perceived weaknesses they are trying to address (or should – in my view – be trying to address) – physical ones, certainly, but also those caused by market failures and power concentration, a lack of rules and the partial Wild West that are the High Seas.

## Physical weaknesses in the network

Cables are at their most vulnerable when they are nearest to the land, or have already made landfall.[14] Landing stations can take the shape of windowless concrete boxes nearer to shore, small industrial warehouses, or even just literal rooms in office buildings, some of which prove not at all impossible to find, even for a less seasoned cable hunter such as myself. They are also frequently lightly monitored and protected, when compared to other critical infrastructure. Manhole covers – in some cases no more than actual lids that one could hypothetically lift, to be found on many a worldwide beach – can similarly lack physical fortifications and be accessed by those with ill intent. There are further concerns about those final littoral stretches the cables need to bridge before they disappear into the hinterland.[15]

Concentrating many cables and their landings relatively closely together is also a weakness. Densely connected cable hubs – such as those along the United Kingdom's west coast, or in places like Singapore – and certain well-trodden cable routes can cluster multiple cables relatively closely together, making it easier to target multiple cables at the same time. Diversifying routes, however, comes with a price tag. They require additional surveying and route preparations, further investment in the land-based infrastructural backbone, and more. Also some of the near-shore security features put in place, which are meant to protect the network can actually make it easier to conduct cable-cutting operations at scale. One illustration of such a measure is the establishment of cable corridors, which are designated specific geographical bands in which undersea cables have a privileged status, and certain higher-risk maritime activities, such as fishing, face restrictions. Australia, in particular, has implemented these cable-first zones.[16] This kind of clustering helpfully reduces accidental damage to cables, but arguably also increases the damage potential of a targeted attack.

The network also faces the opposite issue: not having enough cables and redundancy in a specific place. While the network on the whole can be said to be rather resilient and enjoys a lot of duplication, some places are not well served. Outages in 'thin line' segments of the network, places like the Matsu and Shetland Islands and Tonga can generate global news headlines because their impact on local connectivity is so large – sometimes leaving these places disconnected for prolonged periods of time. Mounting geopolitical tensions can also worsen outcomes: as, for example, countries like the United States and China become more distrustful about relying on each other's mutual cables, this will also see the politically palatable level of redundancy in the network drop, as potential fallback options through which traffic can be rerouted can in practice not actually be called upon.

## Visibility, openness and availability

Another peace dividend legacy that threatens the resilience of the cable network is its relative visibility and the ease of finding and accessing it. The approximate locations of many cables are publicly known and detailed maps have long been made available to a panoply of stakeholders – from regulators, to environmental assessors, to fishermen. There are dedicated fora online of amateur cable hunters, who proudly post pictures and coordinates of their latest landing station discoveries (not infrequently accompanied by a conspicuous dose of big state conspiracy). The cable network is furthermore incredibly expansive, spanning more than 1.4 million kilometres. It is in practice simply not possible to protect the full web of cables at all times or to spot everyone who might be on the look-out for weak spots to potentially exploit. Part of the cable network's beauty is that it is so relatively open and relies on responsible use, cooperative maritime norms and lawful behaviour by all. That is, however, also an ideal easily exploited by bad actors.

Targeting the network is also not especially difficult. While it certainly would require more sophisticated solutions likely only available to the most advanced state actors to bring down large swathes of the network in a coordinated attack, especially if the target were cables laid at greater depths, a smaller operation in shallower waters is fairly simply to execute. The Baltic Sea is on average only around 50 metres deep,[17] well within the range of an anchor (contrast this with the greatest depths of the Atlantic, which can reach 4,000 metres). This leaves shallow seas and areas nearer to land vulnerable to the kind of anchor drag method discussed in the previous chapter. All one really needs is a ship, a willing crew, a rough idea of how cables may be routed and the daring-do to actually execute the act. Though we have, at the time of writing, not yet seen any non-state groups or smaller states successfully try to replicate purported sabotage acts in the Baltic Sea, High North and South China Sea, it is in my view only a matter of time before copycat actions are launched, now that the effectiveness of – and difficulty of attributing – these types of operations has been so clearly demonstrated. It is the democratization of the greyzone attack.

A similarly asymmetric tool to target cables through which smaller actors could potentially generate a lot of impact can be found in the cyber domain. While most of the attention when it comes to sabotage of cables has focused on kinetic methods to sever cables, the actual software and systems that are used to manage traffic flows through cables can also be a target. A thwarted attempt in 2022 to bring down subsea cables in Hawaii focused on trying to disrupt the cable owners' servers, for example.[18] Many of the software systems and networking tools used to manage cable traffic are applied by many companies throughout the telecommunications sector. Finding a weak spot in one of these systems could thus potentially do a lot more damage than physically taking out a cluster of cables.

## Repair and capacity chokepoints

We also see weaknesses in other links in the cable chain – weaknesses, which when exploited could significantly amplify the impact of a targeted attack on subsea cable infrastructure. The repair value chain is one such example. As we discussed in an earlier chapter, while the cable repair and maintenance system generally works well – industry has over the decades erected its own globe-spanning system, distributed cable repair capacity, and has thus managed to keep the number of faults stable, despite the rapid expansion of the network – it is starting to feel under strain. The cracks in the ageing repair ship fleet are beginning to show. Some areas that are less well served, are more fault-prone, or where governments are slow to issue permits can already expect to wait a long time to see their cable repaired: the longest fault repair wait time on recent record lasted nearly a thousand days.[19]

The resilience of the network is not just a function of the ability to repair cables, but also of the speed by which this can be done. This is not just a day-to-day risk, where a lack of investment and capacity, combined with exploding demand for new cables, may make repair times go up. It is also a dangerous vulnerability that could be weaponized as part of a larger-scale attack. It is one thing to cut several cables in one place. It is something else altogether to coordinate the disabling of cables in several dispersed places (in the North and Baltic Sea, further west into the Atlantic, perhaps even in the Mediterranean), if I so happened to want to sow disruption across Europe. This would leave the repair ships on call scrambling to reach all these places at once. If I were then also able to disrupt, or even entirely disable, the small number of repair ships available, restoring connectivity may become a very challenging prospect indeed. The sinking of its repair ships was, as we have seen, a challenge Britain faced during the Second World War, which forced it to rapidly try to convert ships to do the job.

There are more such chokepoints. Repairing cables quickly also necessitates having access to spare length of physical cable. Spare cable is similarly kept in a relatively small number of strategic spots dispersed across the planet. This also serves as a lack of redundancy in the system which could hypothetically be exploited to amplify the impact of an attack. We have an example of this kind of chokepoint manifesting itself inadvertently. The 2024 Francis Scott Key Bridge collapse in Baltimore, caused by a container ship accidentally hitting one of the bridge's piers, killed six and blocked shipping in and out of the Port of Baltimore for eleven weeks. Baltimore also so happens to be home to one of the most important cable depots on the US East Coast – a key resource which could now not be accessed.

While the cable value chain is generally able to withstand multiple faults at the same time, prodding some of these weak spots in the system could dramatically increase the impact of targeted attacks.[20]

## Sea blindness, lawlessness

What adds further vulnerability to the global cable network is the relatively paucity of rules that govern interference and sabotage of this key infrastructure. In yet another case of sea blindness, much of the existing rulebook governing damage to cables is old and, according to many legal experts, no longer up to scratch to address the current context.[21] The nature of much maritime law, which treats most of the High Seas as sitting outside of traditional geographical jurisdictions, furthermore means that bad actors are difficult to hold to account.

The levying of penalties and punishments on those who either deliberately or, far more frequently unintentionally, damage undersea cables has not evolved dramatically from the 1884 Convention for the Protection of Submarine Telegraph Cables,[22] one of the oldest international treaties still in use. Many of the relevant rules and stipulations in the treaty were carried over into UNCLOS, which also has its own limitations. This main framework governing maritime conduct includes only a handful of provisions directly relating to undersea cables and offers little in the way of actual actionable levers to enforce them.

Though treaties like UNCLOS prohibit the wilful damage of cables, when such incidents occur in international waters – which was the case for two out of three recent incidents in the Baltic Sea – their investigation and enforcement are largely left to the country whose flag the offending vessel was sailing under. If the ship in question is acting in the grey zone in furtherance of state interests, that is thus highly unlikely to result in any serious action taken against them. Ships, especially shadow fleet vessels, also frequently sail under so-called 'flags of convenience', managed by countries like Liberia, Panama, the Cook Islands (the one the *Eagle S* used) or even landlocked Mongolia. These countries typically offer lower costs, less regulation and enforcement as well as greater anonymity, allowing the ship's owners to avoid oversight from more stringent jurisdictions.[23] While several governments have made attempts to battle hybrid maritime activity, by more creatively reinterpreting UNCLOS in an effort to overcome these challenges (could these cable incidents be framed as acts of piracy? Threats to the natural environment?), in practice, unless sabotage takes place in a country's territorial waters, holding the culprits to account is frequently a legal dead-end. This combination of weak legal provisions, rather patchy enforcement and outdated rulebooks leaves undersea cables dangerously exposed.

## No playbooks, no red lines

Another weak spot in the network that has little to do with physical cables, but all the more with the legacy of peace dividend thinking, is the lack of defined action plans, processes and assigned responsibilities which would be needed to actually address a serious cable-related crisis. Though some governments are now trying to remedy this, in many regions no clear plan exists for who should do what during a major cable outage. Responsibility is fragmented across borders and agencies, different countries have different rulebooks, coordination between governments and industry remains patchy, and red lines remain ill-defined. This lack of clarity lends itself well to being exploited.

Undersea cables are by nature frequently cross-border, shared infrastructures, necessitating cooperation between countries to, for example, finance the hardening of physical aspects of a system, improve redundancy or facilitate repair. This can be a challenge. Different governments define the threat to cables differently.[24] Where a specific cable can be absolutely pivotal for the connectivity of one country, that same cable could be one of several dozen for another.

We can furthermore wonder how high the appetite for collaboration would be in a situation where a larger number of cables, in dispersed but strategic locations, are damaged at the same time. How do countries prioritize whose connectivity gets restored first and who gets access to finite repair resources? The ones who own the repair ships, or the navy most ready to protect them? Is there a plan in place to establish which cables are most immediately important, and what criteria should such decisions be based on? Will preference be given to cables owned by the well-resourced hyperscalers, or to the ones which serve most customers, or instead to those that ferry strategic and sensitive military and other government traffic? Do we even know which ones those are?

And then there is the matter of who to call in the eventuality of such a calamity. Because also within individual governments themselves the picture of who should be in charge of answering the questions we have just raised is frequently all but clear. Undersea cables are key digital infrastructures, which would suggest they fall under the purview of digital ministries. They are, however, also highly strategic assets and increasingly embroiled in geopolitical competition, demanding the attention of defence ministries, and those tasked with domestic security. There are cyber and interference concerns, which would mean that cyber agencies should have a voice, and then arguably the intelligence services as well. The maritime dimension to cables would bring in navies and coast guards, and departments of transportation.

And there is the pantheon of private sector actors who have a role to play in the protection of cables – from the cable owners, the large telecommunications and content providers, to those that lay and maintain cables, to the insurers and assorted other actors who may be impacted by an outage and involved with restoring connectivity. These companies may have access to the best capabilities and processes to rapidly repair cables, for example, but may not be best placed, or legally able, to do so in an active war zone. Collaboration between these varied private sector actors and governments has been rekindled, especially since the spate of cable incidents that have followed the start of the full-scale invasion of Ukraine, but many open questions remain about the roles and responsibilities each of these entities would have during a crisis situation.[25]

Some of this lack of clarity is already presenting itself in decisions that are being made today. There is a pressure on industry coming from militaries and governments to harden infrastructure, for example by burying cables at greater depths (arguably not the most cost-effective way of improving overall network resilience), and from industry to expand the repair fleet. In both of these cases, it is not evident who should be responsible for footing the bill. This uncertainty reflects a wider shift in the relationship between the private sector and government in an increasingly geopolitically volatile era, where militaries and industry increasingly have to find each other again.

## *Deterring Moscow, protecting the network*

Mounting concerns that these vulnerabilities in the cable network carry the potential to be exploited to disastrous effect, as well as perhaps a growing sense of unease among European publics that their governments did not seem particularly adept at deterring Russia, have led to a flurry of new initiatives to better protect the network. As we will see, these measures involve everything from the deployment of naval frigates and cutting-edge undersea drones patrolling the sea, to – more mundanely, but arguably most effective – renewed investment in increasing redundancy in the network.

The underlying strategy behind this new panoply of interventions can be seen as firstly focusing on reducing opportunity – making it both more difficult and less impactful to damage cables, whether that is through hardening systems (such as burying more segments of cables, even if further away from shore), or intercepting would-be culprits before they can complete their act. The second menu of options looks to impose a higher cost on said culprits, to hopefully deter repeat actions in the future. This cost for the Kremlin could get even higher: European governments are quietly also starting to wonder whether they themselves should not be becoming more entrepreneurial actors in the greyzone domain.

## Patrolling the seas

One way to deter bad actors from deliberately damaging undersea cables and other critical undersea infrastructure, such as power cables, oil pipelines and offshore wind farms, is to increase naval presence and monitor ships exhibiting odd behaviour or taking suspicious routes. This is something both NATO, as well as Taiwan,[26] have started to devote quite substantial resources to. In January 2025, NATO Secretary-General Mark Rutte launched a special mission coordinating these efforts, mere weeks after the *Eagle S* incident, which saw several northern European members of the alliance, from Germany to the Netherlands to affected Finland itself, deploy naval assets to the Baltic to patrol the seas and ward off any Russian shadow fleet members, confused research vessels and other such adventurers.[27]

Since the launch of Baltic Sentry, the handful of frigates zigzagging up and down European waters have not had much to do yet[28] – nearly a year into the operation's launch, no new suspicious cable incidents have taken place (whether that is thanks to increased NATO presence is hard to evidence either way).

Baltic Sentry has invited no small amount of scepticism about the utility and viability of monitoring a network as large as the global, or even just the Baltic, undersea cable network with only a handful of ships. That is arguably also not its aim. We should primarily see operations like Baltic Sentry as attempts to show resolve, as ways of signalling that NATO members, or other countries undertaking similar activities, are aware of Russia's tactics and are not going to let these incidents go unanswered. Or, in the words of Rutte:

> The Russians hate [Baltic Sentry]. They really hate it. So I love it. [The message here is:] 'Hey guys, you have all these merchant ships. They constantly lose their anchors, and then they have the anchor flap over the seabed for 100 miles. We might do a support mission into Russia to teach your commercial fleet how to sail those ships, because it seems to be very difficult for you guys if there is no other intention'.[29]

In the case of NATO, these naval activities are also intended to add heft and credibility to NATO's posture of 'deterrence by denial', whereby European allies aim to show Russia that the chances of success of any possible incursion into the Baltic countries and its nearby waters would be so low that they should not even begin to consider attempting it. Similarly, ensuring both populations and militaries are ready to withstand – or at least not spiral into mass panic about – a successful attack that does take out large swathes of connectivity, follows a similar logic: NATO is ready to respond, takes these kinds of incidents seriously, and cannot simply be pushed around by exploiting weaknesses in global internet infrastructure.

These attempts to bolster monitoring precede the current post-Baltic cable interest: in 2023 the UK government made the novel decision to invest £70 million in converting a former commercial vessel into a special ocean surveillance ship. The RFA *Proteus* has since its launch that same year been explicitly tasked with monitoring suspicious activities near important infrastructure out at sea and experimenting with new ways of surveilling the underwater environment. The vessel, for example, serves as a mothership for dedicated naval drones that aid it in these endeavours.[30]

Some years before that, in 2014, the UK similarly initiated the establishment of the Joint Expeditionary Force (JEF), a grouping of ten naval-minded countries bordering the North and Baltic Seas (traditional continental powers – like Germany and Poland – are not part of the group). The JEF, which can be seen as one of those mini-lateral European formats through which a steady Europeanization of NATO is taking place, has increasingly found its purpose in collaborating much more intensively to prevent further grey zone incursions in their shared waters.[31]

## Drones, drones, drones

To add further credibility to this deterrence posture, and improve the alliance's ability to actually monitor the seas, NATO, as well as many other militaries and governments, from Taiwan to Australia to the United States and Japan, are turning to new technology as a possible cure: undersea drones.

Aerial drones are, according to many military analysts and decision-makers, in the process of revolutionizing the battlefield and altering the very fabric and character of modern warfare. The war in Ukraine, where an estimated 80 per cent of frontline battlefield casualties in 2025 were the result of drone fire,[32] has shown how especially small, low-cost drones can be incredibly powerful force multipliers – and risk leaving large military platforms sitting ducks. It is therefore no surprise that, in a bid to rapidly rebuild their eroded military capacities, European militaries are increasingly looking at unmanned aerial vehicles (UAVs) to solve their triple conundrum of not having enough troops, not having enough money and not having enough time. But drones do not necessarily have to fly.

This interest in drones is increasingly moving into the naval domain as well.[33] Ukraine's clever and highly innovative use of mostly self-developed naval drones has played no small role in allowing the country to match the mighty Russian navy in the Black Sea, while not possessing any traditional naval assets of its own.[34] By using special surface drones, essentially remote-controlled small boats rigged with explosives, which operate in wolf-pack-like patterns, Ukraine has been able to sink a surprising number of Russian naval vessels, and open up the Black Sea for trade. When Secretary-General Rutte announced Baltic Sentry, he also pointed to the importance of the deployment of drones in this operation – both to increase range, as well as an opportunity for the alliance to test these capabilities. NATO is for example experimenting with the use of drones to hover near suspicious ships, where they are used to monitor what is happening on deck, or to communicate directly with the vessel's crew.[35] More novel, and especially complicated, are drones that can operate underwater. One of the reasons why submarines have played such a key role in great power competition since the twentieth century is the degree of stealth that is offered by the opaque deep sea. It is simply very difficult to monitor and make visible things that happen underwater.

Cracking the puzzle of drones, or so-called unmanned underwater vehicles (UUVs) that can monitor underwater, are often presented as the next frontier. Such underwater drones could potentially revolutionize not just the underwater environment but the military balance of power more generally – making it, for example, much more difficult for submarines to operate unnoticed (a key pillar in most nuclear powers' strategies and arsenals). Designing drones that can operate underwater, however, is a lot more challenging than it is to build drones that operate in the air. It is not just that visibility is lower, but it is also far more difficult for the devices to maintain underwater connections and signals, making operating them remotely difficult. To help crack this challenge, many militaries and private investors are now pouring significant amounts of funding into startups that are engineering new kinds of subsea robots and submersibles – a business case that is only becoming stronger, as threats on the seabed increase.

## A data panopticon

But there are more ways the maritime domain can be made more visible. This is why, under the auspices of the Joint Expeditionary Force, northern European countries have now launched operation Nordic Warden,[36] which has the ambition of creating a naval panopticon of sorts that will provide far more visibility over the goings-on in the JEF countries' shared waters, and use AI to actually spot and zero in on potentially suspicious actors that may require attention *before* they can commit their act.

Despite the vastness of our seas and oceans, in very well-trafficked and actively used segments, such as the Baltic Sea and North Sea, there is actually quite a lot of data being collected about what goes on. Vessels traversing these waterways have their own transponders – or automatic identification system (AIS) – which intermittently ping their GPS locations, data which is made publicly available. While it is possible for vessels to turn these transponders off – fishing vessels are known to do this, for example, in order not to give away their good fishing spots, the *Newnew Polar Bear*,

*Yi Peng 3* and *Eagle S* each had theirs turned on. Private sector companies, from offshore wind farms to oil rigs, collect significant amounts of data of their own, and will often have quite a lot of visibility of what is taking place in their infrastructures' direct proximity. Commercial satellite companies monitor vessel movements and other maritime activity. Navies have radar and other data. Port authorities maintain logs about who and what comes in and moves out. Some of these data are publicly available – which is why a lot of the culprit ships involved with the Baltic incidents had already been successfully identified by open source sleuths online – who had been able to match their locations with the timing of the breaks – before they were publicly earmarked as vessels of interest by the authorities.[37]

The problem is therefore less the availability of data, but fusing it all together to paint a useful picture. The private sector keeps a lot of its proprietary data close to its chest. Other sources are rather scattered across different jurisdictions – meaning that if a specific ship is seen suspiciously loitering in one country's territorial waters, that information is frequently not shared with other coast guards, who could have continued to monitor a ship as it traverses their waters next. And that presumes that there are processes in place to act on such information to begin with. This is the kind of thing the JEF coalition, as well as the EU and NATO, are now seeking to resolve.

## Invisibility

While, on the one hand, we see a push to gain more visibility of the activities out at sea, we witness a parallel dynamic where governments are becoming increasingly intent on hiding from view the cables themselves.[38] This can take the form of literally 'hiding' the cables – burying them at greater depths, for example – but this is also increasingly focusing on invisibility in a more figurative sense. For decades, the cable industry has been working hard to better inform fishermen and other frequent cable snaggers about how to avoid dropping their anchors and fishing equipment in the wrong place. These efforts can be as practical as representatives going around in ports and harbours handing out USB sticks with the latest cable maps – far more precise ones than the ones we can find online – to captains and their crews. Some governments are becoming uneasy about this practice, and are now even pre-emptively removing their own data from some of these maps and data platforms, so as not to give away valuable information to potential wrong-doers (in practice, the proverbial cat is arguably already out of the bag on that one – many of these maps have been available for decades). It is a dynamic reminiscent of the Cold War, when protecting cables from far rarer but potentially more impactful deliberate sabotage also started to trump concerns about the day-to-day resilience of the network. The renewed onus on burying and bolstering of cables could similarly be seen as an attempt to once again hide cables from public view.

## Redundancy and building more slack

All of these interventions are intended to better protect the existing network and individual cables – or to deter hostile actors from targeting them. In the end, however, it is simply not possible to protect the full network at all times. It is too large, cables are too exposed, and the ways by which one might target cables are too accessible and broad. The single best solution to improving the resilience of the network, whether it is against incompetent crews, those pretending to be incompetent crews, natural hazards or genuine accidents, however, therefore remains building more redundancy into networks. It may not be the most glamorous solution or one that signals the most geopolitical muscle, but the reason why connectivity was able to withstand the recent – or frankly any – outages so well is the fact that there is sufficient duplication in the network, and an industry apparatus that keeps the network running smoothly (this is not universally the case of course; recall the troubles in the Pacific, West Africa and East Asia).

Governments are increasingly recognizing the value of these kinds of investments into improving redundancy. From Europe to the Indo-Pacific, significant investments are now being made into new cables wiring up underconnected locations and patching gaps in the network.[39] Some are now supporting new repair ships – the US Congress in 2024 commissioned two.[40] The European Commission is mulling doing the same. In this example, we once again see an example of questions of security and resilience, especially during a crisis, outweighing commercial concerns. The cable industry in Europe has become so good and efficient at reducing faults and repairing cables speedily, that the business case for keeping the current number of cable repair ships on call is becoming difficult to sustain – with industry rumblings it may be reduced. The ships simply have too little to do. Reducing the repair fleet would, however, leave even less slack during a crisis.

In another Cold War parallel, there is also a growing interest once more in alternative technologies that may be able to serve as a back-up to – in this case – cables. A hunt for modal redundancy once more. While the satellite, as we have seen, gave way to cables throughout the 1990s, new systems such as Elon Musk's Starlink may provide a powerful source of backup connectivity during a crisis, among other uses. Taiwan has been actively exploring whether it could rely on new satellite tech to serve as a fallback option during a possible invasion. NATO has been investing in a programme called NATO HEIST, a satellite-based system which would help keep different parts of the military connected during a widespread outage.[41] While satellites are nowhere near able to replace cables when it comes to both capacity and latency, new space-based challengers may likely see their role in global connectivity grow in years ahead. We will discuss this in some detail in chapter 9.

## A whole-of-society approach

None of these interventions will matter much if countries do not have access to the people and processes to make them work. An especially critical way of bringing more resilience into the network is by better readying societies and economies for a more geopolitically volatile world. This means dusting off some of the old Cold War playbooks for how to respond to a crisis, but also fundamentally rethinking the role citizens and the private sector play in defending the nation.

The private sector – not just the cable industry – in Europe and elsewhere is frequently still operating through a lens of peace dividend thinking. It is however the private sector that now owns many of the most critical infrastructures needed to keep a country functioning during a crisis – from power plants and electricity grids, to ports and airports, to food distribution and supply chains, to telecommunications systems. Places like the Port of Rotterdam, as Europe's largest port particularly central as a receiving hub for transatlantic NATO reinforcements from, for example, the United States, are already preparing for all sorts of different disruptions and chaos that may come its way in the lead-up to a conflict. In a world of hybrid escalations and potential all-out war – especially one empowered by relatively cheap, ubiquitous but increasingly powerful drones – other private sector actors should similarly expect to be targeted and be thinking about their own contingency planning.

In the cable sphere, there is a need for more practical thinking about the role industry can play during a major outage, and how to proactively prepare for such an eventuality. While it is not very likely that Russia or other actors could cut *all* transatlantic cables – there are too many of them, and they are too dispersed (though I have heard some quiet mumblings that they certainly are not everywhere) – even severing some of the higher capacity systems could already cause real disruption. What would be some of the measures that could be taken to reduce this impact? Some of this could be quite practical and simple. Since it is becoming prohibitively costly in certain geographies to keep the kind of peacetime slack in the repair system in preparation of a possible conflict, the cable industry and navies could work together to train up navy staff to be able to complete cable repairs – a resource that could be called upon in time of war. Trained cable staff, in turn, could sign up to be reservists. Both of these solutions could also help reduce the current challenge of the private sector not being particularly well-equipped – legally or technically – to undertake cable repairs in an active war zone.

The response of the general public matters too. Populations need to be prepared not to react in panic if a disruption does occur. Local access to digital services is unlikely to disappear entirely (most global data stay close to home; though targeting local data centres in tandem may undermine this), but some services will stop working during a cable-cutting outage. Governments in Europe should start to think about how they can best prepare households in taking the kinds of proactive steps they can now take to prepare themselves that are not contingent on access to the internet or other key technologies (do we know the way to the local hospital without GPS?). Countries like Sweden and Finland, until recently non-NATO members (meaning peace dividend thinking never became as pervasive) have long lived with the very real and present danger of a belligerent Russia, have long prepared to mobilize their societies, and can serve as an example.

## Apprehending culprit ships

One reason why some of these hybrid incidents, whether those involving cables or a wider cyber and kinetic sabotage playbook, continue to proliferate and escalate is because the culprits have largely been allowed to get away with it. Governments have been hesitant to publicly attribute responsibility for many of these incidents, because of the difficulty that comes with offering definite proof as well as concerns about escalation. Suspicious ships have been allowed to continue their journeys unimpeded and shadow fleet ships still freely traverse international waters. Financial redress for cable owners is often limited and difficult to obtain, even in cases of genuinely accidental damage.

This may be changing. Countries at the receiving end of increasingly brazen maritime incidents are starting to respond more forcefully, so as to hopefully deter future repeats. Some of this involves more open political attribution, such as Britain's Minister of Defence publicly calling out the actions of the *Yantar*. Some of this is more direct. The shadow fleet especially is facing more scrutiny. From 2023 onwards, G7 countries and partners like the European Union, Australia and South Korea have turned to more conventional tools by adding a growing cadre of shadow fleet ships to their sanction lists,[42] but to little avail: the vast majority of these ships remain able to navigate the seas and tout their wares relatively unfettered, now by some estimates facilitating 83 per cent of Russia's crude oil exports, a vital asset in fuelling Moscow's war machine.[43] Since then, responses have been kicked up a notch, in part motivated by the cable incidents in the Baltic Sea. With each successive incident, Baltic-adjacent countries have become bolder in their responses. The *Newnew Polar Bear* was allowed to leave without ever facing up to a European naval or coast guard vessel at all. The *Yi Peng 3* was monitored for some time, but neither the ship nor its crew was ever apprehended. The *Eagle S* was intercepted, and even nudged to enter Finnish territorial waters – an action not strictly in violation of UNCLOS, but certainly skirting the edges of the norms that have traditionally governed the maritime domain. Since then, Taiwan – closely watching its partners in Europe no doubt – was able to prevent an alleged cable-cutting incident in its waters, and arrested the captain involved.[44] Others are also raising the temperature even further. The German government in July 2025 announced it would stop suspected shadow fleet ships traversing the waters of NATO members, and demand to see their insurance cover – a lack of insurance is a frequent feature of dark fleet vessels.[45] Estonia was that summer even mulling changing its laws so that it would be allowed to sink Russian ships that threaten undersea cables.[46] The Americans boarded and seized two Russian-flagged vessels carrying Venezuelan oil in the early weeks of January 2026, one in the GIUK gap, the other in the Caribbean Sea – actions inviting the political ire (but little tangible action) from Moscow.[47] The French intercepted a sanctioned Russian oil tanker in the Mediterranean Sea several weeks later. None of these ships was necessarily in the sabotage trade, but these actions nonetheless signalled a noteworthy departure from the previous approach to Moscow's maritime mayhem.

One trade-off involved with taking more aggressive action is that it frequently skirts if not fully violates international law in its own right – meaning that it is the countries at the receiving end of Russia's hybrid actions that are now arguably also starting to operate in the grey zone themselves. In a bid to try and improve maritime security, otherwise law-abiding countries can now feel forced to undermine freedom of navigation and other pillars of maritime norms and law. It is a devil's dilemma: do not take action and allow these increasingly brazen violations of international norms to continue largely unchallenged, and even further escalate; do take action, and risk playing into Moscow's hands by violating some of the same norms and rules that underpin the rules-based order the Kremlin has been so aggressively trying to undermine.

## Striking back

Another, even more controversial, option would be returning the favour. As the Russian Federation escalates its greyzone attacks across Europe, some wonder why not strike back? Ukraine, naturally not shackled by the same (semi-) peacetime constraints its European peers are under, has certainly been active on this front. From drones targeting oil refineries and even the Kremlin, to the highly public assassinations of senior generals in central Moscow (competing for headcount with defenestrations), Kyiv has mounted a great many audacious intelligence plots on Russian soil. The spectacular Operation Spider's Web, a June 2025 operation during which Ukraine smuggled commercial drones rigged with explosives deep into Russia and used them to destroy parts of its highly strategic bomber fleet, is considered the crowning achievement.[48] Whether Western intelligence services played any role in any of these activities remains unknown, though some of these incidents have prompted private – and not so private – whispers about at least some Western involvement.

Should European Union member states become more open to deploying such tactics themselves? Should French and Polish intelligence be in the business of blowing up Russian drone factories or cut Russia's submarine cables (or are they perhaps already doing so? Recall the mystery of the cut cable connecting Kaliningrad discussed in the previous chapter). Switch to offensive cyber attacks? Could Europeans take a leaf out of the Kremlin's own playbook and wage disruptive misinformation campaigns in Russia itself – sow concerns about Chinese designs on its lost lands in Siberia, or the imminent fall of the Putin regime?

The answer is not easy. The same dilemma persists: do Europeans start to erode norms simply because others are doing so? Escalation between two nuclear-armed blocs remains a serious risk. And then there is the question of who would be running these operations: covert sabotage operations often require agents on the ground, who would be risking their lives. This is a risk Ukraine – given the existential challenge the country is facing – may be willing to take, but a harder sell in the rest of Europe. Yet some argue that a more geopolitically unshackled Europe, particularly one more actively shaped by the Russia hawks on its eastern flank, may be increasingly willing to let go of such restraint.

Cable sabotage is arguably the most visceral, visible way in which we see the undersea cable network being weaponized. Especially the risk of significant segments of global connectivity being throttled in a war-time scenario is one that demands a more concerted response by governments and militaries alike. Cases of greyzone sabotage, as the incidents in the Baltic Sea and targeting the Matsu Islands may well have been, should in the end, however, be seen as a 'weapons of the weak'. Countries like Russia are willing to engage in these kinds of activities as they have little reputation to lose in the existing global order and are relatively disconnected from the global cable network, making it harder for others to retaliate. Less discussed, but arguably far more powerful, however, are ways in which cables can be weaponized by those actually at the centre of the network. Let us move on to spying.

## *Interfering with cables*

In chapter 1, we briefly discussed Operation Ivy Bells, a daring Cold War operation, which saw an American submarine enter the Soviet-controlled Sea of Okhotsk, off the coast of Siberia, and plant a listening device on a key coaxial cable used by the Soviet Union's Pacific Fleet – an extremely high-risk operation, which required US crews repeatedly entering the USSR's territorial waters (recordings from the wire taps placed on the cables had to be physically retrieved on a regular basis).[49] Ivy Bells was an obvious operational success – the operation ran from 1971 to 1980 and may have continued for much longer, if it were not for Ronald Pelton, a former NSA operative and defector to the Soviet Union, selling Moscow details of the programme.[50] It is also an example of how, in bifurcated systems, the mechanisms through which one can derive strategic value from submarine cable networks can be more limited. Where Britain had been able to rely on its network centrality to listen in on German conversations as they arrived on its doorstep, wiretapping the Soviets required high-risk spy gambits.

Much of the technical detail behind Ivy Bells remains classified. It is, however, generally believed that cables today cannot be interfered with in the same way that they used to be during the Cold War – or at least, not by directly tapping the cables themselves. During the Cold War it had still been possible to place listening devices on old coaxial (copper-core) cables, and remain undetected, as the Ivy Bells example illustrates. Many experts believe that repeating the feat today with modern ultrasensitive fibre optic cables would be almost impossible.[51] Manipulation of the light that travels through the hair-thin fibres would be noticed at the receiving end, or cause noticeable interference. Tapping a cable would require 'bending' light as it moves through the fibre, which would likely cause signal loss or noise that would probably be picked up by network operators. If there are ways to bypass this challenge – there are suggestions it may be possible to insert extraction devices into repeaters, to name one example[52] – they are not reported on in the public domain (though we would of course expect that any entrepreneurial intelligence agency which had been able to crack this puzzle would have little incentive to go around and advertise it). And even if there was currently a government or non-state actor able to reliably overcome this fibre optic tapping challenge, they would soon run into a second complication, which is the nature of the traffic funnelled through modern-day undersea cables.

The sheer volumes of data that travel through even smaller capacity systems are now so unfathomably large,[53] and traffic routed through them follow such unpredictable paths, that attempting to intercept highly specific national security data would be like searching for a needle in a haystack. Compounding the challenge is the fact that much of the most sensitive and therefore in all likelihood most-coveted data intelligence agencies would be after is likely to be encrypted, using methods far more sophisticated than Wilhelmine Germany's printed codebooks, and as such virtually uncrackable – at least when intercepted *en route*. Some hypothesized future technological breakthroughs in, for example, the quantum computing domain could in theory make it possible to crack some of the encryption methods the current internet and banking systems are built on. However, the kind of technological breakthroughs potentially enabling this are seemingly still far off, and especially quantum solutions that can be deployed to decrypt data at scale may well never materialize. Nevertheless, many security experts and governments speculate that intelligence agencies and criminal groups are engaging in so-called 'hack now, decrypt later' operations – storing sensitive encrypted data covertly gathered today, with the view to decrypt them once the technology to do so becomes available.[54] If they are doing so, or attempting to gather any other data routed through cables, it is generally believed this would be taking place at landing sites or further up the land-based bits of cable and network systems. Data collection of this kind would likely also involve the cable owner's consent (so called 'intercept partners', to use Snowden-era parlance). Possible technical backdoors built directly into cables are another possibility.[55]

Whatever the mechanics or method, the United States certainly does believe that it is possible to interfere with traffic that goes through cables, and that China may have become particularly adept at tapping sensitive communications in this way.[56] This would be most easily done by intercepting traffic at the end point – at landing stations, at the network side. But the US security community also speculates that China may indeed be able to insert backdoors or surveillance equipment into cables as part of the cable manufacturing and laying process, or place triggers that could disrupt traffic at some opportune future moment.

These kinds of concerns also raise urgent questions about the implications of Beijing's growing centrality in global technology stacks and supply chains. Washington has been asking them: starting in the late 2010s, the US has become increasingly forceful in warning about what it perceives to be China's insidious presence in communications hardware – including submarine cables.[57]

## *Through the PRISM*

A more cynical interlocutor – and China is certainly one[58] – may throw back at Washington that it takes one to know one. It is well known that the United States and its Five Eyes partners in the past have made, and may well still continue to make, extensive use of 'cable tapping'. It was the 2013 revelations by NSA contractor Edward Snowden that made clear the sheer extent to which the United States and its allies engaged in these types of activities, which – in many cases – also involved the direct interception of fibre optic cable traffic.

The NSA, Snowden revealed, through operations like UPSTREAM, had been able to tap into terrestrial cables in transit – activities condoned by the large telecommunications operators they worked with. Some of these activities also involved undersea cables. Britain's signals intelligence agency GCHQ, through its operation TEMPORA, is believed to have been even more prolific in its bulk collection efforts, enabled by Britain's permissive legal regime and the many cables landing on British shores – reinforcing once again how network power can become permanently embedded in physical geographies (Bude and the Cornish coast were key locations for intercepts).[59] TEMPORA, which relied on Britain's domestic telecom operators being legally compelled to play ball and keep quiet about their involvement, worked by installing interception devices directly at cable landing stations (so not out at sea) – which enabled the agencies to access and scan tens of billions of data points every single day.

Bulk collection as such thus relied on being central in the network. Many of the targets for surveillance undertaken under the banner of the War on Terror – the tracking of potential terrorists was the prime reason for which this surveillance edifice was ultimately primarily erected – were based in places whose data would at some point likely traverse a Five Eyes country. When it comes to monitoring China and Russia, the Five

Eyes are less able to rely on the centrality of their own landing stations as conduits. Both China and Russia have far more closed-off internet loops – with the kind of traffic that might be strategically important to the United States, in particular, presumably far less likely to leave their own respective borders.

Another difficulty that comes with cable tapping is the possible consequences when such operations become known. Just like with Ivy Bells, it was ultimately a whistleblower who made public the sheer extent of America's spying activities, which resulted in not-insignificant global outcry and blowback. The Snowden revelations would not only cause an especially awkward diplomatic fallout with many of its allies (spying on your allies' leaders' private cell phone communications tends to be frowned upon – a fate that befell both Germany's Angela Merkel and Brazil's Dilma Rousseff, among others) but also hand the US's adversaries a powerful moral card to play in future (who was Washington to accuse others of interfering with their traffic?).

The Snowden revelations would also impact the subsea cable network's topology, and in some modest ways began to chip away at America's centrality in it. In 2013, an incensed Dilma Rousseff, then president of Brazil, signed an agreement with the European Commission to lay a new cable, the EllaLink, directly linking Portugal with Brazil, in an explicit effort to bypass the United States.[60] Previously, the vast share of traffic between Europe and South America had been routed through the United States; the completion of the EllaLink cable in 2021 thus reduced the United States' ability to act as a conduit for this intercontinental exchange. Taking stock, a decade after the Snowden revelations, their impact on America's network centrality has, however, overall, arguably been quite limited because of the changing nature of power in the communications realm. Because while the United States may be less geographically central as the network has grown, American companies have only become more dominant across most layers of the internet stack.

## *The ghost in the machine*

American concerns about the susceptibility of digital and data infrastructure to interference go back some time, and did not immediately focus on undersea cables specifically. But they did immediately zero in on Huawei, the Chinese telecoms and technology giant, which from the 2010s onwards has been at the heart of Washington's fixation on the perils of China's technological rise, and the geostrategic agenda that may be driving it. Huawei's maritime arm (since sold off and rebranded HMN Tech, in part because of mounting US pressure) emerged as a major player in the cable sphere some time ago, but it was its rapidly growing footprint in 5G infrastructure roll-out that first invited America's scrutiny. 5G is a catch-all name for next-generation cellular technology and standards which promises (and is already delivering) ubiquitous, very fast and low-latency connectivity that would make possible visions for a far more hyperconnected physical environment.

Any country with serious digital and tech ambitions, i.e. most industrialized and emerging economies, wanted to adopt 5G as rapidly as they could – especially in urban environments. Huawei, as one of the telecommunications equipment market leaders and frequently by far the cheapest option, would be one of the companies at the heart of this infrastructure roll-out: its base stations, routers, and antennas in many places formed the physical backbone underpinning the transition to 5G, and thus promised to become a conduit of the data generated by hundreds of million if not billions of people. This, the fear was, would not only afford Beijing – many in Washington consider Huawei to be an extension of Chinese state power – a lot of control over a key global infrastructure, but would also offer it the opportunity to build potential backdoors into the technology, vulnerabilities which would allow Chinese intelligence to either snoop on or, should it ever wish, even sabotage systems.[61]

So, the United States set out to remove Huawei hardware from its own systems. Soon, this ambition started to focus on its allies too, because sensitive traffic being intercepted in Europe, or in a Five Eyes partner, could quite directly impact America too. Getting all of its partners on board with weeding out Huawei was no easy task, however. One significantly complicating factor was that many countries – including the United States itself – had already invested many billions in rolling out Huawei-made 5G infrastructure, which would effectively now all need to be ripped out and replaced with more expensive alternatives. Another key difficulty was that the United States had no real alternative provider of its own to offer: Huawei's only serious competitors were the European Ericsson and Nokia, considered trustworthy but also expensive, and as non-American companies less directly aligned with Washington's strategic agenda. Here, the US decision, in the wake of the bursting of the dot-com infrastructure bubble, to walk away from what it perceived to be low-margin, low-prestige industries reared its head. Peace dividend thinking had once again resulted in a long-term geopolitical and security vulnerability.

Ripping out and replacing 5G infrastructure that had already been deployed was not only a costly proposition (the estimated cost for Germany alone is around €2.5 billion) but one with quite serious strategic and competitive implications too.[62] Replacing existing infrastructure meant falling behind in the 5G roll-out race, not a welcome prospect especially in European countries, which saw the rapid adoption of 5G as an opportunity to catch up in the digital economy (indeed, many still lag on the 5G front, in part because of the Huawei debate. Trying to access mobile internet in central London these days illustrates that rather viscerally). The push to remove Huawei therefore frequently involved no small bit of diplomatic wrangling, and even coercion to get others to do its bidding (the US allegedly threatened to suspend the UK from Five Eyes intelligence sharing if Huawei remained embedded in its networks).[63] Ultimately Washington's crusade largely succeeded: many of America's key allies across the world have now removed or are committed to removing Huawei from their technology stack. Its wider vendetta against the company has furthermore effectively made it untouchable in most Western markets – at least where critical infrastructure is concerned. Also its consumer-focused smartphones and other hardware have seen their market shares in the West plummet (something it has increasingly been able to make up for in many markets in the Global South, as we will discuss in the next chapter). Washington's ability to influence and steer its large web of global allies once again proved itself an incredibly effective power lever.

## *Team Telecom*

It did not stop with just 5G. In 2020, the first Trump Administration launched the Clean Network Initiative, in an expanded and more formalized effort to exclude Chinese technology companies from global telecommunications and digital infrastructure more generally. Framed as a banner national security effort, the Clean Network sought to prevent companies like Huawei not just from gaining a foothold in 5G networks, but also in other slices of the tech stack, from cloud services, to mobile apps to, indeed, submarine cable systems ('clean cables', if you will).

In the cable sphere, the administration found itself with effective tools to act on this ambition to 'cleanse' the network. In earlier chapters we looked at how the United States, working together with Australia, focused on countering Chinese Belt and Road investment in cable roll-out, for example in the Solomon Islands, by countering such initiatives with its own or its allies' alternative projects. The United States used similar tactics in 2023 to see HMN Tech ousted from the development of the SeaMeWe-6 cable system, a major new cable connecting Singapore to France, which saw its own national champion SubCom take the Chinese company's place.[64] The US approach to accomplishing this diplomatic feat combined both carrot and stick. It reportedly offered co-financing to see SubCom secure the $600 million contract to lay the cable and provided a further arsenal of 'sweeteners' to the more China-minded intermediary cable landing spots along the way. Washington, however, reportedly also made it abundantly clear that if the project *were* to move ahead with this significant Chinese footprint (this was not just about HMN Tech laying the cable, several large Chinese telecommunications companies owned shares in the project), the cable's other owners may well find themselves subject to future licensing, sanctions and national security scrutiny and other threats to its commercial operations. The strategy worked: others budged, and SubCom soon replaced HMN Tech. This switcheroo, no doubt to Washington's delight, saw the other Chinese companies involved with the project walk away from SeaMeWe-6 too, pressured to do so by Beijing. Washington does not like HMN Tech cables; Beijing, in turn, does not want to see strategic Chinese communications ferried through SubCom-led projects.[65]

The US toolbox is not just about cable diplomacy, however. The United States now also regularly uses its ability to veto the laying of cables involving landings on its soil as a potent tool in this cable competition. Here, it is exploiting its regulatory heft, global reach and the extraterritorial power of its technology firms to redraw the map of the global network. Key to this strategy is the clever deployment of 'Team

Telecom', a once sleepy committee tasked with assessing the security risks associated with new cable projects, which now suddenly showed itself to be a useful tool. Any new subsea cable that touches US territory must receive approval from the grouping; given the large share of cables that now involve hyperscaler investments – many of which touch the US at some point – that is now very many of them. The committee has used this leverage to block cable projects that might route data through China or jurisdictions it deems to be too cosy with Beijing, citing national security risks and foreign ownership concerns.

Team Telecom's first major scalp came in 2020, when it partially denied a licence to the Pacific Light Cable Network (PLCN) cable, an ambitious cable project originally designed to connect the US West Coast directly to Hong Kong, which had received significant investments from Meta (then still Facebook) and Google.[66] Hong Kong had traditionally been a stronghold for new cable landings, but that role came under scrutiny when the city state implemented its highly controversial National Security Law, which effectively gave Chinese authorities the ability to gain access to sensitive data passing through Hong Kong, and meant a very serious revision to the idea of a 'one country, two systems', which had allowed Hong Kong to be perceived as a relatively neutral and independent conduit into China.

Team Telecom's decision forced the cable consortium back to the drawing board; the PLCN was eventually completed in 2022, but now no longer landed in Hong Kong. The other proposed segments and landings of the cable – in the Philippines and Taiwan – had instead been approved.[67] The physical cable used for the leg of the project between Taiwan and Hong Kong, which had already been nearly completed by the time Team Telecom's 'nay' arrived, was left lying dormant on the seabed. Team Telecom's decision would not just put a stop to the PLCN cable landing in Hong Kong, it also effectively heralded in the end of Hong Kong as a significant physical cable landing spot for non-Chinese cables. Once one of Asia's cable hub darlings, it has seen itself rapidly being replaced by new, less geopolitically risky challengers, such as the Philippines, Singapore or Indonesia. This combination of Team Telecom and hyperscalers' global influence shows America's networked power in action. Because in many cases, the committee now no longer needs to be involved in decisions to reroute and diversify away cables from China at all. Investors – not wanting to run the risk of seeing their projects delayed, denied or later abandoned, or worse yet, see themselves blocked from working with US companies in future – are proactively diversifying away to new, geopolitically less sensitive locations in Asia in their selection of landing sites.

Not all of Team Telecom's decisions necessarily involve China-linked landing stations directly. Another example was Team Telecom's 2022 decision to deny a licence to the ARCOS-1 cable system, which would have been the first direct cable connection between Cuba and the United States. Though the committee stressed the importance of Cubans gaining access to the global internet, it was concerned about the Cuban government's high degree of control over the state-owned company that would own and operate the cable, as well as its intimate relationship with both the Chinese and Russian governments – which, the committee feared, could see sensitive data on US citizens make its way to Beijing or Moscow.

### *Securitizing cables across the value chain*

These Clean Network efforts are no longer just limited to preventing the laying of new cables landing on US shores that involve Chinese companies, or those that make landfall in China or Hong Kong. Especially under the Biden Administration, weeding China out of the cable network increasingly meant reducing Chinese influence across other links in the cable value chain too, such as the cable repair process or cable manufacturing.

US intelligence services have issued repeated warnings – trying to convince the hyperscalers, senior White House officials, America's allies – that strategically important cables – or better yet any cables – should not be repaired by Chinese ships, warning that their hoisting up would offer CCP-friendly crews an opportunity to place hacking devices or manipulate the cables in such ways their traffic could be interfered with.[68]

These warnings have in particular zeroed in on Sino-British repair services provider S.B. Submarine Systems (SBSS), one of the most important repair providers in the region. According to insider sources reported by the *Wall Street Journal* in 2024, SBSS repair ships have been spotted turning off their transponders in strategically significant positions near Taiwan.[69] The company is furthermore majority-owned by

China Telecom, also a company *non grata* as far as the US government is concerned.[70] Given the nature of the global repair model – which relies on a small patchwork of distributed repair vessels – no longer working with Chinese providers can present a significant resilience challenge for cable owners, especially in Asia, where waiting times are already long. Let us, for example, consider the expansive, fault-prone Yokohama repair zone, which covers a large area in East Asia and relies on one Chinese, one South Korean and one Japanese repair ship. Taking Chinese ships out of the equation reduces capacity by one third – and may significantly slow down repair timelines in an already overstretched but vital region for cable connectivity. Here we once again see the trade-off between day-to-day resilience and national security manifest itself. Similar debates exist around rerouting traffic: if a number of major cables face an outage, how comfortable are the two sides about allowing data to flow through the other's cables? Increasingly less so, as it turns out.

Washington has also turned to yet another form of regulatory muscle-flexing, not the use of its own decision-making bodies this time, but through its continued strength in international governance processes and its ability to rely on its large web of allies (under the Biden Administration at least). One such example was its leading role in the development of the *Joint Statement on the Security and Resilience of Undersea Cables in a Globally Digitalized World*. The Statement, or New York Principles for short, which – as the name suggests – articulates a number of principles for improving the resilience of the global network, was initially signed by thirty countries, on the margins of the 2024 United Nations General Assembly.[71] Though the Statement never singles out Russia or China explicitly, it does specifically call on countries to only work with 'trusted vendors'. To the careful reader, this was a not so subtle nod to the (lack of) trustworthiness of Chinese cable providers. Beijing certainly interpreted it as such, with Foreign Ministry spokesperson Lin Jian stating that 'China firmly opposes the US' unilateral and hegemonic moves to turn undersea cables into a political and security issue'.[72] Though the Principles does not hold any legal weight, it shows how the United States increasingly exports security concerns about Chinese tech abroad.

In July 2025, the FCC, the United States' telecommunications regulator, announced it intends to drive its Clean Cables efforts up a further notch, with Trump's FCC chair Brendan Carr announcing the regulator was in the process of developing new rules that would allow it to ban any Chinese technology from making it into any US-owned cable projects at all – regardless of whether these cables would ever make landfall in or near Mainland China or the United States.[73] A noteworthy detail in the statement was its emphasis on securing and unleashing America's leadership in artificial intelligence – once again showcasing how the country's fixation on winning the AI race is increasingly securitizing the wider digital infrastructure stack.

## *A success?*

The Clean Network[74] programme, which was the Trump Administration's effort to root China out of digital networks, the reinvention of Team Telecom at the vanguard of these activities, and several of the programmes such as the Biden-era Blue Dot programme aimed at strategic infrastructure roll-out, should be seen as part of a multi-pronged strategy by which Washington sought to combine cable diplomacy, economic coercion and the power of its tech industry to limit the reach of China's cable companies. These efforts, which often involved some not too gentle encouragement of third parties, whether it was America's allies or intended cable recipients in the Global South, to do Washington's bidding, have so far borne some fruit.

They have certainly made the lives of executives at Huawei, HMN Tech and other targeted companies a lot more difficult since the late 2010s. A company like Huawei saw its revenues drop by 29 per cent in 2021, in large part due to US pressure, and its sales in most of the West nosedive.[75] In part because of this relentless pressure, it sold off its stake in its cable arm, Huawei Marine, to the Hentong Group in 2020. The company's rebrand to HMN Tech harkens back to its Huawei days – and indeed, despite the sale, Washington's concerns have not been alleviated, and export controls targeting the company remain in place. US efforts to stymie China's cable reach have also not let off.

Undersea cables, in particular, are among those technologies most suited to this kind of coercive diplomatic and economic security approach. There are relatively few of them – every cable has a name, and each newly announced project is an event that is subject to much chatter within the tight-knit cable community. Cables are also static. We know roughly where they are laid, and we know most of the time on whose shores they land. The primary purpose of major, international cable projects is most of the time to interconnect into the wider global network. Over this network the United States – through its hyperscaler power – is able to exert a higher and higher degree of control; you would not want to lay an expensive new cable, and have it barred from the network due to US pressure.

All of this has allowed the US government to keep a close eye on the roll-out of new projects. So much so that it now increasingly no longer has to interfere at all: many actors in the global cable industry – concerned about losing access to the US market and hyperscaler investment – appear to have pre-emptively moved away from working with HMN Tech. By 2019, HMN Tech had been able to eke out a share of approximately 18 per cent of total new cable builds, edging closer to take over the third spot in the global ranking from Japan's NEC. By 2024 its share was down to an estimated 5 per cent of new cable projects.[76] Since the start of Washington's crusade against HMN Tech cables, the company has seen its geographical reach significantly reduced too, with many of its new projects now limited to China's near periphery, instead of the kinds of ambitious, globe-spanning projects like the PEACE cable, discussed earlier in this book.[77]

The growing difficulty the Chinese cable industry now faces is almost physically visible within the small bubble of the industry itself. Large Chinese telecoms and cable companies are still present at cable trade events. They still have a shiny booth with free merchandise, enthusiastic young staffers flown in from Shanghai or Tianjin to tout the company's wares. Their logos feature prominently among the platinum sponsors on banners and brochures. But where the rest of the hall may be filled with buzz, the floorspace near the Chinese booths can feel strangely empty. Industry players know not to touch these partnerships, preferring not to incur the wrath of the Americans, or lose out on future hyperscaler investment. Some of the government and defence sector representatives are even explicitly instructed not to appear in the same picture frame with 'certain companies', thus taking the long way round to the coffee break.

The industry does not universally agree that China, or its cable technology, present a genuine national security risk. Some share American concerns that China may be building backdoors into its hardware, and do not look particularly kindly on the contingent of industry old hands who have gone to work for Chinese companies. Yet others I have spoken to praise the quality of HMN Tech's engineering – and speed by which it developed these skills – and lament the politicization of the cable sphere. This is a technology that is meant to connect after all. Removing China as an alternative source of investment and construction also leaves the market even more beholden to American investment, further entrenching its power.

The upshot of all of this is that, whether hawks or doves, most in the industry recognize that working with Chinese companies means possibly inviting Washington's ire, and may preclude them from receiving future hyperscaler investment. This even extends to cable projects which do not land on US soil and over which Team Telecom thus has no direct influence (yet). The United States does not have to impose secondary sanctions or aggressively try to block cables, as the joint hold of Team Telecom and Big Tech dominance means the industry will largely self-censor. Infrastructural power at its most effective.

## *China strikes back*

Unsurprisingly, China has not let the United States and its allies' efforts to root it out of global digital infrastructure roll-out go unchallenged. In the cable sphere, the country has similarly turned to using national security justifications to prevent the laying of new cables which it deems run counter to its strategic interests. Where Washington uses its Team Telecom rulebook and hyperscaler dominance to block cable projects it does not like, Beijing has instead turned to lawfare of a different kind to, in practice, achieve exactly the same. Rather than focus on the cables themselves, and weeding out US or hyperscaler involvement in wider cable supply chains, Beijing employs its regulatory toolbox to limit or occasionally even ban new roll-out in what it believes to be its, rather expansive, maritime sphere of interest.

Under the banner of protecting national sovereignty and preventing foreign 'interference' with its data, authorities in Beijing now regularly withhold permits or simply deny passage to cable-laying vessels that want to operate near China, especially in the South China Sea.[78] Cable-laying and survey vessels are, for example, now frequently being instructed by the Chinese authorities to seek transit permits to cross the strategic waterway, even when operating in areas considered to be outside of China's direct jurisdiction under most interpretations of maritime law.

Beijing, for example, delayed by several years Japan's NEC laying of the SJC2 cable, which looked to connect Hong Kong to Japan, employing rather similar arguments to those used by the United States to argue that the project may be used as an opportunity to build spying equipment into the cables.[79] The cable – which had been in the works since 2018 – ultimately only went live in July 2025. Survey ships conducting preparatory work for new cable routes – for example ships operating at the behest of the Philippines and Vietnam – have found themselves shadowed and repeatedly obstructed by the Chinese coast guard. This kind of bureaucratic obstruction and intimidation does not target cable-laying directly but does create significant commercial risk and friction for cable operators, who are therefore starting to become more wary of expanding in the strategic sea.

This weaponization of the cable-laying rulebook should be seen as part of Beijing's wider ambition to expand its own maritime jurisdiction across the South China Sea, frequently relying on its own unorthodox interpretation of UNCLOS to do so. Just like in the Arctic, building physical infrastructure in these disputed waters can help strengthen one's claims of sovereignty. Beijing relies on a series of dubious legal and historical claims – combined with regular shows of military force, and greyzone tactics such as the creation of artificial islands – to affirm as its own the area, and islands, within the so-called Nine-Dash Line, an ambiguous set of boundaries which can cover upwards to 90 per cent of the South China Sea. China's increasingly expansive interpretation of the boundaries of its territorial waters and sphere of historical ownership into what most of the international community would consider international waters, and frequently even to be belonging to the exclusive economic zones of its neighbours, has put it at odds with countries from the Philippines to Vietnam to Brunei to Malaysia.

Some of this competition has come concerningly close to blows, for example near the Second Thomas Shoal in the Spratly Islands, where the rusty, slowly disintegrating *Sierra Madre*, a Second World War-era landing craft deliberately grounded there in 1999, permanently manned by a revolving crew of Filipino marines, forms part of the basis of the Philippines sovereignty claim over the largely uninhabited island group. China, which similarly claims the Spratly Islands as its own ('indisputable sovereignty')[80] likes to deploy its belligerent coast guard in attempts to prevent the vessel from being resupplied, which has led to occasional bursts of violence (a 2024 fracas saw a Filipino marine lose a thumb).[81] These types of exchange turn these lawfare strategies into something rather more physical, and threaten to tip into a more significant escalation.

Obstructing the laying and repair of cables may feel comparatively more mundane and less immediately high stakes. This cable politicking does, however, play a role in solidifying Beijing's sovereignty claims in the region, and risks creating an atmosphere of inevitability around China's growing naval dominance. Weaponizing cable permitting also has real, tangible consequences for the cohesion and resilience of the network. The South China Sea is threatening to become a digital *no-go* area for new, non-Chinese cables, with some in the cable industry now largely avoiding the strategic waterway altogether, pivoting instead to new routes south or further east to avoid confrontation or the potential loss of their investments. Meta and Google's Apricot cable and Google's Echo cable were, for example, rerouted in the planning process to instead curve around Indonesia.[82]

This has implications also for other countries in the region, which could see their own cable connectivity become more beholden to and threatened by their larger neighbour. It has consequences for route security and diversity (good and bad – tensions see new routes gain traction, but can also force cables to follow less geologically favourable, fault-prone pathways). It could, in ways not dissimilar to American muscle-flexing in the cable domain, over time lead to the fragmentation of the global cable network, and perhaps even the internet itself.

## *Sensor and sensibility*

Rising competition over undersea cables does not just have an impact on the integrity of the global internet, it can also make it more difficult for countries to collaborate on other critical issues and shared crisis responses. One example of where we see this in action is over the evolving politics around undersea monitoring.

Undersea cables do not just funnel data, they can also be objects that generate data in their own right. Highly valuable data, as it turns out. There is a long tradition of placing sensors and measurement devices on cables, which can be used to, for example, measure temperatures on the seabed, monitor ocean life or analyse acoustics, and track movement in the near proximity of the cable.[83] Some of these sensors serve primarily scientific, environmental or incident monitoring purposes. Others have a distinctly more geopolitical flair. During the Cold War, the United States maintained a large web of underwater 'hydrophones', connected together by dedicated undersea cables, which were deployed to detect the unique fingerprints that would suggest the possible presence of Soviet submarines, among other things.[84] Specialized sensors placed on fibre optic cables – systems such as distributed acoustic sensing (DAS) – are now also increasingly used to monitor the activities in their near proximity (DAS even regularly picks up whale singing), and touted as solutions to alert operators about potential suspicious behaviour, or indeed, identify culprits *in flagrante*.[85]

Another new type of sensor takes the precision of these types of measurements to a next level. So-called SMART (short for Science Monitoring and Reliable Telecommunications) cables have especially sensitive sensors placed on them, which can be used to detect seismic activity and send warning of a possible imminent earthquake that could result in a tsunami. It is this kind of early warning which could provide authorities with critical extra minutes to urge their populations to seek shelter or find higher ground. In the case of tsunamis, in some scenarios even tens of minutes: the kind of lead time that could save thousands of lives. The technology works by placing highly sensitive sensors onto cable repeaters, which report back when they pick up the tell-tale seismic disturbances farther out at sea.

Despite their promise, the actual deployment of SMART cables has, so far, been slow. The first country to deploy the technology at scale, which while powerful, is also expensive, adding approximately 10 to 15 per cent to a cable's cost, is Portugal.[86] There are historical reasons for why the Iberian country would be among the first willing to cover the additional expense of turning their cables SMART. The Great Lisbon earthquake of 1755, which reduced much of the country's capital to rubble and took an estimated 50,000 lives, may have happened several hundred years ago, but still looms large in the Portuguese public imagination, and indeed that of its policymakers. Lisbon, however, does not currently have the sophisticated tsunami monitoring systems in place that more seismically active places like Japan do.[87] It is instead a prime hub for communications cable landings.

Its first SMART cable pilot, which has received funding from the Portuguese government and navy as well as the European Commission, involved the laying of a SMART-enabled cable from mainland Portugal to the Portuguese island of Madeira (the Azores, too, are one of those geographical focal points, which pop up at key moments throughout the undersea cable's history), some 1,000 kilometres away from the Portuguese mainland. A length of coverage which would provide significant additional lead time to respond to an imminent seismic event. Part of what has made Portugal's experiment politically viable is that the cable remains within Lisbon's jurisdiction (or otherwise traverses largely 'empty' international waters) – which removes some of the highly charged geopolitics from the equation. SMART technology would have an even higher utility in the most seismically active geographies such as in the Ring of Fire, but the tense security environment in the West Pacific has made actually deploying the technology controversial.

Japan, still reeling from the 2011 Fukushima disaster, has also been running trials with placing tsunami monitors – but has laid shorter dedicated cables to test the technology, rather than leverage the existing undersea cable network.[88] This is in part because Beijing has reportedly made more geographically dispersed experimentation with SMART cables near its waters difficult. This is not because Chinese authorities do not believe in the technology's scientific merit and utility, but because of concerns that the sensors on cables may pick up far more sensitive signals and vibrations as well, such as submarine movements. These are dual-use tools which can be used to monitor the PLA's maritime activities. These concerns are not entirely unfounded: navies frequently do require potentially interesting data collected by commercial or scientific sensors to be shared with them, lest they accidentally reveal sensitive information on, for example, submarine locations (or fortuitously allow them to glean something on their adversaries). The US Navy, for example, mandates that all such data be pre-sifted before it can be disclosed, as do many other countries.

Because SMART cables, and other such systems, are able to collect such potentially highly strategic information – especially in the high-stakes world of nuclear-armed submarines, whose effectiveness and ability to deter rely on their invisibility – SMART-enabled cables also present a different kind of risk: the prospect of undersea cables becoming legitimate war targets in their own right; not for the traffic going through them but for the sensitivity of the data the sensors placed on them collect.[89] While legal scholars generally agree that cables with a clear military purpose, such as those routing out of naval bases, would make for a legitimate target during a war, what the threshold would be for cables that were – deliberately, or not – picking up signals on war-time naval activity is less clear. Proponents of SMART cables argue that the data these sensors collect is not indiscriminate, and can be limited to mapping the goings-on in countries' respective national waters alone; but in the current heady geopolitical climate, such arguments are unlikely to carry much water. It is yet another example of how high geopolitics can impact resilience, also in other domains.

The upshot of this competition over cable roll-out, and use and abuse of lawfare to limit their reach, is a more fraught cable environment, in which the current dominant communications powers threaten to overplay their hand and undermine the network's overall resilience and cohesion. The ramifications of this we will explore in the next chapter.

# 7

# *Clean Cables*

'Doomed to cooperate'[1] is how Mikhail Gorbachev described the relationship between the United States and the USSR, over a glass of champagne on a Soviet cruise ship docked off the coast of Malta, the venue of a high-stakes bilateral meeting between the Soviet Union's final leader, and then US President George H.W. Bush. It was December 1989, mere weeks after the fall of the Berlin Wall, and two years before the Soviet Union itself would definitively collapse and the need to cooperate would refocus on the orderly unwinding of the USSR, rather than the bipolar rivalry which had so profoundly shaped the global order since the end of the Second World War. While Gorbachev's words may not have been applicable to the Soviet Union for much longer, they would prove more providential for America's relationship with the USSR's erstwhile rival China, and the increasingly close entanglement between the two countries over the decades that followed.

The spirit of peace dividend ensured the two countries' political and business leaders would initially enthusiastically pursue more economic interdependence, especially after China's fateful accession to the World Trade Organization (WTO) in 2001. From the 2010s onwards, the mood within this relationship has decidedly shifted, as both sides have become increasingly concerned about the vulnerabilities this high degree of interdependence brings, and China assumes a more prominent spot on the world stage. The cost of full or significant decoupling, which could alleviate some mutual fears, would be prohibitively high and brings its own risks to economic and geopolitical stability, leaving the pair – and the world – in an increasingly uneasy and perilous stalemate.[2]

Neither the US nor China have proven particularly adept at handling the current moment of transition, where the world is moving from a single hegemon, the United States, towards what may emerge as a new, bipolar Cold War-like settlement, in which two blocs wield hemispheric control, or, more likely, something altogether more multipolar and polyphonic. China has used its growing economic and military heft to increasingly aggressively flex its muscles vis-à-vis its smaller neighbours; its frequent provocative military exercises in the South China Sea and coercive economic practices targeting smaller peers in Asia and Europe,[3] a stark reminder of Beijing's growing military firepower and desire to assert itself. Beijing's habit of flaunting the rules of the economic order that enabled its astronomical growth was never popular. But as the country's economic heft grows, its ballooning production overcapacity of everything from steel to electric vehicles as well as its kneecapping of everyone else's ability to compete are becoming a growing source of global instability and discontent.[4] There are now few industries in which China does not either already dominate, or could soon. This tide will be hard to turn. China's economic expansion now looks less like an aggressive fish in a large pond, but a walrus in a bathtub – leaving little for anyone else.

The United States, fuelled by bipartisan paranoia about losing its position, too, is chipping away at the pillars of the very architecture of the global order it itself has built – from weaponizing its centrality in global financial markets and key technological supply chains,[5] to aggressively cashing in its soft and hard power hold over its allies. All of this is in part an effort to stay ahead of China, but jeopardizes in the process its continued supremacy in each of these spheres – from the role of the US dollar to its military hegemony.

This increasingly tense Sino–US competition is in no small part manifesting itself through an increasingly all-encompassing trade and technology war, in which both sides deploy chokepoints and economic coercion to gain an advantage. The United States is using the tools it has at its disposal to keep China out of highly strategic technology areas it, for now, still dominates and to stunt the PLA's military rise. This focus has especially homed in on the field of AI and its enabling infrastructure, like data centres and specialized chips – a pursuit which has taken on an almost messianic fervour, both in the Beltway and in Silicon Valley.

China, instead – spooked by Washington's aggressive economic playbook and driven by its own ambitions and historical pathologies – has been focusing on indigenizing its supply chains and cultivating its own, alternative global networks of partners, markets and influence it can weaponize.[6] Submarine cables play a multi-faceted role in this rivalry, which increasingly fuses geoeconomics, geopolitics and national security in increasingly complex ways. Undersea cables will at the same time also be heavily impacted by this competition. As the current order erodes, risks of the network bifurcating into separate, cordoned-off blocs – or potentially even entirely parallel cable spheres – are no longer purely academic. In this chapter, we explore what this might mean.

## *Post-Cold War playbook*

As the Cold War drew to a close and the era of peace dividend dawned, submarine cables increasingly turned from weapons of war into tools of economic expansion, used to spread the gospel of neoliberalism and capitalism, rather than a tightly controlled dual-use technology. Restrictions on Russia and China were lifted, as we discussed in chapter 2, and the cable market became a more liberalized, commercial-first one. When there were concerns about interference, spying and sabotage, the United States and its allies were usually the perpetrator, not the victim. But though the United States and its allies may have become a lot less vigilant over this period and – according to many in Washington and Brussels – failed to see the implications of China's rapid and largely unfettered rise, it was this openness and commitment to putting itself at the centre of a liberal, hyper-globalized global order that also provided especially the United States with the tools to fight back.[7]

America's dominant role in global financial markets, through the central role of the dollar and its leading role in institutions like SWIFT (the system that facilitates global inter-bank payments which effectively all global banks – and countries – rely on), allowed it to monitor and control global financial flows, and provided it with the heft to throttle others' access to these indispensable systems and infrastructures. Without access to SWIFT, there can be no full participation in the global economy. Similarly, the global heft of its hyperscalers and wider high-tech industry allowed the United States to wield not just a high degree of control over the roll-out of submarine cables, but also a hammer it could use against many other links of vital global technology supply chains.

Whereas economic blockades of the past had relied on the physical interdiction of goods through naval presence,[8] America's economic warriors in the early 2000s found that the kind of networked power it had over globalization's intangible infrastructures afforded it an incredibly powerful, and bloodless, new lever to persuade others to do its bidding.[9] And better yet: most of it could be implemented from behind a desk. As this toolbox had its clear appeal (especially in a country – then at least – keen to avoid any further military quagmires), economic warfare became an increasingly key pillar of US foreign policy.

Much of this approach focused initially on imposing financial sanctions and economic costs on bad actors in the system. The United States began to hone, expand and turn this financial, networked power against increasingly formidable adversaries. First, there was the targeting of financial flows of terrorist networks in the wake of the September 11 attacks. While organizations like Al-Qaeda were well organized and elusive, they were not centralized bureaucracies with the kinds of levers at their disposal to meaningfully fight back or hedge against this coercion.[10] The next scalp was Iran in the mid-2000s, whose uranium enrichment programme, and apparent nuclear ambitions, the United States has tried to put a decisive halt to. To do this, Washington used its central role in global financial systems to impose a new type of sanction on the regime in Tehran, which limited its ability to derive profits from its oil and gas exports – on which most of the Iranian economy runs. It did this by coercing global banks to limit Tehran's ability to receive payments for its hydrocarbon exports.[11] Russia too became a target, following its invasion of Crimea in 2014 – and then even more forcefully after the full-scale invasion of Ukraine in 2022. As a major, highly interconnected global economy and key actor in the global hydrocarbon market many others relied on, Moscow proved the most ambitious test yet for this approach.[12]

Washington simultaneously also set its sights on China. This would prove an especially existential experiment – not just for proving the efficacy of coercion-over-diplomacy against a very near-peer, but also as policymakers believed America's very pre-eminence as the sole global superpower was at stake. In the case of China, as we shall see, the US approach was not so much centred on sanctions and financial coercion as a means of punishment or forcing a change in behaviour, but rather focused on the use of increasingly more intricate tools to achieve the rather nebulous goal of limiting Beijing's ability to catch up with the US technologically. This approach was not too dissimilar to the export control playbook the US and its allies had deployed against the Soviet Union and Mao's China during the Cold War, which had sought to prevent Moscow and Beijing from accessing strategic innovations. Replicating this for a twenty-first century China, however, would not be an easy task: given the heft of the Chinese economy and its importance in global supply chains – by some accounting measures, when adjusted for purchasing power parity (PPP), China overtook the US economy in 2018[13] – a lot of new, creative thinking about economic and technological levers of influence would soon be required.

The scope of this book does not allow a very detailed play-by-play exposition on the US approach to economic statecraft. What we will do instead is discuss the role undersea cables have played in what I identify to have been the three key characterizing pillars of Washington's China tech statecraft approach in the pre-Trump era (many of these approaches have persisted, or even intensified, under the second Trump Administration, but the rapid vacillations and seeming lack of overarching strategy make it difficult to provide a more durable analysis).

First, there are the export controls, which try to limit China's ability to gain a military (and economic) advantage from accessing cutting-edge technologies, which form the centrepiece of Washington's strategy. We should secondly also see the recent frenzy to bring manufacturing back to the US – whether it is the Biden Administration's rediscovery of industrial policy, or Trump's iconoclastic approach to tariffs – as in large part driven by US competition with China, in a final hour push to reduce dependencies on Chinese supply chains. Lastly, I group together the efforts we discussed in the previous chapter, like the Clean Cables initiative, which push Chinese suppliers like HMN Tech and Huawei out of global telecommunications infrastructure and other technology spheres on national security grounds.

## Chipping away at China's rise

The US export control regime can be said to have been the crown jewel in Washington's broader strategy of economic statecraft aimed at belatedly curbing China's ascent in critical technologies. Its origins lie in the first Trump Administration, but these efforts took on a more existential fervour under Joe Biden. What was at stake here, Washington believed, were the future contours of the global order and who would lead it. The country that controlled key strategic technologies – especially AI and its underpinning building blocks – would be the one to dominate the twenty-first century.[14] To preserve the United States' technological lead and allow it to come out on top in this critical race, it needed to not just keep pushing the technological frontier, but it also had to prevent China from catching up by curbing its companies' access to certain cutting-edge Western technologies.

The Biden Administration's case was unsurprisingly not presented in quite such stark terms. Rather than call for a broad-based decoupling and kneecapping China's ability to innovate in its own right, interventions were framed as targeting a narrow set of specific solutions, which would particularly aid the PLA in its military build-up (the Biden Administration, too, was a firm believer in the pervasiveness of China's civil-military fusion doctrine). As Biden's National Security Adviser Jake Sullivan set out during his now-seminal 'small yard, high fence' speech in 2023: 'Given the foundational nature of certain technologies [those in the small yard], we must maintain as large of a lead as possible [by erecting a high fence, primarily through export controls].'[15]

The focus here was on restricting exports of certain highly strategic technologies, on which the United States was still firmly in the lead. Submarine cables, for example, did not make it into the small yard. This was not because the Administration did not deem them strategic, but because the underlying technology was simply no longer under exclusive Western control. China had already developed domestic capabilities that rivalled those of US firms in this domain – which is why the US relied on cable diplomacy, the long arm of its Team Telecom, and marshalling the hyperscalers' infrastructural power to contain China's operational reach in global telecommunications infrastructure.

The Biden Administration's export control regime was instead geared primarily towards limiting China's access to the most cutting-edge semiconductors and AI chips – the highly sophisticated, intricate hardware building blocks, made by its domestic giants such as Nvidia. It was these kinds of chips that were vital for training frontier AI models, many key military technologies, and much else of particular strategic importance. Semiconductors are a sector where the United States for now still maintains a significant innovation lead over China. The thinking was thus that limiting access would hopefully buy America's own domestic tech champions enough time to 'win the AI race', or at the very least gain a sufficiently large lead.[16] This target of 'gaining an insurmountable lead' remained, and still remains, a rather nebulous one: in a sphere of innovation so subject to continuous evolution, what does it mean for a race to be definitively won? Can export controls ever truly prevent a technology from diffusing? This lack of a real strategic end game notwithstanding, the United States proceeded, and soon identified the tools and chokepoints it needed to actually put this idea into practice.

While the bulk of the world's chips are being manufactured in enormous production plants, so-called foundries, outside of the United States, such as those of Taiwanese TSMC (an important chokepoint in global supply chains in its own right – 65 per cent of global foundry semiconductor production is concentrated in Taiwan, and a far higher share of the most high-end types),[17] much of the design and innovation behind these chips was still taking place in California. Silicon Valley hardware giant Nvidia, whose development of the leading chips used to train AI models allowed it to become, at the time of writing, the world's most valuable company,[18] but does not actually manufacture much at all – the magic is in its designs and ideas. Here, Washington found the cudgel it needed: America's chokepoints in chip and semiconductor supply chains could be found in its control over essential intellectual property and chip design know-how, allowing it a degree of control over effectively all links in the semiconductor and AI value chain.[19]

The economic warriors of the Trump and Biden Administrations weaponized this advantage by leveraging obscure Cold War-era rules, most notably the Foreign Direct Product Rule,[20] which allowed Washington to put restrictions on any product manufactured abroad that uses technology originating in the United States at any point in its supply chain. This in effect globalized the reach of American export controls and forced companies worldwide to abide by this US diktat, lest they lose access to pivotal US intellectual know-how.

The main milestone moment operationalizing this logic came on 7 October 2022, when the US Department of Commerce announced sweeping export controls to restrict China's access to advanced AI chips and the equipment and machinery needed to manufacture them. As a result, leading US chip companies like Nvidia, Intel and AMD, along with many other American and allied producers along the supply chain, saw their ability to export their highest-end products to China heavily restricted. The export of lower-performance, less sensitive chips, was, however, still permitted.

Extensive as it was, the Biden Administration's approach soon proved insufficient. US officials discovered that some of the chipmakers involved had found clever work-arounds to still export nearly-as-good chips to China, if it simply adjusted some of the specifications to remain just under the government-imposed performance thresholds, necessitating a further tightening of the regime.[21] Worse still, Chinese companies could also bypass the need to get hold of physical chips altogether if they could simply remotely access cloud facilities that rented out access to, for example, AI training chips ('compute') in other countries. Convoluted and far from ideal, to be sure, but a workable solution.[22] The clever fox had jumped the fence. Another tightening of the rules and ratcheting up of controls followed. The United States began to place limits further down the supply chain by curbing not just the export of certain chips themselves and the highly specialized machinery used to make them, but also things like the specific chemicals used to clean wafers, the thin slices on which chips are built,[23] thus erecting ever higher fences, guarding an ever larger yard. As we shall see later, both allies and foes bore the brunt of this increased fervour to fill all loopholes.

This push to tighten controls would soon also start to have an impact on the physical geography of AI. For the Biden Administration also began to target the geographical spread of the cloud infrastructure on which AI models were being trained. As one of the Administration's swan song acts, it limited the export of Nvidia's leading-edge Blackwell chips to only a select circle of most-trusted allies – allies in which it had faith they would not provide backdoor access or allow reselling to the competition in China. This list of tier one allies included much of Western Europe but, for example, did not include Saudi Arabia and the United Arab Emirates. It did not even include certain NATO allies like Poland. Without access to cutting-edge GPUs and CPUs, it would now be a lot more difficult to build the kind of AI data centre infrastructure, which the Gulf countries had put at the core of their strategy to establish themselves as AI superpowers. These restrictions would over time presumably also have started to have an impact on the topology of the web of cables the hyperscalers were weaving to facilitate this boom.[24]

We will not get to know if they would have, for the Trump Administration, in its first months back in office, rolled back some of these restrictions included in the AI Diffusion Rule. It has otherwise retained a lot of the Biden-era controls (though Trump himself has on numerous occasions seemingly gone back and forth on the issue) and strong bipartisan support for such policies remains, a sentiment perhaps best expressed by Republican congressman and noted China hawk John Molenaar, who decried that selling high-end AI chips to China 'would be akin [to] giving Iran weapons-grade uranium'.[25] Nevertheless, a second strand of Trumpian thinking on the issue has instead started to embrace an approach of trying to lock others into America's AI stack by actually aggressively exporting the technology and its infrastructural enablers to other countries, and so hopefully convince them to say no to China altogether.[26]

## Back to the factory

A second strand of Washington's economic security agenda regarding China is the growing fixation with restoring America's historical manufacturing prowess. It is in part what motivated the Biden Administration's turn to industrial policy, with its marquee centrepieces of the CHIPS and Science Act, the $280 billion subsidy drive which sought to bring back high-end semiconductor manufacturing to the US (semiconductor innovation largely originates in the US, but the country had lost most of its manufacturing capacity over the 1990s and 2000s to East Asia in particular),[27] as well as the Inflation Reduction Act,[28] which mobilized well over $1 trillion in spending and tax cuts to put the United States at the heart of the green transition, while bringing back middle-class manufacturing jobs to the American heartland.

Trump's radical tariff agenda, which is similarly in part underpinned by a yearning back to an industrial past when America was the factory of the world and a single manufacturing job could sustain a middle-class family, has sought to achieve similar ends. Both were also driven by a recognition of how vulnerable the country had permitted itself to become by allowing its industrial base to erode and by becoming so dependent on China. Though the intellectual bona fides of the Biden approach are rather more robust than those informing the Trump Administration's economic collision course, both agendas shared a joint commitment to reducing dependency on Chinese manufacturing, and other chokepoints that may be weaponized against America in future. Think here, for example, of ensuring America's continued access to high-end chips produced by TSMC, in the event of a successful PLA invasion of Taiwan.[29] If one were seeking justification for Trump's musings about annexing Greenland, accessing the island's vast mineral riches could be another way of getting out of Beijing's stranglehold – its control over supplies of certain critical minerals in this case.

Method notwithstanding, these concerns about dependencies are not unfounded. Though the reasons behind the decline of US manufacturing are long-running and complex, peace dividend thinking, which made possible China's rapid rise, played no small part in accelerating this trend. The same complacency that allowed China to quietly grow the global footprint of its own domestic telecommunications companies throughout the 2000s also enabled the country to rather ruthlessly increase its share in other highly strategic areas of global manufacturing. The West looked on and lined its pockets as it outsourced production to the cheaper East. China accounted for less than 2 per cent of global manufacturing during the period of Deng Xiaoping's opening up of the Chinese economy; it still hovered around a modest 5 per cent by 2000, but reached nearly 30 per cent by 2024 – by some calculations exceeding the share of the G7 countries combined.[30] If the current trajectory of growth continues, China's share could reach a staggering 45 per cent by 2030 – a dominance that would afford the country remarkable global leverage and ability to coerce others; not to mention what this would mean for everyone else's industrial bases (one only needs to consider the fate of Germany's emblematic car industry – which China seeks to supplant with its own electric vehicles).[31]

In the United States, in particular, debates about China's rapidly growing manufacturing share have become increasingly intertwined with national and economic security concerns. Take the specific example of shipbuilding, an industry with high salience to undersea cables. In 2000, Chinese shipyards accounted for around 5 per cent of global shipbuilding. By 2024, this share had already reached 53 per cent. That same year, American shipyards delivered four ocean-going merchant vessels,[32] whereas China's largest manufacturer – the state-owned China State Shipbuilding

Corporation (CSSC) – delivered over 250.[33] US policymakers – certainly not unjustifiably – worry that affording Chinese shipyards such a chokehold on global ship manufacturing would present a significant vulnerability during a potential conflict. This is not just because its access to new ships and ship maintenance would in all likelihood be immediately throttled, but also because China's commercial ship manufacturing base can easily be repurposed for military ends, as per the CCP's civil-military fusion doctrine. Indeed, many of the vessels manufactured in the country are believed to already be built according to military specifications.

These kinds of concerns about the dual-use nature of China's manufacturing juggernaut and infrastructure roll-out – from repair ships to the communications cables connecting to China's nascent web of overseas bases – have become increasingly intertwined with wider national security concerns about embedding Chinese-made tech into critical systems. The securitization of undersea cables and their supply chains is a prime example of this third and final pillar.

## National security everything

Which brings us to the third flavour of Washington's economic security approach: the limiting of Chinese technologies into the US and, allied, tech stacks and critical infrastructure as a national security imperative. Whereas export control regimes in this context usually revolve around preventing a select set of high-end and strategic technologies from going *out* and entering a place (also for national security reasons), this instead is a parallel push to limit Chinese technology – both legacy and cutting-edge – from getting *in*. The Clean Networks programme and its successors, the multi-pronged strategies discussed in the previous chapter by which Washington sought to combine cable diplomacy, economic coercion and the power of its tech companies to limit the reach of China's cable companies, fall squarely within this bucket. As we have seen, these attempts to reduce China's footprint in the cable network are no longer just limited to preventing the laying of new cables by Chinese companies, or having them make landfall in China. The US has increasingly expanded its focus to other links in the cable chain too, such as cable repair and the manufacturing of the cables, repeaters and fibres themselves.

America's securitization of Chinese technology is certainly not limited to the telecommunications realm alone. In recent years, focus has moved to a wide range of technologies with a software component, which – the fear is – could potentially be used to spy on users, or worse yet, be remotely interfered with or potentially even shut down. Who needs submarines to cut cables, if they can be disabled from a distance? We see parallel national security debates surrounding Chinese-manufactured electric vehicles, which some policymakers have referred to as 'driving spy devices'[34] and may even be controlled remotely.[35] There are concerns and restrictions on the roll-out of green energy infrastructure, such as the software involved with managing solar panels – a market China increasingly dominates.[36] Port infrastructure – most of Europe's and the United States' key ports now rely on Chinese-made cranes – was the focus of a Biden-era executive order seeking an investigation about possible kill switches in the technology, a vulnerability which could throttle vital supply chains at an opportune moment.[37]

The key question is whether this approach can actually work. As China's presence in global infrastructure and technology stacks has grown so pervasive in the past three decades, taking any kind of strategic, targeted action to root all of it out again has become simply too difficult and expensive. In some ways, the Rubicon has already been crossed: ripping and replacing all China-linked infrastructure from existing systems is now effectively impossible. Chinese supply chains are too entangled and indispensable in too many areas. Turning every exposure to China into a national security priority, therefore, is arguably not a viable strategy. Because when everything becomes a national security priority, nothing is.[38]

## *Where does this leave us?*

'The core engines of American power are humming', Jake Sullivan said over a plate of tikka masala, in a post-mortem lunch interview with the *Financial Times* after leaving his post in the White House.[39] While the Biden approach certainly had its weaknesses and detractors, elements of it had already shown early successes. The Administration had dusted off the old playbooks from when it last found itself in an existential ideological, economic and military competition, and had started to relearn how to use industrial policy and practise economic statecraft.

With this experiment aborted prematurely – and now partially replaced by something rather more idiosyncratic – it is difficult to say whether Sullivan's words about his Administration's economic security strategy, and approach to what effectively boiled down to a coercive attempt to curtail China's rise as a serious technology challenger, would have borne fruit in the ways intended. There are certainly grounds to be sceptical about the feasibility of this original ambition, for reasons we will soon discuss. The tendency by some commentators to frame the challenge America now faces in China as a new Cold War and battle for ideological and technological supremacy furthermore risks drawing on the wrong historical lessons. The US export control approach, honed as it was during the Cold War, offers useful historical parallels, but the comparison also has its limitations. It is after all being deployed in a very different world and against a very different adversary.

For one, this is not the same global economy as the one in the years immediately following the Second World War, when the members of the newly-minted NATO alliance accounted for over half of global GDP, versus the Warsaw Pact's approximately 15 per cent. While China remains reliant on the West for market access and certain high-end technologies, it now has far more middle- and high-income countries around the world it can trade with – many of which have their own qualms about the West. Several of those parts of the world we would have referred to as non-aligned during the Cold War seem primed for significant future economic growth and could offer fertile ground for market expansion in a more multipolar global order. Also America's own allies and partners may become increasingly less willing to go along with Washington's policy on China and push to decouple, as China's prowess becomes hard to ignore and the United States redeploys its economic warfare toolbox against its own allies.

While export control regimes were never airtight – many a Cold War spy caper involved shadowy import-export men smuggling restricted technology behind the Iron Curtain – the complexity, speed and diversity of today's global economy, as well as the frequently intangible nature of the technologies involved, make it exceedingly difficult to monitor, let alone enforce, restrictions on flows of goods. Indeed, there is growing evidence that smuggling of restricted, high-end chips into China is already happening at scale.[40]

China is furthermore also no USSR, and it is certainly not Mao's China anymore either. The country is a manufacturing giant and far more intertwined into the global economy than either of the United States' main Cold War rivals ever were. In 2023, more than 120 countries around the world counted China as their largest trading partner.[41] Not only is China along almost every dimension a far more open and dynamic economy than the USSR was, it is also no longer a laggard – or at least, not to the same extent. China has proven an increasingly formidable challenger when it comes to driving and exporting its own homegrown innovations. It is becoming indispensable in global supply chains and its top-tier electric vehicles, consumer drones and indeed also undersea cables are in demand, allowing Beijing to increasingly weaponize advantages of its own.

Beyond questions about the effectiveness and coherence of America's economic approach to curtailing an adversary as advanced as China, there is also reason to believe the United States might be undermining its own innovation lead by doing so. Overzealous weaponization of one's centrality in a network can encourage others to go it alone, and can even cause the whole system to fragment – as we have learned from Britain's interwar example. These are also strategies that assume a lead over China can be maintained in the long run – or at least will eventually stabilize. Beaconing oneself off from a country that is now an important source of frontier innovation of its own might in its own way limit America's lead – with the United States the one retreating behind a Chinese wall this time.

## *China strikes back*

Unsurprisingly, China has not looked kindly upon what it perceives to be US-led attempts to curtail its economic rise and ability to take up its 'rightful position' in the new global order. A CCP Foreign Ministry spokesperson, when asked to comment on the signing of the New York Statement, did not mince his words: 'the US has in recent years blatantly contravened international rules and business operation models, built a small yard with high fences targeted at China in the field of undersea cables, and kept abusing state power to go after and suppress Chinese companies, products and technologies'.[42]

China has not left the matter at strongly worded statements but has turned to building the arsenal it needs not just to limit the impact of US economic warfare, but also to wage its own. This is quite visible in the highly strategic undersea cable domain, where China has certainly not yet admitted defeat. HMN Tech continues to lead the – scuppered – growth of China's still-expanding cable network and remains at the heart of Beijing's digital diplomacy efforts.[43] At the beginning of 2025, HMN Tech had four new cable projects in the works, with roll-out in particular focused on the now less accessible South China Sea.[44]

This ambition also extends to many other areas of technological competition. Huawei's setbacks have proven temporary in some domains. While the telecommunications giant has in practice had to cede its market share in most of the West, the company continues to expand its footprint in other geographies, especially in Asia, South America and Africa. After years of flagging profits, Huawei's growth trajectory is back to its pre-sanctions path, in part due to its growing role in China's AI industry.[45] The company has also emerged as one of the stalwarts leading China's efforts to limit the damage of US export controls in the semiconductor industry.[46] Unlike in the undersea cable space, where China operates at the cutting-edge, it does not yet have the same advantages in the semiconductor domain, which is why US-led export controls have presented such a profound challenge. While Huawei has not yet been able to match the performance of the leading-edge Western-designed chips and machinery China has now largely lost access to, the company has come up with creative methods to catch up by doing more with less. There are some early suggestions this strategy has started to pay dividends, with especially the release of a series of surprisingly high-performance and fully homegrown Huawei semiconductors in the autumn of 2024 drawing the attention not just of Washington's economic warriors, but also American chip-making rivals.[47]

This example shows the flip side of export controls and other efforts to weaponize access to technology: while restricting access may provide the country ahead in the race with an initial advantage, it also incentivizes those at the receiving end of restrictions to take matters into their own hands, and innovate themselves out of a dependency. Necessity is the mother of invention, after all. Ironically, there is evidence that this dynamic played *against* China itself in the past: for example, the introduction of rare earth elements export restrictions by China against Japan and others between 2010 and 2015 led to a global surge in innovation in rare-earth element (REE)-intensive downstream sectors outside of China (though not fast enough, as we shall soon see).[48]

Nurturing domestic alternatives is at the heart of China's attempts to mitigate the technology challenge coming from America, but it is not the only strategy Beijing employs. The CCP has also been busy creating alternative structures and cultivating new export markets, preferably those beyond America's reach. Beijing, furthermore, also adheres to the old adage that sometimes the best defence is offence, and has been attempting to strengthen its own hand in the game of economic statecraft, and tighten its economic and technological hold over other countries.

### *Reshoring supply chains and building domestic challengers*

A veritable Sputnik moment, many commentators called it. Markets agreed, sending the stock prices of America's tech darlings briefly tumbling.[49] The luminaries behind national AI champions like Anthropic and OpenAI rushed to pen op-eds in the *Financial Times* and *New York Times*, reassuring investors that not all was lost and that Team America could still win the AI race. Behind this sudden rush of panic was the January 2025 release of DeepSeek's R1, a Chinese open source AI model, which exceeded most expectations about China's progress in developing frontier AI.[50] Though R1 was not quite as good yet as the leading American models like ChatGPT and Claude's most recent offerings, it was getting awfully close for comfort, and – importantly – apparently did so at a fraction of the cost. Not many had seen the arrival of an open Chinese model this good coming, especially not one trained on a combination of older, non-restricted Nvidia chips and potentially even Huawei's own new chip line. The announcement thus raised immediate questions about the efficacy of limiting China's access to top-end chips (it is important to note that significant question marks about the provenance of DeepSeek's GPUs remain, with credible suggestions it in no small part also involved the use of smuggled top-tier American ones).[51]

But there was more that spooked the AI community. There was the fact this was not a solution made by one of China's tech giants, like WeChat or AliBaba, but a tool that had emerged out of a somewhat obscure Hangzhou hedge fund, whose small team of engineers had mostly undergone their training at universities in China, rather than at Stanford, Caltech or MIT. Was it now Chinese companies that were the agile ones, outcompeting a sluggish America, with its closed-off gatekeeper models that cost tens, if not hundreds, of billions of dollars to train and run? Because not only had DeepSeek apparently been cheap to develop, it had also been made available as an open-source model, meaning it was free for others to tinker with and use. American models certainly still performed better, but this breakthrough called into question whether they would in the long run be able to compete with vastly cheaper, free-to-deploy models. What did DeepSeek's success imply about America's big bet on sinking ever more capital into AI infrastructure and compute, if China could just throw an almost just-as-good free model out there soon after?

And what, then, about America's strategy of devising an increasingly intricate web of export controls, had that too been the wrong call? From the vantage point of Silicon Valley and the Beltway, the yard suddenly looked a lot less well-tended than many had previously believed, and the fence guarding it now had a DeepSeek-sized hole in it. The United States had staked its future security, prestige and power on leading the world in artificial intelligence. China had just made it clear that that lead was far from guaranteed.[52]

One of the most important lessons the DeepSeek episode offered was not so much that export controls had failed per se – the company behind DeepSeek had had to rely on less advanced and potentially even covertly acquired chips, a hurdle which had in fact impeded its progress – but that ingenuity, aided by domestically designed alternatives, had allowed a Chinese company to build a credible AI challenger. China's domestic innovation ecosystem had already been increasingly capable of building its own solutions which could not only compete, but frequently also exceed, the West's – especially in technological spheres outside of the AI realm. By restricting access, the White House had not been able to throttle the country's progress, but *had* instead incentivized China to act with more urgency in its attempts to bolster its ability to go it alone.

This was no new ambition. The CCP has long promoted a policy of self-reliance.[53] Not being dependent on the outside world was a core tenet of the Marxist-Leninist thinking that shaped Mao's approach to governing the country.[54] Not wanting to be beholden to the benevolence of outsiders has its antecedents even before then, dating back to the nineteenth century, when Beijing had suffered the humiliation of having unwanted technology from the outside world imposed upon it. The memory of the Century of Humiliation, of Germany and Britain colluding to land telegraph cables on its shores, looms large. It is an idea that still shapes Chinese thinking on foreign dependencies to this day, and forms a key pillar in Xi Jinping's ambitions in the technology sphere. In his speech during the Fifth Plenum in 2020, which set the country's trajectory for the years ahead, Xi once again reconfirmed how creating fully independent supply chains was key to preserving the national interest, and should be a whole-of-society endeavour, in which all of China's industry has to do its bit.[55] China, too, is cleansing its supply chains and opting for self-reliance.

This push for independence stretches far beyond the small yard alone, or technology, but encompasses everything from achieving fully secure access to critical minerals and energy independence, to ensuring food security for its population (an ambition it is pursuing with such fervour, according to some analysts, that it would only be undertaken by a country that expects it may eventually find itself at war).[56]

In the technology realm, China's ambition is to be fully independent, and achieve 'algorithmic sovereignty' across all links in the value chain: starting with input minerals, to reshoring all aspects of the manufacturing process, to the development of alternative software suites to wean China off its dependence on, for example, Microsoft software, which the party sees as a national security risk.[57] The country in 2025 banned the import of the H20 chip, a type of chip Nvidia designed especially for the Chinese market (as it remained under Washington's export control's performance threshold), on security grounds.[58] In a hostile world, everything can be a tool of leverage, or worse still, a kill switch.

This ambition to rid itself of all dependencies has been very present in China's submarine cable strategy too. Even if the global market for its cables has shrunk, China now relies less and less on outside support for the development of the cables it does lay. HMN Tech continues to operate as before, despite the headwinds the company has been facing, and remains a source of innovation in the telecommunications and fibre optics realm. Given its strategic importance, the company can also still count on Beijing's strong financial backing and subsidies. China has also cultivated champions across other links in the supply chain and is now almost fully independent across the full cable-laying and maintenance process.[59]

China has its own cable manufacturer in the Wuhan-based FiberX. China is also home to a growing number of companies that develop and manufacture leading-edge optical fibre technologies and the repeaters that go into the cables. It has been steadily building up its own cable-laying and repair fleet: it now has a modest fleet of four ships. The ominous deep sea cable-cutting submersible which we discussed in previous chapters was less a doomsday device that could cripple the global internet as some fevered media reporting suggested,[60] but instead simply another Chinese step towards further indigenizing its cable repair toolbox (or that was at least how most in the industry interpreted the announcement).

Chinese companies are also investing heavily in other communications technologies, which could in the future potentially serve as either fallback alternatives or complements to undersea cables, such as quantum communications, lasers and new types of satellites. The cudgel the West holds over China in the cable space is therefore now almost entirely a political and diplomatic one. When it comes to technological sophistication and the independence of its supply chains, China can go it alone.

We have seen these kinds of all-of-nation efforts to wiggle out of technological chokepoints before. As we have discussed previously, Wilhelmine Germany was particularly intent on strengthening its own cable industry and tried to leapfrog into experimental new technologies such as wireless to reduce its dependence on Britain's telegraph network. Tools of economic statecraft such as export controls can add urgency to a country's attempts to innovate their way out of this type of grip. The kind of innovative fervour that can drive these efforts may not just lessen the stronghold one country holds over another; it can over time even erode the importance of a chokepoint itself. Fear of conflict and concerns about the weaponization of cables in no small part drove the adoption of radio, as we have seen, which in turn contributed heavily to the demise of Britain's communications hegemony.

### *Create alternative structures*

China – the Middle Kingdom after all, as the cliché goes – has also tried to put itself at the centre of a new web of relationships and structures in which the country itself is the lynchpin. This strategy is intended to nurture new export markets for its chronic production oversupply, but can also help bulletproof it against the worst impact of intensifying US and European efforts to move away from China, and especially the comprehensive sanctions that would most likely follow a long-speculated invasion of Taiwan. China is simultaneously creating new systems and infrastructures which can help reduce its exposure to being barred from using US-controlled global infrastructures. Its cross-border interbank payment system (CIPS) provides an alternative to the global payment system SWIFT.[61] It is trying to lock others into its paradigm and supply chains for AI systems and other technologies.

Scaling Chinese-supported parallel structures also provides ready-made alternatives to other countries, especially those who fear their own actions in the international arena may in the future invite Washington's ire, as has happened to Iran and Russia. As the United States increasingly moves to weaponize its own levers in the global system, betting on China can start to sound like a safer, or at least the more predictable, bet to many governments. By trying to build a new global network of dependencies, China's approach in this regard in many ways follows the classic imperial playbook, but with Chinese characteristics: the British Empire acquired colonies, the United States collected vassal states and a latticework of allies; China does not generally believe in having formal allies, but sees its power in placing itself at the heart of a so-called relational state, in which other countries become increasingly reliant on the new imperial core in Beijing.

China has launched a number of partnerships and parallel networks to give structure and substance to this ambition. The Belt and Road Initiative is unsurprisingly an important part of these activities, with digital diplomacy such as the laying of subsidized submarine cables serving as important tethers to bring others into China's orbit. There is the Shanghai Cooperation Organisation, a membership organization consisting of largely Central Asian countries, initiated by Russia and China in 2001, which can be considered a Eurasian answer to NATO.

The BRICS, the somewhat arbitrary, Goldman Sachs-coined term for the grouping of Brazil, Russia, India, South Africa and China itself, which now counts ten members, is frequently presented as an alternative to the G7. Though it is important not to make more of the BRICS than it really is – an ultimately rather ideologically and geopolitically incoherent talking shop – it is in part through this group that China has started to socialize its CIPS system and its plan for launching a digital yuan,[62] which it believes could over time come to serve as an alternative reserve currency to the US dollar.

Beijing no doubt hopes that these efforts will fare better than the group's aborted plan to lay a BRICS cable, a 34,000 kilometre-long subsea cable, which would have connected Fortaleza in Brazil, to Cape Town, continuing onwards to Chennai in India via Mauritius, routed around Singapore, to Shantou in China to finish in Vladivostok. To be laid by then still Huawei Marine, naturally. The project, announced in 2012 as a means of circumventing US chokepoints in the wake of the Snowden revelations, unlike the EllaLink, never came to fruition.[63]

There are further hurdles to China's approach to creating alternative spheres of influence. Its structures are still new, and China does not have the same soft power appeal the United States enjoyed when it shaped the present world order in its image. The new unpredictability and hostility of the United States on the global stage and retreat from key instruments of power projection such as its development vehicle USAID offer China a window to bolster its reputation. Another opportunity may come from China proactively shaping the norms and infrastructures of the industries of the future, by positioning itself as the leader in the green energy economy and related emerging technologies.

The United States may be walking away from its climate change targets; China will not. China is already the key player in commodity markets and processing of many critical minerals and other resources vital in the newly emerging climate order. It is rapidly electrifying its economy – reducing dependency on fossil fuels. Beijing dominates global markets for photovoltaics, storage batteries and, to a lesser extent, electric vehicles.[64] Visitors to cities from Addis Ababa to Bangalore will find that these places have leapfrogged into these new systems, and increasingly see Chinese-manufactured electric cars, rather than Japanese or German makes, whizzing around. Where the dollar was the currency of the fossil fuel era, China wants the renminbi to be the currency underpinning the new green, electric order.[65]

China has similar ambitions for the digital sphere, where it pushes a comprehensive strategy of exporting standards and solutions, and – indeed, of course – digital infrastructure, which – similar to the hyperscalers' infrastructural power today – could in future lock these countries into Chinese systems.[66] Here, DeepSeek has significance once again. Nvidia, one of the companies bearing most of the brunt of Washington's export control regime, has repeatedly warned that while the United States is busy putting up fences and moats, China is instead markedly effective in diffusing its AI systems and related tech to the rest of the world. As the United States rushes to win the capital-intensive race to the absolute AI frontier, China is focusing on diffusion and actual adoption. Its models may not yet be as good, but they are cheap and for many use cases they are more than good enough; and yet another tool for convincing others to embrace its technology over the incumbents. The upshot of this is that the rest of the world may soon learn to live without American technology; 'Winning the support of mainstream developers everywhere enhances America's economic and national security', according to an Nvidia spokesperson, criticizing Washington's approach. Diffusion and creating dependencies or maintaining a monopoly on the frontier: they are different philosophies – which one will come out on top, remains to be seen.

### *Create chokepoints of its own*

The final prong of China's approach has focused not just on becoming less reliant on others, but on creating interdependencies of its own, and locking others into asymmetrical relationships of which Beijing is the chief beneficiary. If the United States can weaponize the dollar, or China's reliance on high-end chips, or even the machinery to create said chips, Beijing wants to be able to return the favour. The country has become increasingly adept at doing so. By indigenizing supply chains, attracting increasingly more high-end (and consolidating critical lower-end) manufacturing, and growing a global market for the products emerging out of those supply chains, China has over the past three decades quietly but steadily been able to make countries across the world increasingly more reliant on its low-cost manufacturing and market access.

Now that the peace dividend thinking about China's inexorable path towards democratization and opening up has given way to a climate of panic and securitization, it has also become increasingly clear to policymakers and CEOs alike that turning back the clock on these entanglements and dependencies will prove a profound, if not impossible, challenge. Countries, which have learned the lesson that China throttling access to even a seemingly insignificant component can paralyse whole industries,[67] now wait the daunting task of protecting themselves against such risks. This is not entirely a one-way street: China, too, will struggle without access to Western markets. Doomed to cooperate.

Within this economic stranglehold of mutually assured economic destruction, China has been able to strategically home in on and deepen dependencies where the asymmetry is overwhelmingly in its favour. It is so far less able to do so in the high-end technology sphere, though Beijing's decision in the summer of 2024 to impose export controls on its commercial drones, which have proven critical in the war in Ukraine and of which it controls up to 70 per cent of the global market, provides a taste of what may be to come.[68] It is presently extremely difficult to build cheap FPV drones without access to Chinese components, though concerted efforts by Ukraine to rid itself of this dependency has seen the country make rapid progress in fully indigenizing production.[69]

Another area where China already holds particularly strong cards, and has shown an increased appetite for dealing them, is in the space of critical minerals. Critical minerals are a changing set of raw materials and elements which countries consider pivotal to their national security interests, for example because of their use in defence systems or in the green transition. This group includes rare earths, of which China in some cases controls up to 94 per cent of the global supply and processing capacity – an overwhelming dominance it has been able to cement over decades.[70]

As part of the same peace dividend thinking, rich countries were for a long time quite happy to leave the highly toxic and low-margin mining and processing of these minerals to China. It was only when Beijing started to weaponize this dominance in critical mineral supply chains that the rest of the world began to wake up to the worrying dependency they had gotten themselves embroiled in by outsourcing production. While it is certainly not impossible for other countries to develop their own critical mineral supply chains – contrary to what their name suggests, rare earths are not especially rare – rebuilding these capabilities will take time and come at a significant financial and environmental cost.[71] Attempts in the West and elsewhere to gain sovereign access to supplies did not take on sufficient urgency in time to protect against China making use of this chokepoint.

In late 2024, China announced far-reaching export controls on gallium and germanium, two minerals of which it controls up to 97 per cent of the global market. The targets of these export controls were the United States and the Netherlands, as a tit-for-tat for the Biden Administration's intensified controls on semiconductors, which also involved further, even tighter restrictions on the export of highly specialized chip-making machinery made by Dutch ASML. Beijing upped the ante even further in response to the Trump Administration's erratic Liberation Day tariff policy in early 2025, retaliating by announcing restrictions on a host of further minerals, especially those critical for defence and battery technology.[72] It significantly also limited export of the highly-specialized processing machinery that only China now makes.

How soon, and the extent to which, these restrictions will start to impact supply chains remains to be seen. One of the particularly challenging aspects of today's deeply entangled, complex economy, is that it is frequently difficult to map where dependencies and chokepoints may emerge – especially across the full range of goods and processes the most sophisticated economies develop. When we zoom in on submarine cables alone, on first assessment, the impact of Chinese critical mineral restrictions of this kind appears to be fairly limited. Though some of the critical minerals now subject to restrictions, such as tellurium, are used in high-end optics, and others, such as copper, form an important – though replaceable – input into the manufacturing of cables, Western submarine cable supply chains are on the whole quite resilient to this threat. Europe, the United States and several major Asian economies have largely independent cable value chains, all the way up from the manufacturing of new cables to their repair. The minerals involved, as is the case with other critical minerals, can – at a price – usually be found elsewhere, and are only used in smaller quantities. Nevertheless, the global economy runs on more than cables, and China has shown it holds many of the levers to shutter it.

It should, however, be noted that China will in time not find itself immune to the rules of weaponized interdependence and economic coercion either. Just like the United States has seen China, and others, try to innovate themselves out of American chokeholds, China, too, is likely to with time see its lead in critical minerals erode. President Trump's territorial designs on Greenland and Europe's activities in the Arctic township of Kiruna are steps towards this. In the meantime, however, China has found itself in possession of a potent weapon.

### *Good stewards no more*

To summarize: while a hegemon can have a lot of power to bend the parameters of the system in its favour, doing so also carries a degree of risk, and may in the longer run erode its own power. We saw Germany actively try to reduce its dependencies on Britain's communications power, and leapfrog into new technology areas, when it felt it could no longer rely on Britain's good stewardship. We see China attempt to do the same today. As a central actor overplays its hand, it can undermine the power it holds over the overall network – encouraging even neutral parties and allies to limit their own exposure to the central actor. It was Britain targeting Germany which in part encouraged the United States to become a more strategic player in communications networks during the inter-war years. It is also what America's affronted allies, as well as geopolitical swing states, are increasingly seeking to do, now that the US itself appears to be retreating from its own good steward role over many of the institutions and systems that so fundamentally shaped the post-war global order.

### *With a little help from my friends?*

America's coercive, transactional turn may not just impact the long-term vitality of America's web of global alliances and defence partnerships (it has more than eighty in place) and its enduring global influence – if this is something the current Administration still values – it will also significantly undermine the US's ability to weaponize its own global power levers.

The American approach to projecting global power has traditionally relied on close cooperation with other countries. While the United States controlled – and for now still controls – some of the critical intangible financial and normative plumbing that greases the system, and remains an indispensable actor in global technology supply chains, its reach is naturally not absolute. Just like the CoCom regime required frequently rather reluctant allies to play ball to be effective, the cocktail of interventions that have characterized America's recent approach to technological statecraft also relied on the participation of European countries, G7 partners such as Japan and Canada, and others. While the United States may be better placed to go it alone than virtually anyone else (except perhaps China), Washington's ability to rely on and leverage the strengths of its allies has always been a key source of its ability to wield power globally.

Financial sanctions are a lot more effective when enacted by a bloc with the combined heft of over 50 per cent of the global economy. Security concerns raised by the collective NATO allies, which together account for 55 per cent of global military spending, are more likely to be heeded.[73] And then there is the arena of global governance: acting in concert, or at least usually with the approval of, a group of largely democratic countries which nominally abide by international law, has traditionally provided legitimacy for American intervention. Though the United States has shown itself willing to act unilaterally on each of these fronts in recent decades – thus already shaving at the pillars of the liberal international order the country itself had constructed – acting on its own was not always possible, especially when it came to economic coercion tactics. Indeed, especially when targeting highly interconnected China, Washington has had to mobilize its allies and partners to also weaponize their own unique chokepoints in the global economy and supply chains.

Export controls targeting China's ability to acquire cutting-edge semiconductors relied on Japan, South Korea and the Netherlands also limiting access to some of the key solutions and technologies *they* controlled across different links in the AI supply chain. ASML, a Dutch tech giant which holds a global monopoly on some of the pivotal machinery required to create the most bleeding-edge chips, saw itself forced by The Hague to curb exports to China, previously one of its most important customers. This Dutch decision was evidently made at Washington's behest and had involved no small amount of geopolitical pressure. Not only have these curbs come at a significant cost to ASML, and thus the Dutch economy, it has also pushed China to rush to develop its own similar machines (and mount a sizeable economic espionage effort against the company), something it would have had far less incentive to do otherwise. It certainly would not have been as likely to launch a state-backed effort so ambitious it is now often referred to as China's Manhattan Project to build its own (whether it will succeed is another question: by many accounts, ASML's extreme ultraviolet (EUV) lithography machines are the most complex piece of machinery ever made). Just as Chinese companies like Huawei have now started the long journey of building challengers to America's cutting-edge chips, so too do they perhaps over time manage to erode ASML's EUV monopoly – a potentially existential price to ask ASML and by extension the Dutch state, to pay.[74]

Taiwan's chip giant TSMC, which was similarly pushed by the White House – by way of Taipei – to join in on its export controls regime, was also strongly encouraged to set up shop in the United States and support America's reindustrialization. Despite receiving inducements to the tune of $6.8 billion to move some of its manufacturing capacity to Arizona and elsewhere in the United States, this move was not particularly popular in Taipei. The United States has less favourable conditions for chip manufacturing than Taiwan does, with its high labour cost and shortage of skilled workers. More importantly, Taiwanese authorities also feared moving production would also reduce the United States' willingness to defend the islands against a possible PLA invasion, as the nation would now be less reliant on chips supplies from the world's silicon capital.

It was the first Trump Administration which threatened to cut the United Kingdom out of the Five Eyes alliance if it did not comply with removing Huawei from its 5G networks – the estimated £4 billion bill that came with ripping-and-replacing its telecommunications infrastructure to be taken in stride.[75] It was frequently America's allies, from Australia to Japan, who ended up coughing up most of the funding for the US cable diplomacy countering Chinese influence, or have seen their cable projects hampered.

Washington unsurprisingly has not always had an easy time bringing allies on board with such costly requests in order to help America reach its objectives. Rightly or wrongly, up until recently few of America's allies shared Washington's assessment of the threat emanating from China (though this is now changing). America's European and especially Asian allies, however, remain a lot more reliant on access to the Chinese market than the United States is, and fear being singled out and inviting Chinese retaliation if they go along with the White House's wishes. In practice, this has meant that allies' ostensible support for the US economic security agenda, though cloaked in benign language of 'partners and allies', often belied a far more coercive dynamic, in which successive Administrations not all too subtly strong-armed partners into doing their bidding.

Washington may increasingly struggle to do so again in future. The United States was previously able to get its allies to go along with its wishes, because it also offered a lot in return: from access to its indispensable consumer market to its security umbrella. The United States has generally also been a largely reliable steward of the global infrastructures it controlled (minus some awkward blips, like the PRISM revelations and the corrosive societal impact of its Big Tech giants), in the same way that Britain had been seen as a mostly trusted steward of the cable network – even if it occasionally used its dominance over the telegraph for its own ends. An exorbitant privilege, no doubt, but one that also benefitted other players.

During the first 'America First'-tinged year of the second Trump Administration, many policymakers in Washington appear to have abandoned this delicate balance, believing instead that similar – if not better – outcomes can be achieved by taking an approach of very little carrot, and a lot of stick. This is unlikely to pay dividends in the long run. As the Trump White House has started to walk away from America's long-standing security guarantees, wages a mercurial tariff war against all that risks undermining the global role of the dollar and shatters the trust of friends and foe alike, weaponizes its advantages to push for global deregulation and access to resources, and threatens some of its longest-standing allies with territorial conquest and regime change, its partners are likely to become a lot less willing to go along with US demands.

The countries, especially its closest allies, which have proven most dependent and least able to defend themselves against Trump's tactics are at the time of writing largely being presented as effectively vassals, with no choice but to accept the United States cashing in its chips. I predict that this kind of power asymmetry will be far from a durable one, as America's erstwhile partners are now actively diversifying away from America's yoke, focused on decoupling interdependencies, exploring alternative partnerships and strengthening their sovereign capabilities. While the Trump Administration may in the short run be able to derive some profits from this more transactional approach – promises of inbound investment, a global deregulation agenda which benefits its hyperscalers – the US will struggle to rebuild the global influence it is now rapidly losing. One place where we see this play out particularly starkly is in Europe.

## *European alternatives*

European countries have over the post-Second World War period allowed themselves to become profoundly dependent on the good steward, relying heavily on the United States for their security – whether it is the troops stationed on the continent, America's defence-industrial base, or the security provided by its nuclear umbrella. Europe's economic fate is intertwined and dependent on the fortunes of the US economy. The continent is also almost entirely reliant on US technology for many of its most critical systems, both in the civilian and military domain. The three largest hyperscalers – Amazon's AWS, Microsoft and Alphabet – together hold more than 70 per cent of Europeans' data – from their most sensitive health data to those underpinning military operations.[76] Where Finnish Nokia's cell phones were once ubiquitous, there are now no European smartphone makers that enjoy a meaningful market share. The apps that run on top of them were developed in the US or China. Of the twenty largest tech companies by market capitalization, fifteen are American, and only two are in the EU. The EU is even further behind when it comes to many aspects of the AI race, from access to AI hardware and compute to the building of its own frontier models. Europe may be home to one of the leading cable-laying companies in the world with ASN, but commercial investment in new cables now relies increasingly on American hyperscalers, leaving the continent also more beholden in the undersea cable-laying department.

Policymakers in Brussels have long been concerned about the impact this degree of reliance on US technology has on Europe's economic competitiveness – Europe remains a consumer, a market taker in the digital economy, but now builds little of scale of its own, as profits, power and control flow back to the US West Coast. A smaller segment of decisionmakers have also for some time worried about the corrosive influence these unaccountable companies have on the health of its democracies and civil liberties.

To address these kinds of excesses of the digital economy, Europe often turned to regulation as a remedy – relying on the (in)famous Brussels Effect, the idea that the size of Europe's single market and its stringent standards meant that the rules it set would tend to become the global norm – from its landmark General Data Protection Regulation (GDPR), to universal phone chargers.[77] These regulatory interventions have, however, proven to have been of limited impact, and in a time when it is increasingly clear that infrastructure equals power, Europe's lack of its own sovereign digital stack has proven a serious vulnerability.[78] The Trump Administration's decidedly anti-European tendencies have now made viscerally apparent how such dependencies are not just a matter of Europe's long-term economic vitality, but also present a serious national security risk, as it has become clear that the United States may use this over-reliance to turn off Europe's access to technology and data at any moment (such as an escalating stand-off over Greenland?), or use it as leverage in negotiations. The growing intimacy with government and patriotic fervour of some of its tech giants would potentially even further amplify this weapon. Communications hegemony in action.

This concern is certainly no longer academic: the White House's decision in February 2025 to coerce commercial technology companies such as satellite imagery provider Maxar to switch off Ukraine's access,[79] and the dangling of the continued availability of Elon Musk's Starlink system – also vital for Kyiv's war effort – showed the Administration's willingness to use technology dependencies as a coercive bargaining chip. When the Trump Administration imposed sanctions on the lead prosecutors of the International Criminal Court (ICC) in The Hague in response to its sanctioning of Israeli Prime Minister Benjamin Netanyahu, it allegedly also implored Microsoft to turn off the chief prosecutor's cloud access – blocking everything from his email access to his ability to book a plane ticket. The ICC has since expressed intent to move to open source, European alternatives.[80]

The implications of these two moves were clear. If the United States could do this to Kyiv and an influential international institution, it could do the same to London, Berlin, Brussels and Paris. Washington did not need any cable-cutting submersibles to turn the light off. Europe had handed over control over its most vital systems, which could hypothetically be turned off at a whim, critical data compromised or even deleted if the European Union did not abide by the Administration's wishes. Would the Americans play this card? Better not wait to find out, was increasingly the verdict.

In March 2025, the Dutch government called for software independence and announced it would take rapid steps to create its own sovereign cloud, especially for sensitive government data.[81] The Austrian and Dutch militaries have since committed to do the same, and the European Commission too is investing heavily in strengthening independent European cloud providers. In Germany, the Merz government called for achieving European digital sovereignty in its coalition agreement and developing an alternative European technology stack, especially in the strategic growth area of AI.[82] Leading European companies called on the European Commission to invest in sovereign capabilities and to promote a 'Buy Europe' approach. Several governments began to reconsider their agreements to purchase US military equipment and weapon systems, such as F-35 fighter jets, reportedly spooked by concerns about possible 'kill switches' in the Lockheed Martin-manufactured planes, which rely on continued software support and repair.[83]

Some in the cable industry have also suggested that Europe should put muscle behind creating its own commercial cable-owning giant to counter the increased dominance of American hyperscalers – or at least for the existing telecommunications companies to band together. This will likely become a more urgent concern in the years ahead, as the ageing transatlantic cables are increasingly replaced by cables owned by ever fewer American tech companies, further entrenching European dependencies across layers of the technology stack. Because just like cloud services can be shut off, so can traffic going through undersea cables.

Actually de-risking from American tech will naturally provide a profound challenge – once in place, dependencies tend to be hard to unravel – and will require a more ambitious and comprehensive approach to building and scaling European alternatives than what the continent has delivered to date. In many areas, such as defence, the space industry, or in scaling rivals to challenge the cloud dominance of the American hyperscalers, building alternatives may take many years – even decades (though necessity and a growing willingness to accept 'good enough' tech over the less secure frontier can make things move faster). In the meantime, the Trump Administration and the tech giants themselves have expressed increased dismay about these European efforts to disentangle themselves – a confrontation I suspect may come to an acrimonious head in the not too distant future. Nevertheless, Europeans see an opportunity here to not only provide their own, more geopolitically reliable alternatives, but also to position itself as a more trustworthy alternative source of solutions to the rest of the world.[84] If one good steward exits the stage, others may seek to fill the vacuum.

## *Towards a splinternet*

### Hedging no more

What does the increased competition over cables between China and the United States mean for the rest of the world? In the near term, this accelerated decoupling and one-upping can present some benefits for other countries, which can, for example, present themselves as safer, more neutral in-betweens or trusted third poles, or can reap the spoils from the largesse that can result from both camps vying for attention and influence. Depending on the degree of decoupling involved, it may, however, also lead to a more fragmented technology landscape – or even a splinternet – where countries increasingly retreat behind technological walls, and parallel networks may take hold, in which solutions no longer interconnect.

#### What is the splinternet?

'I know it when I see it', was what US Supreme Court Judge Potter Stewart famously said in 1964, when asked to provide a legal definition of 'obscenity'. The term 'splinternet' is often bandied around in similar ways, with its exact meaning in the eye of the beholder. It is worthwhile, therefore, to bring some further specificity and rigour to the term. For internet fragmentation to tip into a *bona fide* splinternet – a world of two or more parallel internets, which can no longer interconnect, I argue it will need to meet a couple of conditions.

First, there needs to be a lack of *interoperability*: despite the many barriers and walls in place between, for example, the Chinese and European internet, users are still able to communicate with each other – the underpinning infrastructures and standards that make the plumbing work are still shared. The emergence of entirely different standards for, for example, routing internet traffic through cables, or future 6G infrastructure, may well not allow such continued interoperability.

A splinternet also needs to be *durable*, meaning that it is not so easy to reverse the splitting up of networks, and that it will be in place for a long time, if not indefinitely. Here too, actions taken by governments lower down the technology stack are more impactful. An authoritarian government may temporarily turn off the internet during a protest, but it can also switch the lever on again. It will instead be much harder to reroute a fibre optic cable, let alone reconcile completely separate technical standards once they take hold (think of this like railroad tracks: a government temporarily blocking trains from crossing its borders can be easily reversed, two neighbouring countries using train gauges with different widths face far more cumbersome barriers).

For us to talk about multiple internets, these different internet spheres also need to cover a significant share of global internet users and *geographies*. North Korea, for all intents and purposes, is already in a far-advanced state of a splinternetification, but is so insignificant a digital actor (though it certainly punches above its weight as far as cybercrime is concerned)[85] that I would not consider its own idiosyncratic version of the internet as a credible, distinct competitor to the dominant internet paradigm. China and Russia fully severing themselves from the internet may begin to meet that threshold. The somewhat peculiar notion of the BRICS creating their own parallel network, which occasionally pops up in discussions, would certainly pass the test.

As the topology of the network changes, we already see alternative (aspiring) cable hubs gaining in importance. Hong Kong, which traditionally was one of the main cable landing nuclei in East Asia, has seen its position rapidly erode since the Sino–American cable tit-for-tat started in earnest in 2019. Alternatives, such as Singapore – which has been keen to present itself as the Switzerland of Asia – the neutral safe haven with whom everyone can do business – has been quick to try to fill the resulting void. Singapore has expressed the intention for twenty-six new fibre optic cables to land in the city state, and has made major investments to attract new data centres (reversing earlier policies which sought to prevent their expansion due to environmental and capacity constraints).[86] By strengthening its digital infrastructure, Singapore can further solidify its growing position in Asia's financial markets, and so also attempt to supplant the increasingly politicized financial sector in Hong Kong.

Another country which has opted for the hedging path – allowing in both China and the United States – is Indonesia, which traditionally had relatively few cable landings or subsea cables connecting it, but has seen itself emerge as a new node in the network. This means that the country is finally finding itself a position in cable networks more commensurate to its size (Indonesia's 17,000 islands span a distance from London to the west of Kazakhstan) and growing demographic and economic heft. Vietnam has been taking the best of what China and the US have to offer to build its own sovereign AI systems – presenting this approach as 'infrastructural non-alignment' – a model that may well work for others too.[87] Turkey, perhaps the most adept of hedgers (few countries could get away with being both a member of NATO and dangling a potential membership of the Shanghai Cooperation Organisation) is emerging as an increasingly more popular terrestrial route to avoid the Red Sea and Suez chokepoints. A lot of this hedging is predicated on the world remaining relatively open, and countries having the ability to deftly navigate and play out one player against another in an open, globalized economy where major partners make competing overtures.

This may not last. We have already started to see the major power begin to push back against this kind of hedging and flex their muscles to force countries to choose. The Gulf countries have been effective hedgers and weaponizers of their own chokepoints (deep coffers, and a significant degree of control over oil prices). Both Saudi Arabia and the United Arab Emirates, as we discussed in chapter 3, are investing heavily in positioning themselves as new AI hubs in a more geopolitically charged world. This involves hefty expenditures on the requisite underpinning digital infrastructure – especially data centres equipped with the highest-end Nvidia chips to train AI – to lay the groundwork for that ambition. The legs of that plan seemed to be sawn from underneath them when the Biden Administration in early 2025 announced it would now only allow a select number of most trusted countries full access to its most high-end chips critical for training AI models, in a bid to prevent chip leakage to China.[88] This list did not include the Gulf. Without Nvidia chips, no post-hydrocarbon AI abundance. The Trump Administration as we saw walked back some of these restrictions, and instead encouraged more AI and data centre investment in the Gulf – under the proviso that the country pick Team USA, naturally. The United States has brought a similar proposal to the United Kingdom, with Washington's coterie of AI champions promising £150 billion of investment in AI infrastructure in the United Kingdom, which has the upshot that the country could see itself even further technologically vassalized to the US and locked into US-provided infrastructures – this at a time when its peers across the Channel are increasingly starting to chart their own course.[89]

As the dividing lines between different camps start to become sharper, the United States and China flex their muscles, and showing allegiance the expectation in return for continued trade relations and military security guarantees, countries may find it harder not to pick sides. Initially, these dividing lines may be primarily political. In a world of actual fragmentation, where competing, non-interoperable standards and technology spheres take hold, the choice may become a physical one.

## *A recipe for war?*

One of the perennial questions international relations scholars and historians struggle with is whether interdependence is a source of stability – the competing parties simply have too much to lose from a rapid decoupling, let alone going to war – or whether it instead lowers the threshold for conflict (with the highly interconnected period leading up to the First World War the usual counterexample used to challenge the notion that mutual dependencies keep the peace). The fact that a globalized, intertwined world offers states more levers through which to target one another – we have explored many in this book, from mysterious sabotage incidents, the covert interception of information, to weaponizing the levers of globalization itself – may perhaps serve to actually defuse tension, with minor provocations taking away the perceived need for more drastic escalation.

If we accept that interdependencies can serve as pressure release valves, decoupling them would by extension therefore risk increasing the chances of conflict. The flipside of throttling China's access to certain technologies is that it will see China become less dependent and less beholden to the United States and its allies. This may inadvertently thus lower the barrier for China to actually seek an invasion of Taiwan, as Beijing sees its adversaries now hold fewer cards to retaliate with.[90] Sanctions bazookas are a lot less painful when the target is largely self-reliant.

One important factor that presently helps maintain the current status quo in Taiwan is that both Beijing and Washington remain heavily reliant on the semiconductor production taking place on the island. This is in part why Taipei has such strong incentives to keep supplying both. An invasion may well see the infrastructure supporting TSMC physically destroyed – a practical concern that factors into China's – and America's – risk calculus. The less dependent China becomes on foreign supply chains for its own chip manufacturing, the less Taiwan's so-called 'Silicon Shield' will hold protective power. The same goes for the United States: though we should be careful not to overestimate the centrality of TSMC in the great power competition over Taiwan, policymakers in Taipei are nonetheless concerned that the United States may become a lot less willing to defend the island once its semiconductors can come from other places too. It was certainly not just a clash in work cultures[91] that made Taipei not too keen on its national champion expanding in Arizona.

Sometimes rushed decoupling can also happen in anticipation of a conflict, and so inadvertently speed up its arrival. The zeal with which the Chinese leadership is pursuing this move towards self-reliance, and its razor focus on achieving food security and other such fundamentals, has unnerved observers in Washington.[92] This is no peace-time planning, they argue, but recalls similar preparations undertaken by Imperial Japan and Nazi Germany in the lead up to the Second World War. Here too, we can find parallels with the telegraph era: recall Wilhelmine Germany's push to develop its own artificial gutta-percha alternative, well aware of how reliant it was on Britain's Malay chokepoint, and the near-certitude that London would make use of it should war break out.

### *Bifurcated, fragmented worlds*

A good steward in global intangible networks risks damaging more than its own role in the network, however. It can also undermine, and fragment, the network overall – potentially even ending it altogether.

Internet fragmentation is as old as the internet itself. From its very inception, countries have tried to cordon off parts of the internet and limit what its citizens are able to see and do online. In some cases, they even restrict access altogether – think here of places like North Korea, Eritrea and increasingly Iran. Others take a more piecemeal approach. Russia, for example, has had long-standing ambitions to wall off its internet from the rest of the world, an effort which it has kicked into second gear since the start of the full-scale invasion of Ukraine. Draconian censorship and the blocking and throttling of most Western social media applications like YouTube and Instagram have moved in lockstep with increased repression in most other aspects of Russian society. Russia's sovereign internet (or 'RUNet') ambitions are motivated less by trying to develop an alternative vision to export to the world but are rather a tool to prevent the Russian domestic public from accessing information and organizing itself online in opposition to Putin's regime.[93]

The same, in a way, goes for China's Great Firewall (though Beijing does encourage others to copy its model – and will gladly provide you with the tools). While the Russian and Chinese internets can indeed be said to be more closed-off (or 'that a digital iron curtain has descended' upon them)[94] and are getting more insular, they can still be circumvented by those with sufficient technical savvy. The underlying standards, norms and technological infrastructures are, for now, still the same. These are not yet true splinternets.

A truly bifurcated global innovation sphere – where it is no longer possible to send one another an email, or make a bank transfer, where our phones no longer automatically work when we get off a plane in a new country – is instead more likely to come about not by deliberate political choice, but by accident, a slow creep of unwinding dependencies, driven by economic warfare, sovereignty efforts and diverging choices made at different forks in the road. Such slow creep bifurcation will prove hard to reverse. While there has been much (occasionally hyperbolic) focus on the potential catastrophic impact sabotaging undersea cables may have on the global internet, damaging cables is ultimately a weapon of the weak – at least during peacetime. It is the most powerful actors in the network undermining the very fundamentals of our interconnectivity that are at greatest risk of bifurcating the cable network, and the global internet with it.

# 8

# *Cables at the Confines of (Supra)planetary Bounds*

As we have seen throughout this book, submarine cables are the slice of the internet stack most tethered to the realities of geography. Cables at the same time also empower a global internet and technology infrastructure that is increasingly creaking at the seams, and running into local – and in time, possibly global – environmental roadblocks. Access to sufficient cheap electricity, land and water and other resources is a growing challenge when it comes to finding new locations for data centres and the other infrastructures at the heart of the current spending frenzy on AI. As countries and companies race to control the technologies of the future, this tension between planetary limits and promises of exponential growth is becoming a growing source of friction.

While undersea cables require both less space and fewer natural resources to function than the data centres and other infrastructures they connect, growth of the cable network could eventually also hit a limit, especially because cables are facing increased competition over seabed 'real estate' from other users, and are subject to climate change-induced upheaval, which could narrow the possible paths new cables can be laid along, and cause more frequent faults.

Threats may also come from much further afield. New challenger technologies, which aim to chip away at the cable's dominance as the main conduit of international data flows, may lift connectivity away from the planetary altogether, up into space. As the geopolitical and geoeconomic battle over cables continues to rage, we also find ourselves in the middle of a budding new space race over emerging satellite technologies, with countries rushing to seize their commercial and military promise.

In this penultimate chapter, we explore some of these planetary and supra-planetary threats to cables, and explore how this new era of great power competition is accelerating these risks.

## *Only connect*

It is the strange beauty of the cable network – the hundreds of thousands of kilometres of garden hoses ferrying light, the beams that underpin our modern world, and connect us together – that first drew me to writing this book. Part of me, however, also felt a nagging sense of unease about the sheer physicality of these cables as they are laid on one of the vanishingly few pristine natural environments we still have left. Is it right that planet Earth's deepest, most mysterious depths, the places we still know far less about than we do about planets hundreds of millions of kilometres away, should be so irreverently bisected by man-made wires? To me at least, there was something impressive but also rather uncanny about the image of fibre optic cables, hung like clothes lines, dangling over canyons and undersea coves. These same cables are now also increasingly wiring up our planet's final frontiers. They have reached the Arctic, they meander along the bends of the Amazon river,[1] and soon will even connect Antarctica, the planet's last true wilderness – the cable engineers like frontiersmen, conquering Earth's last unknowns.

It was therefore somewhat of a relief to find out that the impact of undersea cables on the biotopes they inhabit, and the environment more generally, is actually quite modest.[2] By playing a dual role as sensors important for climate research,[3] cables can even be considered to present a net benefit for the planet (though this is of course hard to quantify). Some experts have told me that the environmental footprint of the overall cable network throughout its full existence – including all cables, their manufacture, the ships involved with laying them, from the 1850s until today – is likely still smaller than the impact generated in an average year by the global fishing industry.

This does not mean we should let the cable industry off the hook; most sectors shine by comparison with the Wild West that is global fishing. There is also more that can be done to reduce submarine telecommunications' environmental footprint. The ageing, predominantly dot-com-era cable-laying fleet is not just a security risk, it is also not as sustainable as it could be, to name but one example.[4] Implementing new technologies and upgrading existing systems could also help reduce the electricity consumption of cables and landing stations.[5] Cables also leave a local mark. Burying cables, especially nearer to shore, for example, inevitably means disturbing marine ecosystems – though there are generally robust planning and permitting processes in place to limit damage (according to some rather too robust – one industry hand I interviewed joked about how one cable landing he worked on in the United Kingdom required the rehoming of half a million cockles).

There is also an ongoing debate between industry and governments about whether the growing web of decommissioned undersea cables should be retrieved from the seabed. The usual practice is for these cables to remain there after their useful lifespan is up, as recovery is costly and hauling cables back up could disturb the intricate habitats that can over time form on top of them.[6] There is currently some 98,000 kilometres worth of decommissioned cable still out there, laying extinguished on the seafloor.[7] Old cables, however, contain non-negligible amounts of reusable, increasingly valuable materials, such as copper. In an era of growing mineral competition, in which countries are seeking to secure their own sovereign supplies and in which recycling is increasingly touted as a geopolitical imperative, retrieving this dormant web could become more interesting. This all notwithstanding, overall it can be said that the cable industry itself is relatively benign and, in the grand scheme of the damage humanity is doing to our marine environments, should perhaps not be the top priority.[8]

Where there are more difficult questions to be answered is around the increasingly outsized impact of the activities the cable network enables. In the same way we have shown that these systems are made up of far more than just physical cables alone, we cannot disregard the wider connectivity stack cables link together. The rapidly rising energy needs required to power the breakneck growth in AI and cloud computing are increasingly eye-watering. The International Energy Agency estimates that data centres collectively accounted for around 1.5 per cent of global electricity consumption in 2024, a number that may more than double by the end of the decade.[9]

The four largest hyperscalers – Microsoft, Meta, Alphabet and Amazon – were predicted to spend an estimated $650 billion on AI infrastructure – the equivalent of the annual GDP of Norway – in 2026 alone.[10] These infrastructure expenditures are increasingly being allocated not just to direct AI inputs such as data centres and specialized chips, but also to new energy infrastructure to support these systems. This rush to build sees hyperscalers don yet another hat: that of energy investors and developers. The tech giants are investing in more climate-neutral sources of power, such as nuclear energy (Microsoft in 2024 announced it would support an effort to recommission Three Mile Island, the Pennsylvania-based nuclear plant, famous for being the site of the most serious nuclear incident in US history),[11] but are also spending big on, for example, natural gas (so much so that there is now a global shortage of gas turbines).[12] Expansion into the Gulf countries similarly sees the data centre energy mix decidedly pivot towards fossil fuels. Given the perceived strategic utility of artificial intelligence and the near-existential importance that is being bestowed on maintaining a competitive edge in the technology, it is not especially likely that this growing footprint will soon be subjected to any serious government scrutiny (or in the words of President Trump, when it comes to the US winning the AI race, it is time to 'drill, baby, drill').[13]

Whether the AI hype will last is an open question. At the time of writing, despite growing jitters in the more clear-headed segments of the market, there are few signs of the hyperscalers slowing down their investments. This should raise some questions for the cable industry about their role in facilitating this energy-guzzling infrastructure build-out, and rewiring of the cable map that comes with it.

## *Impact of climate change on cables*

Undersea cables can contribute to climate change, but are also vulnerable to the increase in storms, floods, droughts, soil erosion and other extreme weather events the projected rise in global temperatures is likely to bring.[14] Though cables are more resilient to climate threats than many other critical infrastructures, researchers have found that submarine cables, and especially cable landing stations, will likely see more frequent and severe faults in the decades ahead.[15]

A rise in sea levels and uptick in major storms, such as typhoons and hurricanes, can cause landing stations to flood and damage cables, especially ones nearer to shore. When Hurricane Maria hit the Caribbean in 2017, it caused widespread devastation, resulting in more than 3,000 deaths and over $90 billion in damages. The tropical cyclone also destroyed important sections of especially Puerto Rico's communications infrastructure, and widespread power blackouts saw the island's cable landing stations go dark.[16] Even if Puerto Rico's cables had proven themselves quite disaster-proof, the electricity grids and other hardware they relied on had not been. In the immediate aftermath, Puerto Ricans found themselves having to resort to using ham radio and other 'obsolete' technologies to reach loved ones abroad and organize emergency relief efforts. Storms like Hurricane Maria are only set to become more frequent and intense as the planet warms.

Extreme temperatures, too, form a threat and can cause landing stations and data centres to overheat. A hotter planet is likely to see more power outages.[17] Coastal erosion could cause especially sandy beaches to retreat. Some of the planet's most iconic beaches, from the Copacabana to Bondi and Miami Beach, are at risk of disappearing within the next few decades. Such erosion could expose previously buried cables to the elements. It will also result in more frequent undersea landslides, which form another menace to cables. The West African cable outages of March 2024, which took out four key cables facilitating the bulk of connectivity serving the region, were the likely result of underwater mudslides. Though damage caused by environmental factors is much rarer than human-made incidents, their fallout tends to be worse and longer-lasting, as they have a tendency to inflict more permanent damage over wider geographies, and can thus affect a much larger number of cables at the same time (the 2011 Tōhoku earthquake and resulting tsunami, most infamous for causing the Fukushima nuclear disaster, also damaged eleven of Japan's undersea cables, to name one example).

Climate change can also negatively impact the resilience of the network in more indirect ways. Rising ocean temperatures are likely to see fish migrate to colder climes, further away from the shores. This will lure the cable community's enemy number one, fishermen, to venture into deeper and deeper waters, where cables tend not to be buried, and are thus more vulnerable.[18] Fishing at greater depths requires heavier anchors and fishing gear, further compounding the risk. All of these factors will make outages more frequent and drive up costs as both planning and cable protection become more complex. This is likely to create even more bottlenecks and fragility in a network that is already finding itself under increased geopolitical and capacity pressure.

These potentially quite far-reaching impacts will not be distributed equally. Some geographies are far more vulnerable to climate upheaval than others. The Pacific Islands – which are already among the least well-served geographies in the global cable network – will be subject to an especially cataclysmic confluence of more frequent extreme weather events, seismic activity, beach erosion and flooding.[19] Some of these islands may become uninhabitable or could even disappear. It is no surprise, then, that Kiribati, an island nation whose population of 140,000 may in future be forced to vacate the archipelago as the seas close in, was one of the founding signatories of the New York Statement on improving cable resilience.

As the number of usable routes and landing spots may start to shrink or become more precarious, climate pressures could further accelerate the fragmentation of the network, and become yet another source of geopolitical tension, as some geographies become more fault-prone. One such example is Taiwan, which does not just find itself at the frontline of global geopolitical tensions, but also is particularly disadvantageously positioned when it comes to seismic activity, tropical storms and seabed geology. As the island considers how it can rapidly improve its resilience to deliberate cable cuts, it has more to worry about than just rogue sand dredgers venturing over from the mainland.

There is an irony in that some of the exact solutions that may help places like Taiwan become more resilient to climate risk are also becoming a source of fragmentation in their own right. Some of the technologies and ways in which cables can actually help us understand and combat the worst impacts of climate change also risk contributing to preventing the kind of collaboration we need to meet this shared challenge. As we have seen in chapter 7, new types of sensors like SMART see their roll-out hampered, as countries like China and the United States warn about their dual-use potential and the very sensitive nature of the data they could collect.

## *It's getting a little crowded in here, isn't it?*

Other solutions aimed at combatting climate change, too, could begin to impact the cable's freedom of movement. Given the vastness of the oceans, six hundred individual submarine cables may not seem like they would take up a particularly noteworthy amount of space on the seabed. Undersea cables may be very long, but they are also thin, and do not require much of a buffer zone – usually only around three metres of seabed needs to be kept clear alongside them. In other words: we would need to be laying unimaginably large numbers of them to start to saturate the ocean floor. But as we have seen, cables are not distributed equally and not all shorelines are equally suitable for landing stations. This means that some geographies are now in fact starting to become rather crowded.

When the first undersea telegraph and power cables were laid in the nineteenth century, they had the seabed largely to themselves. The only other man-made objects a cable would be likely to encounter once settled safely in the deep was the occasional anchor or fishing net. A shipwreck perhaps, or later stray ordinance. That is no longer the case. The first major undersea oil pipeline was laid across the English Channel in the direct aftermath of D-Day to supply the advancing troops with fuel. Today, global seabeds are home to tens of thousands of kilometres worth of oil and gas pipelines, with the density of these pipes especially high in North American and European waters.[20] The first offshore wind farm, erected off the coast of Denmark, became operational in 1991. The North Sea alone is now home to over 40 such parks.[21] Power cable growth, too, continues to increase at pace, as electricity generated in wind turbines offshore needs to be ferried back to land, and countries are starting to interconnect their grids across borders (recall Est-Link 1, one of *Eagle S*'s victims).

We simultaneously also fish more and have in the past few decades unleashed an aquaculture revolution – fish farms now produce 130 million tons of fish biomass annually, more than traditional fishing.[22] Cruise ships, some now the size of horizontal skyscrapers, ferry retirees between the world's great port cities and tropical beaches, and reportedly now cumulatively generate more annual emissions than the equivalent of one billion cars.[23] We trade more – in fact, 90 per cent of international trade of physical goods happens by sea. We still drill for oil and gas. All of these activities mean that, in the past thirty years, the world has been witness to a so-called 'blue acceleration': a rapid intensification of the use of our seas, oceans and seabeds, which has firmly brought the Anthropocene to the maritime domain.[24]

All of these activities will leave the seabed increasingly crowded. This risks becoming a challenge for the laying and security of undersea communications cables, especially in heavily exploited and cable-dense places such as the North Sea. The North Sea offers a prime example of a strategic waterway in which the blue acceleration has been at its most extreme, but also one in which several trade-offs presented by the reconfiguring global order converge. Here, competing objectives around security, energy sovereignty, trade and growth, connectivity and conservation increasingly interlink and clash.

Just as the North Sea (and Baltic Sea) is increasingly an axis around which European military integration has started to take shape, the North Sea countries are also looking at their shared sea as a focal point for economic collaboration.[25] In January 2026, mere weeks before the war in Iran saw the Strait of Hormuz closed, eight North Sea countries committed to together create 'the world's largest clean energy reservoir' by building 100 gigawatts' worth of offshore wind capacity, enough to power between 50 and 100 million homes.[26] The objective is to seize the opportunity offered by offshore renewable energy generation, in particular, as a new engine for decarbonization and rekindling economic growth and reindustrialization in Europe, and, as importantly, achieving energy independence – from Russia, but increasingly also the United States and the now more contingent Gulf countries.

In this neo-Hanseatic vision, offshore wind farms would be able to satisfy as much as 30 per cent of Europe's electricity needs (because if there is one thing the North Sea has a lot of, it is strong wind).[27] New innovations have also made it possible to build these farms further and further out at sea, and to retain the power they generate over greater distances. This opens up more of the sea to potential offshore development, and in turn also necessitates the laying of more and more kilometres of power cable on the seabed to wire them all up. Efforts to build these giant wind parks have run into some speed bumps about the financing of these projects, which has meant that promised investments have not always been unlocked. Nevertheless, it seems this type of renewable energy collaboration will over the long run be the direction of travel, especially as Europe increasingly sees having its own reliable sources of energy as a critical geopolitical imperative.[28]

North Sea countries are also picking up the pace on laying interconnectors among themselves to improve resilience and to reduce the high cost of energy, which has become an increasingly significant competitive challenge for Europe's industry. Such efforts have especially gained momentum in the wake of the war in Ukraine, which not only revealed Europe's over-reliance on cheap Russian gas, but also saw the continent trade this addiction for a new dependency on expensive liquefied natural gas (LNG), shipped over from the United States and countries like Qatar (the offshore terminals that were rapidly erected to receive these LNG shipments are yet another competitor for prime seabed real estate).

There are also more futuristic plans in the works. The governments of Denmark, Belgium and the Netherlands are all interested in building artificial energy islands off their coasts, which could be linked directly to these offshore wind farms, and house data centres and other energy-intensive industries closer to the source of generation. This promises yet more work for the cable.

All of these grand plans will take up physical space in a geography that is already starting to feel more crowded. According to some estimates the physical surface area required to build and operate marine aquaculture, offshore wind, oil and gas infrastructure in the North Sea could increase by as much as fivefold by 2050.[29] The North Sea is already one of the most heavily navigated and fished seas in the world. Oil and gas extraction will also not go away in the short to medium run. Naval activity increases as military tensions mount.

Another, especially controversial, competitor for space, of which the Pacific Ocean is likely to be a prime arena, is seabed mining – the extraction of minerals at depths greater than 200 metres, though generally far deeper. Some stretches of ocean floor are rich in mineral deposits. These can for example be stored in polymetallic nodules, small pellets sprinkled over the seabed, which contain high concentrations of elements like nickel and manganese, and can be hoovered up with specialized tractor-like machines. As countries around the globe race to secure access to critical minerals and other key resources, exploiting these hitherto untapped deposits will become increasingly tempting. The practice is, however, highly controversial. Seabed mining can disturb marine ecosystems and opens up one of the last unspoiled environments we have on earth up to exploitation and invasive human interference.

Environmental scientists and activists have fought hard to prevent the practice from gaining ground, and several dozen governments have called for outright bans or moratoria.[30] This notwithstanding, countries like the United States, China but also Norway have expressed an interest in at least exploring its potential. When conducted at scale, seabed mining, too, will compete for space on the ocean floor, and could cause potential disturbances that could amplify cable breaks, the ICPC has warned.[31]

All of this growth in maritime activity will put even more of an onus on improving cable protection. Because not only could over-saturating the seabed cause an uptick in accidental faults or interference – laying a cable too close to, for example, a power cable can disrupt signals – it may also put a further target on its back when it comes to potential sabotage.

The *Yantar*, which has frequently been caught snooping on undersea communications cable routes, has been spotted doing the same with strategic energy pipelines, wind farms and other critical infrastructures out at sea. The incidents with the *Newnew Polar Bear* and *Eagle S* did not just damage cables, but also a gas pipeline and power cables. It was the still mysterious sabotage of the Nord Stream gas pipelines that started the current flurry of attention to the fragility of our critical maritime infrastructures. Overcrowding the seabed increases the likelihood of accidental spillover, and creates fertile ground for aspiring saboteurs.

Some countries, such as Australia, have tried to shield their cable web from other seabed activities by putting in place so-called 'cable corridors', bands of seabed in which submarine cables are prioritized and other uses restricted. Such protection zones are intended to help prevent interference from other infrastructures and activities, such as fishing. They also place boundaries on the stretches of sea the authorities need to monitor – no small advantage for a country with a shoreline as long as Australia's. Cable corridors can be a good solution in a world where cables are not a tool of geopolitical strife. Deliberately concentrating many cables together, however, also introduces an easy target, some experts in the industry and government warn.

As the pressures on the cable network increase, some readers may wonder whether there aren't any other technologies available that can provide connectivity and are perhaps less beholden to the physical and geopolitical realities of our seas and oceans. Some tech enthusiasts suggest that there might be: amid rapid innovation in satellite technology, is it time to once again look at space for our future connectivity?

### *A threat from the heavens*

*A dark night – too dark, really – the sound of planes flying overhead.*

*Residents in Taiwan's coastal towns notice odd flashes in the distance – blinking a* dot, dot, dot, *far out at sea. Long rows of red and white lights stretching along the pitch-black horizon.*

*They turn to their phones. An earthquake? Have they missed the alert, somehow slept through the first tremors?*

*But when they unlock their home screens, nothing works. The strip on top shows zero bars. Strange. The usual news apps aren't updating. Perhaps they too have been affected by the quake.*

*A loud, droning noise in the distance. An unfamiliar, almost alien, humming.*

*Let's try the BBC World News. If there is something so important that they can't go back to sleep, it will surely be reported abroad too.*

*But the BBC website won't load either. Another error message.*

*Also on their laptops – just the Google Chrome dinosaur, inviting them to play. But they are in no mood for games. Something isn't right.*

*WeChat is slow – is uncle safe? A WhatsApp message to a cousin over in Vancouver – it's still only afternoon there – remains unread, the dreaded connection wheel spinning.*

*Didn't they use to have one of those old little wind-up radios? Would those not work? No, that one got donated ages ago.*

*They turn back to the kitchen window. The little red lights in the distance seem to be increasing in number, an orange flare arcing through the sky, like fireworks.*

*It couldn't be, could it?*

*Was this then finally the one?*

*If only they could manage to access some news.*

This is a real scenario military planners in Taipei, in Washington, Tokyo, Canberra and elsewhere need to reckon with. As of 2026, there are fifteen international cables that connect Taiwan to the rest of the world.[32] This is not an especially low number when it comes to redundancy, and reflects Taiwan's important role as a digital hub. But this seemingly robust cable web belies a rather concerning fragility underneath.

Several of Taiwan's cables make landfall on the Chinese mainland – meaning that they are anything but secure during a possible escalation involving its irredentist neighbour. If it were to ever come to a possible Chinese naval invasion or siege of the island it should be assumed that Taiwan's cable network would be a primary initial target, and an extraordinarily difficult one to defend too.

Surrounded as it is by water, Taiwan is almost entirely reliant on subsea cables for the bulk of its international connections. The cutting of the cables would leave the islands largely disconnected from the rest of the world, relying on less reliable and low-bandwidth satellite connections. Regardless of whether the PLA would choose to try and seize Taiwan swiftly, or instead lay a prolonged naval blockade, Taiwan and its supporters would likely not be able to reach the faults and restore cable-based internet connectivity anytime soon.

In the absence of fallback connectivity, mounting a successful military and civilian counter-response would become a lot more difficult. Taiwan's authorities would be significantly hampered in their ability to coordinate both military and civilian responses, especially if local communications systems were jammed in tandem. As news and communications from the outside world would slow to a trickle, it should be expected that panic would break out among the general public.

Taiwan is planning for this eventuality. Following the 2023 incident involving damage to the cables connecting to the Matsu Islands – the one where Chinese vessels severed the small islands' two main subsea links, leaving them without internet for nearly two months – Taipei announced it would not only try to bolster cable connectivity to its more sparsely populated, outlying islands, but would also explore alternative technological solutions to bring more redundancy to its overall network.[33]

One possible solution which has been gaining traction is the use of so-called lower Earth orbit (or LEO, for short) satellites, near-earth constellations of smaller satellites which can be easily deployed more or less anywhere in the world to deliver high-speed internet. Elon Musk's Starlink is the most famous, and currently the most mature and widely used, example of the current crop of LEO satellite systems.[34] Though LEO satellites cannot yet – and by most level-headed expert assessments, likely never will – replace the bandwidth provided by cables, they could offer stopgap connectivity in times of a large-scale outage. These small satellites also have a growing military utility, as we shall soon see.

As there is a growing awareness about subsea cables as a prime target – both in the grey zone, as well as in more conventional conflicts – it should come as no surprise that governments are looking elsewhere for alternatives, as we discussed in chapter 6. This security-driven hunt for what we have dubbed 'modal redundancy', as well as efforts to leapfrog into promising new areas of technological development, to rid oneself of a dependency or vulnerability, are not new.

This is exactly what Germany and the United States sought to achieve with their early, risky investments in wireless telegraphy, which they saw as providing an opportunity to disentangle themselves from the strictures of Britain's dominance over the telegraph cable network. There are currently no challenger technologies that could replace the fibre optic cable as the main conduit for international data traffic. The recent success of LEO satellites, however, has seen several governments across the world now race to develop their own sovereign capacity in this domain.

## *Lower Earth orbit revolution*

It is not so long ago that satellites still played an important role in global communications and connectivity networks. They would, however, begin to rapidly give way to fibre optic cables over the late-1980s and 1990s. By the early 2010s, their share had dwindled to a measly 1 per cent.

The primary reason for why satellites lost out to the same technology they had superseded (at least in the public imagination) some decades before was primarily efficiency. New fibre optic cables proved incredibly effective at moving the exponentially growing amounts of data generated in the digital economy to far-flung places. And they could do so much faster than satellites could – and much more cheaply too. The connectivity gap between cables and satellites is now vast: total global satellite capacity in 2026 stood at around 50 terabits per second.[35] Contrast that with subsea cables, which had a potential capacity of around 8,750 terabits per second.[36] Satellites similarly cannot compete with cables on latency – the inevitable delay involved with getting a packet from A to B: satellite traffic has to travel several tens of thousands of kilometres up into space, away from Earth, and then back again before it reaches its intended destination.

This challenge of high latency was already a source of grievance before the advent of the internet. Telecommunications companies wanted international telephone calls to be speedy – we have all experienced how disruptive and noticeable even a minor delay or echo on a phone call can be. Latency issues truly became a headache, however, as the new digital era began to demand anything from near-instantaneous financial flows to high-quality video calls and streaming.

The reason why communications satellites cannot offer this type of speed is in part because the majority of them are deployed in geostationary orbit, around 36,000 kilometres from Earth – where satellites move at the same speed as the Earth's rotation. Positioning satellites in geostationary orbit has many advantages. It allows them to stay at the same fixed point with respect to Earth, meaning ground-based infrastructure does not have to adjust. And because they are so far away, their signals can cover large swathes of territory, along the earth's curvature, limiting the number of satellites needed to provide wide coverage. Positioning satellites at such a distance, however, also means that data has to travel a long time to reach a satellite, and take a similarly long time to be beamed back again to its intended recipient back on earth.

To resolve these issues of limited bandwidth and high latency, it has long been hypothesized that relying on larger quantities of smaller satellites positioned much closer to Earth could provide a solution. So-called lower Earth orbit satellites, or LEOs, are placed in orbits of less than 2,000 kilometres from Earth. Here, they are deployed in large clouds, or constellations, which enable these nimbler satellites to cover the same amount of ground their far larger geostationary cousins do, while dramatically increasing speed and capacity, as bandwidth is now distributed over a much higher number of objects.

This is not the first time we have seen experimentation with LEO satellites. In the late 1990s, alongside the ill-fated boom in fibre optic cable roll-out, a wave of startup companies like Iridium and the Bill Gates-backed Teledesic attracted billions in funding to try and make satellites fit for the internet age, by moving satellite deployment down to lower-Earth orbit. But a lack of maturity of the technology itself, eye-watering costs, and, soon after, the dramatic bursting of the dot-com bubble saw these efforts crash back to Earth.[37]

From the early 2010s onwards, a new wave of companies has tried to rekindle this dream, benefitting from new technological advances, increased demand for hyper low-latency connectivity, and steep drop in costs (it is, according to industry assessments, now around 100 times less expensive to launch 1 gigabit into space than it was two decades ago).[38]

Early mover OneWeb, initially a British startup since acquired by French Eutelsat, was launched in 2012 – and by 2026 had a constellation of around 600 satellites up in LEO and MEO,[39] making it the second largest provider. In 2019, Amazon founder Jeff Bezos launched Project Kuiper, since renamed Amazon LEO, which now also has its first satellites up in LEO. China, too, has several domestic challengers of its own, such as the state-backed, dual-use GuoWang and Qianfan, which are presently still some way behind, and initially focused primarily on the Chinese market. Most famous and advanced, however, is Elon Musk's Starlink, which launched its first LEO satellites in 2019, benefitting from its mother company SpaceX's ability to provide it with cheap launch capacity to drive down costs. As of March 2026, there were some 10,000 live Starlink satellites up in LEO,[40] and the company had over 10 million subscribers.

While LEO satellites are a promising technology, they are currently neither powerful nor cheap enough to provide a serious alternative to undersea cables as the backbone of global connectivity. We should thus see them primarily as a powerful addition to cables, there to fill the gaps the undersea network cannot. They can help bridge the digital divide, for example, by bringing high speed connectivity to places where laying cables – whether terrestrial or undersea – is prohibitively expensive or complex. Starlink, for example, now provides connectivity to Antarctica, though a $200 million US-government funded undersea cable may in future replace it.[41] The system is also increasingly popular in rural areas where bandwidth access is limited. Some fans of the outdoors bring the receiver terminals with them on camping trips. Systems like OneWeb and Starlink were initially also conceived as a solution for bridging Africa's pernicious connectivity gap.

LEO satellites can also bring reliable, high-speed internet to moving platforms, such as trains and airplanes (forcing our eyeballs onto our phones in one of the few remaining places that had remained mercifully disconnected). They are providing connections to cruise ships – in the same way that Marconi's wireless would bring news and entertainment to the passengers of the transatlantic ocean liners.

LEO satellites are also particularly useful for providing backup connectivity in the wake of crises such as natural disasters. This is the kind of use government and military officials tasked with the response to large-scale cable outages are watching particularly closely. Musk famously offered Starlink to Ukraine right at the start of Russia's full-scale invasion, as the invading Russian army put (and continues to put) enormous strain on Ukraine's internet infrastructure.[42] He took to X to offer the same to Gazans in the wake of the IDF's invasion of the land strip,[43] and to the residents of Los Angeles during the devastating forest fires of early 2025. When Tonga was left in the dark in the aftermath of a 2022 earthquake which destroyed its cables, Starlink offered limited respite.[44] Some traffic was diverted through Starlink systems following the sinking of the *Rubymar* in the Red Sea as well.

But the domain where we have perhaps seen most interest, especially from governments and militaries, is in LEO satellite's use on the battlefield. The successful and highly innovative deployment of Starlink systems by the Ukrainian army – and, through deft evasion of restrictions, to a lesser extent by the Russian army as well – has shown that the kind of hyperconnectivity enabled by LEO satellites can be a gamechanger in modern warfare.

They allow troops on the ground to be far more mobile, while allowing them a lot more real-time visibility of what is happening on the battlefield. More importantly, they are also a crucial enabler of the extensive drone operations that have come to define the war in Ukraine. By early 2025, both sides were producing over 200,000 drones a month, with innovation happening so fast new solutions to either attack or defend against drones were becoming obsolete within a matter of weeks.[45] A reported 70 per cent of battlefield casualties in Ukraine are now caused by UAVs.[46]

The most visceral manifestation of the first true drone war is perhaps the Baudrillardian, technobeat-accompanied social media videos of soldiers being chased through trenches by first-person view (FPV) drones. Both these remote detonations and their recording are frequently made possible by Starlink connectivity. Especially during the early stages of the war, LEO satellite systems also proved more resilient to electronic warfare and jamming than traditional military communications solutions like radio, because signals have shorter distances to travel and can be moved ('beam hop') between different terminals.[47] All of this has certainly not gone unnoticed in defence ministries around the world.

## *Space race 2.0*

The highly effective use of Starlink in Ukraine has fuelled a rush among governments to procure LEO satellite capacity of their own, as part of a wider rekindled race to dominate commercial and military space technologies. This push, however, also runs the risk of introducing its own new dependencies and vulnerabilities. Like many of the drones being used in Ukraine (though Kyiv has increasingly indigenized this production), also many of the space-based solutions deployed in the conflict originate in the private sector. There is Starlink but, for example, also much of the satellite imagery used for reconnaissance and identifying targets is provided by commercial space actors. This has created another situation in which private companies – or in some cases a single individual – can wield an enormous amount of power over increasingly critical functions and infrastructures countries rely on for their security and survival.

In a now notorious incident in September 2022, Musk is reported to have personally intervened to prevent the Ukrainian military from using its Starlink systems in an operation in Russian-occupied Crimea.[48] In February 2025, the US government reportedly again threatened to turn off Ukraine's access to Starlink – all of it, this time – in an apparent attempt to coerce Ukrainian President Zelensky into agreeing to a disadvantageous critical minerals deal.[49] This was no idle threat: Ukraine remains extremely reliant on the technology for key military operations. Kyiv has long been acutely aware of its dependency on Starlink. In the absence of viable, proven alternatives, it has, however, proven difficult to diversify away to other providers. Ukraine is certainly not the only one concerned about entangling themselves into a new dependency which can be weaponized against them by opting for Starlink. Following Musk's X threats, Ukraine and its European supporters rushed to find alternatives – and soon turned to less mature and still smaller, but what they perceived to be more politically dependable European rivals like Eutelsat's OneWeb constellation.[50] The Franco-British satellite operator saw its stock price soar over 500 per cent in response[51] – and has since signed further deals with places with similar concerns, like Greenland.[52] As we have seen throughout this book, weaponizing dependencies can be a powerful lever in the geopolitical arena, but overplaying one's hand can also erode an advantage.

Also Taipei is acutely aware of the risks that come with relying on a single, not exactly apolitical, provider. Taiwan's concern reportedly centred around Musk's reliance on China in his various business dealings.[53] In particular, Tesla, the electric car company the billionaire is most famous for, is deeply intertwined with both Chinese manufacturing supply lines and export markets (though Tesla faces increasingly formidable domestic competitors in the country). This entanglement has raised questions in the Taiwanese government about its ability to rely on Starlink should China ever decide to pull the proverbial trigger.[54]

When describing Taiwan's original initiative to procure LEO satellites, Audrey Tang, the island's illustrious former digital minister, famous for spearheading Taiwan's pioneering digital government efforts, cautioned against 'addressing one vulnerability by creating another'.[55] This is why Taipei has also turned to currently still less well-established providers, such as Eutelsat and Amazon LEO, and is now also launching its own domestic provider.[56] Tang, in an interview with Bloomberg, clarified that the island would be working with multiple providers from multiple jurisdictions; this not just to bring redundancy and reduce coercive levers, but also to 'make it very difficult to jam or disrupt all those different satellite systems belonging to different countries at once'.[57]

Taiwan sees purchasing LEO satellite capacity from a wider range of suppliers as a path towards resilience as it aims to launch its own. Others too are rushing to build their own sovereign LEO satellite systems. As part of its broader strategic autonomy agenda, ambitions to gain independent access to space and revive its flagging commercial space industry, the European Union has committed to funding IRIS², its own sovereign satellite constellation.[58] The project, which involves the likes of Airbus, Eutelsat and several of the continent's telecom giants, will cost an estimated €10.2 billion. The IRIS² constellation is planned to consist of a comparatively modest 290 satellites which will be deployed both in lower Earth and medium Earth orbit. Once ready, the system will bring high-speed satellite internet to European citizens, but importantly also provide Europe's militaries with reliable, encrypted communications. Also in Europe, it is these kinds of dual-use benefits that increasingly drive the agenda.

Achieving consensus and buy-in when it comes to actually adopting $IRIS^2$ has, however, proven more difficult. The project will not be completed until 2030, which in 2025 led the Italian government, under the leadership of Prime Minister Giorgia Meloni, to consider spending over €1 billion on acquiring Starlink access to facilitate both military and government communications. While Meloni was then one of the few European leaders who enjoyed a warm relationship with Musk and the Trump White House, critics in Italy and Europe worried about the security implications of relying on a non-sovereign system for a key ally's most sensitive communications.[59] The heated debate that resulted from the deal – which has since been put on hold – illustrated the difficult trade-off Europe now faces: disentangling oneself from a dependency often comes with a higher cost and quality compromises, and could leave Europeans temporarily vulnerable before their own systems fully mature.

China, unsurprisingly, is similarly eyeing its own sovereign capabilities. Though Beijing has announced several initiatives, not much is known about the progress on China's LEO satellite ambitions. What is known is that Beijing has secured permission from the ITU, which also governs the deployment of new satellites, to launch more than 200,000 of them into space. In 2024, it launched its first rockets to support its plans to have its first 1,300 LEO satellites up in orbit by 2027.[60]

The Pentagon, which runs one of the most tech-mediated militaries and certainly the best-resourced one, unsurprisingly has been especially interested in bringing LEO satellite connectivity into its technology stack. Under the Biden Administration, it, too, started to have reservations about becoming too dependent on commercial providers.[61] This is even more so, because Elon Musk already played an outsized role in Pentagon military contracting, with especially SpaceX's capabilities increasingly indispensable for NASA and the US military's ability to operate in space.[62] To address these concerns – which came to a head after the tensions over the use of Starlink in Crimea – SpaceX in 2022 announced it was launching Starshield, a military-grade, more secure version of Starlink, specifically designed with the US military (which is a major customer) in mind, which hands more – but still not full – control to the Pentagon. But even though we now see some of these safeguards be put in place, the infrastructural power at play here remains profound. The symbiotic relationship between the private sector and the Pentagon is reminiscent of the Cold War days discussed in chapter 4, though the advantage this time appears to be tipped in favour of the tech giants, not the government.

## *'Rumours of the cable's death have been greatly exaggerated'*

If you were to take a ruler and try to find the point where a survivor of a shipwreck would find herself with the longest possible distance to have to swim to get back to land, triangulation would find you a spot – a so-called pole of inaccessibility – deep in the Pacific Ocean. We call this place Point Nemo. Point Nemo is the spot where ageing satellites and spaceships come to die: the end station after a careful, controlled landing back to Earth, as far from civilization, and thus risk, as possible. Nemo is where Soviet space station Mir was laid to rest, along with over 250 other space vessels. It is also the spot where the International Space Station (ISS) is scheduled to deorbit and crash into the ocean after its planned retirement in the early 2030s.[63]

Point Nemo may be among the most visceral, physical points where the High Seas and space meet. But it is certainly not the only one. There are a striking number of similarities and overlaps between the space and maritime domains – from rulebooks that can resemble the Wild West, to concerns about overcrowding, to increased geopolitical competition and greyzone activity. It is in many of these parallels where we will also find the limitations of LEO satellites, and their ability to become a serious challenger to the undersea cable.

LEO connectivity is not only still comparatively expensive, it would require an incredible amount of individual satellites to function at scale and achieve the kind of bandwidth and coverage cables can now provide. Some readers may have seen the distinct chains of Starlink terminals pass by in the night sky, like a neat train of ducks cutting through a stream. Now imagine a murmuration of lit-up starlings fully saturating the skies: to generate enough connectivity to satisfy global demand would require the deployment of orders of magnitude more of the small satellites than are currently up there. So many, in fact, that they could start to overwhelm the orbit they operate in – which is already the most crowded.

As of early 2026, there were over 14,000 satellites deployed in space, of which 84 per cent orbit in LEO. In 2020, that number was still only 3,000. In 1990 it was about 450. If all the LEO satellites currently queued up for ITU approval actually get launched, it would bring us to over *one million* satellites.[64] This, according to many experts, is not sustainable. Overcrowding LEO risks leaving the orbits we rely on unusable, and by extension the growing pantheon of space activities heavily constrained, if not rendered impossible. Space, incongruous as it may sound, can, like our seas and oceans, become too crowded. The orbits most useful for space activities are finite – and it is especially lower Earth orbit that is at risk.

Having too many satellites and other space objects up in lower Earth orbit is a growing concern among scientists, who worry these new mega-constellations will light up the skies to such an extent it would make astronomical observation prohibitively difficult.[65] America and China's goal of having the first astronauts (and taikonauts) set foot on the moon in generations, or Elon Musk's even more ambitious mission of colonizing Mars, could also be hindered by the oversaturation of near-space. Satellites also serve more purposes than just communications. Lower Earth orbit is a critical one, which provides a home to everything from the ISS, to the satellites enabling GPS, climate and weather monitoring, to those serving military needs critical for intelligence-gathering and command and control. There is now even increasingly more concrete talk in tech circles about launching solar-powered data centres into orbit.[66]

A compounding challenge is that many of these new LEO satellite systems do not have a long lifespan. A Starlink satellite needs replacing every five years, after which they are designed to make their way back to Earth.[67] Contrast this with cables, which can last twenty-five years. Given the volumes of satellites required to make a dent in cable connectivity, the environmental implications of this speak for themselves. These short lifespans also present a more significant challenge: the domain of space, like the High Seas which cables traverse, is very thinly regulated when it comes to the deployment of new space objects, but importantly also their removal.[68]

While space objects are engineered to either burn up in the atmosphere or make their way back to Earth – in places like Point Nemo – that process does not always go equally well, and can cause debris to get stuck in orbit. The proliferation of so-called 'space junk' – leftover bits and parts of space objects – is an under-appreciated but serious issue, only set to worsen if the fevered visions for space-based hyperconnectivity come to fruition. There are at the time of writing some 8,000 pieces and fragments of space objects stuck in orbit. Some of this space junk is condemned to circle and circle around our planet in perpetuity.[69]

This cosmic debris can take on such a velocity that even a tiny screw or finger-nail-sized speck of paint can do an incredible amount of damage to the objects they collide with. Dotting the skies with ever more satellites increases the risk of such collisions happening, especially when the satellite's deployment is done in haste, amid accelerating commercial and geopolitical competition over control of space and supremacy in the space economy. Such collisions are even hypothesized to be able to set in motion a chain reaction, which could take out with it a cascading amount of space objects in its wake. This so-called 'Kessler syndrome' could create a cloud of space debris so wide and so fast-moving it could effectively mean the end of humanity's ability to use a specific orbit, or possibly even outer space, at all.

The risk of space debris is aggravated by a lack of internationally recognized governance and accountability mechanisms. There are efforts by the United Nations to bring together the major space powers, like the United States, China, Russia and the European Union, to agree on norms and rules around responsible behaviour in space and prevent – or otherwise clean up – cosmic junk. The commons-nature of space, its growing geostrategic importance, as well as the current geopolitically tense climate, leave the chances of these global governance initiatives making significant headway rather slim.

Competition in space shows similarities to the weaponization of the seabed and High Seas, with countries taking an increasingly more belligerent and provocative stance. Russia, back in 2021, controversially destroyed one of its own satellites as part of an anti-satellite weapons test, creating a cloud of debris that briefly forced the crew of the ISS – which at the time included two Russians – to seek shelter.[70]

In 2007, China similarly deliberately destroyed one of its own satellites, an event which has generally been perceived in the West as a show of force to showcase Beijing's ability to take down space objects during a future war.[71] NATO adopted space as a fourth domain of war fighting in 2019, and the United States launched a dedicated space force during the first Trump Administration, both decisions that showcase how strategically significant space has once again become.

Hybrid activity, too, is increasing in the space domain, with cyberattacks (targeting especially ground stations), the jamming of signals and spoofing to, for example, disrupt GPS, and reportedly also so-called 'proximity operations' – deliberate near-misses of space objects – growing in frequency. In another analogue with cables, the design of commercial space objects and infrastructure, too, has been the product of a peace dividend mindset, meaning they are frequently not yet designed with these kinds of escalations in mind.

All of this means that though LEO satellites can serve as a useful back-up technology to cables during times of crises and bring new uses, the technology is far from resilient against some of the same forces that threaten the cable. Technological limitations will also limit their immediate uptake. But just as we saw at the advent of wireless, which, too, was an initially expensive technology beset by technological hurdles: when an innovation proves to have significant strategic and military utility, practical concerns about cost and reliability, let alone responsible use, may well conveniently be brushed aside.

# 9

# *Future Cables*

When crowds gathered in Europe and North America to celebrate the successful landing of the first transatlantic telegraph cable, the gravity of the historical moment they were sharing must have been palpable. This was a paradigm shift for humanity, a decisive victory of technology over distance. The future had arrived. In the century and a half since, we have begun to take the undersea cable, and the near-instantaneous global communications it enables, for granted.

The cable's fading from the public imagination would not take long. By the turn of the twentieth century, attention had already started to shift towards communications technologies that seemed to belong even more firmly in the realm of science fiction than submarine cables' Vernian deep-sea mystique. First, there was wireless telegraphy and radio, which captured a *Zeitgeist* consumed by the paranormal and the occult. Some decades later, we fell for the glamour of the space race, Sputnik, and the satellite. With the birth of the internet and all that it enabled, our awareness of the physical engineering underpinning it became even more superficial, reduced to a vague, ethereal notion of 'the cloud'.

In some ways, the invisibility of the network is a byproduct of its own triumph. As we have seen throughout this book, undersea cables – with all the human ingenuity, graft, collaboration and technological innovation involved in making them work – show a remarkable degree of resilience. If you have ever experienced a serious internet or service outage, a screen going dark, it was most likely not caused by an undersea cable fault. We do not see – never had to see – undersea cables, because they essentially always work. It would almost make us forget that this is a physical network routed through the depths of our oceans, garden hoses laid bare on the seabed, light shooting through them through infinitesimally thin fibres, pulses representing unfathomably large amounts of data, of information, carried to us, away from us, anywhere we want it to, within the blink of an eye. It shouldn't work, and yet it does.

But this lack of awareness of the vital physical infrastructures that make our world spin has also introduced dangerous fragilities. Indeed, decades of peace dividend thinking, relatively low geopolitical tension, and a by and large collective commitment to maintaining open trade and lines of communications have left us complacent. Eroding international norms, the weaponization of dependencies, climate upheaval and the rising spectre of global bifurcation and conflict have, however, left this economic model of driving down cost at the expense of resilience, diversity and decentralization increasingly precious.

It is this same model that has resulted in our currently hyper-centralized technology sphere – where a handful of firms control virtually all layers of the stack. When one of the major cloud providers suffers an outage, hospitals, airports and banks around the world ground to a halt. Many of the products and services we use every day – from search engines to 'smart' fridges to booking doctors' appointments – increasingly feel like they are no longer working as well as they used to,[1] but alternatives are now vanishingly few. The skilled maintainers are retiring from the workforce in droves. In a world where innovation is the leitmotif and the archetype of the lone genius inventor is praised above all else, we do not always sufficiently value the critical importance of the systems and people that keep things running and secure – let alone find ourselves willing to bear their cost.

In this book, we have also explored the recent spate of incidents involving damage to cables, from the Arctic, to the Baltic, from Taiwan to the Red Sea, and the escalating greyzone phoney war between Europe, the United States, Russia, China and Iran and their proxies, that have catapulted undersea communications cables to the forefront of public discourse again, after more than a century of near absence. These incidents, too, have revealed the danger of peace dividend thinking and have started to make us once again aware of the perils of leaving little slack and redundancy in systems. We now live in a more dangerous, uncertain world, in which a polyphony of intersecting crises has increasingly begun to leave its mark on the contours of the network. Submarine cables may not be inherently fragile, but the world they operate in increasingly is.

Given the role cables play in enabling and upholding the post-war global order, they are uniquely vulnerable to its retreat. Undersea cables have always been harbingers, perhaps even preconditions, of globalization. The telegraph cable helped give rise to what we now consider the first wave of globalization, shaped in Britain's image – a period of hyper-imperialism and increased international trade and financial entanglement, which birthed an order which found its final demise in the trenches of the Great War. The extensive cutting of cables during the First World War can perhaps be seen as symbolic of the severed tethers to that lost world. The fibre optic cable, too, came of age in an era of increased globalization, a period of post-Wall exuberance, increased international commerce and borderless trade, financialization, and the internet – all of which the undersea cable in part enabled. I am finishing this book at a moment when that second wave of globalization similarly appears to be reaching the end of its rope, or at the very least, sees the rules that govern it dramatically rewritten, in no small part by their very author. The weaponization of undersea cables is set to once again play an important role in this unravelling, and in several ways exemplifies its retreat.

The cable network as we currently know it has relied for its global expansion on a relatively open, free and secure maritime domain, underpinned by Pax Americana. This was a world in which all countries, especially the most powerful ones, took responsibility for keeping trade routes open, and on the whole did not overly greedily make use of the chokepoints and their ability to control activity in their respective territorial waters. The waning power and weight of international agreements like the Law of the Seas, the more general decline of multilateral institutions like the United Nations, and a reduced willingness to guarantee maritime security by key actors actively undermine this now fragile balance.

The cable network in no small part also relies on us *wanting to be* interconnected. It is why we lay them to begin with. The whole global edifice of companies, organizations and operators there to make the network function only survives because there is so much demand for funnelling increasingly large amounts of data to other places. That this demand persists is not a given. We are in the early stages of a growing global push towards more technological sovereignty, where countries keep data close to home, prefer cloud infrastructure to be on their own soil and nurture their own insulated technology stacks, and more generally seek economic and political decoupling. All of this could see the demand for international exchange start to dwindle.

Maintaining a truly global, interoperable and shared subsea cable network ultimately relies on cooperation and trust. Governments and companies across the world together ensure there is shared repair capacity. They collectively agree to uphold norms and laws that posit that cables are not to be interfered with – whether that takes the form of sabotage, or the tapping of sensitive communications (commitment to the latter, of course, has in the past already proven more fungible). We appear to no longer be living in that world. On the seabed, war is already raging. Previously core cable geographies start to be avoided and supply chains disentangled, further laying the groundwork for an increased bifurcation of the global network, which could eventually see it split altogether.

## *The great unwinding*

These threats to the network, and the increased spectre of fragmentation, are happening against the backdrop of a rapidly unwinding global order. We appear to find ourselves at one of those inflection points in history, when the tectonic plates of alliances and power are rapidly reconfiguring, but where it is not yet clear where the new balance might stabilize, or who will end up on top in the new status quo. To paraphrase a Gramscian maxim: we are in an interregnum, in which the old world is dying, and the new has yet to be born.

These kinds of moments, as history has shown us, can be incredibly dangerous. The world has arguably not been closer to a full-scale global conflagration since the end of the Second World War. Rapid technological and demographic change is sparking domestic and international tension, and undermines political stability and the social contract in countries across the world. Wars of territorial conquest are no longer a thing of the past. The spectre of an even wider escalation looms large, as the erstwhile hegemon retreats and others rush to rebuild their military capacity, try to reduce their dependencies on one another, or – better yet – make use of the ones they themselves already hold.[2] In this already tense environment it is especially difficult to imagine a stable endpoint to the increasingly heated competition between China and the United States (and now the latter's relationship with its nominal allies too) – a new balance in which all powers would find themselves content and with dignity intact.

As I have aimed to show throughout this book, undersea cables feature remarkably frequently in this increasingly multifaceted tug-of-war over global position and influence. The different ways in which the network is being weaponized are not only varied, they can also be said to reflect the distinctive pathologies and ways in which (would-be) great powers are seeking to balance the wobbling icebergs of the emerging order in their favour.

The United States sees the advantages and unprecedented power it has wielded since the end of the Second World War under threat by the rise of China, and the emergence of a more multipolar world. The three key pillars of America's hegemony – its overwhelming military might, technological and economic leadership, and the global role of the US dollar – are no longer beyond dispute. To maintain its position, the country, under successive administrations, has been throwing all the levers its current central role has endowed it with to buy itself time and ensure the old balance of power is maintained. If there is to be a reconfigured order, the thinking goes, it should continue to have the United States at its core.

Under the Biden Administration, bipartisan efforts to maintain US technological supremacy – at the core of American grand strategy since at least the early Cold War – and outcompete China took on an almost existential fervour, in which national security and economic statecraft became increasingly one and the same. Hundreds of billions were mobilized to ensure the United States could rebuild and secure its industrial capacity in semiconductors and other strategic industries. National security concerns drove an ever-larger number of technologies to become subject to export controls. Expensive political capital was cashed in with long-standing allies such as Japan and the Netherlands to strong-arm them into participating in these efforts.

This approach has found its reflection in the undersea cable domain too. The Trump and Biden Administrations have proven ruthlessly adept at using America's own central role in the digital economy, its powerful web of allies, technological heft and control of trade flows to push Chinese cable companies out of the global cable market. The infrastructural power wielded by its hyperscalers was deftly leveraged to 'de-risk' the network from perceived threats of Chinese interference and to lay new strategic cables. As the relationship between Washington and Silicon Valley grows ever more intimate, its ability to wield power through this emerging tech-industrial complex will only intensify, with deeply concerning implications for everyone else dependent on its technology.

The second Trump Administration is no less concerned about America's role on the global stage, but has taken a decidedly different view when it comes to identifying the remedies that may ensure America's continued hegemony. Where the Biden Administration's approach was built around working closely with allies – even if this rhetoric frequently belied an in practice more coercive dynamic – Trump's America First has approached its relationships with the rest of the world as transactional, if not outright hostile. This is to be a world of regional supremacy and – in the words of Secretary of State Marco Rubio – a return to the historical 'normalcy' of multipolarity, in which different great powers reign supreme in their respective spheres of influence.[3] It paints a world in which the United States is more insular, protects its own interests first, wages wars of choice, and no longer foots the bill for acting as the world's policeman and good steward. The erratic way in which the Administration has gone about accomplishing this – and the amount of global distrust it has sown in the process – suggests we are witnessing something more akin to hegemonic suicide than a budding hemispheric supremacy. What this will mean for the global undersea cable network – which is unlikely to thrive in such a geopolitical climate and without its chief protector – remains to be seen.

Russia never had the requisite economic strength, strategic coherence, or firm hold over global chokepoints to allow it to enjoy the kind of pervading, networked power the United States and increasingly also China wield.

Perhaps aware of its limitations for a change, Russia, rather than positioning itself as the single global hegemon in its own right, has instead focused on pursuing multipolarity, and has done so with an almost messianic zeal.[4] For Moscow, which sees itself as unduly disrespected in the current system, to once again enjoy the great power status it believes it is owed, it wants to see the world move back to an international arrangement more akin to the Concert of Vienna, where countries have their own spheres of influence – and can apparently wage genocidal wars to protect them. In achieving this, the Kremlin has not shied away from using all the asymmetric levers of chaos and disruption it has at its disposal to undermine the current order and will this new future into existence.

These tactics are reflected in the country's actions in the cable domain. Russia – a bit part player when it comes to undersea cables, and increasingly isolated from global communications networks more generally – has relatively little to lose from undermining trust and the security of the network. Most of its cable connectivity is terrestrial, and the country is taking increasingly more aggressive and far-reaching steps to limit its citizens' access to the global internet.

The alleged sabotage incidents targeting cable infrastructure in the Baltic Sea and High North, which as we have seen many believe the country is behind, and Russia's frequent escapades in NATO waters, not only serve to undermine morale in the countries targeted, but also force these countries to compromise on important values underpinning the current order, such as the freedom of navigation and the more general pursuit of maritime collaboration and openness. Russia as the spoiler and disruptor – literally and figuratively.

China, too, sees the current moment as an opportunity to right historical wrongs, but does not see itself as a spoiler, but rather as a new pole in its own right – the literal Middle Kingdom's rightful place in the world to be restored, at the heart of a whole new set of global networks.[5] Beijing does not so much want to destroy the current order and its associated rulebook, but rather to alter, and significantly strengthen its role in it. One way in which the country has aimed to do so is by making itself increasingly economically indispensable.

China has been biding its time, and has steadily but effectively positioned itself to dominate the industries of the future. From leading in critical mineral, photovoltaics and electric vehicles to shaping the rules and new institutions: China wants to set the parameters for the new electrified, green energy order – in the same way the United States was able to do for the petro-order in the aftermath of the Second World War.[6] The current closure of the Strait of Hormuz may speed up this epochal transition. China is also becoming an increasingly formidable player in the innovation sphere. According to the Australian Strategic Policy Institute, China now leads in the development of fifty-seven out of the sixty-four critical emerging technologies the institute tracks.[7] Where the United States is increasingly betting the house on AI, China is taking a more diversified approach.

Beijing's strategy is not just focused on putting China at the forefront of technological developments in anything from AI to quantum to biotechnology but also looks to leverage this new dominance to create its own interdependencies of which the PRC will be the prime beneficiary. The renminbi, it hopes, will be able to play the role in the renewable energy order that the US dollar for now still plays in the fossil economy.[8] By setting standards and exporting its vision, and the tools, for cyberspace, China plans to further draw other countries into its innovation sphere and make them dependent on its supply chains.

Telecommunications, including undersea cables, have – as we have seen – long been core to this strategy. Influential CCP voices over the years have not only called telecoms infrastructure a critical enabler for spurring domestic technological innovation and adoption, but also a key tool for expanding China's global influence.[9] The roll-out of cables allows China to weave other countries into its web, while its dubious interpretation of its maritime jurisdiction has seen Beijing push yet others out of what it perceives to be its sovereign, historical sphere of influence.

China's path ahead – ridden with domestic economic and demographic pressures, growing global pushback, and a persistent soft power deficit internationally – may not be as smooth as it is often presented. The current seemingly chaotic retreat of the United States from its global role will, however, offer opportunities.

Whether a Chinese-led world order would bring the kind of Pax Sinica and stability Pax Americana and Pax Britannica did at their apex remains to be seen. As it stands, China does not seem especially interested in donning the mantle of the good steward in the global system. Where the United States brought us Bretton Woods and the WTO, China brings oversupply and market distortion. Where both Britain and the United States were (up to recently) willing to police maritime trade routes and keep global lines of communications open, Beijing seemed to have treated the closure of the Red Sea to Western ships as a welcome opportunity to improve the competitiveness of its own shipping industry.

Another power which could potentially benefit from the current moment of uncertainty and polycrisis to strengthen its geopolitical position in the world and fill the vacuum left by the United States apparently ceding its leadership role, is Europe. Europe, at least when acting in a unified fashion, is arguably the only other pole with the requisite economic heft and global influence to challenge the China–US binary that currently seems primed to form the axle around which the new multipolar world turns. The European Union especially has an opportunity to present itself as the trusted, predictable safe haven, which adheres to the rule of law – which could allow the continent to strengthen anything from the role of the Euro in the global system, its ability to attract long-term investment and global talent, to a chance to form a third paradigm for innovation and trustworthy technology. A more offensive, hard power-focused strand of this thinking also sees Europe take back its traditional military and geopolitical role in the world – high levels of defence spending since the start of the war in Ukraine, a budding sense of pan-European patriotism, and growing animosity and distrust towards the United States add fervour to these pursuits.

So far, however, Europe has primarily been at the receiving end of what Commission President von der Leyen has referred to as a hyper-competitive and hyper-transactional new global order.[10] The return of territorial conquest to its soil, the increasingly hostile and coercive external forces chipping away at its security and economic competitiveness, chaotic retreat from past certainties and eighty years of American patronage, an ageing, declining population and growing public discontent about the seeming inability of its leaders to respond to these challenges, have shaken the continent's confidence.

This lack of confidence and leadership is reflected in its difficulty to find itself a vision and story to tell on the global stage. Indeed, it seems its geopolitical approach continues to vacillate between the – naive though noble – hope that old norms, alliances and institutions can be maintained, and its emerging strategic autonomy agenda, which seeks to set out a vision for a more strategic, independent and ultimately more powerful global role for the Union, and seize the opportunities offered by others' retreat.

Europe has been showcasing a growing willingness to chart its own sovereign course in the technological realm, after being shocked into action when it saw its profound military and software dependencies weaponized against it, but at the same time remains wary of antagonizing the US government or giving preferential treatment to its homegrown solutions.

We see this play out in the undersea cable domain too. In order to make a fist against both hyperscaler dominance and China's Digital Silk Road spending and growing innovation footprint, Europe has also upped its game in the cable diplomacy realm. The funding of strategic cables in Europe's hinterland, from the Arctic to the Mediterranean to the Black Sea, but also further afield in places where the EU seeks to strengthen its diplomatic and economic ties, has allowed the continent to grow its global influence, but has also invited – in my view misguided – domestic accusations of Europe joining the neo-colonial arms race for global power.

This fightback also has a security dimension. It was not just the return of war to the European continent, but also the increasingly brazen shadow war campaign waged against it that once again made clear that Europe's multi-decade geopolitical holiday was truly over. These incidents have contributed in what can be said to be a steady, quiet and therefore easily written off Europeanization of NATO, and a growing comfort with the continent taking more forceful action on its own.

It also exemplifies Europeans' core dilemma: by seizing suspicious ships, assets or – bolder yet – returning the favour, Europe is increasingly forced to itself operate in the grey zone, and so too abandon the pillars of the rules-based global order. In a world where old norms are rapidly crumbling, does it still serve to play by the rules and hold on to what was?

Others, so-called middle powers – from the United Kingdom to the Gulf, India, Canada, Brazil and Turkey – may not have the same great power pretensions (yet), but look to work with others or seize the opportunities they can as they balance the diverging icebergs, straddling and positioning themselves to avoid getting stuck in the maelstrom or to improve their lot. While for many the sudden falling away of the US security umbrella presents a serious threat, a more multipolar, diverse order in which more countries can have their voices and concerns heard, and can wield new levers of power the emerging order could introduce, could also serve many of these small and mid-sized actors well.

We already see middle powers leveraging the asymmetric advantages they have at their disposal – for example by controlling new chokepoints,[11] or by building new economies, and dependencies around the resources that may start to become more important in a post-hydrocarbon world.[12] In the cable space, middle powers have presented themselves as new, more secure or neutral cable hubs ('little Switzerlands'), as sources of cheap energy and abundant land for new AI infrastructure, or have stretched the powers bestowed upon them by the Law of the Seas to maximum effect. Others see an opportunity to hedge between the competing camps to derive maximum advantage, for example by courting geopolitically motivated cable investments and subsidies.

## *Lessons from history*

We have seen how the increased entanglement of the undersea cable network in wider geopolitical competition over the shape of the new global order can also undermine its integrity. Though the entry of China and the hyperscalers has quite dramatically changed the balance of power of the network, cable routes have shown themselves remarkably sticky – the products of historical inertia, geographical constraints and economic inequalities. But they are not immutable. Routes can and do change – even the most pernicious chokepoints can erode. The key players behind the increasingly escalatory weaponization of cable routing and other maritime activities in the Red Sea risk overplaying their hand, for example. Their actions will, however, likely primarily impact their own individual hubs and spokes in the network, which over time could see them bypassed and the chokepoints they control lose their potency. When the *communications hegemon*, instead, abandons its good stewardship over a network in the name of security and consolidating its own power, the consequences can be a lot more profound.

Here, we may take lessons from the British example. During the early communications revolution of the nineteenth and early twentieth centuries, Britain was the unmistakable superpower in the network. It held this advantage for decades. Laying a telegraph cable, funding a cable, running a cable, repairing it: all involved Britain one way or another. For most, the idea that London would in the future not be at the heart of effectively all facets of global communications would have been unimaginable. And when a challenger in the shape of Marconi's wireless did arrive to challenge the All Red Line's global supremacy, the Admiralty simply saw to it that Britain would dominate this new technology too. The incredible centrality Britain enjoyed in the network was not just the product of its market dominance combined with deft strategic thinking and generous subsidies in Whitehall, but also relied on its peers, which all benefitted from Britain's largesse and protection of global telegraphy, willingly handing it this stewardship role.

Britain was long aware it would be able to translate this overwhelming network centrality into a serious and destructive weapon should the need ever arise. Though not always the most responsible steward over the network before the First World War (which had seen some of its hold already start to loosen), Britain long held its powder dry and chose to deploy the nuclear option of cutting Germany out of the global network only when its impact would be greatest. Indeed, the contribution severing Germany's communications made to the outcome of the war is arguably an underestimated one. Britain playing this card to such devastating effect – and by extension making it abundantly clear that London would be able to do the same to others – however, also meant other countries would now increasingly start to try to limit their dependency on British communications benevolence. Everyone had seen the damage that could be done.

This episode offers lessons for today. Weaponizing one's dominance in shared systems comes at a cost – especially in the longer run. America has for decades disproportionately benefitted from its leading role in global networks, an advantage it has been able to translate into a potent weapon. The Snowden revelations revealed how the United States and its Five Eyes partners could make use of their geographical centrality in the cable network to undertake expansive surveillance operations. Washington has been able to use its infrastructural power over the internet and related technologies to push China out of telecommunications infrastructures, from 5G roll-out to, indeed, submarine cables. It learned how to leverage the might of the US dollar – and the deep insight into global financial flows it allowed – to place sanctions on rogue actors like Iran and Russia.

After the return of Trump to the White House, the use of these networked weapons has taken on an even more coercive turn – and now just as frequently targets America's long-standing allies as it does its foes. The United States has used its overwhelming dominance over technology, tariff threats and the indispensability of its market to secure deals and to force vassalized allies to water down regulations its tech giants did not like. It dangled its security umbrella and weapon exports as bargaining chips to secure market and resource access. As I finalize this manuscript in the early months of the Administration's second year, it can be said that, for now, the US has left its good steward role well and truly behind.

Not only is Washington already beginning to see its own power in networks and global influence begin to be questioned because of this new approach, its actions have also started to set in motion the decline of these same architectures it has so long controlled. Even America's allies are now making rapid moves to reduce their reliance on US technology and weapon systems and build their own sovereign alternatives – which may well see the dominance of hyperscalers over all layers of the tech stack start to wane. New technologies – such as lower Earth orbit satellites – may once again supplant the old. The role of the once unassailable dollar is now for the first time being questioned. New financial structures and other alternative institutions, such as those being proposed under the auspices of the BRICS, may see their influence grow.

The United States is not entirely alone in this: China, too, has started to use the dependencies it has quietly built to coerce others. This, too, will spur others to, for example, speed up the development of their own alternative sources of critical minerals, or reconfigure supply chains. Weaponizing interdependencies is showing itself one of the more powerful levers of influence in an interconnected, globalized world, but is a weapon that needs to be used with caution. It is single-use – so use it well.

## *Context collapse*

We do not yet know what kind of world we might be moving towards – whether it is a world of deglobalization and rushed fragmentation, of bifurcated continents and power blocs, or new forms of intertwined multipolarity. But what is clear is that the trajectory certainly does not appear to be towards more openness and collaboration. What that means for the undersea cable, the ultimate symbol of the interconnected world, only time can tell.

And that is perhaps the main message of this book. Undersea cables, as we have seen, are both objects and subjects of power. They are above all, however, tools of mutual understanding – the medium that conveys the message. And it is exactly that role that is now under pressure. When the aforementioned crowds lined the shores to witness the first transatlantic cable landings, they marvelled not so much about the gutta-percha and copper, but about the ghosts in the machine – the words coming to them from thousands of kilometres away, the actual meaning behind the *rat tat tats* of the telegraph. When the internet shrugged off its military-industrial antecedents, we celebrated not the tubes and wires, not (just) the billions to be earned by the tech moguls, but the – now arguably horribly naive – promise that the internet would turn us all into one global village.

The whole assemblage of physical infrastructures, the edifices of our connectivity – the rubber, glass and copper, the grey boxes that house data centres, the revived Three Mile Islands,[13] the IXPs and ISPs, even the device you may be reading this on: they are important because of what they enable. The flows of communications, the ability to share and exchange with others across the world, the complete demystification of the far-away, the removal of barriers and informational gatekeepers. It is from these data and information flows that cables ultimately derive their power.

We are currently living through a moment when it is becoming increasingly clear just exactly how much power that truly is. Revolutions in communications as profound as the one enabled by the internet inevitably bring great upheaval. While the internet's far-reaching impact has been felt for decades now, it has only been in the past few years that the sheer magnitude of change the internet has brought has truly started to manifest itself. Indeed, virtually all of the tectonic forces of change we have discussed in this chapter are either catalysed by or have their roots in this digital revolution. The current moment of great power transition is in a significant way rooted in a battle over data-driven technological supremacy, which the players involved believe will determine the new global haves and have-nots.

Though the internet has also brought much good, its corrosive influence on democracies and shared sense of purpose and truth mean that the existing post-war political consensus that has kept most of the Western world historically stable for nearly eight decades is rapidly coming to an end. As I finish this book, we are also witnessing in real-time the unprecedented fusion between the world's most powerful presidency and military, and Silicon Valley, home to the richest and most influential companies – a marriage which may deliver a whole new type of information-mediated hyperpower altogether.[14] It is impossible to fully understand the impact of these kinds of epoch-defining moments of change when one is living through them: is this the birth of something entirely novel, or are we instead witnessing the final hurray of these information empires, the final manic dance before the bubble bursts and with it perhaps even the relentless forward expansion of communications technology?

Seventy-seven years passed between Gutenberg's invention of the printing press in 1440 and his compatriot Martin Luther hammering his ninety-five theses on a church door in Wittenberg. The dissemination of Luther's ideas – made possible by that same printing press – would set in motion a series of events, including one of the most lethal wars the continent has ever seen, which would radically transform Europe, and soon after the world. Since Gutenberg, we have been on a more or less relentless trajectory of intensification of communications and democratization of access to information, with successive innovations allowing the sometimes steady, sometimes very rapid, reduction of distance and time. First information conquered land, then found its way through seas and oceans, then moved into space: the next frontier we can perhaps find in the accelerationist visions of AI-enabled hyperconnectivity and omnipotent machine intelligence sold to us by technology companies and supporting act of assorted futurists and evangelists.[15] Given this hitherto relentless push forward, it is easy to assume that this whiggish path towards ever more connectivity will always continue. It is certainly not something we consider likely to ever reverse.

The fragmentation and deglobalization of the internet is, however, already taking place, and is impacting ever more layers of the connectivity stack, from governments censuring free flows of information,[16] all the way down to the hidden but no less fractious competition over undersea cables. Though we are not there yet, we may eventually find ourselves in a bifurcated world, of wholly separate technology spheres, where doing something as mundane as sending an email to a friend abroad may simply no longer be possible.

It is hard to imagine what such a world would look like, but that should not mean we should rule out the possibility. Messengers could relay letters from Rome to the empire's furthest outposts in as little as ten days during the apex of the Roman Empire's power[17] – enabled by a system of well-maintained and guarded roads and imperial outposts, semaphores, sea and riverine routes, like proto-landing stations and communications cables projecting its might. By the early Middle Ages most of this system was already lost – the same journey now taking weeks, if not months. This was not just due to the declining physical state and maintenance of the Roman *viae* themselves, but also the loss of security, of norms, of a societal consensus that this was a system to be preserved, enforced and protected. As both the digital and maritime domain are becoming increasingly contested, the bar to abusing the network's openness continues to be lowered, and the sea lanes that make possible the current order crumble, undersea cables, too, could become a relic of a lost world.

# *Notes*

**Introduction**

1 C. Bueger and T.P. Edmunds, *Understanding Maritime Security* (New York: Oxford University Press, 2024).
2 United Nations Conference on Trade and Development (UNCTAD), *Shipping data: UNCTAD releases new seaborne trade statistics*, 2024. https://unctad.org/news/shipping-data-unctad-releases-new-seaborne-trade-statistics.
3 David E. Sanger and Eric Schmitt, 'Russian presence near undersea cables concerns US', *The New York Times*, 25 October 2015.
4 Sebastian Moss, 'Project Waterworth: Meta announces world's longest subsea cable project spanning five continents', *Data Center Dynamics*, 14 February 2025.
5 TeleGeography, 'Submarine cable FAQs (frequently asked questions)', TeleGeography. https://www2.telegeography.com/submarine-cable-faqs-frequently-asked-questions.
6 TeleGeography, 'Submarine cable map'. https://www.submarinecablemap.com/.
7 Allison Marsh, 'The first transatlantic telegraph cable was a bold, beautiful failure', *IEEE Spectrum*, 31 October 2019.
8 'Dunant – Submarine networks'. https://www.submarinenetworks.com/en/systems/trans-atlantic/dunant.

**1 A Global Revolution**

1 M. Schwartz and J. Hayes, 'A history of transatlantic cables', *IEEE Communications Magazine* 46, no. 9 (2008): 42–8.
2 Daniel R. Headrick, *The Invisible Weapon: Telecommunications and International Politics, 1851–1945* (New York: Oxford University Press, 1991).
3 Christopher Hoag, 'The Atlantic telegraph cable and capital market information flows', *Journal of Economic History* 66, no. 2 (2006): 342–53.
4 Simone M. Müller and Heidi J.S. Tworek, '"The telegraph and the bank": on the interdependence of global communications and capitalism, 1866–1914', *Journal of Global History* 10, no. 2 (2015): 259–83.
5 Jill Hills, *The Struggle for Control of Global Communication: The Formative Century* (Urbana: University of Illinois Press, 2002).
6 Rudyard Kipling, 'The deep-sea cables', in *The Seven Seas*, 1896 via the Kipling Society. https://www.kiplingsociety.co.uk/poem/poems_cables.htm.
7 Ivan Roussev, 'The telegraph in the Crimean War', in *The Routledge Handbook of the Crimean War* (London: Routledge, 2021).
8 David Paul Nickles, *Under the Wire: How the Telegraph Changed Diplomacy* (Cambridge, MA: Harvard University Press, 2003).
9 Orlando Figes, *The Europeans: Three Lives and the Making of a Cosmopolitan Culture* (London: Allen Lane, 2019).

10 Daniel R. Headrick and Pascal Griset, 'Submarine telegraph cables: business and politics, 1838–1939', *Business History Review* 75, no. 3 (2001): 543–78.
11 Dwayne Winseck, 'Submarine telegraphs, telegraph news, and the global financial crisis of 1873', *Journal of Cultural Economy* 5, no. 2 (2012): 197–212.
12 P.M. Kennedy, 'Imperial cable communications and strategy, 1870–1914', *English Historical Review* 86, no. 341 (1971): 728–52.
13 Headrick, *The Invisible Weapon.*
14 Nicole Starosielski, *The Undersea Network* (Durham, NC: Duke University Press, 2015).
15 John Tully, 'A Victorian ecological disaster: imperialism, the telegraph, and Gutta-Percha', *Journal of World History* 20, no. 4 (2009): 559–79.
16 Headrick and Griset, 'Submarine telegraph cables'.
17 Headrick, *The Invisible Weapon.*
18 Ibid.
19 Jeffrey G. Williamson and Kevin H. O'Rourke, *Globalization and History: The Evolution of a Nineteenth-Century Atlantic Economy* (Cambridge, MA: MIT Press, 1999).
20 Nickles, *Under the Wire.*
21 Ibid.
22 Kennedy, 'Imperial cable communications and strategy, 1870–1914'.
23 Starosielski, *The Undersea Network.*
24 Headrick and Griset, 'Submarine telegraph cables'.
25 Tully, 'A Victorian ecological disaster'.
26 Daniel R. Headrick, 'The tools of imperialism: technology and the expansion of European colonial empires in the nineteenth century', *Journal of Modern History* 51, no. 2 (1979): 231–63.
27 'Captain Bowman H. McCalla's Lessons of the Late War, 1899'. https://www.history.navy.mil/content/history/nhhc/research/publications/documentary-histories/united-states-navy-s/telegraphy-and-cable/captain-bowman-h-mcc.html.
28 Headrick, 'The tools of imperialism'.
29 Daniel R. Headrick, 'Strategic and military aspects of submarine telegraph cables, 1851–1945', in Bernard Finn and Daqing Yang (eds) *Communications Under the Seas: The Evolving Cable Network and Its Implications* (Cambridge, MA: MIT Press, 2009).
30 House of Commons Parliamentary Papers, Cd. 1056, 'Cable Communications Report of the Inter-departmental Committee on Cable Communications' (1902).
31 Heidi J.S. Tworek, 'How not to build a world wireless network: German–British rivalry and visions of global communications in the early twentieth century', *History and Technology* 32, no. 2 (2016): 178–200.
32 House of Commons Parliamentary Papers, Cd. 1056.
33 Hills, *The Struggle for Control of Global Communication.*
34 Kennedy, 'Imperial cable communications and strategy, 1870–1914'.
35 Winseck, 'Submarine telegraphs, telegraph news, and the global financial crisis of 1873'.
36 Starosielski, *The Undersea Network.*
37 Kennedy, 'Imperial cable communications and strategy, 1870–1914'.
38 Conducted in 1911 by the successor Committee for Imperial Defence.
39 Ibid.
40 Heidi J.S. Evans, '"The path to freedom"? Transocean and German wireless telegraphy, 1914–1922', *Historical Social Research/Historische Sozialforschung* 35, no. 1 (2010), 209–33.

41 Headrick and Griset, 'Submarine telegraph cables'.
42 Headrick, *The Invisible Weapon.*
43 Jonathan Reed Winkler, *Nexus: Strategic Communications and American Security in World War I* (Cambridge, MA: Harvard University Press, 2008).
44 'Captain Bowman H. McCalla's Lessons of the Late War, 1899'.
45 Evans, '"The path to freedom"?'.
46 Pascal Griset, 'Je t'aime, moi non plus: the development of Atlantic submarine cables and the complexity of the French–American Dialogue, 1870–1960', in Bernard Finn and Daqing Yang (eds) *Communications Under the Seas: The Evolving Cable Network and Its Implications* (Cambridge, MA: MIT Press, 2009).
47 Philipp Blom, *The Vertigo Years: Europe, 1900–1914* (New York: Basic Books, 2008).
48 Erik Larson, *Thunderstruck* (London: Random House Large Print, 2006).
49 Elizabeth Bruton and Paul Coleman, 'Listening in the dark: audio surveillance, communication technologies, and the submarine threat during the First World War', *History and Technology* 32, no. 3 (2016): 245–68.
50 Rick Umback, 'Huawei and Telefunken: communications enterprises and rising power strategies'. Australian Strategic Policy Institute, 2019.
51 Jonathan Reed Winkler, 'Bridging the gap: the cable and its challengers, 1918–1988', in Bernard Finn and Daqing Yang (eds) *Communications Under the Seas: The Evolving Cable Network and Its Implications* (Cambridge, MA: MIT Press, 2009).
52 Nickles, *Under the Wire.*
53 Tworek, 'How not to build a world wireless network'.
54 John Ferris, 'Before "Room 40": the British Empire and signals intelligence, 1898–1914', *Journal of Strategic Studies* 12, no. 4 (1989): 431–57.
55 Nicholas Hiley, 'The strategic origins of Room 40', *Intelligence and National Security* 2, no. 2 (1987): 245–73.
56 Nicholas Mulder, *The Economic Weapon: The Rise of Sanctions as a Tool of Modern War* (New Haven, CT: Yale University Press, 2022).
57 Nicholas A. Lambert, *Planning Armageddon: British Economic Warfare and the First World War* (Cambridge, MA: Harvard University Press, 2012).
58 Mulder, *The Economic Weapon.*
59 Marc Frey, 'Trade, ships, and the neutrality of the Netherlands in the First World War', *International History Review* 19, no. 3 (1997): 541–62.
60 Evans, '"The path to freedom"?'.
61 Frey, 'Trade, ships, and the neutrality of the Netherlands'.
62 Ibid.
63 Alexander Watson, *Ring of Steel: Germany and Austria-Hungary at War, 1914–1918* (London: Allen Lane, 2014).
64 Barbara W. Tuchman, *The Zimmermann Telegram* (London: Ballantine Books, 1985).
65 Kennedy, 'Imperial cable communications and strategy, 1870–1914'.
66 Winkler, *Nexus: Strategic Communications and American Security in World War I.*
67 Ibid.
68 Ibid.
69 Ibid.
70 Stephen B. Adams, 'Arc of Empire: The Federal Telegraph Company, the US Navy, and the beginnings of Silicon Valley', *The Business History Review* 91, no. 2 (2017): 329–59.

71 Winkler, 'Bridging the gap'.
72 Ibid.
73 Document 16: ADM 116/4594: Provision of a Gibraltar-Madeira cable – 1942.
74 Document 12: ADM 116/5443: Cable communications and cable ships: repairs Eastern Mediterranean, loss of cable ship FARADAY, strategic cable requirements, etc. v – 1941–1945.
75 Document 40: ADM 116/3360: Emergency requirements for communications facilities between Admiralty and ports, establishments etc. From National Archives.
76 ADM 116/5445: Naval W/T and D/F station in Azores: transfer to United States Navy, disposal of equipment, site, etc. From National Archives.
77 Daniel Immerwahr, 'Twilight of Empire', *Modern American History* 1, no. 1 (2018): 129–33.
78 Ruth Oldenziel, 'Islands: the United States as networked empire', in Gabrielle Hecht (ed.) *Entangled Geographies: Empire and Technopolitics in the Global Cold War* (Cambridge, MA: MIT Press, 2011), pp. 13–42.
79 Asif Siddiqi, 'Sputnik 50 years later: new evidence on its origins', *Acta Astronautica* 63, nos. 1–4 (2008): 529–39.
80 Aaron Bateman, 'Information security in the space age: Britain's Skynet satellite communications program and the evolution of modern command and control networks', *Journal of Strategic Studies* 47, no. 1 (2023): 5–28.
81 Frederick R. Kappel, Oral History Interview – JFK#1, 11/08/1965, From John F. Kennedy Presidential Library.
82 President Eisenhower, 'Merry Christmas from space!', Pieces of History (blog), 19 December 2012.
83 Hugh R. Slotten, 'Satellite communications, globalization, and the Cold War', *Technology and Culture* 43, no. 2 (2002): 315–50.
84 Ibid.
85 Winkler, 'Bridging the gap'.
86 CIA-RDP79T01149A000300130004: submarine communication cables of the Soviet bloc and other nations of potential Soviet invasion, 20 November 1952.
87 A.C. Wilson, 'A thousand years of postal and telecommunications services in Russia', *New Zealand Slavonic Journal* (1989): 135–66.
88 Ibid.
89 Robert Campbell, *Soviet and Post-Soviet Telecommunications: An Industry under Reform* (Boulder, CO: Westview Press, 1995).
90 Michael Goodman and Huw Dylan, 'British intelligence and the fear of a Soviet attack on Allied communications', *Cryptologia* 40, no. 1 (2016): 15–32.
91 Ibid.
92 Review of NATO telecommunications system – 1956 SGWM-172-56. From NATO Archives.
93 Aaron Bateman, 'The weakest link: the vulnerability of US and Allied global information networks in the nuclear age', *Journal of Strategic Studies* 48, no.1 (2025): 156–85.
94 NATO: SUBJECT: Protection for the Shore Ends of Submarine Cables 1953SGM-0738-53. From NATO Archives.
95 'Review of NATO Telecommunications System – 1956'.

96 David Edgerton, *The Shock of the Old: Technology and Global History Since 1900* (Oxford: Oxford University Press, 2007).
97 Starosielski, *The Undersea Network*.
98 Goodman and Dylan, 'British intelligence and the fear of a Soviet attack'.
99 Desmond Ball, 'Improving communications links between Moscow and Washington', *Journal of Peace Research* 28, no. 2 (1991): 135–59.
100 Ibid.
101 Ibid.

**2 Peace Dividend**

1 Winkler, 'Bridging the gap'.
2 Jeff Hecht, *City of Light: The Story of Fiber Optics* (Oxford: Oxford University Press, 1999).
3 Peter Runge, Oral History Interview, AIP. https://repository.aip.org/node/129779.
4 Hecht, *City of Light*.
5 Ibid.
6 Peter Runge, Oral History Interview.
7 Ibid.
8 International Cable Protection Committee, 'Sharks don't dine on subsea fibre-optic cables, says ICPC', *Fibre Systems*, 1 July 2015.
9 Patrick Juggerst, 'AT&T's undersea fiber-optic cable systems', *Sea Technology* 36, no. 7 (1995): 29–30, 32–4.
10 Rush Doshi, *The Long Game: China's Grand Strategy to Displace American Order* (Oxford: Oxford University Press, 2021).
11 Cable & Wireless Communications, 'Our History', Liberty Caribbean Communications.
12 Bill Clinton, 'Full text of Clinton's speech on China Trade Bill'. Speech, Paul H. Nitze School of Advanced International Studies, Johns Hopkins University, Washington, DC, 9 March 2000.
13 Margaret Thatcher letter to Keith Joseph (Cable & Wireless/GEC applications for export licenses for equipment to lay fibre optic cables across Soviet Union) ['Project Marathon': reason for refusal]. Released July 2018. Margaret Thatcher Foundation archives.
14 Michael Mastanduno, 'Strategies of economic containment: US trade relations with the Soviet Union', *World Politics* 37, no. 4 (1985): 503–31.
15 Margaret Thatcher letter to Keith Joseph ('Marathon' project) [defends Government decision not to grant export license; suggest meeting of officials with representatives of the Marathon partners]. Released July 2018. Margaret Thatcher Foundation archives.
16 'Coordinating Committee for Multilateral Export Controls (CoCom): Exports of Fibre Optic . . .', 1 December 1992. FCO 177/644.
17 Steven Greenhouse, 'US and Allies move to ease Cold War limits on exports', *The New York Times*, 25 May 1991.
18 Antony J. Blinken, 'Cold War static on fiber optics', *The New York Times*, 4 January 1992.
19 Al Gore, Speech at the inauguration of the First World Telecommunication Development Conference (WTDC-94), 21 March 1994.
20 Andrew Blum, *Tubes: A Journey to the Center of the Internet* (New York: Ecco, 2012).
21 Starosielski, *The Undersea Network*.
22 Damien Cave, 'Dot-com party madness', Salon, 25 April 2000.

23 Dwayne Winseck, 'The geopolitical economy of the global internet infrastructure', *Journal of Information Policy* 7 (2017): 228–67.
24 Jeff Hecht, 'Boom, bubble, bust: the fiber optic mania', *Optics and Photonics News* (October 2016): 47–53.
25 Areppim AG, *Internet users in the world: Growth statistics and 2010 forecast.* https://stats.areppim.com/stats/stats_internetxfcstx2010.htm.
26 Brian Duignan, 'Dot-com bubble', *Encyclopaedia Britannica.* https://www.britannica.com/money/dot-com-bubble.
27 Brookings Institution, *The telecommunications crash: What to do now?* (2003).
28 Ibid.
29 Hecht, 'Boom, bubble, bust'.
30 Jeff Hecht, 'The bubble legacy', *Physics World* 23, no. 5 (2010): 36.
31 Winseck, 'The geopolitical economy of the global internet infrastructure'.
32 Thomas Donahue, 'The worst possible day: US telecommunications and Huawei', *PRISM* 8, no. 3 (2019): 14–35.
33 Winseck, 'The geopolitical economy of the global internet infrastructure'.
34 Josh Dzieza, 'The internet's undersea deep repair ships', *The Verge*, 16 April 2024.
35 Submarine Networks, 'Statistics on subsea cable fault and repair'.
36 KIS-ORCA, 'Maintenance & repair operations'.
37 Josh Dzieza, 'The internet's undersea deep repair ships'.
38 Dan Swinhoe, 'The cable ship capacity crunch', *Data Center Dynamics*, 6 December 2022.
39 Ibid.
40 Jianqing Chen, 'From Cold War geopolitics to the crisis of global capitalism: the history of Chinese wireless network infrastructures (1987–2020)', *The China Quarterly* 255 (2023): 644–62.
41 Edward J. Malecki and Hu Wei, 'A wired world: the evolving geography of submarine cables and the shift to Asia', *Annals of the Association of American Geographers* 99, no. 2 (2009): 360–82.
42 Ibid.
43 CAICT, 'Report on China's Participation in the Construction and Protection of International Communication Submarine Cables' (2025).
44 TeleGeography, *Chinese vs U.S. Network Infrastructure in Asia, From Cloud to Cables* (2024).
45 Richard Wray, 'Ten years after the crash, the dotcom boom can finally come of age', *The Observer*, 14 March 2010.
46 Carlota Perez, 'Unleashing a golden age after the financial collapse: drawing lessons from history', *Environmental Innovation and Societal Transitions* (2013): 9–23.
47 David Jagielski, 'Amazon is an e-commerce beast, but this much smaller segment makes up 60% of its operating profit', *The Motley Fool*, 16 November 2024.
48 Dan Swinhoe, 'Submarine cables find new impetus under hyperscalers', *Data Center Dynamics*, 23 November 2021.
49 Alan Mauldin, 'A (refreshed) list of content providers' submarine cable holdings', TeleGeography, 27 June 2024.
50 Dunant has a capacity of 250 *tera*bits per second, almost a million times larger than TAT-8's 280 megabits per second.

51 Stephen Burton, 'Submarine cable launch numbers have surged since 2020 and another 68 cables are expected by 2027', Analysys Mason, 16 May 2024.
52 Swinhoe, 'Submarine cables find new impetus under hyperscalers'.
53 Katja Bego, 'A vision for the future internet', Nesta, September 2020.
54 For example, Paul Lipscombe, 'Keeping fiber shortages in check', *Data Center Dynamics*, 5 May 2023.
55 Harry Baldock, 'Hyperscalers: seizing the reins of the submarine cable industry', Total Telecom, 18 February 2025.
56 Amber Jackson, 'Moody's AI spending surge will keep driving hyperscaler race', *Data Centre Magazine*, 1 July 2025.
57 Jesse Noffsinger et al., 'The cost of compute: a $7 trillion race to scale data centers', McKinsey & Company, 28 April 2025.
58 Vantage Markets, 'How the Magnificent Seven stocks shape the S&P 500', 12 December 2025.
59 Baldock, 'Hyperscalers: seizing the reins of the submarine cable industry'.
60 https://www.iscpc.org/.
61 Deutsche Welle, 'Two Baltic Sea cables repaired after suspected sabotage', Deutsche Welle, 1 June 2025.

**3 Contours of the Network**

1 National Science Foundation, 'Antarctic subsea cable', National Science Foundation, US Government. https://www.nsf.gov/geo/opp/ant/antarctic-subsea-cable.
2 Allegra Rosenberg, 'How Antarctica's history of isolation is ending – thanks to Starlink', *MIT Technology Review*, 26 February 2024.
3 Winston Qiu, 'Google to build Umoja subsea cable connecting Africa with Australia'. Submarine Cable Networks, 24 May 2024.
4 Jet Propulsion Laboratory, 'Next-generation water satellite maps seafloor from space'. *NASA JPL News*, 19 March 2025.
5 In fact, the wider maritime research community has benefitted greatly from both the longevity and sophistication of the cable industry and its prolific seabed mappers.
6 Submarine networks and ICPC statistics.
7 BBC News, 'Asia communications hit by quake', BBC News, 27 December 2006.
8 Winston Qiu, 'Cables cut by Taiwan earthquake and typhoon Morakot', Submarine Networks, 19 March 2011.
9 Tom Bateman, 'Tonga is finally back online. Here's why it took 5 weeks to fix its volcano-damaged Internet cable', euronews, 23 February 2022.
10 Meaghan Tobin and Marian Kupu, 'Four months offline: post-quake, many Tongans are still without Internet', Rest of World, 30 May 2022.
11 Jonas Franken, Thomas Reinhold, Lilian Reichert and Christian Reuter, 'The digital divide in state vulnerability to submarine communications cable failure', *International Journal of Critical Infrastructure Protection* 38 (2022): 100522.
12 The Maritime Executive, 'Internet outages highlight Africa's few and faulty subsea cables'.
13 Matt Burgess, 'Why Egypt became one of the biggest chokepoints for Internet cables'. *Ars Technica*, 3 November 2022.

14 Sebastian Moss, 'Egypt's submarine cable stranglehold', *Data Center Dynamics*, 15 September 2022.
15 Ibid.
16 Dhanashree Thorat, 'Colonial topographies of Internet infrastructure: the sedimented and linked networks of the telegraph and submarine fiber optic Internet', *South Asian Review* 40, no. 3 (2019): 252–67.
17 Jess Auerbach Jahajeeah, 'Undersea cables for Africa's internet retrace history and leave digital gaps as they connect continents', *The Conversation*, 15 March 2024.
18 European Central Bank, *The International Role of the Euro* (Luxembourg: Publications Office, 2017).
19 Arnaud Mehl, Barry Eichengreen and Romain Lafarguette, 'Cables, sharks and servers: technology and the geography of the foreign exchange market', Working Paper Series 1889, European Central Bank (2016).
20 David Souden, *Voices Over the Horizon: Tales from Cable and Wireless* (London: Granta, 1999).
21 Perez, 'Unleashing a golden age after the financial collapse'.
22 I grew up not far from said ISP – a windowless colossus, under round-the-clock security protection. Local myth had it that a radiation spill in the 1950s had left the site – a then largely fallow field (now university campus) not far from the centre of Amsterdam – so toxic, the frogs in the nearby pond had six legs and eyes the size of marbles. Though I never found any of said frogs, perhaps it did spur my early fascination with the physicality of the internet's underpinnings.
23 Blum, *Tubes: A Journey to the Center of the Internet.*
24 Gordon Corera, *Intercept: The Secret History of Computers and Spies* (London: Weidenfeld & Nicolson, 2015).
25 Dan Swinhoe, 'The future of Virginia Post-Loudoun', *Data Center Dynamics*, 4 November 2024.
26 Ana Faguy, 'A humming annoyance or jobs boom? Life next to 199 data centres', BBC News, 26 October 2025.
27 Matthew Gooding, 'The ongoing impact of Amsterdam's data center moratorium', *Data Center Dynamics*, 22 August 2024.
28 Josh Saul et al., 'AI data centers and electricity prices', *Bloomberg Technology*, 29 September 2025.
29 Dan Swinhoe, 'AI could drive $6.7 trillion investment in data centers, maybe, claims McKinsey', *Data Center Dynamics*, 2 May 2025.
30 Note: data centres used for AI interference, rather than training, do follow the traditional laws of proximity.
31 ICIS, 'Data centres hungry for power', *ICIS Explore.*
32 Saudi Vision 2030. *Kingdom of Saudi Arabia, Vision 2030.* https://www.vision2030.gov.sa/en.
33 Paul Cochrane, 'How Saudi Arabia is redrawing the map of the future with fibre-optic cables', *Middle East Eye*, 5 April 2023.
34 Deryck Fay, *Connecting a Nation: The Story of Telecommunications in Ireland* (Dubin: Trinity Dublin University Press, 2021).
35 Document 40: ADM 116/3360: Emergency requirements for communications facilities between Admiralty and ports, establishments etc.

36 'Review of NATO telecommunications system – 1956 SGWM-172-56' and 'Study into Gibraltar – Sardinia cable 1 ENCLOSURE: Report on submarine cables'. From NATO Archives.
37 Winston Qiu, 'Google's Blue-Raman cable to create new Eurasia route across Israel', Submarine Cable Networks, 15 April 2020.
38 Paul Cochrane, 'Israeli-backed Internet cable aims to link country to Saudi Arabia and Gulf States'. *Middle East Eye*, 3 April 2023.
39 'Israel hopes new data cables can make friends of former enemies', *The Economist*, 5 March 2022.
40 Paul Cochrane, 'UAE landing station confirmed for fibre optic cable set to link Israel to Gulf States', *Middle East Eye*, 22 September 2023.
41 Dealroom, 'Country guide: Israel'. https://dealroom.co/guides/israel.
42 Michelle Mohney, 'Impact of the Venezuelan crisis on the country's Internet', Northwestern Engineering, 23 July 2024.
43 Doug Madory, 'Cuba and the geopolitics of submarine cables', Kentik, 13 January 2023.
44 US Department of Justice, 'Team Telecom recommends the FCC deny application to directly connect the United States to Cuba through subsea cable', 30 November 2022.
45 Reuters, 'Cuba and French telecoms operator Orange begin work on subsea cable to Martinique', Reuters, 8 December 2022.
46 Robert Greene and Paul Triolo, 'Will China control the global internet via its digital Silk Road?', The China Project, 8 May 2020.
47 Starosielski, *The Undersea Network*.
48 Mateusz Kaczmarek, 'Eritrea's digital desert: inside the world's most isolated Internet – and the satellite lifeline on the horizon', 12 June 2025.
49 Convention for the Protection of Submarine Telegraph Cables (Paris, 14 March 1884).
50 Though the US never signed the 1982 Treaty, it adheres to most of its rules. It has, however, made it difficult for the US to credibly call out violations of UNCLOS by other actors.
51 Jeanne-Mây Desurmont, 'Territorial claims and subsea cables: the geopolitics of invisible lines in the South China Sea', Bloomsbury Intelligence and Security Institute, 21 May 2024.
52 Liliya Khasanova and Katharin Tai, 'Shades of authoritarian digital sovereignty: divergences in Russian and Chinese data localisation regimes', *Journal of Cyber Policy* 9, no. 1 (2024): 70–94.
53 Regulation (EU) 2016/679 of the European Parliament and of the Council of 27 April 2016 on the protection of natural persons with regard to the processing of personal data and on the free movement of such data, and repealing Directive 95/46/EC (General Data Protection Regulation). *Official Journal of the European Union* L 119, 4 May 2016.
54 Rahul Rao, 'Europe's quest for cloud sovereignty faces growing pains', *IEEE Spectrum*, 17 March 2026.
55 Rich Miller, 'Brexit prep has boosted data centers, subsea cables. But what now?', Data Center Frontier, 25 October 2019.
56 Such warnings had even preceded the incident itself: 'Houthis may sabotage Western Internet cables in Red Sea, Yemen telecoms firms warn', *The Guardian*, 5 February 2024.
57 Maria Grazia Attinasi et al., 'Sailing through storms: the fallout of Red Sea disruptions for global trade and inflation', *VoxEU (CEPR)*, 26 April 2024.

58 Patrick Wintour, 'Houthis may sabotage Western internet cables in Red Sea, Yemen telecoms firms warn', *The Guardian*, 5 February 2024.
59 Patrick Wintour, 'Houthis deny targeting underwater cables amid marine disaster warning', *The Guardian*, 28 February 2024.
60 Bloomberg, 'Full repairs to damaged Red Sea Internet cables delayed by Yemen political splits', gCaptain, 7 May 2024.
61 The Economist, 'The Houthis' moneymaking machine', *The Economist*, 18 January 2025.
62 Dan Swinhoe, 'Houthi crisis in Red Sea spurs interest in alternative fiber routes', *Data Center Dynamics*, 18 April 2024.

**4 Cable Power**

1 John Keegan, *A History of Warfare* (New York: Alfred A. Knopf, 1993).
2 Amjad Iraqi, '"Lavender": the AI machine directing Israel's bombing spree in Gaza', *+972 Magazine* (blog), 3 April 2024.
3 The Economist, 'How Elon Musk's satellites have saved Ukraine and changed warfare', *The Economist*, 5 January 2023.
4 Thomas G. Mahnken, *Technology and the American Way of War since 1945* (New York: Columbia University Press, 2008).
5 Winseck, 'The geopolitical economy of the global internet infrastructure'.
6 European Commission, 'Additional €142 million to support submarine networks and connectivity infrastructure under Connecting Europe Facility (CEF) Digital', European Commission, 5 December 2024.
7 Joe Brock, 'Special Report: Inside the subsea cable firm secretly helping America take on China', Reuters, 6 July 2023.
8 The Five Eyes are an intelligence alliance, with its formal origins in the early Cold War. The term Five Eyes itself originated from For AUS/CAN/NZ/UK/US Eyes Only – referring to the respective intelligence agencies of these countries.
9 Nicole Carter, 'Protection of undersea telecommunication cables: issues for Congress', 7 August 2023. https://www.congress.gov/crs-product/R47648.
10 Xtera, 'Xtera completes the final splice on DISA's Guantanamo–Puerto Rico submarine cable system', Xtera, 15 November 2018.
11 Chris Knowlton, 'The Cold War: history of the SOund SUrveillance System (SOSUS)', Discovery of Sound in the Sea, 14 January 2022.
12 Brock, 'Special Report'.
13 US Navy, 'USNS Zeus Military Sealift Command'. https://www.msc.usff.navy.mil/Press-Room/Photo-Gallery/igphoto/2002479551/.
14 Adams, 'Arc of Empire'.
15 Leander Kahney, 'The FBI wanted a back door to the iPhone. Tim Cook said no', Wired, 16 April 2019.
16 Thomas Heinrich, 'Cold War armory: military contracting in Silicon Valley', *Enterprise & Society* 3, no. 2 (2002): 247–84.
17 Stuart W. Leslie, *The Cold War and American Science: The Military-Industrial-Academic Complex at MIT and Stanford* (New York: Columbia University Press, 1993.
18 Raj M. Shah and Christopher Kirchhoff, *Unit X: How the Pentagon and Silicon Valley are Transforming the Future of War* (New York: Scribner, 2024).

19 Kahney, 'The FBI wanted a back door to the iPhone'.
20 Shah and Kirchhoff, *Unit X*.
21 Bernd Debusmann Jr., 'Who is paying for Trump's White House ballroom? Full donor list revealed', BBC News, 21 October 2025.
22 Katja Bego, 'Silicon Valley's national security pivot will only accelerate under the new Trump administration', Chatham House, November 2024.
23 Laura Bratton, 'The Pentagon is spending billions on Big Tech and Silicon Valley startups as it goes all-in on AI', 13 May 2024.
24 Connor Echols, 'Killer AI is a patriotic duty? Silicon Valley comes to Washington', Responsible Statecraft, 2 May 2024.
25 Will Feuer, 'Palantir CEO only wants employees who agree with mission to boost the West', *Wall Street Journal*, 18 January 2023.
26 Jacob Helberg, *The Wires of War: Technology and the Global Struggle for Power* (New York: Avid Reader Press, 2021).
27 Bego, 'Silicon Valley's national security pivot'.
28 Joe Biden, 'Farewell Address to the Nation', White House, 15 January 2025.
29 Andrew Blum and Carey Baraka, 'Google and Meta's underwater cables up the stakes on internet control', Rest of World, 10 May 2022.
30 Kate Irwin, 'Google is building massive fiber optic cable network from Africa to Australia', *PC Mag*, 23 May 2024.
31 Niva Yadav, 'Meta to build around-the-world subsea cable – report', *Data Center Dynamics*, 24 October 2024.
32 Joe Brock, 'Inside the subsea cable firm secretly helping American take on China', Reuters, 6 July 2023.
33 Juan Ortiz Freuler, 'The weaponization of private corporate infrastructure: Internet fragmentation and coercive diplomacy in the 21st century', *Global Media and China* 8, no. 1 (2023): 6–23.
34 Katja Bego, 'The latest frontier in global power dynamics: the complex network of undersea cables', in Carlo Secchi and Alessandro Gili (eds) *Infrastructure Grids and Networks: The Challenges Ahead, amid Security and Efficiency* (Milan: ISPI, 2025).
35 Jonathan E. Hillman, *The Digital Silk Road: China's Quest to Wire the World and Win the Future* (London: Profile Books, 2021).
36 Doshi, *The Long Game*.
37 Hillman, *The Digital Silk Road*.
38 https://www.peacecable.com/.
39 Times of India, 'China's BRI losing steam as loans turn sour, new investments decline: Report', *The Times of India*, 7 September 2023.
40 'China Inc. is recalibrating its approach to its overseas footprint as the BRI turns 10 years old', Merics, 27 September 2023.
41 Ibid.
42 Sameer Patil and Prithvi Gupta, 'The Digital Silk Road in the Indo-Pacific: mapping China's vision for global tech expansion'. ORF Issue Brief No. 683 (January 2024).
43 Halford Mackinder's Heartland Theory argued that whoever controlled the central landmass of Eurasia – especially Eastern Europe, Russia and Central Asia – would possess the geographic advantage to dominate Europe, Asia, and so ultimately wield global power, because this vast 'Heartland' was both rich in resources and difficult for sea powers to

invade. See Halford J. Mackinder, 'The geographical pivot of history', *The Geographical Journal* 23, no. 4 (1904): 421–37.

44 Seth Schindler, Ilias Alami, Jessica DiCarlo et al., 'The Second Cold War: US–China competition for centrality in infrastructure, digital, production, and finance networks', *Geopolitics* 29, no. 4 (2024): 1083–120.

45 Elsa B. Kania and Lorand Laskai, 'Myths and realities of China's military-civil fusion strategy', Center for a New American Security, 28 January 2021.

46 Ibid.

47 Rick Umback, 'Huawei and Telefunken: communications enterprises and rising power strategies' (Australian Strategic Policy Institute, 2019).

48 Djibouti is somewhat of military hub – also the Italians, Americans and French maintain bases here.

49 Jacob Mardell, 'The BRI in Pakistan: China's flagship economic corridor', Merics, 20 May 2020.

50 Hillman, *The Digital Silk Road.*

51 Greene and Triolo, 'Will China control the global Internet via its digital Silk Road?'.

52 Katja Bego, 'A vision for the future internet: a vision for a more democratic, resilient, sustainable, trustworthy and inclusive internet by 2030', Nesta, July 2020.

53 Greg Noone, 'How Huawei is winning over the global south', Tech Monitor, 22 December 2022.

54 Hillman, *The Digital Silk Road.*

55 Mihai Sora, Jessica Collins and Meg Keen, 'The Great Game in the Pacific Islands', Lowy Institute, August 2024.

56 April Herlevi, 'China's strategic space in the digital undersea', National Bureau of Asian Research, 14 March 2024.

57 Ibid.

58 Amy Remeikis, 'Australia supplants China to build undersea cable for Solomon Islands', *The Guardian*, 13 June 2018.

59 AP Via SCMP, 'Huawei out, Australia in: Solomons drop Chinese for billion-dollar cable', *South China Morning Post*, 13 June 2018.

60 G7 Development Ministers, 'Factsheet on the G7 Partnership for Global Infrastructure and Investment (PGII)', G7 Research Group, University of Toronto, 23 October 2024.

61 Lisa Curtis and Martijn Rasser, 'A techno-diplomacy strategy for telecommunications in the Indo-Pacific', Quad Tech Network QTN Series, September 2021.

62 Ursula von der Leyen, 'Statement by Executive Vice-President Vestager and Commissioner Breton on the EU's Connectivity Package', European Commission, 1 December 2021.

63 Ursula von der Leyen, 'Speech by President-elect von der Leyen in the European Parliament Plenary on the occasion of the presentation of her College of Commissioners and their programme', European Commission, 27 November 2019.

64 Council of the EU, 'Global Gateway: Council endorses flagship project list for 2026', 10 December 2025.

65 Olivier Pinaud, '"Strategic" submarine telecom cable manufacturer ASN nationalized by France', *Le Monde*, 5 November 2024.

66 Winston Qiu, 'EU adopts TEAM EUROPE strategy on subsea cable security and resilience', Submarine Networks, 26 March 2026.

67 European Commission, 'Joint communication to strengthen the security and resilience of submarine cables', Shaping Europe's Digital Future, 20 March 2026.
68 'Digital Gateway between the Atlantic and the Mediterranean – Medusa submarine cable system', 12 March 2024.
69 European Investment Bank, 'The EU and EIB Global team up to upgrade digital connectivity to the southern neighbourhood'.
70 Belgacem Tahchi, 'Algerian gas to strengthen energy security of the European Union: policy, capacity and strategy', *Energy Reports* 11 (2024): 3600–13.
71 European Investment Bank, 'Black Sea digital connectivity'. https://www.eib.org/en/projects/all/20210614.
72 Anna Gross, Chris Campbell and Alexandra Heal, 'EU plans Black Sea Internet cable to reduce reliance on Russia', *Financial Times*, 12 May 2023.
73 EU NeighboursEast, 'More Georgians than ever trust the EU, according to latest opinion poll', EU NeighboursEast, 11 November 2024.
74 Press release: 'Europe's largest deposit of rare earth metals located in Kiruna', 12 January 2023.
75 Euractiv, 'Sweden announces discovery of Europe's biggest deposit of rare earth metals', 12 January 2023.
76 Atle Staalesen, '"Human activity" behind Svalbard cable disruption', *The Barents Observer*, 11 February 2022.
77 Copenhagen Economics, 'The economic value of submarine cables in the Arctic'.
78 NORDUnet, CSC – IT Center for Science (Finland), Sunet, and DeiC, 'Vision 2030: a resilient submarine cable system through the Arctic equipped with sensing: the importance and the opportunities', 31 January 2024.
79 Lars Fischer, 'Built-in resilience for Arctic subsea cables'. NORDUnet (blog), 15 March 2024.
80 Alexandra Middleton and Bjørn Rønning, 'Geopolitics of subsea cables in the Arctic'. The Arctic Institute – Center for Circumpolar Security Studies, 2 August 2022.
81 Isabelle Bousquette, 'What will it take to connect the Arctic? $1.2 billion, 10,000 miles of fiber-optic cable and patience', *Wall Street Journal*, 10 March 2023.
82 Paul Lipscombe, 'Arctic sea ice cuts subsea cable, causing lengthy broadband outages in Alaska', *Data Center Dynamics*, 14 June 2023.
83 European Commission, 'New projects signed under CEF digital to enhance and strengthen submarine cable infrastructure across and to the EU', Shaping Europe's Digital Future, 5 December 2024.
84 Elizabeth Buchanan, 'Russia's gains in the Great Arctic Race', War on the Rocks, 4 May 2023.
85 Gabriela Baczynska, 'Veteran explorer stakes Russia's claim over the Arctic', Reuters, 27 February 2013.
86 'China unveils vision for "Polar Silk Road" across Arctic', Reuters, 26 January 2018.
87 David Bandurski, 'Polar Silk Road', China Media Project, 19 January 2026.
88 Johan Wicklén, Sharon Jåma and Diana Olofsson, 'FOI varnar för svenskt rymdsamarbete med Kina', *SVT Nyheter*, 13 January 2019.
89 Thomas Nilsen, 'FSB signs maritime security cooperation with China in Murmansk', *The Barents Observer*, 25 April 2023; TASS, 'Russia and China ready to cooperate on development of northern sea route — Putin'. https://tass.com/economy/1592391.

90 Jeremy Greenwood and Shuxian Luo, 'Could the Arctic be a wedge between Russia and China?', War on the Rocks, 4 April 2022.
91 Paul Josephson, 'The deep historical roots of Russia's militarisation of the Arctic', Engelsberg Ideas, 9 October 2024.
92 Magnus Nordenman, 'Back to the gap', *The RUSI Journal* 162, no. 1 (2017): 24–30.
93 Elizabeth Buchanan, *Red Arctic: Russian Strategy under Putin* (Washington, DC: Brookings Institution Press, 2023).
94 NATO, '"Knowledge is power, character is more" – Speech by Admiral Rob Bauer, Chair of the NATO Military Committee Canadian Forces College – Joint Command and Staff Programme and National Security Programme', 16 November 2022.

**5 Anatomy of a Fault**

1 The case still remains unresolved; in the words of one former UK intelligence official I asked about the matter: 'sometimes it's best not to inquire too deeply'.
2 Radio Free Europe/Radio Liberty, 'Finland opens probe into possible "intentional damaging" of Baltic Sea pipeline', Radio Free Europe/Radio Liberty, 11 October 2023.
3 Ibid.
4 NATO, 'Doorstep statement by NATO Secretary General Jens Stoltenberg following the extraordinary NAC meeting', NATO, 11 October 2023.
5 European Commission, 'Balticconnector gas pipeline up and running since 1 January 2020', European Commission, 8 January 2020.
6 Reuters, 'Putin dismisses as "rubbish" idea Russia attacked Baltic pipeline', Reuters, 13 October 2023.
7 Ali Abbas Ahmadi, 'Finland says gas pipeline damage probably caused by dragging anchor', BBC News, 24 October 2023.
8 Atle Staalesen, 'Runaway ship Newnew Polar Bear, suspected of sabotage in Baltic Sea, is sailing into Russian Arctic waters', *The Barents Observer*, 26 October 2023.
9 Atle Staalesen, 'Newnew Polar Bear sails towards Bering Strait', *The Barents Observer*, 6 November 2023.
10 Gasgrid, 'Balticconnector's repair work completed — next on to commissioning', Gasgrid, 4 April 2024.
11 Anne Kauranen and Andrius Sytas, 'China ship is focus of pipeline damage probe, Finland says', Reuters, 20 October 2023.
12 ERR News, 'China admits container ship Newnew Polar Bear damaged undersea gas pipeline', ERR News, 12 August 2024.
13 The Maritime Executive, 'Captain appears in Hong Kong court on charges from 2023 pipeline break', The Maritime Executive, 9 May 2025.
14 Reuters, 'Sweden urges Chinese ship to return for undersea cable investigation', Reuters, 27 November 2024.
15 Sam Breazeale, '"Incredibly difficult to prove": two Baltic Sea Internet cables were damaged within 24 hours. Was it Russian "hybrid warfare" or just a coincidence?', Meduza, 25 November 2024.
16 Gabrielius Landsbergis (@GLandsbergis), post on X (formerly Twitter), 21 November 2024. https://x.com/GLandsbergis/status/1859239391668953524.
17 DW, 'Russia denies cutting Baltic Sea cables as tensions rise', DW, 20 November 2024.

18 Christy Cooney, 'Sweden asks China to co-operate over severed cables', BBC News, 29 November 2024.
19 Miranda Bryant, 'China refused investigation into ship linked to severed Baltic cables, says Sweden', *The Guardian*, 23 December 2024.
20 International Maritime Organization, 'Casualty'. https://www.imo.org/en/ourwork/iiis/pages/casualty.aspx.
21 Mack DeGeurin, 'The mystery surrounding two severed Baltic subsea internet cables is getting murkier', *Popular Science*, 23 December 2024.
22 Lukas Trakimavičius, 'The hidden threat to Baltic undersea power cables', NATO Energy Security Centre of Excellence, December 2021.
23 Michelle Wiese Bockmann, 'Finland police seize Russian-linked dark fleet tanker Eagle S in cable-cutting investigation', Lloyd's List, 26 December 2024.
24 Julia Webster, Emily Thomson, Temra Baydono, Olof Konig, Kerry B. Contini, Sunny Mann and Junko Suetomi, 'G7 sets price cap for Russian oil at USD 60 per barrel', Global Sanctions and Export Controls Blog, 9 December 2022.
25 Michelle Wiese Bockmann, 'Russia-linked cable-cutting tanker seized by Finland was loaded with spying equipment', Lloyd's List, 27 December 2024.
26 Bockmann, 'Finland police seize Russian-linked dark fleet tanker'.
27 TT News Agency, 'Finland releases underwater images of Eagle S', *Sweden Herald*, 31 December 2024.
28 Reuters, 'Finnish coastguard boards tanker suspected of causing power and internet cable outages', *Guardian*, 26 December 2024.
29 NATO, 'NATO launches Baltic Sentry to increase critical infrastructure security', NATO, 14 January 2025.
30 Nadja Skopljak, 'Damaged Finland-Estonia subsea link to resume operations earlier than planned', Offshore Energy, 6 June 2025.
31 ICPC, 'How do subsea cables get cut?: The International Cable Protection Committee responds to recent subsea cable damage in the Baltic Sea, ICPC, 27 November 2024.
32 Greg Miller, Robyn Dixon and Isaac Stanley-Becker, 'Accidents, not Russian sabotage behind cable damage, officials say', *Washington Post*, 19 January 2025.
33 TT News Agency, 'Expert on cables: accident explanation is nonsense', *Sweden Herald*, 23 January 2025.
34 Paul Lipscombe, 'No signs that Baltic subsea cuts were deliberate, says Swedish authorities', *Data Center Dynamics*, 23 April 2025.
35 auonsson, 'There is an estimated 1 in 10k – 100k years chance that all 8 of the Nov 2024 – Jan 2025 Baltic Sea cable breaks are coincidental', Bluesky, 15 February 2025.
36 Brendan Cole, 'Russia issues ominous warning about undersea internet cables', *Newsweek*, 12 November 2024.
37 Tom Bennett, 'Baltic states unplug from Russia and join EU power grid', BBC News, 9 February 2025.
38 Håvard Gulldahl and Inghild Eriksen, 'This is what the damaged Svalbard cable looked like when it came up from the depths', NRK, 26 May 2024.
39 Tim Stronge, 'Is it sabotage? Unraveling the mystery of undersea cable breaks', TeleGeography, 3 February 2025.
40 Olena Goncharova, 'Russia says its undersea telecom cable in Baltic Sea damaged by external impact', *Kyiv Independent*, 9 February 2025.

41 Thomas Rid, *Active Measures: The Secret History of Disinformation and Political Warfare* (New York: Farrar, Straus and Giroux, 2020).
42 MI5, 'Director General Ken McCallum gives latest threat update', 8 October 2024.
43 Mark Rutte, 'NATO chief Mark Rutte warns Russia could use military force against alliance in five years', Chatham House, 9 June 2025.
44 NATO, 'Building a better NATO', 10 June 2025.
45 Secrétariat général de la défense et de la sécurité nationale, 'National Strategic Review 2025', 13 July 2025.
46 Kremlin, 'Address by the President of the Russian Federation', Kremlin, 21 February 2022.
47 Radio Free Europe/Radio Liberty, 'Estonia hit by "Moscow Cyber War"', Radio Free Europe/Radio Liberty, 17 May 2007.
48 Rain Ottis, 'Analysis of the 2007 cyber attacks against Estonia from the information warfare perspective', Cooperative Cyber Defence Centre of Excellence, 2008.
49 Alexandra Wiktorek Sarlo, 'Fighting disinformation in the Baltic States', Foreign Policy Research Institute, 6 July 2017.
50 Charles Clover, 'How Russia is jamming GPS around Europe', *Financial Times*, 3 September 2025.
51 Sam Mullins, 'The role of non-state actors as proxies in irregular warfare and malign state influence', Irregular Warfare Center, 9 December 2024.
52 Radio Free Europe/Radio Liberty, 'Russia suspected in sabotage campaign that led to DHL cargo plane crash in Lithuania', Radio Free Europe/Radio Liberty, 2 December 2024.
53 Csongor Körömi, 'Russia used Belarusian refugee as spy to start Warsaw mall fire, prosecutor says', Politico Europe, 2024.
54 Andrew Harding, 'Hand of Moscow? The men jailed for vandalism in French hybrid warfare case', BBC News, 1 November 2025.
55 Nette Nöstlinger and Jürgen Klöckner, 'Russia started Berlin factory fire as part of hybrid war on Europe, report says', Politico Europe, 24 June 2024.
56 Kate Connolly, 'US reportedly foiled Russian plot to kill boss of German arms firm supplying Ukraine', *The Guardian*, 11 July 2024.
57 Nette Nöstlinger and Jürgen Klöckner, 'Train cable fire at NATO summit sparks fears of sabotage in Netherlands', Politico Europe, 2024.
58 Kelly M. Greenhill, 'When migrants become weapons: the long history and worrying future of a coercive tactic', Foreign Affairs, March/April 2022.
59 George Right, 'Russia's removal of border markers "unacceptable" – EU', BBC News, 24 May 2024.
60 Dan Sabbagh, 'French military detain two after boarding Russia-linked oil tanker suspected of launching drones', *The Guardian*, 1 October 2025.
61 Daniela Richterova, Elena Grossfeld, Magda Long and Patrick Bury, 'Russian sabotage in the gig-economy era', *The RUSI Journal* 169, no. 5 (2024): 10–21.
62 Sebastian Clapp, 'Eastern flank watch and European drone wall', European Parliamentary Research Service, October 2025.
63 Stew Magnuson, 'Baltic Sea Now Called a "NATO Lake"', *National Defense Magazine*, 10 July 2024.

64 Deutsche Welle, 'Poland, Baltic States back away from Land Mine Treaty', Deutsche Welle, 2025.
65 Matthew Gooding, 'Ship's captain from China jailed for three years in Taiwan over subsea cable sabotage', *Data Center Dynamics*, 13 June 2025.
66 Ben Blanchard and Yimou Lee, 'Fear of the dark: Taiwan sees wartime frailty in communication links with world', Reuters, 15 March 2023.
67 Noah Robertson, 'How DC became obsessed with a potential 2027 Chinese invasion of Taiwan', *Defense News*, 7 May 2024.
68 Koh Ew, 'Taiwan jails China captain for undersea cable sabotage in landmark case', BBC News, 12 June 2025.
69 Minna Ålander, 'The resilience dilemma', Phillips P. O'Brien Substack, 4 October 2025.
70 HC Deb, 'Russian maritime activity and UK response', House of Commons Hansard, 22 January 2025.
71 The general narrative is that we have not seen war-time cable-cutting since the Second World War. The US and UK Armies are generally believed to have cut terrestrial cables during the Gulf Wars. Some experts I spoke to for this book also suggest it may have been a more common practice during other recent conflicts, such as Libya.
72 Christian Bueger, Tobias Liebetrau and Jonas Franken, 'Security threats to undersea communications cables and infrastructure – consequences for the EU', European Parliament, Policy Department for External Relations, April 2022.

**6 Cutting the Cord**

1 Sanger and Schmitt, 'Russian presence near undersea cables'.
2 Rishi Sunak, 'Undersea cables: indispensable, insecure', Policy Exchange, 1 December 2017.
3 Jonathan Beale, 'Russia a "risk" to undersea cables, defence chief warns', BBC News, 15 December 2017.
4 Ministry of Defense of France, Seabed Warfare Strategy, 2022.
5 Atle Staalesen, '"Human activity" behind Svalbard cable disruption', *The Barents Observer*, 11 February 2022.
6 Malte Humpert, 'Nord Stream pipeline sabotage mirrors Svalbard cable incident', High North News, 29 September 2022.
7 Håvard Gulldahl and Inghild Eriksen, 'This is what the damaged Svalbard cable looked like when it came up from the depths', NRK, 26 May 2024.
8 Patrick Bury and David Murphy, 'No time to hide: the future for Irish defense and security and how our partners can help', War on the Rocks, 3 March 2023.
9 Tom Dunlop, 'Sinn Féin say Irish reliance on British forces "embarrassing"', *UK Defence Journal*, 23 December 2023.
10 Conor Gallagher, 'Russian intelligence ship located in Irish-controlled waters not responding to communication', *The Irish Times*, 10 April 2025.
11 Department of Defence, 'Tánaiste addresses Valentia Island subsea cable security and resilience symposium', Government of Ireland, 11 October 2024.
12 Robert McCabe and Brendan Flynn, 'Under the radar: Ireland, maritime security capacity, and the governance of subsea infrastructure', *European Security* 33, no. 2 (2023): 324–44.

13 SubTel Forum, 'Industry Report', SubTel Forum. https://subtelforum.com/industry-report/.
14 Camino Kavanagh, 'Wading murky waters: subsea communications cables and responsible state behaviour', United Nations Institute for Disarmament Research, 30 March 2023.
15 Ibid.
16 Mike Clare, 'Submarine cable protection and the environment', International Cable Protection Committee, October 2024.
17 Finnish Environment Institute, 'The Baltic Sea in numbers', Finnish Environment Institute.
18 A.J. Vicens, 'DHS investigators say they foiled cyberattack on undersea internet cable in Hawaii', CyberScoop, 13 April 2022.
19 International Cable Protection Committee, '2024 Plenary Highlights', 3 May 2024.
20 European Subsea Cables Association, https://www.escaeu.org/.
21 Tara Davenport, 'Submarine cables, cybersecurity and international law: an intersectional analysis', *Catholic University Journal of Law and Technology* 24, no. 1 (2015): 57–109.
22 Centre for International Law, '1884 Convention for the Protection of Submarine Telegraph Cables', Centre for International Law, National University of Singapore, 14 March 1884.
23 Christian Bueger and Timothy Edmunds, *Understanding Maritime Security* (New York: Oxford University Press, 2024).
24 Camino Kavanagh, Jonas Franken and Wenting He, 'Achieving depth: subsea telecommunications cables as critical infrastructure', United Nations Institute for Disarmament Research, 23 April 2025.
25 European Commission, 'Recommendation on the security and resilience of submarine cable infrastructures', European Commission, 21 February 2024.
26 The Maritime Executive, 'Taiwan increases monitoring of offshore cables, boarding suspicious vessels', The Maritime Executive, 15 January 2025.
27 NATO, 'Joint Press Conference by NATO Secretary General Mark Rutte with President of Finland Alexander Stubb and Prime Minister of Estonia Kristen Michal', NATO, 14 January 2025.
28 Sam Breazeale, 'Surveilling Putin's shadow fleet', Meduza, 3 April 2025.
29 https://www.nato.int/cps/en/natohq/opinions_236426.htm?selectedLocale=en.
30 RFA Proteus, Royal Navy, https://www.royalnavy.mod.uk/organisation/units-and-squadrons/support-ships/rfa-proteus.
31 Joint Expeditionary Force, https://jefnations.org/.
32 Marc Santora et al., 'A thousand snipers in the sky: the new war in Ukraine', *The New York Times*, 3 March 2025.
33 For example, https://www.royalnavy.mod.uk/news/2024/september/20/240920-royal-navy-tests-technology-in-portugal and https://www.diana.nato.int/faq/diana-priority-focus.html.
34 David Kirichenko, 'Ukraine's marauding sea drones bewilder Russia', Center for European Policy Analysis, 30 January 2025.
35 Anna Desmarais, 'NATO may turn to using a fleet of sea drones to protect vulnerable Internet cables in the Baltic Sea', Euronews, 19 December 2024.

36 Ministry of Defence and Foreign, Commonwealth & Development Office, 'Joint Expeditionary Force activates UK-led reaction system to track threats to undersea infrastructure and monitor Russian shadow fleet', GOV.UK, 6 January 2025.
37 Jane van Tienen, 'OSINT's role when geopolitics cuts deep', OSINT Combine, 20 March 2025.
38 ICPC, 'Charting submarine cables is critical for maritime safety and infrastructure protection', International Cable Protection Committee.
39 European Commission, 'Joint Communication to strengthen the security'.
40 https://www.congress.gov/bill/118th-congress/house-bill/1189/text.
41 HEIST NATO SPS Project, 'HEIST: Hardening and Enhancing Infrastructure for Submarine cable Technology', HEIST NATO SPS Project.
42 Foreign, Commonwealth & Development Office, 'UK imposes new wave of sanctions choking Russian oil revenues with Foreign Secretary arriving in Italy for G7', GOV.UK, 25 November 2024.
43 Kyiv School of Economics, 'Russian oil revenues decline despite active shadow fleet and higher oil prices', May 2024.
44 Ew, 'Taiwan jails China captain'.
45 The Maritime Executive, 'Germany and Sweden join in crackdown on shadow fleet vessels in Baltic', The Maritime Executive, 1 July 2025.
46 Alexander Martin, 'Estonia considers allowing Navy to sink merchant ships threatening submarine cables', The Record, 9 April 2025.
47 Jaroslav Lukiv, 'US seizes two "shadow fleet" tankers linked to Venezuelan oil', BBC News, 7 January 2026.
48 Katja Bego, 'Ukraine's Operation Spider's Web is a game-changer for modern drone warfare. NATO should pay attention', Chatham House, 17 July 2025.
49 Sherry Sontag and Christopher Drew with Annette Lawrence Drew, *Blind Man's Bluff: The Untold Story of American Submarine Espionage* (New York: HarperCollins, 1999). p. 167.
50 CIA Reading Room, Document CIA-RDP90-00965R000605140023-4.
51 Bryan Clark, 'Undersea cables and the future of submarine competition', *Bulletin of the Atomic Scientists* 72, no. 4 (2016): 234–7.
52 Ibid.
53 An exception here could be highly specific, low-volume cables such as the new cable splice to Diego Garcia discussed in chapter 3, for which it is likely that a large share of the traffic would have a national security relevance.
54 Jonathan Greig, '"Store now, decrypt later": US leaders prep for quantum cryptography concerns', The Record, 28 August 2024.
55 Ewen Macaskill and Gabriel Dance, 'The Snowden NSA files decoded', *The Guardian*, 1 November 2013.
56 Lane Burdette, 'Leveraging submarine cables for political gain: US responses to Chinese strategy', *Princeton Journal of Public & International Affairs*, 5 May 2021.
57 US Department of Justice, 'Team Telecom recommends that the FCC Deny Pacific Light Cable Network system's Hong Kong undersea cable connection to the United States', 17 June 2020.
58 Reuters, 'China accuses US of cyber security hypocrisy amid Snowden dispute', Reuters, 27 June 2013.

59 Ewen MacAskill, Julian Borger, Nick Hopkins, Nick Davies and James Ball, 'GCHQ taps fibre-optic cables for secret access to world's communications', *The Guardian*, 21 June 2013.
60 Sebastián Moss, 'Spanish and Brazilian governments team up for submarine cable', *Data Center Dynamics*, 26 April 2017.
61 NATO Cooperative Cyber Defence Centre of Excellence (CCDCOE), 'Huawei, 5G, and China as a security threat', CCDCOE, 28 March 2019.
62 Nick Wood, 'Germany finally gets round to banning Huawei, sort of', Telecoms.com, 11 July 2024.
63 Jonathan Swan, 'Huawei threatens America's closest relationship', Axios, 26 January 2020.
64 Robert Clark, 'US hardball drove Chinese vendor from huge cable project, reports', Light Reading, 27 March 2023.
65 Joe Brock, 'How Washington cut Huawei out of the undersea cable business', Reuters, 24 March 2023.
66 US Department of Justice, 'Team Telecom recommends'.
67 Winston Qiu, 'FCC approves license for PLCN', Submarine Networks, 13 February 2022.
68 Dustin Volz and Drew FitzGerald, 'US fears undersea cables are vulnerable to espionage from Chinese repair ships', *The Wall Street Journal*, 19 May 2024.
69 Ibid.
70 House Select Committee on the Chinese Communist Party, 'House Committee subpoenas Chinese telecom giants after refusal to disclose CCP ties', House Select Committee on the Chinese Communist Party, 24 April 2025.
71 'The New York Joint Statement on the Security and Resilience of Undersea Cables in a Globally Digitalized World', European Commission, 26 September 2024.
72 Global Times, 'US politicization of undersea cables opposed', *Global Times*, 24 September 2024.
73 Federal Communications Commission, 'Protecting against national security threats to the communications supply chain through FCC programs', Federal Communications Commission, 2024.
74 US Department of State, 'The Clean Network', US Department of State, 2020.
75 AFP, 'Sanction-hit Huawei says revenues down 29% this year', *The Guardian*, 31 December 2021.
76 Patrick Christian, 'Chinese vs. US network infrastructure in Asia, from cloud to cables', TeleGeography, 17 October 2024.
77 Anna Gross et al., 'How the US is pushing China out of the internet's plumbing', *Financial Times*, 23 June 2023.
78 Jeanne-Mây Desurmont, 'Territorial claims and subsea cables: the geopolitics of invisible lines in the South China Sea', Bloomsbury Intelligence and Security Institute, 21 May 2024.
79 Ibid.
80 Nick Danby, 'By, with, and through at the Second Thomas Shoal', War on the Rocks, 20 May 2024.
81 South China Morning Post, 'Filipino sailor recounts how thumb was torn off in South China Sea clash', *South China Morning Post*, 26 June 2024.

82 Elina Noor, 'Subsea communication cables in Southeast Asia: a comprehensive approach is needed', Carnegie Endowment for International Peace, 18 December 2024.
83 UNEP-WCMC, 'Keeping connected: submarine communications cables and ocean life', UNEP-WCMC, April 2025.
84 Mizuho Kajiwara, 'Maritime security and underwater surveillance technology: lessons from the Cold War', Indo-Pacific Outlook, 24 January 2024.
85 AP Sensing, 'Continuous subsea power cable monitoring', AP Sensing.
86 Alka Tripathy-Lang, 'Making underwater cables SMART with sensors', Eos, 12 December 2022.
87 Vitor Silva, Amir Taherian and Carlod Sousa Oliveira, 'Earthquake early warning for Portugal: part 1 – Where does it matter?', *Bulletin of Earthquake Engineering* 20 (2022): 5545–65.
88 SubTel Forum, 'Japan agency uses submarine cable to detect tsunami', SubTel Forum.
89 Bronte Munro and Iain MacGillivray, 'Reconsider using undersea cables as military sensors', *National Defense Magazine*, 29 September 2023.

**7 Clean Cables**

1 Kristina Spohr, *Post Wall, Post Square: How Bush, Gorbachev, Kohl, and Deng Shaped the World after 1989* (New Haven, CT: Yale University Press, 2019).
2 Michael J. Mazarr, 'Understanding competition: great power rivalry in a changing international order: concepts and theories', RAND Corporation, March 2022.
3 Aya Adachi, Alexander Brown, Francesca Ghiretti, Mikko Huotari, Jan Weidenfeld and Max J. Zenglein, 'Dealing with China's economic coercion – the case of Lithuania and insights from East Asia and Australia', Mercator Institute for China Studies (Merics), 20 December 2021.
4 Aya Adachi, 'China's overcapacity and the Global South: an opportunity for the EU', *Internationale Politik Quarterly*, 26 March 2025.
5 Henry Farrell and Abraham L. Newman, 'Weaponized interdependence: how global economic networks shape state coercion', *International Security* 44, no. 1 (2019): 42–79.
6 Elizabeth Economy, 'China's alternative order', Foreign Affairs, 23 April 2024.
7 Edward Fishman, *Chokepoints: How the Global Economy Became a Weapon of War* (London: Elliott & Thompson Limited/Portfolio, 2025).
8 Mulder, *The Economic Weapon.*
9 Ibid.
10 US Department of the Treasury, 'Terrorist Finance Tracking Program (TFTP)', US Department of the Treasury. https://home.treasury.gov/policy-issues/terrorism-and-illicit-finance/terrorist-finance-tracking-program-tftp.
11 Laura MacInnis and Roberta Rampton, 'Obama tightens sanctions on banks helping Iran sell oil', Reuters, 1 August 2012.
12 Katja Bego, 'Chokepoints: how the global economy became a weapon of war', *International Affairs* 101, no. 4 (2025): 1534–5.
13 Jérémie Cohen-Setton, 'Blogs Review: China's GDP (PPP) to surpass the United States?', Bruegel, 12 May 2014.
14 It was ironically Vladimir Putin in a 2017 speech, who was the first world leader to openly proclaim AI leadership as the deciding lever of geopolitical power of the twenty-first

century. Pursuing artificial intelligence development rather than wars of conquest would certainly have been a more positive path forward for the Russian civilizational project.

15 Jake Sullivan, 'Remarks by National Security Advisor Jake Sullivan on renewing American economic leadership at the Brookings Institution', The White House, 27 April 2023.
16 Mark Kennedy, 'America's AI strategy: playing defense while China plays to win', Wilson Center, 24 January 2025.
17 The Economist, 'The semiconductor choke point', *The Economist*, 13 June 2024.
18 Mitchell Labiak, 'AI frenzy makes Nvidia the world's most valuable company', BBC News, 18 June 2024.
19 Chris Miller, *Chip War: The Fight for the World's Most Critical Technology* (New York: Simon & Schuster, 2022).
20 George W. Thompson, 'The foreign-direct product rule', Thompson & Associates, PLLC, 29 March 2022.
21 Karen Freifeld and Fanny Potkin, 'US ordered TSMC to halt shipments to China of chips used in AI applications', Reuters, 10 November 2024.
22 Eleanor Olcott and Qianer Liu, 'Chinese AI groups use cloud services to evade US chip export controls', *Financial Times*, 9 March 2023.
23 ASML, 'ASML statement on updated US export restrictions', ASML, 2 December 2024.
24 Fang-Wei Lin and Barath Harithas, 'The AI diffusion framework and the foundry due diligence rule: a compliance perspective', Center for Strategic and International Studies, 27 March 2025.
25 New York Times, 'As Trump weighs sale of advanced AI chips to China, critics sound alarm', *The New York Times*, 29 October 2025.
26 The White House, *America's AI Action Plan* (Washington, DC: The White House, 2025).
27 US Congress, H.R.4346 – CHIPS and Science Act, Congress.gov, 9 August 2022. https://www.congress.gov/bill/117th-congress/house-bill/4346.
28 US Congress, H.R.5376 – Inflation Reduction Act of 2022, Congress.gov, 16 August 2022. https://www.congress.gov/bill/117th-congress/house-bill/5376/text.
29 Bloomberg, 'Taiwan officials urge US to calm rhetoric about "unsafe" chip reliance in event of a Chinese invasion', *South China Morning Post*, 21 April 2023.
30 China Power Team, 'Measuring China's manufacturing might', ChinaPower Project, 17 December 2024.
31 Ibid.
32 It should be noted that the United States has not been a powerhouse in ship manufacturing since the Second World War (high labour costs, cumbersome legislation such as the Jones Act, and preference for higher-margin industries are at the root of this). China's growing share has come at the expense of, in particular, South Korea and Japan, and markets in Europe such as the Netherlands, Germany and Italy.
33 Matthew P. Funaiole, Brian Hart and Aidan Powers-Riggs, 'Murky waters: navigating the risks of China's dual-use shipyards', Center for Strategic and International Studies (CSIS), 25 March 2025.
34 Edward Helmore, 'Biden issues rules to ban Chinese-made cars amid spying fears', *The Guardian*, 22 September 2024.
35 AP with Euronews, 'Chinese-made buses in Norway can be halted remotely, spurring increased security', Euronews, 6 November 2025.

36 Council on Foreign Relations, 'China overseas ports tracker'. https://www.cfr.org/tracker/china-overseas-ports.
37 The White House, 'Fact Sheet: Biden-Harris Administration announces initiative to bolster cybersecurity of US ports', The White House, 21 February 2024.
38 Daniel W. Drezner, 'How everything became national security', Foreign Affairs, September/October 2023.
39 Demetri Sevastopulo, 'Former national security adviser Jake Sullivan: "The core engines of American power are humming"', *Financial Times*, 31 January 2025.
40 Osmond Chia, 'Trio charged over alleged plot to smuggle Nvidia chips from US to China', BBC News, 20 March 2026.
41 Mark A. Green, 'China is the top trading partner to more than 120 countries', Wilson Center, 17 January 2023.
42 Global Times, 'US politicization of undersea cables opposed', *Global Times*, 24 September 2024.
43 China Academy of Information and Communications Technology, *Report on China's Participation in the Construction and Protection of International Communication Submarine Cables* (2025).
44 Data from: TeleGeography, 'Submarine Cable Map', TeleGeography, https://www.submarinecablemap.com/.
45 Rob Davies, 'Huawei shrugs off US sanctions with fastest growth in four years', *The Guardian*, 29 March 2024.
46 Huawei Investment & Holding Co., Ltd., '2023 Annual Report'. https://www.huawei.com/en/annual-report/2023.
47 Qianer Liu, 'How Huawei surprised the US with a cutting-edge chip made in China', *Financial Times*, 30 November 2023.
48 Laura Alfaro, Harald Fadinger, Jan S. Schymik and Gede Virananda, 'Trade and industrial policy in supply chains: directed technological change in rare earths', Working Paper, May 2025.
49 Sinead Carew, 'China's DeepSeek sets off AI market rout', Reuters, 27 January 2025.
50 Jordan Schneider, 'ChinaTalk: DeepSeek — what it means and what happens next', Lawfare, 30 January 2025.
51 The Information Staff, 'DeepSeek is using banned Nvidia chips in race to build next model', The Information, 2025.
52 Ananya Bhattacharya, 'Non-Western founders say DeepSeek is proof that innovation need not cost billions of dollars', Rest of World, 30 January 2025.
53 Meia Nouwens, 'China's economic and technological self-reliance', International Institute for Strategic Studies (IISS), November 2020.
54 Frank Dikötter, *China After Mao: The Rise of a Superpower* (New York: Bloomsbury Publishing, 2022).
55 Nouwens, 'China's economic and technological self-reliance'.
56 Max J. Zenglein and Jacob Gunter, 'The Party knows best: aligning economic actors with China's strategic goals', Merics (Mercator Institute for China Studies), 12 October 2023.
57 Ryan McMorrow and Nian Liu, 'China blocks use of Intel and AMD chips in government computers', *Financial Times*, 24 March 2024.
58 This ban was likely more a case of political signalling, that it did not need America's tech

scraps, than it was about actual national security concerns; China does still allow the import of many other similar products.

59 Cheng Ting-Fang, Lauly Li, Tsubasa Suruga and Shunsuke Tabeta, 'China's undersea cable drive defies US sanctions', *Nikkei Asia*, 26 June 2024.
60 Stephen Chen, 'China unveils a powerful deep-sea cable cutter that could reset the world order', *South China Morning Post*, 22 March 2025.
61 Emily Jin, 'Why China's CIPS matters (and not for the reasons you think)', Center for a New American Security, 5 April 2022.
62 Reuters, 'China's central bank says to promote digital yuan in multi-polar currency system', Reuters, 18 June 2025.
63 Jackson School of International Studies, 'Reactions to US cybersecurity policy: BRIC and the undersea cable', Jackson School of International Studies, University of Washington.
64 Nik Martin, 'From solar to EVs: How China is overproducing green tech', Deutsche Welle.
65 Zoe Liu Zongyuan, 'China wants to ditch the dollar', *Noema Magazine*, 11 January 2024.
66 Hillman, *The Digital Silk Road*.
67 Reuters, 'How the Nexperia chip crisis upended auto supply chains again', Reuters, 24 November 2025.
68 Mark Bergen, 'China is cutting off drone supplies critical to Ukraine war effort', Bloomberg, 9 December 2024.
69 Maria Varenikova, 'Ukraine drones China', *The New York Times*, 11 March 2026.
70 East Asia Forum, 'How China is weaponising its dominance in critical minerals trade', East Asia Forum, 19 February 2025.
71 Julie Michelle Klinger, *Rare Earth Frontiers: From Terrestrial Subsoils to Lunar Landscapes* (Ithaca, NY: Cornell University Press, 2017).
72 Reuters, 'China hits back at US tariffs with rare earth export controls', Reuters, 4 April 2025.
73 Ministry of Defence, 'Finance and Economics Annual Statistical Bulletin: International Defence 2024', GOV.UK, 15 August 2024.
74 Stefano Lovati, 'China invests €37 billion to develop domestic EUV lithography systems', Power Electronics News.
75 The Register, 'Germany to cut Huawei from networks irrespective of costs', The Register, 18 August 2023.
76 Katja Bego, 'Europe must organise itself to counter the technological blackmail of the Trump Administration', *Le Monde*, 18 March 2025.
77 Anu Bradford, 'The Brussels Effect', *Northwestern University Law Review* 107, no. 1 (2012): 1–67.
78 Katja Bego, 'Public digital infrastructure should be at the core of Europe's tech sovereignty strategy', Nesta, 14 July 2021.
79 Ibid.
80 Maximilian Henning, 'International Criminal Court to ditch Microsoft Office for European open source alternative', Euractiv, 30 October 2025.
81 Dutch Government, 'Non-paper: strengthening cloud sovereignty of public administrations', Rijksoverheid, 15 July 2025.

82 Théophane Hartmann, 'European industry scores big win as Germany and France both support sovereign EU-based tech infrastructure', Euractiv, 10 April 2025.
83 Military Watch Magazine, 'Kill switch concerns: Portugal considering abandoning F-35 for Gripen', Military Watch Magazine.
84 European Commission, 'EU sets out its international digital strategy', European Commission Digital Strategy.
85 Joe Tidy, 'North Korean hackers increasingly targeting wealthy crypto holders', BBC News, 7 October 2025.
86 Tsubasa Suruga, 'Singapore to double subsea cable landings in digitization push', Nikkei Asia, 5 June 2023.
87 Dang Nguyen, 'A third path for AI beyond the US–China binary', Noema Magazine, 16 September 2025.
88 The White House, 'Fact Sheet: ensuring US security and economic strength in the age of artificial intelligence', The White House, 13 January 2025.
89 Department for Science, Innovation and Technology, 'US–UK pact will boost advances in drug discovery, create tens of thousands of jobs and transform lives', GOV.UK, 16 September 2025.
90 The Diplomat, 'Silicon Shield 2.0: a Taiwan perspective', The Diplomat, September 2024.
91 Ibid.
92 The Economist, 'Why is Xi Jinping building secret commodity stockpiles?', *The Economist*, 23 July 2024.
93 A. Mikadze, 'Digital Iron Curtain: Russia's quest for internet sovereignty', Riddle Russia, 14 September 2023.

**8 Cables at the Confines of (Supra)planetary Bounds**

1 In The Field Stories, 'Optical cable is laid in the bed of the Amazon River', In The Field Stories, March 2022.
2 UNEP-WCMC, 'Keeping connected: submarine communications cables and ocean life', UN Environment Programme World Conservation Monitoring Centre, April 2025.
3 Dan Swinhoe, 'Making subsea cables smart and helping save the planet', *Data Center Dynamics*, 7 June 2022.
4 International Cable Protection Committee, 'Submarine cable protection and the environment', October 2024.
5 Ibid.
6 Ibid.
7 SubTel Forum, 'Industry Report 2024–2025', Submarine Telecoms Forum. https://subtelforum.com/industry-report/.
8 UNEP-WCMC, 'Keeping connected'.
9 IEA, 'Energy and AI: energy demand from AI', International Energy Agency, April 2025.
10 Reuters, 'Big Tech to Invest About $650 Billion in AI in 2026, Bridgewater Says', Reuters, 23 February 2026.
11 Richard Luscombe, 'Three Mile Island nuclear reactor to restart to power Microsoft AI operations', *The Guardian*, 20 September 2024.
12 Stephen Stapczynski, Akshat Rathi and Josh Saul, 'AI-driven demand for gas turbines risks a new energy crunch', Bloomberg, 2 October 2025.

13 Mohar Chatterjee, 'Trump picks Burgum to put AI at heart of energy policy', Politico, 15 November 2024.
14 M.A. Clare, I.A. Yeo, L. Bricheno, et al., 'Climate change hotspots and implications for the global subsea telecommunications network', *Earth-Science Reviews* 237 (2023): 104296.
15 Ibid.
16 Associated Press, 'Puerto Ricans hunt for precious Wi-Fi and cell signals', Voice of America (VOA News), 25 September 2017.
17 Georgia Butler, 'The tide comes in for subsea cable networks', *Data Center Dynamics*, 12 December 2023.
18 Clare et al., 'Climate change hotspots'.
19 IPCC, Sixth Assessment Report. https://www.ipcc.ch/assessment-report/ar6/.
20 Mohammed Hussein, 'Mapping the world's oil and gas pipelines: interactive', Al Jazeera, 16 December 2021.
21 The Economist, 'Floating wind turbines could rise to great heights', *The Economist*, 21 July 2021.
22 Marc Verdegem, Alejandro H. Buschmann, U. Win Latt, Anne J.T. Dalsgaard and Alessandro Lovatelli, 'The contribution of aquaculture systems to global aquaculture production', *Journal of the World Aquaculture Society* 54, no. 2 (2023): 206–50.
23 Constance Dijkstra and Valentin Simon, 'The return of the cruise: how luxury cruises are polluting Europe's cities', *Transport & Environment*, June 2023.
24 Bueger and Edmunds, *Understanding Maritime Security*.
25 The Economist, 'Can the North Sea become Europe's new economic powerhouse?', *The Economist*, 1 January 2023.
26 UK Government, 'UK and Europe sign historic pact to drive clean energy future', January 2026.
27 Ibid.
28 Nora Buli and Stine Jacobsen, 'Failed offshore auction highlights how Denmark missed wind's change', Reuters, 6 December 2024.
29 Swiss Re, 'No room left – competition for space generates infrastructure accumulation risks', 12 June 2024.
30 Deep Sea Conservation Coalition, 'No Deep-Sea Mining'.
31 Bob Wallace, 'Deep seabed mining a threat to global subsea cable network safety, environment', Submarine Telecoms Forum, 12 July 2024.
32 TeleGeography, 'Submarine cable map'. https://www.submarinecablemap.com/.
33 Kathrin Hille, 'Taiwan in talks with Amazon's Kuiper on satellite communications amid China fears', *Financial Times*, 17 December 2024.
34 International Telecommunication Union, 'Space Connect: the rise of LEO satellite constellations', February 2025.
35 Dan Swinhoe, 'NATO funds subsea & satellite connectivity resilience project – report', *Data Center Dynamics*, 10 July 2024.
36 Ibid.
37 Eric Rosenbaum, 'The space-linked investing idea Bill Gates has chased since the 1990s', CNBC, 24 March 2022.
38 Goldman Sachs, 'The global satellite market is forecast to become seven times bigger', 5 March 2025.

39 Eutelsat, 'About Eutelsat'. https://www.eutelsat.com/about-eutelsat.
40 Planet4589, 'Space statistics'. https://planet4589.org/space/con/star/stats.html.
41 Rosenberg, 'How Antarctica's history of isolation is ending'.
42 Michael Sheetz, 'Elon Musk's SpaceX sent thousands of Starlink satellite internet dishes to Ukraine', CNBC, 22 March 2022.
43 Deutsche Welle, 'Musk activates Starlink Internet service in Gaza Hospital', Deutsche Welle, 24 July 2024.
44 Kalafi Moala, 'Parts of Tonga without Internet after cables damaged and Starlink ordered to cease operations', *The Guardian*, 16 July 2024.
45 Georgetown Security Studies Review, 'A first-person view: examining Ukraine's drone industry', 15 May 2025.
46 Paul Adams, 'Kill Russian soldiers, win points: is Ukraine's new drone scheme gamifying war?', BBC News, 18 July 2025.
47 The New Voice of Ukraine, 'Russian EW disrupts Starlink near frontlines, says military expert', 2 June 2024.
48 Dearbail Jordan, 'Elon Musk says he withheld Starlink over Crimea to avoid escalation', BBC News, 8 September 2023.
49 Reuters, 'US could cut Ukraine's access to Starlink over minerals, say sources', Reuters, 22 February 2025.
50 Reuters, 'Could Europe's Eutelsat help replace Starlink in Ukraine?', Reuters, 5 March 2025.
51 Matthew Loh, 'Fears of Starlink troubles in Ukraine have sent a smaller French competitor's stock soaring over 500%', Business Insider, 6 March 2025.
52 Laurence Russell, 'Eutelsat signs deal with Greenland national telco Tusass for LEO services', *Data Center Dynamics*, 8 October 2025.
53 Edward White, 'Elon Musk: the "wild card" in Trump's dealings with China', *Financial Times*, 29 November 2024.
54 Hille, 'Taiwan in talks with Amazon's Kuiper'.
55 David E. Sanger, 'Musk ultimatum imperils Taiwan's push to "war-proof" its internet', Bloomberg, 6 July 2023.
56 'Taiwan running out of time for satellite communications, space chief tells AFP', *France 24*, 19 September 2025.
57 Kelvin Chen, 'Taiwan ramps up efforts to finish backup satellite network', Taiwan News, 23 September 2023.
58 European Commission, 'IRIS$^2$ secure connectivity', EU Space Programme.
59 Nicolas Camut, 'Italy Starlink talks at standstill amid political tensions', *Politico Europe*, 22 March 2025.
60 Shannon Vaughn, 'LEO Wars: China's orbital challenge to the US-led digital order', Foreign Policy Research Institute, April 2025.
61 Konstanin Toropin, 'Pentagon silent on Elon Musk and Starlink risks as military use expands', Military.com, 15 November 2024.
62 Joseph Trevithick and Tyler Rogoway, 'This is how the US national security apparatus is dependent on SpaceX', *The War Zone*, 6 June 2025.
63 NASA, 'International Space Station transition plan FAQs'. https://www.nasa.gov/faqs-the-international-space-station-transition-plan/.
64 European Space Agency, 'ESA Space Environment Report 2024', 2024.

65 Georgina Rannard, 'Musk's satellites "blocking" view of the universe', BBC News, 16 September 2024.
66 Sebastian Moss, 'NVIDIA announces space compute modules including Vera Rubin', *Data Center Dynamics*, 16 March 2026.
67 Tereza Pultarova, 'Starlink satellites: facts, tracking and impact on astronomy', Space .com, February 2026.
68 Marilyn Harbert and Asha Balakrishnan,'Space debris, FCC regulation, and orbital sustainability', *Issues in Science and Technology*, 2023.
69 The Editors, 'Space trash threatens the global economy', *Scientific American*, 17 May 2024.
70 Christian Roulette, 'Russian satellite blast sends debris cloud into orbit', Reuters, 27 June 2024.
71 Shirley Kan, 'China's anti-satellite weapon test', Library of Congress, 23 April 2007.

**9 Future Cables**

1 Cory Doctorow, 'My McLuhan lecture on enshittification', *Medium*, January 2024.
2 Stockholm International Peace Research Institute (SIPRI), 'Unprecedented rise in global military expenditure; European and Middle East spending surges', SIPRI, 2025.
3 US Department of State, 'Secretary Marco Rubio with Megyn Kelly of The Megyn Kelly Show', 30 January 2025.
4 Sergei Karaganov and Dmitry Suslov, 'A new world order: a view from Russia', Russian International Affairs Council, October 2018.
5 Doshi, *The Long Game*.
6 Zongyuan, 'China wants to ditch the dollar'.
7 Jennifer Wong Leung and Stephan Robin, 'Critical technology tracker', 2025.
8 Zongyuan, 'China wants to ditch the dollar'.
9 Hillman, *The Digital Silk Road*.
10 European Commission, 'Speech by President von der Leyen at the EU Ambassadors Conference 2025', 4 February 2025.
11 Ioannis Kotoulas and Wolfgang Pusztai, *Migration as a Weapon: Turkey's Hybrid Warfare against the European Union* (Athens: Foreign Affairs Institute, 2020).
12 Matthieu Salomon et al., 'Indonesia's energy transition ambitions: nickel downstreaming and beyond', Natural Resource Governance Institute, 30 January 2025.
13 Natalie Sherman, 'Microsoft chooses infamous nuclear site for AI power', BBC News, 20 September 2024.
14 Bego, 'Silicon Valley's national security pivot'.
15 Daniel Kokotajko, 'AI 2027 forecast scenario', *AI-2027 Project*, 3 April 2025.
16 Freedom House, 'Freedom on the Net', 2025.
17 A.M. Ramsay, 'The speed of the Roman imperial post', *The Journal of Roman Studies* 15 (1925): 60–74.

# Index